The Scene of the Voice

SUNY series in Contemporary Continental Philosophy
―――――――
Dennis J. Schmidt, editor

The Scene of the Voice
Thinking Language after Affect

Michael Eng

SUNY PRESS

Published by State University of New York Press, Albany

© 2023 State University of New York

All rights reserved

Printed in the United States of America

No part of this book may be used or reproduced in any manner whatsoever without written permission. No part of this book may be stored in a retrieval system or transmitted in any form or by any means including electronic, electrostatic, magnetic tape, mechanical, photocopying, recording, or otherwise without the prior permission in writing of the publisher.

For information, contact State University of New York Press, Albany, NY
www.sunypress.edu

Library of Congress Cataloging-in-Publication Data

Name: Eng, Michael, author.
Title: The scene of the voice : thinking language after affect / Michael Eng.
Description: Albany : State University of New York Press, [2023] | Series: SUNY series in Contemporary Continental Philosophy | Includes bibliographical references and index.
Identifiers: ISBN 9781438492520 (hardcover : alk. paper) | ISBN 9781438492537 (ebook) | ISBN 9781438492513 (pbk. : alk. paper)
Further information is available at the Library of Congress.

10 9 8 7 6 5 4 3 2 1

*For Kim and Lady,
and our sharing voices*

Contents

Preface ix

Introduction 1

Part 1. Heidegger

1 The Voice: Sounding the Scene of Finitude 29

2 From *Phonē* to *Logos*: The Antagonism of Language and the Figuration of the Voice 47

3 A Finite Scene? Heidegger's Antigones and the Returns of the Voice 67

Part 2. Nancy and Lacoue-Labarthe

4 Figuration and Finitude: Ontological Mimesis and Onto-typology between Nancy and Lacoue-Labarthe 103

Part 3. Blanchot

5 The Other Night of the Voice: *Désoeuvrement*, Effacement, and the Limit-Experience of the Outside 153

Part 4. Deleuze

6 Deleuze and the Voice of Simulacra	189
Epilogue: Thinking and Language after Affect	229
Notes	241
Bibliography	277
Index	295

Preface

"*Écoutez et répétez!*" instructed the anonymous male voice from the cassette recorder. This particular moment took place in my seventh-grade French class many years ago, but the memory is still palpable. We were having one of those lessons in which we listened to a taped dialogue of an everyday encounter between friends. After playing the entire dialogue through, which was usually a couple of minutes or so, the tape played the dialogue again in snippets, which we were to repeat.

I wanted to be good at French, and I took it up initially because it was one of the languages my mother had studied when she was younger (no psychoanalytic connections there, I'm sure), but I found it slow going. At the time of the event I am recounting, I was just starting out, and I was nowhere near able to think in French yet. I don't recall being particularly enthusiastic about this day's exercise, but I listened and repeated along with my classmates, dutifully following the instructions of the tape.

The recording that day was different, however. This particular dialogue was set not in France but in one of France's former colonies or in one of its current overseas departments. I do not recall which, but it could have been Martinique, for all I know. I actually didn't take too much note of it because in seventh grade my knowledge and awareness of colonialism were basically nonexistent. I could tell, however, that the voices we were listening to were not those of the typical European (i.e., white) characters to which we were accustomed. Their accents were different, and these voices sounded heavier in tone. They also spoke more slowly, which I welcomed because it was easier to follow the dialogue unassisted by printed text.

I could tell that both my classmates and French teacher noticed these differences as well because they began to laugh as the recording played. I did not know what exactly they were laughing at until I realized that they were all looking at each other exchanging knowing glances. At that moment, our teacher said (nodding toward me) that the voices sounded like "David" (my adopted "French" name). This was followed by more laughter.

Interestingly enough, while I know I didn't laugh along with everyone else, I also recall that I didn't quite understand what was happening at the time. Although I thought I had been listening to myself as I attempted to speak in French (kind of a prerequisite for language learning, I would think), I guess I hadn't been doing it well enough. I just hadn't understood how my voice sounded like the voices on the tape. It's not until now, as I reflect on the long journey of composing *The Scene of the Voice*, that I can appreciate that this journey has been much longer than I ever realized. This is perhaps fitting given Heidegger's conviction that we are claimed by the matter—*die Sache, la chose*—of thinking before we ever choose to think. I couldn't comprehend until now the injury induced by the connection my teacher and classmates made between my voice and the voices of these colonized subjects depicted by the lesson tape. But as the only nonwhite person in the room at the time, I don't believe I thought their connection was a coincidence, and the memory of that experience tells me that *The Scene of the Voice* is not just some project among many I could have written. Rather, events like the one I am recounting (it was hardly a primal scene) help me understand that my thinking had long been claimed by this study's central themes of voice, language, affect, and mimesis. They also help connect the analysis I develop in the following pages to my work, developed elsewhere, in the possibility of speech within groups and institutions, in affective identifications with the institutional voice, and in the aestheticization of difference in the forms of race, gender, and the body in space. Given these long-held commitments, I think it would be fair to characterize *The Scene of the Voice* as an attempt to open a scene of questioning, one that is attuned, however, to voices that are as much collective as they are individuated.

In keeping with that theme of a collective voice, I want to acknowledge the many voices that have helped me shape and nurture the questioning that unfolds in the pages contained here, and in so doing, form and listen to my own voice: among those that I have carried with me, perhaps the strongest is that of Christopher Fynsk, whose teaching, mentorship, and friendship cannot be adequately measured. I am most grateful for his unwavering encouragement and philosophical companionship.

I would like to extend my gratitude to Gisela Brinker-Gabler, William Haver, Ingeborg Majer-O'Sickey, and Stephen David Ross for the gift of their teaching, as well as appreciation for the generous intellectual spirit shared by those I have the privilege of counting among my fellow travelers: Javier Anguera, Sushmita Chatterjee, Steve DeCaroli, Deniz Durmuş, Frances Kunreuther, Renée Green, Josh Hayes, Ann Holder, Lynne Huffer, Jennifer McWeeny, Lorraine Markotic, Brendan Moran, Dorothea Olkowski, Mariana Ortega, Mickaella Perina, Falguni Sheth, Elizabeth Sikes, Sam Talcott, Paul Venet, and Jason Wirth.

I wish to thank Michael Rinella at State University of New York Press for supporting the project and shepherding the manuscript through the publication process, Contemporary Continental Philosophy series editor Dennis Schmidt for his support of my work, as well as the three anonymous reviewers whose critical responses to the original draft of the manuscript proved invaluable to sharpening the focus of my argument. My great appreciation goes to Susan Geraghty, Alicia Brady, and Aimee Harrison for their work in guiding the manuscript through the editorial, production, and marketing stages.

Kimberly Lamm, to whom I dedicate *The Scene of the Voice*, along with our dear, sweet girl Lady, has been an unending source of support, encouragement, and intellectual inspiration. I am grateful for her many readings of the manuscript throughout the course of its development.

Finally, I wish to express my profound gratitude to my mother Cecilia and to my late father Thomas Eng. I wish with all my heart that this book could have appeared when he was still with us. Even more, I wish that my younger sister Michelle, who we lost all too soon shortly after our father passed away, could be here still. It is within the echoes of their voices that I composed these pages.

Introduction

The Scene of the Voice; or,
What to Do with Language after Affect

These days, it may seem odd or even quaint to be undertaking a study on the voice. Studying the voice inevitably means engaging with language, and recent research in the humanities and interpretive social sciences testifies to a decisive turn away from the concern with language that characterized postmodern and poststructuralist thought. Continental philosophy is currently in the thralls of speculative realism and object-oriented ontology, movements that are imagined to be breaks with what they describe as the straitjacketed "correlationalism" of post-Kantian philosophy.[1] Elsewhere along the contemporary theoretical horizon, one encounters invocations of a "new materialism" that would finally dispense with critical theory's anthropocentric nature.[2] Interwoven among these developments are the turn to affect and the so-called return to the aesthetic, which emphasize embodied forms of belonging and ideas of trans-, nonindividualized, and shared sensibility.[3]

From the perspective of these recent critical occupations, the engagement with language cultivated by poststructuralist thought—for example, as in deconstruction and psychoanalysis—does too much and yet not enough. Too much in the sense that Jacques Derrida's famous phrase "*Il n'y a pas de hors-texte*" ("There is nothing outside of the text" / "There is no outside-text")[4] gave rise to anxieties of linguistic and social determinism, of speaking subjects suddenly rendered imaginary fictions, thus robbing actual persons of voice, rights, and responsibilities. Too little, then, in the sense that with the turn to language, the body, it was said, was also done away with and thus the world, nature, and matter along with it. Purportedly trapped in the representative structures of language and culture, many have felt it imperative to regain the supposedly lost external world and, with it, the certainty and freedom that the idea of material existence promises. In response to such perceived trappings, speculative realism and new materialism hold out hope of engaging once again with objects themselves rather than the interiority of the mind, of which language is supposedly a mere expression. Similarly, the affective and aesthetic turns affirm the fact that we have bodies, whose capacities for sensibility cannot be spoken away.

Given this supposed legacy of poststructuralist thought and the current attempts to overcome that legacy, what could be gained from a return to the voice, much less from theorizing a "scene of the voice"? In this study, I contend that a reconsideration of the voice corrects some of the presuppositions at work in contemporary theory's latest turns. I include among these presuppositions not only an idea of poststructuralism's conception of language but more importantly, the self-evident opposition of language to affect and materiality. When we look at the voice as it appears in one of poststructuralism's guiding texts—Martin Heidegger's *Being and Time*—these presuppositions are revealed to be untenable.

Beginning with its conceptualization in Heidegger's project of fundamental ontology in *Being and Time*, and continuing with its reception by French post-Heideggerian philosophers, the voice realizes the social-political and ethical ambitions at the heart of critical thought's most recent projects by affirming language as a condition for the affective and aesthetic conceptualization of difference. Without a reconsideration of the voice and without attention to what I describe as the "scene" of the relation between language and the sensibility of existence Heidegger calls human finitude (our understanding and interpretation of the sense/meaning of Being that precedes and makes possible affective and aesthetic sensibility), the pursuit by the contemporary turns to affect and the aesthetic to regain an experience of difference remains incomplete. By eschewing the question of language, these turns, I argue, end up blocking their access to the very object to which they lay claim.

The Scene of the Voice analyzes the figure of the voice in contemporary Continental thought in order to reassess, trouble, and ultimately rewrite the exclusion of language from the material and bodily concerns the currently circulated notions of affect, sensibility, and the aesthetic are intended to signal. Heidegger's importance for the poststructuralist tradition makes his oeuvre—and specifically his conception of the voice—a logical starting point for this rewriting. More crucially, I argue, the destiny of the voice in Heidegger and post-Heideggerian Continental thought shows that these recent turns to affect and the aesthetic are mistaken in their conviction regarding the priority of affect over language. The voice shows that this relationship is actually the reverse. Or, more precisely, while the image of language as representation or communication may be an abstraction in comparison to the supposed immediacy of affective sensibility (though that is far from proven), the image of language embodied by the figure of the voice testifies to the human being's fundamental (or what Heidegger calls "originary") understanding and interpretation of the sense/meaning of Being. It is an image of language that not only makes possible signifying communication; it is also one that makes possible the form of sensibility that is said to be captured by the concept of affect.

For Heidegger, the voice names an experience with language that reveals its formational role in human existence. To exist is to interpret one's existence from an originary understanding of the sense/meaning of Being. Since this fundamental relationship of human finitude seldom appears before us in our quotidian dealings in the world when we are in commerce with beings (and in fact is typically suppressed or overlooked as a condition of our dealings with the world and as a condition of "having" a "world" filled with meaning in the first place), the human being needs to be "re-called" to this fact of the sense/meaning of Being and our interpretative relationship to it, which is always-already underway as a condition of our existence. The voice arrives to us—calls us, claims us, affectively—to confront us with the fact of the sense/meaning of Being and our interpretive relationship to it through the fact of language, the fact that language exists at all. By opening on to an experience with the fact of language, the voice reveals the fact of Being (that there are beings[5]), and the fact that our interpretive relationship to the sense/meaning of Being makes possible our engagement with materiality, including that materiality supposedly "signified" by affect.

Just as the Heideggerian voice reveals a relation to language that precedes and grounds representation and the conventional meanings of voice previously indicated, and just as it reveals a fundamental sensibility that precedes and grounds the conception of sensibility promoted by the affective and aesthetic turns, it also harbors a conception of shared sensibility (a sharing of the sense/meaning of Being between human beings) more fundamental than the one presupposed by the affective and aesthetic turns. As we will see, it is a sharing so radical that it is not a sharing between subjects but an originary "Being-with" that gives rise to subjective relationality. Moreover, as a figure, the voice serves as a scene for this constellation of language, sensibility, and human finitude. The voice is a figure for the appearance of the sense/meaning of Being and the human interpretive relation to it.

This "scene of the voice" in Heidegger is so radical that it does not belong to the speaking subject but instead calls the subject out and places a "claim" on the subject; the voice is a scene of the subject's dispossession, an event in which the human being is revealed in its exposure to the sense/meaning of Being and whose existence is constituted by this very exposure. Still, it is exactly this dispossession that Heidegger theorizes as a condition of human freedom, of existence as possibility. For Heidegger, the voice reveals human existence as an experience of freedom that is born out of an intimate relation to Being, an intimacy also simultaneously and unavoidably shared with other human beings.

The voice plays a crucial role as a vehicle of materiality and freedom: as a figure, the voice is an appearance of the human being's freedom to itself, as well as the human being's interpretation of its freedom, which Heidegger calls "facticity." The voice is a testimony to human existence as open, self-interpreting possibility. Showing how Heidegger works out this conception of the voice is the central project of this book. But it is also devoted to examining the critical pressures French post-Heideggerian thought has placed on Heidegger's theorization of the voice, particularly with regard to the voice's figural dimension, which, due to the centrality of the self-interpretation of human existence, Heidegger posits as necessary to the structure of human finitude.

Since, in Heidegger's view, the voice appears to the human being in order to testify to the human's self-interpreting relation to Being, it is consequently inseparable from its opening as a scene of appearance, which is to say, presentation. And although this scene of presentation reveals the ways the human subject is always-already outside of itself—in what Heidegger describes as an ecstatic relation that also places into radical question the assumptions made by the entire Western metaphysical tradition regarding the human subject's self-presence—the voice's scenic/figural character nonetheless renders it vulnerable as a site of specular capture. As a figure of the human relation to Being, it offers the temptation to think that this relation can be mastered through this very figure or image. Hence, there is a threat that the voice serves as yet another moment of speculative thought's drive to spectacularize Being, a drive often seen as exemplified by Hegel where the ambition is to fix an image of Being in order to know it and to know it in order to master it.

The role of spectacularization in the metaphysical impulse to master Being extends to the political sphere, specifically in the drive to master social existence through a fictive or mythic image of community, such as *das Volk* ("the People") or "the Nation," which invite affective identification. Heidegger's emphasis on the voice as a figure of the shared sense of Being, culminating in what he describes in *Being and Time* as the human Dasein's historical destiny in *das Volk*, not only suggests a possible spectacularization of community in his text but also his thought's close and uncomfortable proximity to the ideology of National Socialism, which of course traded on that very spectacularization of community.[6]

Rather than having the possibility of its share in the spectacularization of Being and community disqualify it from having any critical purchase on the contemporary theoretical landscape, this fraught character of the Heideggerian voice allows it to do the opposite. To substantiate this claim, I draw on critiques by Jean-Luc Nancy and Philippe Lacoue-Labarthe, who identify the figure of the voice in Heidegger as a site that makes his thought vulnerable to the ideology of National Socialism but also debate whether this particular fate of Heidegger's thought means that all attempts to think difference are destined to speculative capture. Their debate constitutes a critical moment in *The Scene of the Voice*, for it shows, contra the presuppositions of the affective and aesthetic turns, that what connects language and affect and what makes their severability from each other untenable is a contestation around mimesis. Not mimesis defined as imitation but mimesis as the name for radical, dissimulating difference. The opposition between language and affect that drives the affective and aesthetic turns is thus not a matter of which has access to "the really Real" (language or affect) but is instead a contest over which can name the relation to difference. Where the debate between Nancy and Lacoue-Labarthe indicates an awareness of this fact by post-Heideggerian thinkers of the voice and especially the dangers of specular capture that hover around it, proponents of the affective and aesthetic turns miss the fact of the contestation over mimesis altogether. As I go on to argue, this allows these turns to succumb to their own specular capture, both in the form of an artificial separation of language from affect (resulting in a reifying figuration of the latter) and in uncritical mimetic identifications with—and indeed, unconscious, affective investments in— various disciplinary voices that tend to be given authoritative deference in certain provinces of American academia, most immediately those of "Philosophy" and "Theory."

The debate between Nancy and Lacoue-Labarthe turns out to be critical for *The Scene of the Voice* because not only does it lay bare the social-political and ethical stakes of the opposition between language and affect but also delineates at least two paths that I argue post-Heideggerian thought follows in its reception of the Heideggerian voice. Two thinkers who I identify as following these paths are Maurice Blanchot and Gilles Deleuze. By analyzing the respective efforts Blanchot and Deleuze undertook to respond to and reconceive the problem of the voice in Heidegger's text, specifically with respect to the issues Nancy and Lacoue-Labarthe's debate exposes regarding the voice's scenic/figural dimension, *The Scene of the Voice* demonstrates the need to invent new engagements with language in the form of new modes of writing in order to honor the fundamental relation to the sense/meaning of Being while also guarding against the dangers of specular capture. As such, *The Scene of the Voice* also indicates untapped resources in Continental reflections on language for addressing contradictions at work in contemporary theories of affect and the aesthetic, which, in their respective drives to capture the really Real, end up only capturing their own self-fascination with their figurations of sensibility.

Before I outline the analysis I undertake here in *The Scene of the Voice*, I would like to map out the assumptions and contradictions that I see operating in the affective turn and the return to the aesthetic. Although it is not the purpose of this book to engage with the writings making up these movements directly, I do want to devote some space to delineating what I see are the lacunae present in them in order to illustrate what is at stake in taking up again the question of language in Heidegger and post-Heideggerian thought. For the purposes of this introduction, I will focus on those two trends that presently occupy the theoretical imaginary involving affect and the aesthetic, particularly as they intersect with each other. I have chosen to leave to the side the movements of new materialism, speculative realism, and object-oriented ontology previously noted. Although, as I have suggested, all these turns and movements share some basic assumptions about materiality and a desire for freedom,[7] speculative realism and object-oriented ontology especially involve a quite specialist debate with the legacy of post-Kantian Continental philosophy. New materialism calls for a rehearsal of the so-called older materialisms of Marxism and particularly Marxist-feminism. Tarrying with the complexities of those debates, I feel, would take us too far afield when my main goal is to provide a more general critical horizon that reaches across the humanities and interpretive social sciences, one whose expanse I would like readers to see *The Scene of the Voice* as questioning.[8]

The following section gives a thumbnail sketch of the affective turn, the return to the aesthetic, and their intersection. While I refrain from a critical assessment of them, I outline the contours of these turns in such a way as to stress what, to my ears, are specific resonances they share with Heidegger's work. Of particular note are regular evocations of such Heideggerian themes as sensibility, world, and dwelling, which, for Heidegger, coalesce in the question of language. Remarkably, Heidegger's name almost never accompanies these evocations; yet they appear frequently enough that it is possible to wonder whether there is not a simultaneous reliance upon and repression of Heidegger's *texte* in the construction of these turns. In any case, I will maintain that a recovery of these subterranean "Heideggerianisms" is called for, for they reveal the reality of the desire animating these recent turns across the contemporary theoretical horizon and thus point the way for these turns to, in spite of themselves, actually think the object they seek.

The Turn to Affect and the Return of the Aesthetic

From the viewpoint of its proponents, the affective turn announces an involvement with the body and a promise to correct the body's exclusion from the history of thought. Because of its materiality and contingency, the body has been considered an unreliable basis upon which to ground philosophical truth, which, since Plato, has been projected as unchanging and transcendent. Since the affective turn has appeared relatively recently on the critical scene, we are led to believe that the history of the body's exclusion runs right up to the twentieth century and includes those intellectual movements that have immediately preceded the turn to affect. In his foreword to *The Affective Turn*, a collection of essays edited by Patricia Ticineto Clough with Jean Halley, Michael Hardt refers to these prior movements as the linguistic and cultural turns. Although he does not identify specific thinkers with these movements, his characterization of the affective turn as "introduc[ing] an important shift" in research that "refer[s] equally to the body and the mind" stakes out the basic antagonism between the current attention to affect and those previous academic concerns; while those previous turns were caught up exclusively with reason, the affective turn corrects that imbalance.[9] Furthermore, by involving both "reason and the passions" in the Spinozist sense, affect, says Hardt, allows us to (finally) enter the "realm of causality" (ix). Implied with this statement, then, is the idea that the linguistic and cultural turns' preoccupation with representation and ideology sequesters us in the imaginary, where nothing is really real and from within which we are unable to affect the world.

For Clough, the challenge is to think of affect in active rather than passive terms. In her introduction to the volume, Clough mirrors Hardt's characterization of the affective turn, although she goes into greater detail contextualizing it as a development from previous theoretical pursuits. One of these pursuits is the psychoanalytic treatment of trauma that was ubiquitous in academic discourse in the 1990s. For Clough, this treatment represents an early occupation with affect, but in her estimation, it suffered from a number of fatal oversights. The first of these oversights was in working with a conception of the body as something individualized, contained, and discrete (11); the second has to do with a self-imposed limitation on how psychoanalysis can talk about (i.e., represent) trauma. Since its conception of the body insists on a fixed distinction between nature (as body) and culture, or, in other words, between matter and form, psychoanalysis can only understand trauma as an experience that repeatedly happens to the body, which the body is unable to overcome (7–8). Thus, according to Clough, the psychoanalytically conceived traumatic body is trapped in a fatal affect, which can only yield a form of expression that retreads without end a traumatic wounding, providing no opening for transformation or change. All attempts at writing about trauma from the basis of this exclusively passive psychoanalytic conception of the body can only reproduce a form of testimony (or perhaps a kind of voice) afflicted by absence and loss (4–5).

Against this supposedly mistaken view adopted by psychoanalysis, Clough invokes the Deleuzian conception of the body (from his readings of Bergson and Spinoza, and from his collaborations with Félix Guattari) as a "machinic assemblage" composed of a concentration of forces and relations that includes the inhuman as much as the human, the inorganic as much as the organic (1–4). The Deleuzian body is not a rationalized, atomic unit, but a networked site open to being affected as much as it affects other bodies, a site of relation with and between other bodies as well as their environments. Unlike the supposed solely passive body of psychoanalysis, the Deleuzian body is active. With the Deleuzian body, trauma is no longer a final interruption of the body but a moment in the body's process of perpetual becoming (11). Following Keith Ansell Pearson's reconstruction of Deleuze's critique of Freud, and particularly his outline of Deleuze's "biophilosophy," Clough submits that the Deleuzian body and the affective relations it presupposes entail a radical reconceptualization of matter, which includes information and reveals the body as "better understood as a machinic assemblage," "neither organic nor mechanical," and, quoting Pearson, "approaching a 'techno-ontological threshold'" (12).[10] For

Clough, then, it is not the case that psychoanalysis has no conception of affect; rather, as the Freudian conception of trauma shows, its conception is inadequate to a thought of becoming (and therefore freedom) and what she claims, again, following Pearson, is the emergence of a "postbiological" human evolution (12).

According to Clough, this postbiological emergence can be gleaned from the fact that, within "the social" today, "a new configuration of bodies, technology, and matter" requires critical theory to respond differently than it has in the past, to "shift . . . from privileging the organic body to exploring non-organic life" (2). If the Deleuzian conception of the body allows for a more complex understanding of affect, one that exceeds the individual human body and includes the human body's nonhierarchical, networked interface with other bodies, human and nonhuman alike, then we must see the body as a product of social-political forces, not something we can separate from history at our choosing. These forces include those of capitalism and information technologies, Clough maintains, which have produced a body whose affective capacities they exploit in order to train the body for work, as well as consumption (16–17). This is the body of global capitalism and neoliberalism, showing that, though affect promotes an image of open becoming, the becoming that results is not always the desired kind. It is a most perplexing contradiction given the freedom attributed to affect by theorists of the affective turn. But without a theorization of affect, Clough submits, it will not be possible to confront the social as it is currently configured and modulated through these manipulations, and we will hamper our abilities to act effectively within it as a consequence (20).

Another collection dedicated to marking out a space for affect studies is *The Affect Theory Reader*, edited by Melissa Gregg and Gregory J. Seigworth. Published two years after Clough's volume, *The Affect Theory Reader* is similarly based in a Deleuzian-Spinozist approach to affect, even though it curiously features well-known affect theorists (most notably, Sara Ahmed and Lauren Berlant) who do not adhere to that particular conception of affect. Nonetheless, in their introduction, Gregg and Seigworth invoke the phrase from Spinoza's *Ethics* made famous by Deleuze and elaborated by Deleuzian affect theorists such as Brian Massumi: "No one has yet determined what the body can do."[11] Gregg and Seigworth's invocation is intended as much as a comment on the open-endedness of affect as on the status of affect studies itself. Spinoza's theorization of affect as pertaining to an infinite capacity for the body to be affected and to affect other bodies serves as the basis upon which Gregg and Seigworth submit affect as both an opening on to difference as well as a concept of existence that resists any final conceptualization. "There is no single, generalizable theory of affect," they write, "not yet, and (thankfully) there never will be" (3). Because of its infinite openness, affect is characterized as a perpetual "*inbetween-ness*," and as such, is a name for "those forces—visceral forces beneath, alongside, or generally *other than* conscious knowing, vital forces insisting beyond emotion—that can serve to drive us toward movement" (1). "Indeed," Gregg and Seigworth say, "affect is persistent proof of a body's never less than ongoing immersion in and among the world's obstinacies and rhythms, its refusals as much as its invitations" (1). Like Hardt's and Clough's remarks in *The Affective Turn*, Gregg and Seigworth cast affect as anchoring the human in (nonlinear) causality and processes of becoming but in a way that cannot be captured by the supposed lawlike structures of consciousness and rationality. Here again, affect means contingency, possibility of the new, and ultimately, freedom.

In contrast to *The Affective Turn*, which assembles a particular set of papers written by Clough's students that amounts to a very specific approach to affect, *The Affect Theory Reader* offers a wider survey of the turn to affect across the disciplines composing the humanities and interpretive social sciences. Nonetheless, a few themes remain consistent between the two collections: in addition to the association of affect with the noncognitive and its identification with becoming and freedom, the idea that the turn to affect constitutes a simultaneous turn away from the linguistic turn "and its attendant social constructionisms" appears in Gregg and Seigworth's introduction as well (7). Like Clough, who has an essay in *The Affect Theory Reader* also, Gregg and Seigworth maintain that affect promises the possibility of fashioning "a much wider definition for the social and cultural" (presumably less deterministic) than what was allowed under the linguistic turn (8). This is one of the claims *The Scene of the Voice* will test in its attention to Heidegger's conception of language. As I will show through his figuring of the voice, Heidegger's relation to language is decidedly not deterministic; the relation to language is instead a condition for any possibility of freedom.

Like the affective turn, the return to the aesthetic also imagines a more expansive social and political sphere. The name most associated with this return is that of Jacques Rancière, whose *Disagreement* (1999 [*La Mésentente* (1995)]) and *The Politics of Aesthetics* (2004 [*Le Partage du sensible* (2000)]) redirect philosophical research back to the concern with aesthetics and the senses that characterized much of eighteenth- and nineteenth-century European thought. Rancière enacts this return, however, in order to provoke a consideration of what he describes as a fundamental connection between aesthetics and politics, putting forth the claim that all politics are grounded in an aesthetic contestation, or in what he calls "the distribution of the sensible."[12] Although Rancière does not construct his position as a response to the linguistic turn, he does characterize post-Heideggerian approaches to theorizing the political as wrongheaded and can thus be seen as seeking to correct those approaches (or, as he says, as attempting to "save" us from them).[13] As with the affective turn, there have been attempts to capture the idea of the return to the aesthetic in various edited collections. Taking their inspiration from Rancière's interventions, they align with affect theorists in their regard of the social as governed by a structure of shared sensibility.[14]

Before enumerating the ways that the voice exposes lacunae in the above conceptions of affect and the aesthetic, I want to discuss some critiques of the affective turn, which I believe touch also on the return to the aesthetic. Especially noteworthy is the critique Clare Hemmings puts forth, analyzing in particular claims made by Eve Kosofsky Sedgwick and Brian Massumi in their respective theorizations of affect.[15] This approach in itself is interesting, for they each represent quite different theoretical positions vis-à-vis affect: Sedgwick, a pioneer of queer theory, pursues a path staked out by Silvan Tomkins and crafts her approach to affect in close dialogue with Melanie Klein. By contrast, Massumi is a well-known interpreter of Deleuze and of Deleuze's collaborations with Guattari, and so elaborates a conception of affect from out of their engagement with Spinoza. Despite this stark difference, their writings consistently appear as guiding texts in the work of affect theorists, and Hemmings is able to demonstrate how these two paths taken by Sedgwick and Massumi toward affect share some common theoretical assumptions and tendencies.

As Hemmings notes, in addition to reversing the mind-body hierarchy (but still retaining the hierarchy), the affective turn works with an unquestioned ontology of affect. It conceives affect as essentially disruptive and good, and as essentially good because it is disruptive (549–51). Confirming also that this valuation of affect takes place as a response to what is felt as the domineering and nihilistic critique of poststructuralist theory, particularly deconstruction, Hemmings questions the idiosyncratic character of the causal freedom affect is taken to manifest. With respect to Sedgwick, Hemmings questions her characterization of affect as that which escapes linear causality. She is equally suspicious of Massumi's description of affect as autonomous, showing how these conceptions betray "an attitude or faith in something other than the social and cultural . . . [a] *trust that* there is something outside culture" (563; original emphasis). Although she does not give a name to this faith or trust, we might recognize it as the reappearance of the Kantian belief in noumenal causality. Such a reappearance should not be welcomed by critical discourse, it should seem, as it cordons off human freedom into a space of the ineffable and the mystical and invites an epistemological quietism.

In her critique of the affective turn, Ruth Leys also questions the characterization of affect as nonrational, asignifying, and prepersonal, saying that this expresses a metaphysical assumption regarding the mind's separation from the body, as well as "a false dichotomy between mind and matter."[16] However, she then builds further on Hemmings's observation of affect theorists' automatic equation of affect with newness and "the Real," particularly as the real site of politics and locus of political transformation (451). As I previously noted, this assumption leads to a contradiction, which Hemmings touches on as well in her analysis, and that is seemingly unknowingly articulated by Clough in her introduction to *The Affective Turn*—namely, that affect names both the possibility of the new and also the terrain upon which social manipulation and control are exerted (460–61).[17]

It is with affect's contradictory status that we might see another intersection between affect studies and the return to the aesthetic. Rancière's theorization of the aesthetic ground of the political provides a possible explanation of how affect can be a force of both homogenization and revolutionary newness, of identity and difference. Any distribution of the sensible requires, according to Rancière, a demarcation between those who are identified as capable of receiving that particular partition of sense (the sense, for example, of belonging to a given community) and those who are identified as incapable of (and ineligible to) receive that partition. Rancière points to Aristotle's explanation for why the slave is ineligible to participate in political life as an exemplar of the distribution of the sensible. The contradiction, of course, lies in the fact that the slave is both inside and outside the given distribution. Although he lacks the capacity to comprehend the given distribution of sensibility, thereby excluding him from it, he must still be able to understand enough within this distribution in order to obey commands from those who have been identified as belonging to that distribution.[18]

What Rancière himself takes for granted, however, is the very fact of this "sharing-distribution" (*partage*) of sense, of the sensible's "distributability," which then renders the assumptions he makes in his theorization of the political's aesthetic ground in league with the assumptions animating the affective turn. For both the affective turn and the return to the aesthetic presume a fundamental "shareability" of affect and sense, but they do not explain how this is possible or what accounts for it. When we search for such an explanation, we might find ourselves thrown from Rancière back to affect theory's description of "the world" as that which mediates the transmission and sharing of affect and sense. "Indeed," write Gregg and Seigworth, "affect is persistent proof of a body's never less than ongoing immersion in and among the world's obstinacies and rhythms, its refusals as much as its invitations" (1). However, this merely pushes the search further, for their conception of world is not an empirical one. In the very same passage, they will refer to affect as that which "circulate[s] about, between, and sometimes stick[s] to bodies and *worlds*" (1; emphasis added). What is "world" for them, then? Apparently, a shared sensibility.

I have demonstrated elsewhere that the sense of "sense" informing Rancière's conception of *partage* possesses a Heideggerian valence, which he takes great efforts to suppress.[19] In this way, Rancière shares with affect theory what Hemmings describes as a willful misreading of the poststructuralist tradition as part of the process of constructing their critical positions.[20] Both presuppose sense as something shared and transmitted among bodies, but neither provide an explanation for its shared character other than to define it as such. And although Rancière may limit any other "Heideggerianisms" from slipping into his discourse, the texts associated with affect theory have been less vigilant. In addition to "world," one finds repeated invocations of "dwelling" with decidedly existential intonations.[21] I contend that these invocations remain conceptually vague absent any contestation with Heidegger's thought, and especially without any engagement with the Heideggerian voice, which figures the relation to finitude connoted by the concepts of "world" and "dwelling."

As I explained previously, my intention in pointing out these lacunae is not to dismiss either the affective turn or the return to the aesthetic. As I hope to show, I have a deep allegiance with these projects' theoretical and political commitments. If I have a complaint, it concerns the ways these projects establish their critical positions in opposition to post-Heideggerian thought on language even as their work makes use of its major concepts.

Rather than diminish these scholars' aims, an explicit elaboration of Heidegger's conceptualization of the voice can actually enhance them and help them achieve what I argue is being expressed by their drive to theorize affect and the aesthetic: namely, a desire to encounter existence as an experience of difference. Yet, by identifying language strictly with "conscious knowing" and rationality, the affective turn robs itself of the opportunity to capitalize on Heidegger's theorization of language as an experience that exceeds signifying communication and representation. Relatedly, by overlooking Heidegger's reflections on human finitude as an originary relation to the sense/meaning of Being, the notion of sensibility invoked by both the affective turn and the return to the aesthetic remains merely that—a notion, if not altogether an empty abstraction. Heidegger's conceptualization of the voice, I argue, reveals that the sensibility to which the affective and the aesthetic turns appeal is grounded first in a relation to language as a gathering of the sense/meaning of Being—and not the other way around.

Furthermore, Heidegger's stress on the scenic dimension of the voice provides a way to address the contradictions that confront the affective turn. Specifically, his emphasis that it is through the voice that human beings confirm their understanding of the sense of existence and have that understanding reflected back to them in and through the figure helps explain how the sensibility that affect names can be alternately both an experience of freedom as well as a site of manipulation. Indeed, as Heidegger's French readers have shown, this inextricable scenic dimension of the voice accounts for his own infamous capture by the ideology of National Socialism, even as he offered it as an opening to "destructure" Western metaphysics. Their critical assessment of how the voice can equally serve as an affective vehicle not only for repeating a speculative longing endemic to the very tradition that Heidegger sought to dismantle but also for allowing oneself to be captured by the metaphysics of presence to which fascist politics subscribes makes it clear that the voice—as figure, scene, and screen—delineates a site with which any thought attending to the political grounds of social existence must contend. Despite succumbing to specular capture himself, Heidegger's theorization of the voice (and the question of language it harbors) nonetheless reveals this hazard of figuration, and as *The Scene of the Voice* shows, it also maps approaches for negotiating this hazard. By eschewing the questions of language, the affective turn and the return to the aesthetic effectively block themselves from appreciating their own trade in figuration and ultimately from reaching the realms of affect and the aesthetic to which they lay claim.

From Finitude's Scenic Dimension to (Un)writing the Figure

"World," "dwelling," "inbetweenness," "*partage*," even "body"—in addition to carrying Heideggerian inflections, these concepts that populate the discourses of the affective turn and the return to the aesthetic are unquestionably figures through which these discourses attempt to get at the social ground of existence. However, unlike Heidegger's figuration of the shared sense of Being in the voice, the employment of these terms by affect theorists and the new aestheticians lacks a self-awareness of these terms' figural character. For even if affect escapes rationalization, the thought of such an escape must pass through and appear in language. This simple fact seems to continue to be overlooked. What marks the voice in Heidegger as singular is the fact that by testifying to the human being's fundamental understanding of the sense/meaning of Being, the voice serves as a figure of human finitude. It is an event of human finitude appearing to itself; it is a figure for finitude's figuration, in a movement Heidegger names "facticity." The voice thus testifies to the fact that human finitude and its (self-)figuration are inseparable. "Affect" is simply another name for a thought of human finitude—of being in the world from an understanding of the sense/meaning of Being. As such, we will see that "affect" cannot shed either its participation in the sense/meaning of Being or its accompanying figural dimension.

The Scene of the Voice argues in fact that it is precisely finitude's figuration in and as a relation to language that underlies the sense of existence as an affective and aesthetic event—not the other way around. Throughout this study, I examine how Heidegger establishes the voice as the figuration of finitude, and I explore how this figuration is based in a fundamental experience of language. But it is an experience of language conceived not in a derivative mode of representation or signification, to which theorists of the affective turn and the return to the aesthetic reduce language. It is an experience of language as Heidegger shows is revealed in the voice—as a relation to the fundamental (i.e., originary) sense/meaning of Being that is the condition for existence. This examination of Heidegger's theorization of the voice as an experience of language organizes the book's first three chapters, which move from the voice's appearance in *Being and Time* (1927) to what I argue are its reappearances and transformations in "The Origin of the Work of Art" (1935–36, published 1950 and 1960), *Introduction to Metaphysics* (1935, published 1953), and *Hölderlin's Hymn "The Ister"* (1942, published 1984).

After establishing the ways Heidegger figures the voice as the intersection of language and finitude in these works, I then go on to examine how thinkers of the post-Heideggerian Continental tradition engage with the social-political implications of Heidegger's theorization of the voice. The question animating the second half of the book is the following: if part of being human means having our finitude appear before us in the voice, then does this mean human existence requires a figure—or scene—in order to appear? An affirmative answer to this question underscores the centrality of sensible presentation to human existence. However, as indicated earlier, dangerous implications arise from this possibility, most immediately, the problem of specular, affective capture by the figure—or what Jean-Luc Nancy and Philippe Lacoue-Labarthe have called "myth." This threat of figural capture, which Nancy and Lacoue-Labarthe view as subtending mythic structures of community, such as the kind promulgated by National Socialism and the one that Nancy and Lacoue-Labarthe argue appears in Heidegger's conception of the voice, outlines a fundamental tension between the necessity of figuration to human existence and the possibility (or perhaps inevitability) of a specular fascination that masquerades as an encounter with existence and difference.

As also noted previously, however, this tension Nancy and Lacoue-Labarthe uncover and debate in their analysis of the Heideggerian voice reveals most immediately that what is actually at stake in the opposition of language and affect is the question of mimesis. Language, affect, figure, voice, human finitude, and community all meet in the question of how to respond to the demand of mimesis, which Nancy and Lacoue-Labarthe's debate shows is the demand of difference as such—specifically, how to think and affirm difference without attempting to master it through the figure. This question of mimesis thus serves as a frame through which *The Scene of the Voice* then explores how other thinkers within the post-Heideggerian Continental tradition have received the Heideggerian problematic of the voice and devised new modes of writing to navigate the hazards of figuration. Between Maurice Blanchot and Gilles Deleuze, we encounter two modes of writing that reconfigure the Heideggerian voice and respond to the problem of the figure and the demand of mimesis: for Blanchot, the writing known as literature is a scene for the figure's effacement through the dissimulating force of what he names "the narrative voice," while for Deleuze, writing is a way to solicit the voice as the univocity of Being, which he theorizes as a process of becoming that gives rise to ever more figures. In the last two chapters of the book, I consider the ways Blanchot's and Deleuze's respective responses to Heidegger uphold his conception of the centrality of figuration and affectivity in the experience of finitude while also critically revising the configuration of voice, language, affect, and finitude.

Chapter 1 establishes the figurative and affective dimensions of the voice through a reading of its appearance in *Being and Time* as the call of conscience. Existing commentaries tend to focus on Heidegger's description of the voice of conscience as a call that comes from Dasein addressed to itself, which they interpret as aligning with commonplace conceptions of conscience as an ideal, interior monologue. However, as I show in my reconstruction of the role the call of conscience plays in the structure of Dasein's finitude, which I analyze through Heidegger's concept of "finite transcendence," the voice possesses an essential affective and figurative character that cannot be separated from the way Heidegger contends it shocks the human Dasein back to the fact of its existence and from its forgetting of the fact that it always-already has an understanding of the sense/meaning of Being. By highlighting the connection between Heidegger's conceptualization of *die Stimmung* (mood or attunement) and the voice as *die Stimme* in *Being and Time*, chapter 1 draws attention to a thought of affect in Heidegger as a relation that exceeds the individual subject but that also shows the inextricable relationship of sense and sensibility at the heart of the human Dasein's understanding of the sense/meaning of Being. The connection between *die Stimmung* and *die Stimme* also underscores the voice as an affective, figurative echo and return of human finitude to itself, one that points to a fundamental relation to the question of language.

Staying with *Being and Time*, chapter 2 expands the analysis of the first chapter by bringing out the ways Heidegger's aesthetic figuration of the voice strikes a critical distinction between an instrumental, communicative conception of language (voice as mere speech or *phonē*) and a relation to language as an affective experience of finitude (voice as *logos*). This "antagonism of language," as I name it in this chapter, performs two tasks in Heidegger's conceptualization of the voice: First, it uncovers an existential "speaking" of language by opening onto an experience with language as a site of the sensible presentation of finitude, an experience of language as an affective scene of the human being's relation to the sense/meaning of Being, where language exceeds its conventional role as a tool of communication or representation. Secondly, this antagonism stresses the relational dimension of language, emphasizing the voice as an opening of finitude that is shared with the other human being, an emphasis I draw out with the aid of Jean-Luc Nancy's *Le Partage des voix* (1982) [which was translated into English as a long essay entitled "Sharing Voices" (1990)]. Together, the book's first two chapters demonstrate how the Heideggerian voice figures a fundamental relation between language and existence that reveals an image of Heideggerian affect that precedes the meaningfulness and shared quality of affect as it is presupposed in the affective and aesthetic turns of contemporary thought. The incorporation of Nancy's intervention on the shared scene of human finitude also shows that the Heideggerian voice is not an internal psychic event but an externally directed, collective experience.

Once we begin to see the essential role the aesthetic figure of the voice plays in the shared experience of human finitude, a number of questions emerge: How does the voice's aesthetic character relate to Heidegger's more explicit reflections on aesthetics, specifically to his conception of the work of art? And does the voice appear in his reflections on the work of art, or does the figure of the voice recede as Heidegger's thought develops? If the voice can be said to appear in Heidegger's conceptualization of the work of art, then in what ways, if any, might those appearances constitute a transformation in Heidegger's theorization of the voice?

Chapter 3 investigates these questions through a reading of Heidegger's "The Origin of the Work of Art" and his interpretations of Sophocles's *Antigone* in *An Introduction to Metaphysics* and *Hölderlin's Hymn "The Ister."* In "The Origin of the Work of Art," we find Heidegger arguing explicitly for the centrality of figuration to human finitude, and we witness the voice reappear through the figuration of the "strife" between world and earth, for which the artwork provides a stage or scene. Following Heidegger's contention in "The Origin of the Work of Art" that poetry is the art form par excellence, I then trace the voice's travel to Heidegger's interpretations of tragedy, specifically in terms of his sustained engagement with *Antigone*. It is in this travel from *An Introduction to Metaphysics* to *Hölderlin's Hymn "The Ister"* that we view two transformations of the voice emerge in Heidegger's thinking: the first is an image of the voice as a historical saying of a people (in this case, that of the Greek Dasein), and the second is an image built upon a possible merging of the voice with the feminine in the character of Antigone herself.

In addition to connecting to Nancy's elaboration of the voice in Heidegger as a collective sharing and as giving rise to ever new figures, both of these transformations will revitalize questions about the place of the voice in the Western metaphysical tradition and the social and political implications that unfold from this, which the chapters that follow pursue more directly. Against the backdrop of those questions, however, this third chapter shows how the voice's persistence in Heidegger's conception of the work of art mobilizes what Heidegger describes as the artwork's dissimulating or "aletheiac" force and its staging of human finitude. Ultimately, I argue in this chapter that, for Heidegger, the work of art makes sensible the necessity of presentation in the human being's experience of finitude. In other words, the artwork serves as a scene *of the* scene of the human relation to the sense/meaning of Being—a scene *of the* scene of the voice.

After the first three chapters analyze Heidegger's conception of the voice, and the inextricable connection among language, affect, finitude, and figuration it expresses, chapter 4 turns to an examination of the voice's critical reception by Heidegger's French readers. It focuses on the metaphysical hazards of figuration and their social and political implications as revealed in Jean-Luc Nancy's and Philippe Lacoue-Labarthe's engagement with Heidegger and the question of the relationship of his thought to his involvement with National Socialism. Given what appears to be the necessity of figuration (or what Nancy and Lacoue-Labarthe debate as the scenic) to human existence, a question arises as to the extent to which philosophical thought can resist specular capture. Nancy names such capture "myth," particularly in terms of an identification with the myth of community, and Lacoue-Labarthe describes it in terms of the impulse to master Being by fixing it in a figure, a drive Lacoue-Labarthe names "onto-typology."

As previously noted, Nancy's and Lacoue-Labarthe's respective positions regarding the problem of the scenic in Heidegger, and in philosophy more generally, do not align; in fact, their respective positions form the basis of a decades-long debate that they sustain concerning the ability of critical thought to guard against the threat of specular capture. While Nancy acknowledges Heidegger's apparent subscription to onto-typology as a serious issue, particularly as it informs Heidegger's apparent projection of the human being's destiny in an image of community, he approaches the matter as a question of mythic writing that requires repeated interruption and the rewriting of community, what we will see him refer to as a kind of "ontological mimesis." As also previously stated, Nancy's position will suggest that at the heart of his disagreement with Lacoue-Labarthe lies the problem of mimesis, or rather, the problem of the problem of mimesis—the history of mimesis as a problem (or threat) of difference that "Philosophy" regards itself as authorized to resolve via prohibition and control but particularly through the mastery supposedly afforded through figuration. Thus, from that standpoint, Lacoue-Labarthe is much more skeptical than Nancy regarding the ability of philosophical thought to ever be rid of figuration and therefore remain free of specular capture and the social-political and ethical implications that follow: the most immediate of which is the possibility that by creating figures through which to encounter and welcome difference, philosophical thought ends up consolidating its domination of it. To the extent that the debate between Nancy and Lacoue-Labarthe reveals that the problem of mimesis is *the* problem at stake in the question of language, affect, finitude, and figuration, what reason is there to suspect that the embrace of affect and the aesthetic by the (speculative) turns of contemporary thought are not also unwittingly implicated in the problem of mimesis?

Chapter 4 thus constitutes a pivotal moment in *The Scene of the Voice* and delineates the lines of thought it pursues in its final two chapters, as well as the epilogue that closes the book. As we will see, the debate between Nancy and Lacoue-Labarthe offers two competing views on how to respond to the problem of figuration while still honoring the desire to encounter difference *as difference* and Heidegger's original intuition that the relation to difference—of Being, of the other human being—appears in the intersection of language and finitude. Both views rest on conceiving new images of writing: on the one hand, as mentioned, Nancy proffers a conception of writing (and of community) as perpetual interruption. From Lacoue-Labarthe, we receive the imperative to write as a mode of effacement, one that casts suspicion on all forms of mythic belonging by undoing the figure and achieving a "caesura of the speculative," a notion Lacoue-Labarthe adopts from Friedrich Hölderlin in order to promote a suspension of onto-typology. These two positions delineated by Nancy and Lacoue-Labarthe provide coordinates to approach the work of Blanchot and Deleuze in the final two chapters of the study, making it possible to view them as not only critical readers of the Heideggerian voice but also to regard them as each realizing new forms of writing that align with the opposing imperatives staked out by Nancy and Lacoue-Labarthe.

Chapter 5 is dedicated to examining Blanchot's pursuit of the question of literature as both a reconfiguration of the Heideggerian voice and as an instance of the writing of effacement which Lacoue-Labarthe calls for in his debate with Nancy. With Blanchot, we see an intensification of the thought of the experience with language that Heidegger opens up in his work. Literature, for Blanchot, is a site of exposure so severe that it refuses the human being access to language as a refuge for subjectivity. Through the movement of what Blanchot calls "unworking" (*désoeuvrement*), which is also a link to Nancy, literature exiles the human subject to what he describes as the "night" of "the outside," denying the human being any claim to experience as such, much less to thinking. In contrast to the Heideggerian voice, which for Heidegger ultimately returns to the human being as a form of self-address, Blanchot clears a space for what he names the "narrative voice" of literature, which leaves the human being bereft of language, and therefore bereft of a voice as well, constituting a scene of their affective withdrawal. Focusing on writings often regarded as the most formative in Blanchot's thought, including "Literature and the Right to Death" (1949), *The Space of Literature* (1955), and *The Infinite Conversation* (1969), as well as "Artaud" (1956), a brief but important piece (notably influential for Deleuze as well), I retrace how each step Blanchot takes in staging the scene of effacement occurs in direct response to, and as revisions of, the Heideggerian constellation of voice, language, affect, the work of art, and of thinking itself. Through this staging, Blanchot recovers (without trying to master) the dissimulating force of mimesis that Nancy and Lacoue-Labarthe's debate reveals is at stake in the Heideggerian voice.

Standing in contrast to the scene of effacement enacted by Blanchot are Deleuze's conceptualizations of univocity and simulacra, which chapter 6 argues can be regarded as constituting an altogether different reception and revision of the Heideggerian voice. After reconstructing Deleuze's theorization of univocity in *Difference and Repetition* (1968), which he partly undertakes through an explicit citation and reading of Heidegger, I follow him as he elaborates the concept further in *The Logic of Sense* (1969) in relation to the figure of simulacra, which I read as figures for mimesis, thus connecting back to the fundamental question identified by Nancy and Lacoue-Labarthe in their debate with one another. Together, univocity and simulacra delineate ways that I contend Deleuze attempts to figure the Heideggerian question of the relationship between human being and the sense/meaning of Being. At the same time, I also argue that these concepts in Deleuze resonate with Nancy's assertion that what is called for in response to the problem of figuration is an embrace of its inevitability and the need for thought to fashion ever new figures for conceptualizing human finitude. In yet another respect, Nancy's elaboration of the shared scene of human finitude, established in my reading in chapter 2, will suggest correspondences between the Heideggerian and Deleuzean theorizations of affect.

Attending to Heidegger's role in what is considered Deleuze's "mature" philosophical writings of *Difference and Repetition* and *The Logic of Sense*, chapter 6 suggests the possibility of opening new approaches to Deleuze's corpus, encouraging us to see him as a dedicated reader of Heidegger (as well as Blanchot). Should this hypothesis hold, then implications follow for how we might read anew Deleuze's theorizations of the work of art and of literature in terms of how they might engage both Heidegger and Blanchot but also in terms of how they might offer another variation of the constellation among voice, language, affect, and finitude. The focus on this constellation in Deleuze will allow us to attune ourselves to how it appears in Deleuze's later works in aesthetics, such as *Francis Bacon: The Logic of Sensation* (1981) and in the second volume of his *Cinema* books, *The Time-Image* (1985).

But perhaps more provocatively (at least as far as self-identifying Deleuzean theorists are concerned), I also suggest in chapter 6 that the formative presence of Heidegger for Deleuze's conceptualization of univocity invites us to entertain the idea of counting Deleuze as a philosopher of language in the post-Heideggerian tradition. Such a view, I contend, helps illuminate differently how we should understand Deleuze's later collaborations with Guattari, particularly their theorization of a "minor literature" and the role of the animal voice in it. But, more pertinent to the present study, the possibility of assessing Deleuze's status as a philosopher of language holds significant implications for affect studies and its self-authorizing narrative, which identifies Deleuze as one of the pioneers of its field. For if, as I argue in this chapter, Deleuze's conceptualization of affect rests on a theorization of the voice, then this reliance upsets affect studies' foundational claim about the primacy of affect over language. More crucially, Deleuze's theorization of simulacra helps us see that he belongs among the post-Heideggerian thinkers who grapple with the problem of language and affect as really concerning the problem of mimesis, thus shifting the debate to what *The Scene of the Voice* holds is the more essential question at the heart of the opposition between language and affect.

At this point, it may be worth including an acknowledgment of both the ambitions and limitations of the book's final two chapters. Each are certainly ambitious in what they are trying to argue, although in different ways. While Blanchot's engagement with Heidegger's thought is readily known, the idea that his theorization of the question of literature, as well as the literary practice he realized, constitutes a writing of effacement that Lacoue-Labarthe advocates in his response to the problem of the scenic in Heidegger may seem to imply that Blanchot represents an example of an application of Lacoue-Labarthe's thinking. In fact, it is the reverse: Blanchot is a strong influence in Lacoue-Labarthe's thought. My decision to present these readings in this order is not so much to suggest a linear line of reception of Heidegger by his French readers as it is to offer a particular interpretation of Blanchot using the frame of the debate between Nancy and Lacoue-Labarthe. The nonlinearity of this interpretation becomes clearer if one takes into account as well that Nancy's employment of the concept of *désoeuvrement* comes originally from Blanchot and that the "mapping" I suggest with the final two chapters (Blanchot as expanding upon Lacoue-Labarthe, Deleuze as expanding upon Nancy) can come across neater than I actually intend when we note that the problem of community, and specifically what Blanchot refers to in a critical response to Nancy as "the apocalyptic voice" of community, demarcates another debate within post-Heideggerian thought, in this case, one between Nancy and Blanchot that is much more fraught than the one I focus on between Nancy and Lacoue-Labarthe.[22]

Similarly, of all the chapters in *The Scene of the Voice*, chapter 6 is the most experimental, not only in terms of the mapping of Deleuze and Nancy from which it sets out but also in being an intentional staging of an *Auseinandersetzung* or *explication* (in the sense Jacques Derrida has used such terms[23]) of Heidegger and Deleuze. While the chapter documents existing instances where scholars have noted affinities between Heidegger and Deleuze, I press a stronger claim regarding inheritance, which, as I show, Deleuze himself indicates. At the same time, chapter 6 can be said to simply be testing the hypothesis that Deleuze was a serious reader of Heidegger, specifically on the concept of the voice. Nonetheless, given Deleuze's limited references to Heidegger in his writings, and what many view as the inconsistencies between their thought, regarding Deleuze as a reader of Heidegger entails reading Deleuze against himself at times. The particular points of debate will include the degree to which Heidegger and Deleuze can be said to share similar understandings of the major themes with which *The Scene of the Voice* is concerned, namely: voice, language, finitude, and affect. Here in this introduction, I simply want to note the challenge of assessing this degree of a shared understanding while also asserting confidence that such an assessment is called for. Part of that confidence is established by chapter 4's uncovering of the fundamental problem of mimesis as that which connects the Heideggerian voice to Deleuze's philosophical project.

This confidence also extends to the argument I unfold in these last two chapters that holds that both Blanchot and Deleuze share a concern with the connection that the question of human finitude has to the possibility of thinking itself. Both Blanchot and Deleuze inherit this problem from Heidegger as part of their inheritance of the Heideggerian voice, particularly in terms of the link Heidegger projects between the call of the voice and the call of thinking (the call *that is* thinking). In this shared concern among Heidegger, Blanchot, and Deleuze, we actually witness a triangulation take shape, with Blanchot revising in a profound manner the relation between the call of the voice and the call of thinking and Deleuze elaborating their relation even further after his own engagement with Blanchot's thought.

These intricate lines of inheritance converge to underscore the fact that what is at stake in the constellation of language, finitude, figuration, and affect embodied by the voice is the possibility of a form of thinking that is able to break free from the self-affirming narcissisms of representation and encounter the dissimulating force of difference as such.

As a meditation on these stakes concerning language, thinking, and the narcissisms of representation, *The Scene of the Voice* closes with a brief epilogue that reads Blanchot's "Thought and the Exigency of Discontinuity," the essay that opens *The Infinite Conversation*. Reflecting on both the language of research and its ideal figures—the teacher, the writer, the professor, the philosopher, the scientist, etc.—Blanchot argues in that piece that as long as the language of research avoids posing the question of (its) language, it betrays the originary encounter with alterity that gave rise to it, exchanging the task of thinking for a fable of progress and a fantasy of access to difference. I thus use Blanchot's essay, in combination with the lessons presented by the debate between Nancy and Lacoue-Labarthe, as an opportunity to return to the concerns I enumerated at the outset of this study regarding the discourses of the affective turn and the return to the aesthetic and to present some concluding thoughts on what their exclusion of language costs these discourses. In my estimation, Blanchot's text gives pause to the impulse to celebrate these discourses as cutting-edge research, and it offers sobering warnings about what the drive to master difference yields for the possibility of speech—as well as the reification of community—within the contemporary University.

Other Voices

My hope is that *The Scene of the Voice* will help dislodge a certain sedimented understanding of the post-Heideggerian engagement with language, which, as I have tried to indicate, has been used as a kind of productive amnesia to establish the conceptual footing of various turns in critical thought following Heidegger.

Other names certainly belong to this legacy and will, at times, intersect with the readings I offer in this book. The one who perhaps comes most immediately to mind is Jacques Derrida, who in *Of Grammatology* touches on the Heideggerian conception of the voice as an echo of the philosophical logos and the metaphysics of presence the logos presupposes (23–24).[24] As I hope my outline in this introduction makes clear, this study takes a different approach to Heidegger's conception of the voice by first taking seriously Heidegger's casting of the voice as an affective—and necessary—figuration of human finitude and then tracing out the tensions that follow from such a relation of necessity. I thus do not take issue with Derrida's critique but rather follow certain reverberations of Heidegger's text, and of the texts of his readers, that overlap with Derrida's critique. If anything, I would say this volume is composed of readings that occupy different but related and less traveled regions of the horizon Derrida inhabited in his reflections on Heidegger's text.

It is precisely because the name "Derrida" is so readily identified with the legacy I am trying to productively read against in this study that I feel it is more effective to pursue the reception of the voice by thinkers who also take seriously the particular logic of the voice's necessary figuration and its attendant challenges for conceptualizing the political. I have sought to engage especially those thinkers not typically associated with the Heideggerian tradition, or at least those who occupy its periphery. This will force a reassessment of the discursive history so neatly packaged by the critical turns I survey above. Although Blanchot is understood to have taken up many Heideggerian themes in his corpus, few commentaries attend to his conceptions of writing and the work of art as specific responses to the problem of the Heideggerian voice. Certainly, Deleuze is almost never viewed as a reader of Heidegger. Nor is he thought of as a philosopher of language in the post-Heideggerian vein. Among my hopes for *The Scene of the Voice* is to introduce a need to reconsider this posture toward Deleuze's text and, ultimately, to provoke some general uneasiness with the certainty that we are done with the question of language.

Part 1
Heidegger

Chapter 1

The Voice

Sounding the Scene of Finitude

In my introduction, I spoke of the need to read against the common perception of Heidegger and post-Heideggerian thought as reducing "everything" to language. As I tried to show, this is a perception that has been repeated in an uncritical manner by theorists of the affective turn and the return to the aesthetic, even as they rely on Heideggerian figures of finitude to establish their claims about affect and the aesthetic. Heidegger's conception of the voice, however, undoes such a narrative. The voice in Heidegger not only indicates a relation to language that is inseparable from the affective and the aesthetic but also reveals the relation to finitude as grounded in this originary relation to language.

By theorizing the voice as a saying in which human finitude—the human being's understanding of the sense/meaning of Being—appears before itself and calls the human back to the fact of its existence, Heidegger urges us toward a nonlinguistic (i.e., nonsignifying, noncommunicative—relation to language). For Heidegger, this relation to language exists prior to our ability to use it as a tool of signification or communication. In calling the human being back to the fact of their existence, the voice both points to this relation to language as an opening of finitude and serves as an affective and aesthetic witness to the human being's relationship to Being.

In this opening chapter, I reconstruct Heidegger's conceptualization of the voice in *Being and Time* and the role he assigns it in the structure of human finitude, a rhythmic movement he names "finite transcendence."

Finite transcendence is the relation between Being and human being that constitutes human existence as "Dasein"—literally, "Being-there," but also "Being-thrown-ahead." Human beings' finitude (their understanding of Being) allows them to encounter individual beings, including their own being, thus enabling them to live their existence in a futural direction as one of possibility (e.g., living their lives one way instead of another). In being-ahead of itself in this way, the human Dasein's finitude is a form of transcendence; to be human is to be thrown ahead, ecstatic. The issue, I will show, is that Dasein's transcendence also results in Dasein forgetting that it has an understanding of Being, which is where Heidegger describes the voice as intervening in order to call Dasein back to the fact of its finitude, hence the notion of Dasein's existence as a rhythmic movement. Dasein's existence is marked by a pulsation back and forth between its understanding of Being and forgetting the fact of its understanding. (Notice I do not say forgetting the sense/meaning of Being, which, by definition, is not possible for Dasein.)

The main aim of this chapter is to arrive at an appreciation of the voice as not only an affective experience that, in calling Dasein back to the fact of its finitude, jars Dasein out of the forms of complacency it can fall into regarding its existence. It is to also understand the affective claim of the voice on the human Dasein as a (circular) "echo" of the originary affective relation, as it appears through the human Dasein's "moods" or *Stimmungen*, to the sense/meaning of Being. The voice, as *die Stimme*, is a sensible figure (in both senses of the term "sense") of this affective relation or scene of finitude, as well as a relation to language that is extra-linguistic. After establishing the voice as an affective, figural experience of language, I dedicate chapter 2 to elucidating the concept or theory of language Heidegger is working with in his conception of the voice, and I devote my efforts in chapter 3 to exploring the contours of the voice as figure.

As it may be becoming clear, reengaging Heidegger's conception of the voice will require a sustained encounter with the intricacies of Heidegger's text and its challenging terminology, an encounter that typically only acolytes of Heidegger's thought are willing to pursue. My position, however, is that, without such a sustained—and patient—engagement, a full appreciation of the way the Heideggerian voice intervenes in the question of finitude's relation to language will remain elusive. As a result, evocations of human finitude, such as those that populate the current theoretical horizon of affect studies and the return to the aesthetic, will remain vague.

Finitude and Finite Transcendence

The voice occupies a curious place in Heidegger's oeuvre. Most commentaries on Heidegger, particularly in the Anglo-American reception of his thought, tend to divide his writings into two main periods, an early and a late period. The voice is most readily recognized in the form of "the voice of conscience" as it appears in *Being and Time*, which is considered Heidegger's early period. However, the voice appears again in the later period, the period from the 1930s onward that is largely considered a turn away from the emphasis on the human Dasein in *Being and Time* and toward the question of language. It is in the late period that Heidegger speaks of "the voice of Being" itself. Most conventional accounts satisfy themselves with describing this "turn" in Heidegger's thought as a recognition on Heidegger's part that his focus on the human Dasein in his early work relied too much on the metaphysics of subjectivity, which is what the project of *Being and Time* expressly aimed at escaping.[1] The thematization of the voice of Being, unmediated by Dasein's conscience, is thus regarded by conventional readings of Heidegger as a correction to this early failure to break with metaphysics.

Yet there is one major problem with such conventional accounts: namely, how to understand the concept of the voice in and between each so-called period. What happens to the voice between its two appearances? Is it the same voice? Are they different voices? How does one tell?

My aim is to trouble the idea of such a stark division in Heidegger's thought and to set the conditions for a reassessment of that posture toward Heidegger's corpus based on the idea of a continuity of the voice in his work. As such, I regard the two appearances of the voice in the early and later periods of Heidegger's oeuvre not as distinct voices but as differing moments or inflections of the finite transcendence of Dasein. Within Heidegger scholarship, such a position is somewhat controversial since finite transcendence seems to be localized in the early period of Heidegger's thought and particularly that period's concern with the human Dasein's understanding of Being. I share, however, the contention that a minority of Heidegger scholars hold, which is that Heidegger's occupation with the relationship between human being and Being never dissipates. In order to understand therefore the role the voice plays throughout the course of Heidegger's thought, I maintain that it is essential to grasp first what Heidegger means by the concept of finite transcendence.

Although finite transcendence has been invoked often in Heidegger scholarship, it has been treated only sporadically, mainly referred to but not fully defined. To this day, Heidegger scholars are still coming to terms with it as a concept Heidegger develops in the project of fundamental ontology that Heidegger inaugurates in *Being and Time*.[2] The main reason for this scholarly ambivalence is that the concept is only sketched out in *Being and Time*, named explicitly in work where Heidegger elaborates the project from *Being and Time*, and then recedes from view in the later writings. As Christopher Fynsk has noted, however, the problem of the relation between human beings and Being haunts Heidegger throughout his thought, whether in the form of finite transcendence or in terms of what Heidegger named in the later writings "the appropriating event" (*Ereignis*). As Fynsk shows, Heidegger himself acknowledged this haunting.[3]

Finite transcendence explains how Dasein's finitude—its understanding of Being—implies a fundamental relation to Being as a condition of its existence and yet also how this fundamental relation leads to Dasein taking for granted its existence and thus a forgetting of (its understanding of) Being. The concept of finite transcendence thus names and underscores the human being's inextricable relation to Being, a relation that nonetheless results in the human being's forgetting of this relation. The voice in *Being and Time* calls Dasein back to the fact of its finitude and presents to Dasein the fact that it has an understanding of Being.

In *Being and Time*, Heidegger describes the finitude of Dasein as a transcendence, and he conceives this transcendence in terms of temporality. Being *is* time: it only "is" through appearing, and in appearing, in taking place, Being becomes present. Furthermore, Being is finite to the extent that it becomes present, in time, in the "thatness and whatness" of individual beings.[4] Thus to speak of Being is always to speak of it as "the Being of beings." Yet Being only discloses itself and becomes recognizable as finite if there is already the understanding of Being, which is only to be found in the being of Dasein. Dasein is that being who "in its being . . . is concerned *about* its very being" and who therefore has an a priori relation to Being (S10). Dasein is the "site of the understanding of Being" (S 7n), writes Heidegger, and "only as long as [Dasein] *is* . . . 'is there' [B]eing" (S196).[5]

In *Kant and the Problem of Metaphysics* (1929), Heidegger offers a summary statement of how Dasein's finitude makes possible the appearance of beings. The encounter with the finitude of Being takes place through Dasein's commerce with beings, but this commerce is predicated on Dasein's finitude (its understanding of Being):

> As a mode of Being, existence is itself finitude, and as such it is only possible on the basis of the understanding of Being. . . .

> On the grounds of the understanding of Being, the human is the there, with whose being occurs the opening irruption into beings so that it can express itself as such as a Self. *More original than the human is the finitude of the Dasein in it.*[6]

The Da (the "there" of "Being-there") is the indication of Dasein's finitude, of Dasein's existence as thrownness. To be concerned about its being means that Dasein is in a relation of "being-ahead-of-itself" (S §41), being thrown and open toward possibility—toward both the possibilities of Being and its own possibilities, the greatest possibility of which is that of impossibility or death (S §§31, 50).

Here it is important to note that in elaborating Dasein's finitude Heidegger stresses the active, temporal connotation of thrownness. It is not the fact that Dasein dies that determines Dasein's finitude. Rather, Dasein is finite because, concerned about its being, in a relation Heidegger consequently names "care," Dasein is thrown toward death as "its ownmost potentiality-for-Being" (SZ 163). Dasein is always-already thrown ahead and into the concern of its "totality of involvements" (MR 415), which Heidegger calls "world."

The finitude of Dasein thus becomes the (non)ground of its transcendence: To be finite is to be concerned about one's being, which throws one ecstatically ahead of oneself, beyond oneself. In its concern about its existence, Dasein transcends itself and encounters beings. At the same time, in being thrown, the "ecstasis" (SZ 329) of Dasein's existence (that *is* Dasein's existence) and the relation to Being this presupposes causes Dasein to transcend beings as such.

In comparison to other beings, Dasein alone is finite; Dasein alone has an understanding of Being that allows it to "temporalize itself" (MR 417), revealing time as the horizon of its existence. As a result, finitude radically individualizes Dasein and designates Dasein singularly as not just another being among beings: "The Dasein in the human determines it as that being which, [b]eing in the midst of beings, comports itself to them as such. Further, as this comportment to beings, the human is determined in its own [b]eing as essentially other than all remaining beings which are manifest in Dasein" (*Kant* 164/234, translation modified).[7] In fact, as Heidegger states in *Being and Time*, Dasein's transcendence becomes the condition without which no comportment to beings is possible: "If the thematization of what is objectively present—the scientific project of nature—is to become possible, [*Dasein*] *must transcend* the beings thematized. Transcendence does not consist in objectivation, but is rather presupposed by it. But if the thematization of innerworldly beings objectively present is a changeover from taking care which circumspectly discovers, then a transcendence of [Dasein] must already underlie 'practical' being together with things at hand" (S 332/SZ 363–64; original emphasis). The terms of finite transcendence thus presuppose one another: To be finite means to be transcendent (thrown ahead, ecstatic, beyond beings as such). To be transcendent means to be finite (temporal, concerned about one's being).[8] Both finitude and transcendence presuppose an understanding of, and therefore a relation to, Being.

The circularity of finite transcendence comes to a "close" in a more fundamental (i.e., "originary") circle, which many readers of Heidegger have called and continue to call "hermeneutic":[9] Dasein *is* temporal (it exists or "ex-ists" and is finite) because it has an understanding of Being, and "the understanding of Being [is] projected upon time from out of the ground of the finitude of Dasein in human beings" (*Kant* 166/243, translation modified). At the same time, Dasein is capable of having an understanding of Being as temporality because it itself, in its thrownness, is temporal (BT/SZ §5).

Part of my aim in the opening chapters of this book is to draw out the significance of the circle as a figure of finite transcendence. What I wish to stress here is that the circle figures finite transcendence as a relation before relation. That is to say, finite transcendence is that relation that makes possible any and all of Dasein's subsequent relations—any self-relation, including the relation to itself as that being concerned about its being but also any relation to beings (human or otherwise) Dasein encounters "in the world."[10] Finite transcendence makes "world" as such possible for Dasein.

Forgetting as Finitude

The terms Heidegger employs to characterize Dasein's existence—thrownness, Being-in-the-world—connote activity and movement. Heidegger sees Dasein's existence as active in another way as well. In his conception, Dasein has always-already "chosen" its existence ontologically. It has already decided in favor of its existence in a movement Heidegger calls "resoluteness" or "decisiveness" (*Entschlossenheit*) (SZ §54). "Only the particular Dasein decides its existence, whether it does so by taking hold or neglecting," Heidegger declares. "The question of existence never gets straightened out except through existing itself" (MR 33/SZ 12).[11] Dasein cannot *not* choose in favor of its existence. Since Dasein's existence rests on its understanding of

Being, this means that Dasein always-already has an understanding of Being. There is, however, the possibility—and in fact, inevitability—of Dasein forgetting the question of the sense/meaning of Being (and thereby forgetting that its being is characterized by the fact that its being is a question for it). This is what Dasein, paradoxically, is destined to commit on the everyday ontic register as a result of its finitude.

Dasein's finitude makes possible the slope of Dasein's ontic existence, its thrownness into the totality of its concerns in everydayness. Yet its preoccupation with "factual circumstances" causes Dasein to "lose itself" to the anonymity of tradition and "the 'they'" (*das Man*) (MR 309; 43/SZ 265; 21). Dasein's ontic state is that of being fallen, inauthentic, and having its identity inflected through others. "The Self of everyday Dasein," Heidegger writes, "is the *they-self* [*das Man-selbst*]" (MR 167/SZ 129). The "they-self" is a state where "[e]veryone is the other, and no is himself" (MR 165/SZ 128).

Fallen, Dasein not only forgets the fact of its finitude, and, as a result, the fact of its understanding of the sense/meaning of Being. Dasein forgets that it has forgotten. Again, there is no forgetting the sense/meaning of Being on Dasein's part, for this is the condition for the possibility of its thrownness; Dasein can only forget the fact of its understanding of the sense/meaning of Being. Tradition and everydayness are partial aspects of Dasein's existence; when Dasein mistakes these partial aspects of its existence as self-evident and for the whole of its existence, Dasein becomes distracted from reflecting upon the fact of its finitude (MR 43/SZ 21). Mistaking these partial, ontic aspects of its life for the whole of its existence, Dasein either forgets the fact of its understanding of the sense/meaning of Being or flees from this fact (MR 69/SZ 44). This is why Heidegger still regards the neglecting of one's existence as a decision about one's existence.

Nonetheless, if tradition and everydayness, and therefore forgetting and fleeing, are inevitable aspects of Dasein's thrownness, it must be the case also that forgetting is part of the meaning of Dasein's existence. Forgetting the question of the sense/meaning of Being must belong to both the finitude of Dasein and the history of Being itself. Heidegger thus declares, "The finitude of Dasein—the understanding of Being—lies in forgetfulness. . . . The basic fundamental-ontological act of the Metaphysics of Dasein as the laying of the ground for metaphysics is hence a 'remembering again'" (Kant 159).[12] This is also why Heidegger says authentic Being-one's-Self is not "an exceptional condition of the subject, a condition that has been detached from the 'they'; it is rather an existentiell modification of the 'they'—of the 'they' as an essential existentiale" (MR 168/SZ 130). We will see momentarily how important this qualification is between the "existentiell" and the "existentiale." Nonetheless, it must be possible—even necessary—for Dasein to "remember again" its understanding of Being within the ontic structures of its existence. If it is true that there is no forgetting the sense/meaning of Being, only the forgetting of the fact of our understanding of it (and the forgetting of this forgetting), then it must be possible to show how Dasein, in its ontic-existentiell structures, already "knows" its ontological-existential status and furthermore how it attests this fact to itself (MR 311/SZ 267). Heidegger posits the voice as serving as Dasein's attestation to the fact of its finitude. Its call shocks Dasein back to the fact that it always-already has an understanding of Being and that it has already chosen its existence from the ground of this understanding. This means that Dasein's finitude is grounded in an affective relation to the sense of Being and that the voice (*die Stimme*) appears as part of, and testimony to, a circular relation between the sense/meaning of Being and the sensibility (in the form, as we shall see, of mood [*Stimmung*]) to the sense/meaning of Being.

The Ontic-Ontological Constitution of Dasein and the Task of the Existential Analytic

The voice comes to serve as Dasein's testimony regarding its finitude, but before going on to show how Heidegger establishes the voice as fulfilling this role, two questions first need to be explained: Why is such testimony necessary? And what does this testimony sound like?

In answer to the first question, Dasein needs to testify to the fact of its finitude due to the ontic-ontological structure of its being. In §4 of *Being and Time*, Heidegger writes, "The roots of the existential analytic . . . are ultimately *existentiell*, that is, *ontical*. Only if the inquiry of philosophical research is itself seized upon in an existentiell manner as a possibility of the Being of each existing Dasein, does it become at all possible to disclose the existentiality of existence and to undertake an adequately founded ontological problematic" (MR 34/SZ 13–14; original emphasis). The character of Dasein is that of being ontic-ontological simultaneously and "equiprimordially," Heidegger argues a few lines above this passage. Ontically, "Dasein is an entity whose Being has the determinate character of existence" (MR 34/SZ 13): that is, Dasein exists. Ontologically, Dasein's "existence is thus determinative for it" (MR 34/SZ 13): its existence determines Dasein's understanding of itself *as* possibility (MR 33/SZ 12). There is no severing of these two slopes of

Dasein's being, thus making Dasein singular in its existence. As Heidegger states, "Dasein is ontically distinctive in that it *is* ontological" (MR 32/SZ 12; original emphasis). As such, Dasein "takes priority over all other entities." This priority allows it to serve as the "ground" of all or any other (future) ontologies (MR 34/SZ 13). But in order to explicate the manner of this ground, the existential analytic must trace the ontic-ontological structure of Dasein's being and follow it in the movement Heidegger refers to as the "hermeneutical Situation" or circle of Dasein's being.[13]

We have already begun to see some of the implications of Dasein's circularity in finite transcendence, the most cutting being the paradoxical structure of "Being-there": Dasein's finitude results in the forgetting of its finitude; its understanding of Being results in the forgetting of the fact of this understanding.

Still another inflection of this paradoxical character of Dasein's existence is that the whole of Dasein's being—its "potentiality-for-Being-a-whole" (MR 276/SZ 233)—is attained through the assumption of its fragmentary being. Finite transcendence means that Dasein is never present to itself in the way the subject of metaphysics is (or is posited to be). Contrary to the Cartesian cogito, Dasein is not master of its existence because its existence requires its dependence on that which is outside it (Being and the understanding of Being's sense/meaning).[14] Finite transcendence also makes Dasein's being as possibility possible. As possibility, Heidegger says, Dasein's being is incomplete; it is characterized by a "not yet" (MR 276/SZ 233). Inasmuch as it exists, Dasein is not yet. At the same time, however, the relation of finite transcendence constitutes Dasein's ontological status, its "potentiality-for-Being-a-whole," which Heidegger calls the "authentic Being-one's-Self" (*das eigentliche Selbstsein*) of Dasein (MR 168/SZ 130 §27). If in order to be a whole and be one's authentic "Self" means "assuming" one's finitude in the mode of a decision, then it must also mean assuming—that is, deciding in favor of—one's essential incompleteness.[15] If Dasein is to testify to the fact of its finitude, then it must offer a testimony that captures both the ontic and ontological sides of its existence. Any testimony targeting just one side of Dasein's existence—its wholeness as a Self or its fragmentary nature as a "not yet"—will remain decidedly incomplete.

What form, then, should testimony take? If the ontic and the ontological are inextricably linked in Dasein's being (if this inextricability *is* the singular character of Dasein's being, of Dasein *as* Dasein), and if there is no escape from the paradoxical consequences of this inextricability, then the task of the existential analytic is not simply a matter of pulling Dasein back from the ontic to the ontological (the inextricability we have touched on makes such an option nonsensical), "enlightening" Dasein as it were. The ontological cannot be an exceptional condition of Dasein's existence to which Dasein returns since Dasein never "leaves" the ontological.

Nor can it be the aim of the existential analytic to resolve the paradoxical character of Dasein's finitude. Instead, its aim must be to uncover how the ontological conditions the ontic and how this fact is disclosed to Dasein in the ontic. The "strategy" of the existential analytic is to trace this circular structure and to show how this circularity is itself (and as such) a tracing of Dasein's relation in/of finite transcendence. "*Dasein is its disclosedness*," Heidegger tells us (MR 171/SZ 133; original emphasis). Dasein's existence, the existential analytic will reveal, is nothing other than the tracing of the circularity of its existence.

The movement between the ontic and ontological may also be described as a perpetual call and response, or ebb and flow, between the two registers. I myself have been attracted to the German phrase *hin und her* to describe this movement, in which occupation with one side of the existential problematic necessitates occupation with the other side, only to be called back again to its "opposite." As I move on to trace the voice's appearance to Dasein, I will emphasize the voice's affective and aesthetic dimension in terms of this *hin und her* rhythm, particularly with respect to the circular echoing among the affective sensibility or *die Stimmung* of the figure of the voice as *die Stimme des Gewissens* (the voice of conscience), the sense/meaning communicated by the voice, and Dasein's understanding of the sense/meaning of Being for which the voice figures.

The Appearance of the Voice

Thus far, I have been tracing the movement of Dasein's finitude and what I suggest is its *hin und her* rhythm: Dasein's understanding of Being propels Dasein forward to choose its existence through its everyday ontic engagements, but these very engagements also lead Dasein to forget the fact of its finitude. Thus, Dasein has to be called—in fact, shocked—back to this fact. The voice appears to Dasein in order to fulfill this task.

In its everyday ontic engagements, Dasein's being is fragmented across its various concerns; Dasein's attention is not on its own being but on the existence of those objects external to it. This fragmentation not only causes Dasein to forget the fact of its finitude; it causes Dasein to mistake its isolated concerns as encompassing the whole of its being. Heidegger confronts this capacity for Dasein to misrecognize its being in his analysis of care (*Sorge*), which is the term Heidegger uses to characterize Dasein's self-relation as it is propelled ahead of itself from out of its understanding of Being. Care is not just one quality among many of Dasein's being; Dasein's being is that of care.

As care, Dasein transcends and distinguishes itself from all other "modes of Being (readiness-to-hand, presence-at-hand, Reality) which characterize entities with a character other than that of Dasein" (MR 275/SZ 230). Care marks Dasein as singular and is an expression of its transcendence of beings. "But," Heidegger asks, "*is* the phenomenon of care one in which the most primordial existential-ontological state of Dasein is disclosed? And has the structural manifoldness which lies in this phenomenon, presented us with the most primordial totality of factical Dasein's Being? Has our investigation up to this point ever brought Dasein into view *as a whole?*" (MR 275/SZ 230; original emphasis). Even though Dasein's being is that of care, does the analysis of care reveal the whole of Dasein's being? According to Heidegger, the answer is no, or at least, not yet. Heidegger states: "One thing has become unmistakable: *our existential analysis of Dasein up till now cannot lay claim to primordiality*. Its fore-having never included more than the *inauthentic* Being of Dasein, and of Dasein as *less* than a *whole* [*als unganzes*]. If the Interpretation of Dasein's Being is to become primordial, as a foundation for working out the basic question of ontology, then it must first have brought to light existentially the Being of Dasein in its possibilities of *authenticity* and *totality*" (MR 276/SZ 233; original emphasis). Because Dasein's being as care only comes into view when Dasein is pursuing specific possibilities of its existence, the analysis of care will only offer a partial picture of Dasein's potentiality-for-Being. From the standpoint of care, where Dasein is always in situation with its projects, Dasein's being is dispersed along the horizon of its everyday concerns. As care, Dasein's being is fragmented and therefore incomplete. When Dasein is engaged with a concern, it activates its being as possibility but only realizes one possibility, never the whole possibility of its being.

If care does not reveal Dasein's being as a whole, then what does? Heidegger's answer is Dasein's relation to its own death. In care, Dasein is thrown ahead toward possibilities of its being. The ultimate possibility of Dasein's being is the possibility that it becomes no longer possible: the possibility, in other words, that it ceases to exist. Therefore, Dasein's being only comes into view as a whole at the moment of its death. Dasein's being is a Being-towards-death.

"Nevertheless," writes Heidegger,

> this existentially "possible" Being-towards-death remains, from the existentiell point of view, a fantastical exaction [*eine phantastische Zumutung*]. The fact that an authentic potentiality-for-Being-a-whole is ontologically possible for Dasein, signifies nothing, so long as a corresponding ontical potentiality-for-Being has not been demonstrated in Dasein itself. Does Dasein ever factically throw itself into such a Being-towards-death? Does Dasein *demand*, even by reason of its ownmost Being, an authentic potentiality-for-Being determined by anticipation?
>
> Before answering these questions, we must investigate whether to *any* extent and in any way Dasein *gives testimony*, from its ownmost potentiality-for-Being, as to a possible *authenticity* of its existence, so that it not only makes known that in an existentiell manner such authenticity is possible, but *demands* this of itself. (MR 311/SZ 266–67; original emphasis)

According to Heidegger, Dasein's ontological state of Being-towards-death means very little if it cannot be shown that Dasein testifies to itself (i.e., is a witness to) its Being-towards-death in its everyday existence. If Dasein did not produce such testimony to itself, then, Heidegger argues, Dasein would not be able to make a demand (*Zumutung*) of itself that it break free from its lostness in the *they* (*das Man*) and recover its potentiality for being a whole (MR 311). If Dasein did not testify to itself its Being-towards-death, then not only would its potentiality for being a whole never appear to it, but it would never free itself from the grasp of the *they*. Dasein's existence would always belong to others, never to itself. It would merely be a subject, not a Self.

As Heidegger explains, the *they* has the power of diluting Dasein's experience, to the extent that it becomes unclear "who" chooses in favor of Dasein's existence (MR 312/SZ 268). Does Dasein decide its existence, or does the *they*? The difficulty of answering this question is influenced by the fact that Dasein's Being-in-the-world is shared with other Daseins, so "world" always-already carries with it commerce with others. However, the depth of Dasein's imbrication with others determines also just how lost Dasein can be—and often is—in the *they*. It is easier for Dasein to give the burden of having to decide its existence over to others than for Dasein to take it up as its ownmost existential project. "Because Dasein is *lost* in the 'they,'" writes

Heidegger, "it must first *find* itself. In order to find *itself* at all, it must be 'shown' to itself in its possible authenticity. In terms of *possibility*, Dasein *is* already a potentiality-for-Being-its-Self, but it needs to have this potentiality attested" (MR 313/SZ 268; original emphasis). In order for Dasein to extract itself from its capture by the *they*, Dasein must be shown that its existence is one of possibility and that the expression of this possibility is not to be found in the self of the *they* (the "*they*-self"), which, by definition is inauthentic (*uneigentlich*, improper), but in Dasein's authentic (*eigentliches*, proper) Self. This demonstration, however, cannot come from outside of Dasein, for that would mean it comes from the region of the *they*. This demonstration must come instead from Dasein itself. Only then can it count as a form of authentic testimony, and such testimony, Heidegger tells us, appears in the figure of the voice of conscience, which belongs to "Dasein's everyday interpretation of itself [*Selbstauslegung*]" (MR 313/SZ 268).

By linking the voice to *Auslegung* (interpretation), Heidegger provides a connection between the ontic and ontological registers of Dasein's existence and thereby establishes the basis for how Dasein might attest to the fact of its ontological condition from within the ontic aspects of its everyday existence. Interpretation, as Heidegger describes earlier in *Being and Time*, is a mode of understanding (*Verstehen*). Together with *Befindlichkeit* (state-of-mind) and *Rede* (discourse), understanding forms the essential, "equiprimoridal" modes ("*existentialia*") of Dasein's Being-in-the-world (MR 203/SZ 160). They are at once ways in which "world" is disclosed to Dasein and indications that Dasein's being is one of having world disclosed to it. As Heidegger puts it, "*Dasein is its disclosedness*" (MR 171/SZ 133; original emphasis). In order for Dasein to pursue its possibilities for being, however, it must understand what it is capable of (MR 184/SZ 144). And in order for Dasein to understand what it is capable of, it must develop its understanding by interpreting its possibilities for being (MR 188/SZ 148). Dasein's Being-in-the-world entails the fact that it is always-already engaged in a mode of self-interpretation.

What distinguishes the form of interpretation that constitutes the voice of conscience from the other forms of Dasein's everyday interpretations is the fact that the voice of conscience is not a type of discourse between two Daseins but a speaking of Dasein to itself. "*In conscience Dasein calls itself*," states Heidegger, "The call comes *from* me and yet *from beyond me* [*Der Ruf kommt* aus *mir und doch* über *mich*]" (MR 320/SZ 275; original emphasis). Furthermore, what Dasein says to itself through the voice is, strictly speaking, nothing. The voice calls by staying silent, says Heidegger (MR 322/SZ 277). If it were to communicate some type of information, it would operate along the ontic register and within the province of the *they*, which take Being for granted and treat it as ready-to-hand; this is why the voice must remain silent.

What kind of voice speaks by remaining silent? An uncanny one, says Heidegger. Even though the voice comes from Dasein itself, it appears anonymously, as an impersonal call. " 'It' calls [*'Es' ruft*], against our expectations and even against our will," writes Heidegger (MR 320/SZ 275). The "it" of the voice of conscience is like the *es* of *es regnet* (it's raining) or of *es gibt* (there is), or even the *es* designating the id in Freud's psychic topography. The voice's impersonal character, however, is not the result of its uncanniness. The voice is uncanny, Heidegger says, because Dasein itself is uncanny in its very being. Thus, Dasein's experience of the voice as impersonal implies an inability on Dasein's part to recognize the voice as issuing from itself.

Why wouldn't Dasein be able to recognize the uncanniness of the voice as its own—that is, as its own voice and as its own uncanniness? Heidegger refers us again to the analysis of Dasein's Being-in-the-world that he conducted earlier in *Being and Time*, in which he describes Dasein's thrownness as propelling Dasein constantly ahead and outside of itself (in the mode of an ecstasis) toward its potentiality-for-Being. Existentially, then, Dasein is "not at home" (*Un-zuhause*), "uncanny" (*unheimlich*) (MR 233/SZ 188). Yet, Dasein only realizes its existential condition of uncanniness in anxiety, which is an unpleasant feeling from which Dasein seeks insulation and comfort. This insulation and comfort are provided by the *they*, which functions as a home where Dasein "can dwell in tranquillized familiarity" (MR 234). The *they* provides a destination to which Dasein can flee the anxiety brought about by its uncanniness, which according to Heidegger "pursues Dasein constantly" (MR 234).

While Dasein may find shelter in the *they*, this is a false comfort because the self Dasein occupies in the *they* is that of the inauthentic (*uneigentliches*) *they*-self, not Dasein's authentic (*eigentliches*) Self. What is more, the defenses the *they* provide against Dasein's anxiety only last so long. At some point, Dasein is called/calls itself back to the fact that its home is really that of not being at home, of being thrown into the fact "*that-it-is*," faced "with the 'nothing' of the world" (MR 321). By "the 'nothing,' " however, Heidegger does not have in mind anything like a nihilistic outlook on the world. In fact, he means quite the opposite: that there is a nothingness or nullity—a fundamental "notness" (*Nichtheit*) (MR 331), an essential not-yet—at the ground of Dasein's existence. Such a null ground must exist at the heart of Dasein's being; otherwise, Dasein's existence would not be one of possibility (MR 331/SZ 285). In a decisive passage, Heidegger describes how the voice calls Dasein back to the fact of its nullity:

> The appeal calls back by calling forth: it calls Dasein *forth* to the possibility of taking over, in existing, even that thrown entity which it is; it calls Dasein *back* to its thrownness so as to understand this thrownness as the null basis which it has to take up into existence. This calling-back in which conscience calls forth, gives Dasein to understand that Dasein itself—the null basis for its null projection, standing in the possibility of its Being—is to bring itself back to itself from its lostness in the "they"; and this means that it *is guilty*. (MR 333/SZ 287; original emphasis)

Like the call of conscience itself, guilt here means something more fundamental than its common, everyday sense. Heidegger does not mean moral or legal guilt. He does not mean that Dasein owes something to others, even as he acknowledges Dasein's intertwined existence in Being-with-others (MR 328/SZ 282). He is evoking rather an idea of guilt that is tied to "Dasein's kind of Being" (MR 328/SZ 283), which is to say, to the nullity that is the nonground of Dasein's existence. Dasein's being—its finitude—is that of thrownness from out of an understanding of Being. Dasein has no choice about its thrownness, yet it lives its projects on the basis of its existence as thrownness. "[Dasein] is never existent *before* its basis," writes Heidegger, "but only *from it* and *as this basis*. Thus 'Being-a-basis' means *never* to have power over one's ownmost Being from the ground up. This '*not*' belongs to the existential meaning of 'thrownness'. It itself, being a basis, *is* a nullity of itself" (MR 330/SZ 284; original emphasis). Since it is always-already thrown ahead of itself into situations and taking up possibilities, Dasein can never offer a justification of its existence prior to its Being-in-the-world. Ultimately, there is no reason for Dasein's existence; yet it is responsible for its existence nonetheless.

However, when Dasein resorts to the shelter of the *they* and believes its home is there, not only does Dasein overlook its fundamental uncanniness; it overlooks the fact of its existential guilt and gives responsibility for its existence over to the *they*. In dwelling in the *they*, Dasein chooses not to choose its existence. Yet by calling Dasein back to the nullity of its being, the voice calls Dasein back to the fact "that it is." This means both the fact that Dasein is thrown in its existence and that the character of Dasein's thrownness is one of care. That is to say, Dasein has already chosen in favor of its existence, whether it realizes it or not, whether it wants to or not. It cannot not choose itself because it already has chosen itself. For Dasein to give its existence over to the *they* amounts to a fleeing from the fact that it has already chosen its existence.

The fact that Dasein has already chosen its existence stems from Dasein's finitude—its understanding of Being, which allows Dasein to take its being as its concern and propels it ahead of itself into possibilities for being. Brought back, then, to the fact "that it is" in hearing the call of conscience, Dasein understands itself as its ownmost potentiality-for-Being. "In understanding the call," Heidegger writes, "Dasein is *in thrall [hörig] to its ownmost possibility of existence*. It has chosen itself" (MR 333–34/SZ 287; original emphasis). Dasein's heeding the call of conscience, furthermore, means Dasein "*wanting to have a conscience*" (MR 314/SZ 270 and MR 334/SZ 288; original emphasis), thereby "*making up for not choosing*" in the *they* (MR 313/SZ 268; original emphasis). The voice tears Dasein away from its lostness in the *they* and brings Dasein back to its ontological constitution as that being who, having an understanding of Being, takes its being as its concern. In understanding the call of conscience, Dasein assumes its finitude, the nullity at the heart of its thrownness. Dasein's understanding the call of conscience is thus its taking over the groundlessness of its existence. "The ground," Heidegger writes, "is never anything but the ground for an entity whose Being has to take over Being-a-ground" (MR 330–31/SZ 285, translation modified). In being-thrown, Dasein becomes its own ground. The voice attests to this fact, and in hearing the voice, Dasein affirms it. In affirming this fact, Dasein takes over its Being-a-ground for its existence, rather than giving this ground over to the *they*.

But what if Dasein does not hear the call of conscience, or in hearing it, does not understand it? According to Heidegger, that is not possible. "Indeed," says Heidegger, "hearing constitutes the primary and authentic way in which Dasein is open for its ownmost potentiality-for-Being. . . . Dasein hears because it understands" (MR 206/SZ 163). Since Dasein's finitude is grounded in a fundamental understanding—namely, of the sense of Being—it is existentially predisposed to hear. Dasein's capacity to be "in thrall [*hörig*] to its ownmost possibility of existence" is tied to its ability to hear (*hören*). Furthermore, because the voice comes from Dasein itself, it is not possible for Dasein not to hear the call or not to understand it. It is only possible for Dasein to flee its voice and drown it out with the noise of the *they*. But no matter what Dasein might do to flee its finitude, it carries its understanding of Being with it, and it also carries its ability to be interpellated by—that is, its capacity to be exposed to and by—the voice of conscience, "as in hearing the voice of the friend whom every Dasein carries with it" (MR 206/SZ 163).

This last phrase proclaiming the voice of the friend is one of the more famously enigmatic lines in *Being and Time*.[16] Although it seems to be designed to clarify the connection between Dasein's understanding of Being and its openness to this understanding, the formulation reintroduces a relation of alterity into Dasein's self-relation. Unless, of course, it doesn't; for what remains unclear is whether the figure of the friend's voice is that of another Dasein, or whether it is a doubling of Dasein itself. Is the figure of the friend's voice a figure of Dasein's ecstasis or uncanniness? Or is it not a figure at all? Is it an actual voice of alterity that speaks to Dasein? And what is the relationship between the friend's voice and the voice of conscience? How many voices actually populate Dasein's being?

Because it testifies to Dasein's understanding of Being, the voice is fundamentally a figuration of Dasein's finitude. Whether this figuration is what Michel Haar has called alternately an "autology" or an "autoaffection" of Dasein,[17] or is the trace of the other Dasein whose finitude is imbricated in Dasein's own and who effectively haunts the being of Dasein, as Christopher Fynsk has argued,[18] the figure of the voice certainly names an affective relation at the heart of Dasein's being. If the voice jolts Dasein to an experience of its uncanniness, re-calling Dasein to the fact of its finitude, this is because Dasein's understanding of Being, as we saw, is already an affective event; it is an *aisthesis* of Being as sense. This much is confirmed in Heidegger's description of understanding and state-of-mind as "equiprimordial" (*gleichursprünglich*) to the "there" of Dasein (MR 172/SZ 133). And it is confirmed more specifically in the ways in which Heidegger states that Dasein's "moods" (*Stimmungen*) and forms of "Being-attuned" (*Gestimmtsein*), as everyday (i.e., ontic) instances of state-of-mind, are modes through which Dasein's being, its thrownness, "is disclosed to itself *prior to* all cognition and volition, and *beyond* their range of disclosure" (MR 175; original emphasis). At the same time, in a gesture that reveals affinities between Heidegger's conception of affect and the more Deleuzean-inflected image of affect that populates the contemporary turn to affect, Heidegger is very careful to emphasize that a mood (*Stimmung*) is not a subjective psychological phenomenon but an indication of a more fundamental, external relation, namely the relation to the sense/meaning of Being (MR 178).

This makes the voice (*die Stimme*) an affective, figural, and circular return or 'echo' of the originary affective relation that is Dasein's understanding of the sense/meaning of Being.[19]

Yet, as Heidegger also indicates in this section of *Being and Time*, "state-of-mind and understanding are characterized equiprimordially by *discourse [die Rede]*" (MR 172/SZ 133; original emphasis), so we will need to examine how the voice, as a call that testifies to Dasein's being, not only connects to the question of language as it appears in *Being and Time* but also how it constitutes a very specific experience of language insofar as it calls without saying anything, without imparting any information. Implied in the figure of the voice is a form of speech that exceeds instrumental modes of language, a speech that is extra-linguistic. With his conception of the voice, then, Heidegger offers a provocative scene of human finitude, one that combines figuration, affect, and language into an event that he identifies as fundamental to the human essence. To be human is to be called by the voice.[20] As I explain in the introduction to this study, it is this fundamental scene that current critical projects embracing affect over the exclusion of language have missed, and this is why it is important to return to the scene of the voice in Heidegger's thought.

In the following chapters, I elaborate the two other parts of the constellation constituting Heidegger's conception of the voice—language and figuration. Having reconstructed in this chapter the affective link Heidegger establishes between the voice and human finitude, I dedicate chapter 2 to drawing out the image of language upon which this link rests. This image, which I call "the antagonism of language," shows Heidegger was concerned quite early on in his thought with the problem of the metaphysics of language (and relatedly, the language of metaphysics), and that the voice, as figure, serves a specific role in Heidegger's effort to think the closure of metaphysics.

Chapter 2

From *Phonē* to *Logos*

The Antagonism of Language and the Figuration of the Voice

Chapter 1 reviewed Heidegger's conceptualization of the voice and reconstructed the central role it plays in his project of fundamental ontology. As the call of conscience, it shocks the human Dasein back to its ontological ground, which Dasein loses hold of due to the structure of human finitude. In my reading of *Being and Time*, I described Dasein's movement between forgetting its finitude and being shocked back to it by the voice in rhythmic terms: Dasein's finitude (its understanding of Being) makes possible Dasein's finite transcendence (its encounter with beings), propelling it ahead of itself. This movement enables Dasein to pursue projects and to possess its existence as a form of futurity. Yet at the same time, Dasein's finite transcendence leads Dasein to lose itself in its projects, causing Dasein to forget both the fact of its understanding of Being and the fact that its understanding of Being is always-already disclosed to Dasein as part of its existence. Heidegger thus conceives the voice of conscience as a form of testimony—from Dasein to itself—that calls Dasein back to the fact of its finitude. As I have been arguing, the voice's testimony is an affective and aesthetic event that shocks Dasein back to the fact of its finitude. However, it is Dasein's finitude—its sensibility to the sense/meaning of Being—that makes such an affective and aesthetic experience of the voice's figuration possible in the first place. The voice (*die Stimme*) is thus an affective, figurative echo or return of the human Dasein's relation to the sense and sensibility (*die Stimmung*) of

Being—the fact that, as Dasein, the human being always-already possesses, and is captured by, an understanding of the sense/meaning of Being.

In chapter 1's concluding sections, I suggested that Heidegger's conceptualization of the voice harbors a theory of language that, while not yet explicit in *Being and Time*, constitutes the groundwork for the reflections on language he pursues in his later thought. Heidegger's casting of the voice as a call that says nothing rests on an image of language that does not conform to models that conceive language as an instrument of communication or a vehicle of information. Such models rely upon an economy of representation in which language is used as a tool for representing an object for thought, thus subsuming language within a metaphysics of presence. So instead of communicating a specific sense or meaning through an act of representation, the voice testifies affectively to the fact of sense—specifically, the fact that there is sense of Being. What is more, the voice affirms the fact that Dasein "ex-ists" as thrown ahead of itself because it always-already possesses an affective understanding of the sense of Being.

My claim in this chapter is thus twofold: First, that the voice in Heidegger's thought rests on what I wish to call an "antagonism of language," on a struggle between the metaphysical and nonmetaphysical images of language just described. Secondly, by exceeding the economy of representation, the voice acts as a figure for this antagonism. As a figure, the voice presents (and returns) Dasein to a scene of the relation between its finitude and the fact of sense—at once the sensibility of sense/meaning and the sense/meaning of sensibility.

Since the voice is animated by the antagonism of language, the affective experience Dasein undergoes in hearing its call is a singular event. By this I do not mean an event that individualizes Dasein, reinstalling it as a metaphysical subject who "has" experiences but singular in the way Jean-Luc Nancy has identified its meaning: as an experience of radical exposure.[1] Maurice Blanchot names this singular experience of language the "limit-experience," an experience of the limit of experience.[2] The measure of the voice's affective and aesthetic effect must be taken on this level; otherwise, it would be just one experience among others. In this experience (before experience), Dasein is brought face-to-face with the fact that the only thing that grounds its existence is its understanding of the sense/meaning of Being, which it always-already has but which is not a sense/meaning that gives itself to representation. (It is rather the condition for the possibility of representation.) One clear implication of Heidegger's conceptualization of the voice, then, is that it figures for a constellation of finitude, language, and affect that is essential to the character of human existence. As I have been arguing, it is this constellation that the contemporary fields of affect studies and the return to the aesthetic presuppose yet routinely overlook.

There is a specific cost to overlooking the antagonism of language in Heidegger's figuration of the voice and to overlooking this antagonism's role in the voice's affective and aesthetic character. That cost is the reinscription of the metaphysics of presence. Both the affective turn and the return to the aesthetic claim to undo the metaphysics of presence through their respective theorizations of becoming. However, it is difficult to square such a claim with the metaphysics of subjective experience they seem to assume. Furthermore, by eschewing the question of language in their theorizations, the affective turn and the return to the aesthetic imply their discourses are exempt from the regime of representation, which, at best, is a contradictory stance. Heidegger's figuration of the voice, by contrast, offers a way to think becoming as a movement not in strict opposition to representation but in excess of it. For the sensibility to which the voice attests is the ground for any act of representation whatsoever. More importantly, the image of language harbored by Heidegger's conception of the voice provides a relational account of sensibility—to the becoming of Being, and, as we will see, to the other Dasein—that discourses of the affective turn and the return to the aesthetic can only assert dogmatically. In order to understand the relational account of sensibility and its importance, though, we must attend more closely to the image of language Heidegger crafts in figuring the voice.

The first part of this chapter reconstructs this image of language by retracing the way Heidegger grounds his conception of the voice in two key sets of distinctions: on the one hand, between language (*die Sprache*) and discourse (*die Rede*); and on the other hand, between *phonē* and *logos*. Each pair consists of metaphysical and nonmetaphysical terms, with the nonmetaphysical terms (discourse and logos, respectively) constituting the foundation from which the voice receives its uncanny, dissimulating force. It is from these nonmetaphysical modes of language, then, that the voice gains its affective and aesthetic characteristics. By seeing how discourse and logos make it possible for the voice to shock Dasein back to the fact of its finitude, we can offer an account of how affect and the aesthetic "have" sense in the ways presupposed by the affective turn and the return to the aesthetic.

Yet while Heidegger's conception of the voice shows how any thought of a relationship among affect, the aesthetic, and finitude remains incomplete without a consideration of the question of language, it does not carve a clean path for escaping the regime of metaphysics. As will become clear, the most obvious impediment to the voice making possible such an escape is Heidegger's grounding of it in the philosophical logos. As much as Heidegger would want to hold that this grounding is a reappropriation and reinterpretation of logos—and therefore part of his project of destructuring the history of metaphysics—we cannot simply take his word for it. Instead, we must see how his reinterpretation of logos contributes to the voice as a figure of the antagonism of language. At stake will be a tension between logos understood traditionally as the ground of logical, signifying communication, and logos as a power inherent to language to allow the appearance of Being.

The stress, I submit, must be on this tension the phrase the antagonism of language connotes. When felt on that register, human finitude will be seen as a struggle between the metaphysical and nonmetaphysical. To be more precise—the extra-metaphysical, insofar as Heidegger's aim is to open an experience (again, at the limit of experience) of that which exceeds the regime of the metaphysics of presence. Following from this, the voice, I argue, should be understood as staging this struggle between metaphysics and its excess. The voice ought to be viewed as a *scene* of human finitude.

As I have been suggesting, Heidegger is less than explicit in documenting the antagonism of language at work in his conception of the voice. He is even more opaque in indicating the voice's figural dimension, and so this aspect needs to be read for with even greater care. Thus, after reconstructing the place that the antagonism of language occupies in the structure of the voice, I will devote the second part of this chapter to bringing out the voice's status as a figure or scene of human finitude. For this aspect of my analysis, I will engage in a sustained reading of Jean-Luc Nancy's essay "Sharing Voices" (*Le Partage des voix*), a foundational text that traces the theme of the voice from the hermeneutic relation to logos in *Being and Time* to the later writings on language. In so doing, this early essay by Nancy helps confirm my intuition regarding the continuity of the theme of language throughout Heidegger's oeuvre.

However, there is an even more inventive intervention "Sharing Voices" contributes to the present study and that is its assertion of the voice as a figure that constantly makes way for more and more figures—from logos to the hermeneutic circle to the dialogue—spanning the entirety of Heidegger's thought. We will see Nancy draw out a number of implications from this observation: First, as a figure, the voice points to the fact that Dasein's finitude propels it into interpretation (*Auslegung*). Which is to say that Dasein does not exist first and then interpret its existence. Dasein's existence is one of interpretation, and the abundance of figures testifies to all the ways Dasein interprets the presentation of the sense of Being. Second, interpretation presupposes a relation and exposure to alterity—both the alterity of the sense of Being and, Nancy argues, that of the other Dasein (the other human being), who also makes up Dasein's world. Third, this means that human finitude (the understanding of the sense/meaning of Being) is always-already shared/divided (*partagé*) and that the multiplicity of figures cannot be reduced to a single Dasein alone but is instead the product of other Daseins as well, of plural voices. Fourth, and finally, the essential connection between interpretation and figuration suggests the latter belongs to human finitude and is required by it. To be finite means to be "en-scened."

The essential relation Nancy's "Sharing Voices" establishes between figuration and interpretation plays a central role in our understanding of Heidegger's appeal to the philosophical logos. If there is a proliferation of figures of the voice in Heidegger, then his text can be regarded as performing the scene of human finitude. In other words, the text itself is a scene of the voice, even as it explicates this scene. Furthermore, insofar as Heidegger's text performs the scene of the voice, it cannot help but perform the antagonism of language I wish to argue inheres in the voice's structure. Thus, while Heidegger's reappropriation of the philosophical logos in his conceptualization of the voice risks a reinscription of metaphysics, the performative dimension of his writing resists this risk to the extent the voice cannot be traced back to a metaphysical subject who would be its origin.

Let me now turn to examining how the antagonism of language animates the voice and how this antagonism brings with it Heidegger's reclamation of the philosophical logos. From there we will then be able to engage with Nancy's scenic intervention in "Sharing Voices."

The Silent Voice and the Antagonism of Language

One of the more enigmatic characteristics of the voice as Heidegger conceives it has to do with the nature of its call to Dasein. Heidegger describes it as a silent one: "The call does not report events; it calls without uttering anything. The call discourses in the uncanny mode of *keeping silent*. And it does this only because, in calling the one to whom the appeal is made, it does not call him into the public idle talk [*Gerede*] of the 'they,' but *calls* him *back* from this *into the reticence of his existent* potentiality-for-Being" (MR 322/SZ 277; original emphasis). There are a number of reasons why the voice cannot call in an everyday sense. If it did, it would belong to the sphere of communication, which is exclusively the realm of the *they*. And if the call were from the *they*, from the realm in which Dasein loses itself, then it would not be able to shock Dasein back to the fact of its finitude. Thus, the call cannot be a public one.

Furthermore, one only encounters a public kind of speaking in the *they*, which Heidegger characterizes as idle talk—anonymous murmurings, gossip, noise. Beneath the significations that circulate and that are exchanged in the everyday sphere of the *they* lies Dasein's finitude, its understanding of the sense/meaning of Being, without which the public creation and exchange of signification would not be possible. Since Dasein's finitude is its understanding of the sense/meaning of Being, which it always-already has, there is no moment when this understanding is communicated to Dasein as if it were a piece of information. In its testimony to Dasein's finitude, the call of conscience is a form of authentic speaking, but one which is silent compared to the noisy, inauthentic mutterings of the *they*.

Heidegger presents a parallel of his distinction between the inauthentic "idle talk" of the *they* and the authentic call of the voice in his description of how Dasein hears the voice's call. Bringing Dasein back from its lostness in the *they* and originating from Dasein itself (from its Self), the call of conscience issues an address Dasein cannot *not* hear and cannot *not* understand. Delineating such an authentic mode of hearing is essential to showing how Dasein attests to its ownmost potentiality-for-Being (MR 324). As Heidegger asserts, "If in each case the caller and he to whom the appeal is made are *at the same time* one's own Dasein *themselves*, then in any failure to hear the call or any incorrect hearing of *oneself*, there lies a *definite kind* of Dasein's *Being*. A free-floating call from which 'nothing ensues' is an impossible fiction when seen existentially. With regard to Dasein, 'that *nothing* ensues' signifies something *positive*" (MR 324/SZ 279; original emphasis). In one respect, then, even failing to hear the call of the voice in the everyday ontic register says something about Dasein's state of being, namely its relation to its potentiality-for-Being. If Dasein fails to hear the call of conscience, it is because its relation to its existence as a thrown being has been obscured, which means that its failing to hear is still a decision on Dasein's part to remain ignorant of the kind of being that it is. In this regard, from the ontological standpoint, Dasein still hears—and understands—the call even when it fails to hear it ontically. This is why it would be an "impossible fiction" for Dasein not to hear the call of the voice.

Because the voice calls Dasein back to its existential ground, it is clear Heidegger is promoting an ontological (as opposed to an ontic) sense of the modes in which Dasein relates to the voice—an authentic form of hearing, keeping silent, and a communication that is not a communication. Less clear is that these formulations also hinge on an ontological image of language that, as I submit, is invoked and relied upon consistently by Heidegger in *Being and Time*, yet which only achieves a faint outline in the work.[3] Nonetheless, the opposition between ontic and ontological conceptions of language constitutes what I am calling the antagonism of language structuring the voice. Without an understanding of this antagonism, the above characteristics of the voice and its call will remain enigmatic, or even worse, dogmatic.

As I state at the outset of this chapter, the antagonism of language is expressed in a tension between two sets of terms that Heidegger deploys in *Being and Time*: language (*die Sprache*) and discourse (*die Rede*), and *phonē* and *logos*. Heidegger privileges the latter of each pairing and then constructs the voice upon them. The schema I wish to present reconstructs how the voice relies upon the qualities of discourse, which itself relies on the qualities of logos. Logos, I will show, will bring us full circle back to the voice, for it is a retranslation of the Aristotelian distinction between the animal voice (*phonē*) and human reason (*logos*). The entire schema shapes the antagonism of language and constitutes the voice's existential force.

In *Being and Time*, language is the ontic expression of discourse, and discourse is not only language's ontological ground but is also equiprimordial with the other existential modes or "existentialia" (specifically, understanding and state-of-mind) through which Dasein's Being-in-the-world is disclosed to it. Discourse, understanding, and state-of-mind are the fundamental ways Heidegger says Dasein discovers its existence in the world. As the ontic expression of discourse, language is derivative from it and names the general arena in which everyday linguistic activities such as communication and assertion take place (MR 204/SZ 161). Language is thus the realm in which the *they* operates.

As a mode through which Dasein's Being-in-the-world is disclosed (i.e., appears) to it, discourse is not, Heidegger emphasizes, present-at-hand (*vorhanden*) in the world. It therefore does not make itself available as an object ready to be manipulated (*zuhanden*, ready-to-hand). Instead, discourse only makes its appearance in the world as language, which does lend itself to being manipulated (MR 204/SZ 161). As with any of the ontic-ontological distinctions Heidegger makes throughout *Being and Time*, it is possible, even inevitable, for Dasein to lose itself in the ontic and forget its ontological relations. The same loss takes place with respect to discourse anytime Dasein mistakes language and its "totality-of-significations" (*Bedeutungsganze*) for the totality of what can be articulated (MR 204).

On the contrary, discourse articulates what can be asserted in language; discourse is a condition of linguistic communication. According to Heidegger, articulation is the process of recognizing the sense (*Sinn*) of something in order that Dasein may interpret it as part of its existence. "The intelligibility of something [*Verständlichkeit*]," Heidegger explains, "has always been articulated [*gegliedert*], even before there is any appropriative interpretation [*zueigenenden Auslegung*] of it. Discourse is the Articulation [*die Artikulation*] of intelligibility. Therefore it underlies both interpretation and assertion. That which can be articulated in interpretation, and thus even more primordially in discourse, is what we have called 'meaning' [*Sinn*]" (MR 203–4/SZ 161). Discourse identifies what is capable of becoming intelligible and what is subsequently (i.e., derivatively) capable of being articulated in interpretation. Discourse designates what is meaningful (*sinnvoll*) as such and what can then take on specific meanings (*Bedeutungen*) for deployment in communication (MR 195 and 204/SZ 153 and 161).

Yet if discourse is not an object present-at-hand in the world, then how does it disclose Dasein's Being-in-the-world? If it is ontologically the condition of meaning and not a means by which to communicate meaning on the ontic register, then how does Dasein's relation to it appear? In two ways, according to Heidegger: Hearing (*Hören*) and keeping silent (*Schweigen*).

Through hearing, as we will recall from having touched on it briefly at the conclusion of chapter 1, Dasein becomes open to its existence as possibility, which is why Dasein cannot not hear the call of conscience. Heidegger's declaration regarding the existential character of hearing appears, though, in his description of the ontological status of discourse, which Heidegger says hearing helps constitute. The full passage reads as follows: "Hearing is constitutive for discourse. And just as linguistic utterance is based on discourse, so is acoustic perception on hearing. Listening to [*Hören auf*] . . . is Dasein's existential way of Being-open as Being-with for Others. Indeed, hearing constitutes the primary and authentic way in which Dasein is open for its ownmost-potentiality-for-Being—as in hearing the voice of the friend whom every Dasein carries with it" (MR 206/SZ 163). In order for Dasein to hear authentically, however, it must be able to keep silent.

Heidegger thus enhances the passivity implied in hearing with a kind of active passivity of keeping silent, which in turn assumes discourse:

> Keeping silent authentically is possible only in genuine discoursing. To be able to keep silent, Dasein must have something to say—that is, it must have at its disposal an authentic and rich disclosedness of itself. In that case one's reticence makes something manifest [*macht offenbar*], and does away with 'idle talk' ["*Gerede*"]. As a mode of discoursing, reticence Articulates [*artikuliert*] the intelligibility of Dasein in so primordial a manner that it gives rise to a potentiality-for-hearing which is genuine, and to a Being-with-one-another which is transparent. (MR 208/SZ 165)

Both passages oppose the noisy, idle talk of language to the silent openness of discourse, setting up the qualities Heidegger attributes to the voice when he turns to the call of conscience later in *Being and Time*. The distinction between language and discourse allows Heidegger to classify the voice as an authentic saying of Dasein's finitude, and the characteristics of hearing and keeping silent that constitute discourse map on to the voice as a silent communication that Dasein cannot not hear. But what is most interesting for the present study is that since the voice testifies to the fact of Dasein's finitude, such testimony would not be possible without Dasein's relation to discourse. Dasein's recovery of the fact of its finitude and to the sensibility (*die Stimmung*) it harbors, relies on a fundamental relation to this originary, nonlinguistic, and extra-metaphysical event of sense named discourse.[4] Also discernible in the previous passages is the claim that authentic Being-with takes place in the relation to discourse, which is one of the central themes we will see Nancy pursue in "Sharing Voices."

Discourse is essential to the power of the voice to attest to the fact of Dasein's finitude. However, it is not quite clear how exactly the aspects of hearing and keeping silent that shape Dasein's relation to the voice reveal to Dasein the fact of its finitude. In fact, it is not clear how the voice, reliant as it is on discourse and its articulation of intelligibility, reveals anything at all.

Yet we receive a clue in Heidegger's claim in the above passage on keeping silent when he remarks that Dasein's "reticence makes something manifest" (*macht offenbar*). This claim hints at the distinction Heidegger makes later in the text in the sections exclusively devoted to the character of the call of conscience. In those sections, Heidegger explicitly connects the discussion of discourse to the voice, categorizing the voice's call as a "mode of discourse" (MR 316/SZ 271). After restating the idea that "[d]iscourse articulates intelligibility," he says it "must not be overlooked" that "vocal utterance . . . is not essential for discourse" (MR 316/SZ 271). The voice is not a vocal utterance, but rather a "giving-to-understand" (MR 316/SZ 271).

The difference between a mere vocal utterance and a "giving-to-understand" harkens back to the introductory section of *Being and Time* where Heidegger argues for a return to a more originary meaning of logos as part of a more fundamental conception of the project of phenomenology. Logos is not simply the "science of" something, as it is commonly understood when it is appended to some object (e.g., biology as the science of life). Nor is it, Heidegger lists, " 'reason,' 'judgment,' 'concept,' 'definition,' 'ground,' or 'relationship,' " for these are already translations (i.e., interpretations) that do not capture the essence of logos (MR 55). Logos, Heidegger says, comes from *legein* (discourse), which in turn is *apophansis*—"letting something be seen" (MR 47, 56).

That discourse maps (back) onto logos, and vice versa, in the project of *Being and Time* ought not be surprising. Just as discourse designates the ontological ground of language, "mak[ing] something manifest" so that something may be signified subsequently in language, logos names an ontological condition allowing phenomena to appear as such (MR 56). However, this is where things get a bit murky. Heidegger then writes, "When fully concrete, discoursing (letting something be seen) has the character of speaking [Sprechens]—vocal proclamation in words. The λόγος [*logos*] is φωνή [*phonē*], and indeed, φωνή μετὰ φαντασίασ [*phonē meta phantasias*]—an utterance in which something is sighted in each case" (MR 56). As the ontological ground of language, discourse, Heidegger says, does not require a vocal utterance and is able to communicate by keeping silent. This is how the voice of conscience can call silently while also saying nothing. Since logos is discourse, one might then expect Heidegger to describe logos as a silent voice, an ontological form of *phonē*. But as the above passage indicates, this is not what Heidegger does. He instead calls it an utterance and implies that rather than *phonē* being a derivative form of logos, logos is a form of phonē with something added to it. Something happens, in other words, in the movement between these ontic-ontological pairings: language and discourse; phonē and logos.

Or rather, something doesn't happen. For what seems to remain consistent in the set of relations Heidegger works with in constructing the voice is the ontological hierarchy, traditionally enforced since Aristotle, of logos, defined as rational speech possessed by human beings, over phonē, defined as mere animal voice.[5] In fact, Heidegger bases his characterization of discourse and logos as events of apophansis ("letting something be seen") in Aristotle's distinction between *logos semantikos* (a signifying discourse) and *logos apophantikos* (a theoretical discourse in the sense of *theorein*, a seeing/observing/apprehending discourse).[6] Although Heidegger implies he is departing from the Platonic and Aristotelian inheritance of logos as it has been transmitted through the history of philosophy, his conceptualization of the relation between discourse and logos through Aristotle says otherwise.

It is certainly possible to go into great detail dissecting this intricate repetition of Aristotle's distinctions between forms of logos in *Being and Time*, as others have done.[7] No doubt we would arrive at conclusions similar to those of these others scholars and be moved to agree that, in repeating Aristotle's conceptual schema regarding logos, Heidegger does not seem to destructure the history of ontology in the way he promises but instead appears to reinscribe this history, and therefore, the metaphysics of presence.[8]

There is one exception within this genre of critique and its argument, however (within, that is to say, the deconstructive genre), and that is Nancy's "Sharing Voices."[9] The account Nancy offers of the Heideggerian voice in this early essay invites us to consider more carefully how profoundly—and unstably—Heidegger occupies the space between metaphysics and what has been referred to as its closure (the task of thinking the end of metaphysics from within the metaphysical tradition).[10] Without denying the critique that the metaphysics of presence reenters Heidegger's text through the voice, Nancy will nonetheless focus on the ways the voice's figural dimension helps it avoid fully doing so. In my next section, I analyze Nancy's argument that the voice's status as figure: (1) denies the view of logos as ground; (2) reveals the shared aspect of human finitude (which is to say, the relation to the sense/meaning of Being as always-already a collective sensibility among Daseins); and (3) implies a performative character to Heidegger's text. Taking Nancy's reading to suggest that Heidegger's reflections on the voice constitute their own "scene of the voice," I want to move toward the idea that there is an essential relationship between finitude and the multiplicity of figuration.

"Sharing Voices" and the Figuration of the Voice

Nancy's "Sharing Voices" opens with a protest against what he calls the modern interpretation of "interpretation." This interpretation, according to Nancy, is first of all a misinterpretation. In his account, modernity is the age of the hermeneutic turn, which replaces "truth" (the idea that there are discoverable, independent facts of the world) with "interpretation" (the idea that there is only meaning). Thus, instead of pursuing truth, philosophy pursues meaning—our creation of it and our participation in it. Such a turn away from truth ought to have made for a decentering of the metaphysics of presence. However, in a sweeping genealogy of modern hermeneutics that he outlines from "[Friedrich] Schleiermacher to [Hans-Georg] Gadamer" (248n1) in which he includes Nietzsche, Freud, and Heidegger but also Wilhelm Dilthey, Rudolf Bultmann, and Paul Ricoeur, Nancy contends that the desire for presence nonetheless persists in the hermeneutical turn. By positing meaning as a process that one is already participating in and reproducing, even as one is engaged in trying to discover it, modern hermeneutics, he says, ends up presupposing an original meaning, and is thereby "haunted [. . . by] the thought of returning to the origin" (214). Modern hermeneutics thus makes way for the return of metaphysics because it simply reinstalls the subject of representation, privileging, Nancy states, "the subject of meaning and the meaning of a subject" (214).

According to Nancy, though, modern hermeneutics' misinterpretation of interpretation is less a symptom of hermeneutics itself than the result of a mistaken reception of Heidegger's thematization of the hermeneutic circle.[11] To see where this misinterpretation takes place, Nancy brings us back to the first appearance of the circle in *Being and Time*. It is in the second section of the work's introduction, where Heidegger enters into the apparent circularity of the question of Being, and it is not a coincidence that this circularity appears (or rather, appears to appear) in the very same passage in which Heidegger also introduces us to Dasein. For in order to ask the question of Being, Heidegger contends that we need to analyze the Being of that being for whom their being (and therefore Being) is a question. That being is Dasein (MR 26–27/SZ 7).

Inaugurated here is the project of fundamental ontology and the task of reconstructing the ways Dasein's being appears to it as a question. Heidegger acknowledges the project's apparent circularity—posing the question of Being by investigating that being for whom its being is a question. Wouldn't we have to already know the meaning of Being in order to define the being of Dasein? And if we already do know the meaning of Being, then why would we need to pose the question of Being? (MR 27/SZ 7).

Heidegger immediately answers that such a form of circularity only appears if Being is taken as a concept that grounds one's encounter with beings and that is assumed to be something one possesses beforehand (MR 27–8/SZ 8). The question of Being, he says, does not involve asking about a concept but rather asking about the conditions for the appearance of the question (MR 28/SZ 8). The chief condition of the question of Being, of posing it, is the existence of that being (Dasein) for whom its being (and therefore Being) is a concern. How else would the question of Being be posed if it were not a concern? And for whom is Being a concern? The answer, Heidegger states, is essentially Dasein; the question of Being belongs to the essence of Dasein (MR 28/SZ 8).

It is this answer from Heidegger that Nancy takes up and that he says is missed by the modern hermeneutic tradition in its reception of *Being and Time*. Particularly egregious in this act of misunderstanding are those most famously responsible for shaping the tradition, such as Ricoeur and Gadamer, who, in Nancy's view, stake out a hermeneutic "method" as a search for meaning ("Sharing" 212–18). Such a search signals a profound misinterpretation of *what* the turn to interpretation indicates. "Being," Nancy writes in elaborating Heidegger's rejoinder, "is not presupposed as another thing, only as the relation to being—of being-there. . . . Being is presupposed as the relation to being which makes the being of being-there. It is presupposed as being-there itself, as the facticity of being-there" ("Sharing" 217–18). It is incorrect to regard the turn to interpretation as a problem of the presupposition of meaning; the turn to interpretation is rather an announcement *that there is meaning* and that the fact of meaning is connected fundamentally to existence.

By treating the question of Being as an investigation into an object, Nancy suggests the modern hermeneutic tradition approaches the question from a speculative, metaphysical understanding, which then leads to the problem of circularity because such an understanding assumes the existence (i.e., being) of the thing (Being) one is investigating. However what if, as Nancy submits, the question of Being were not a metaphysical question but an existential one? What if the question of Being did not point to an object but instead pointed to itself as a way to make visible the facticity of Dasein, which is to say the fact of Dasein and the fact of its thrownness and finitude as the interpretation (*Auslegung*) of its being from its understanding of the sense/meaning of Being—which are made possible from Dasein posing the question of Being? The point, in other words, is not for there to be an answer to the question of Being but for the question of Being "to display itself" ("Sharing" 218). And in displaying itself, the question of Being displays Dasein's facticity. The question of Being stages the scene of Dasein's finitude—the scene, that is to say, *that is* Dasein's finitude.

In *Being and Time*, Heidegger defines Dasein's facticity as the fact that Dasein is—"'that it is and has to be'" (MR 173/SZ 134). But the fact of Dasein's existence, he qualifies, is not the same as the fact that an object present-at-hand exists: say, for instance, a rock. What differentiates the fact of Dasein's existence from that of a rock's is that Dasein relates to its being as a question. Dasein never finds itself existing generally, in the abstract; it always exists as thrown or as engaged in a circumstance—and with its own being a concern for it (MR 83/SZ 56). Dasein, in other words, cannot be separated from its finitude, from its understanding of the sense/meaning of Being, which in turn allows it to project its existence ahead of itself as part of a world.

Accordingly, Heidegger writes, "The concept of 'facticity' implies that an entity 'within-the-world' has Being-in-the-world in such a way that it can understand itself as bound up in its 'destiny' with the Being of those entities which it encounters within the world" (MR 82/SZ 56). Heidegger's use of the term "destiny" (*Geschick*) in this passage is not arbitrary, of course. However, bracketing for the moment its larger significance in his thought, we can simply note that he is connecting Dasein's Being-in-the-world with a sense of movement, evoking Dasein's thrownness (*schicken*, the root of *Geschick*, means "to send").[12] By tying this movement to Dasein's commerce with beings, moreover, this passage from *Being and Time* rehearses the finite transcendence of Dasein as it is propelled from Dasein's understanding of Being. Yet this understanding carries with it an understanding Dasein has—or rather, interprets—of its own being: "As understanding, Dasein projects its Being upon possibilities. This *Being-towards-possibilities* which understands is itself a potentiality-for-Being, and it is so because of the way these possibilities, as disclosed, exert their counter-thrust upon Dasein. The projecting of the understanding has its own possibility—that of developing itself. This development of the understanding we call 'interpretation'" (MR 188/SZ 148). Facticity thus names an interpretive constellation in which Dasein interprets its being (and therefore Being) as it is thrown ahead in its existence toward possibilities. In displaying Dasein's facticity, the question of Being is a staging of Dasein's existence as interpretation. If the project of *Being and Time* is a hermeneutical one, Nancy thus comments, it is because it takes *hermēneia* (interpretation) as one of its central problems. Interpretation is not a method to be employed as a means to answer the question of Being; rather, the question of Being points to the task of explaining interpretation as the ground of Dasein's existence. This is why, Nancy argues, Heidegger seeks to recover *hermēneia* in its originary sense ("Sharing" 219).

It turns out, of course, that the originary sense of *hermēneia* is that of an originary relation to sense itself or as such—the sense (*Sinn*, *sens*) of Being as originary relation. In this way, we are brought back to the connection Heidegger draws among interpretation (*Auslegung*, laying something out), logos as *legein* ("letting-something-be-seen"), and the phenomenology of Dasein ("Sharing" 219; MR 58/SZ 34). "Here," observes Nancy, "phenomenology receives a discreet but decisive inflection.... It is no longer a question of showing the constitution of a world for a subject, but of letting be seen what the manifestation *is*, on the one hand, and, on the other hand, of letting it be seen that a comprehension is *already* comprehension of being" ("Sharing" 220; original emphasis). Rather than the "science of" phenomena, phenomenology is an appearing of logos as a scene of understanding interpretation, of the relation that is human finitude.

By reconstructing the problem of interpretation as a problem of the scene of human finitude, Nancy troubles the criticisms that habitually charge Heidegger with reinscribing the metaphysics of presence through his appropriation of logos. Logos in Heidegger's text is not a metaphysical concept but the scene of facticity, a scene of the voice. The hermeneutic circle, then, does not so much designate a method or concept of interpretation (as the modern hermeneutic tradition misinterpreted it as) than stand, as Nancy says, as an "image" or "figure" of the scene of human finitude ("Sharing" 222). It is this figure, Nancy writes, "that distributes our 'human' scene to us" (*qui nous répartit sur notre scène "humaine"*) ("Sharing" 212; *Partage* 12). The hermeneutic circle figures human finitude as a scene of facticity—a movement of interpretation that appears to itself in its very movement.[13] When the voice of conscience calls Dasein back to the fact of its finitude from its lostness in the *they*, it is to this scene that the voice testifies.

The figuration of logos is not the only way that Heidegger prevents himself from falling (fully) back into the metaphysics of presence. Nancy goes on to contend that this figure is dialogic and that its "dialogicity" ("Sharing" 227) constitutes another aspect of Heidegger's conceptualization of logos that resists metaphysical reinscription: a fundamental—and unending—exposure to alterity. From this viewpoint, the hermeneutic circle is not a figure of returning to or recovering a lost origin; it is instead an image of the event of meaning as a perpetual opening onto difference (or, as Nancy suggests in a reference to Derrida, *différance*) ("Sharing" 224). "The opening of *hermēneuein* [interpreting] is, in this sense," states Nancy,

> the opening of the meaning and in the meaning as *other*: not an 'other' meaning, superior, transcendent, or more original, but a meaning itself as other, an alterity defining meaning. Just as the being-in-question of [B]eing in its own being defined being-there [Dasein], according to an alterity and an alteration of its presence, its subsistence, and its identity, *hermēneuein* determines—or rather announces—that the meaning, this meaning *in question*, is always *other*, in every sense of the expression. ("Sharing" 224; original emphasis)

Nancy is not describing simply the existence of different meanings. He is describing here an alterity—or differentiation—at the heart of the relation to meaning as such. He is invoking the ontological difference, the relation of Being to human being. Dasein relates out of a concern (i.e., meaningfully) to its being from a fundamental understanding of the sense/meaning of Being. Something *other* makes possible Dasein's relation to its being as well as to other beings or existing things (as we have seen from the structure of finite transcendence). This *something other* is of course Being. Since Dasein never encounters Being in abstraction, however, Being only appears or "announces itself" in Dasein's engagement with the becoming that characterizes Dasein's thrown existence ("Sharing" 224). This is why Nancy will proclaim that there is always an "other of the other" ("Sharing" 246). This experience of difference (before, or at the limit of experience) is essential to the relation to meaning. Without alterity, there would be no meaning. If what is other were completely transparent to understanding, if Dasein could interpret thoroughly and without remainder the sense/meaning of Being (and therefore the meaning of its being/its being as meaning), then there would be no interpretive movement at all for Dasein, which is to say Dasein would not "ex-ist."

The fact that Dasein's relation to meaning resists all final attempts at assimilation or mastery supports the idea that Dasein is not the metaphysical subject or the subject of representation. But the dialogic character of interpretation includes for Nancy another aspect encompassed by the ontological difference, and that is the relation to the other Dasein. In stressing this sense of the dialogic, Nancy pushes against the modern hermeneutical tradition's conception that interpretation is directed at deciphering the meaning of the other person, for that, too, subscribes to a metaphysical picture of intersubjectivity and in no way thinks of meaning as a primordial relation that precedes all other forms of relation ("Sharing" 225). With the concept of the dialogic, Nancy is therefore alluding to the image of a *dia-logos*, of an event of meaning that is always-already divided/shared (*partagé*) among Daseins.

This turn to the dialogic may seem an odd addition on Nancy's part. Although Heidegger does not seem to make this relation to alterity explicit in *Being and Time*, we have encountered moments where the presence of alterity—in the form of the other Dasein and in Dasein's relation to itself—presses in upon the phenomenology of Dasein. The call of the voice comes from Dasein itself, but it arrives ecstatically and reaches Dasein uncannily, as if from someone other. Remember, too, the enigmatic formulation Heidegger offers in his description of Dasein's primordial comportment in hearing, which he says constitutes Dasein's openness to the call, "as in hearing the voice of the friend whom every Dasein carries with it" (MR 206/SZ 163).

Nancy reads these moments in *Being and Time* as eruptions of otherness that Heidegger, whether knowingly or not, acknowledges yet also quickly suppresses. For Nancy, however, these eruptions nonetheless testify to the fact that Dasein's interpretive understanding—its existential *Aus-legung* or laying out—is never a solitary one, never a *Selbstauslegung* (self-interpretation). Or to be more precise, Dasein's *Selbstauslegung* is made possible by a fundamental accompaniment of otherness: a Being-with (*Mitsein*) that Dasein cannot cast off. When meaning makes its presentation, it always does so in a communal way divided/shared among others. As such, Nancy writes, "*Logos* is not a *phonē sēmantikē* [signifying voice], it is not a voice endowed with signification, it is not a meaning, and it will not be able to be 'interpreted.' It is, on the other hand, the articulation before the voices, in which, nevertheless, the voices are conjoined already, and divided (separated)" ("Sharing" 244). Meaning, according to Nancy, is nothing other than this division/sharing among others, which accounts for the multiplicity of meaning and its unceasing alterity. But this multiplicity and unceasing alterity of voices also links "us" together in a community of sense:

> It is from there that it is necessary, from now on, to understand the hermeneutic opening of the question of being, and its circular character. If we are in motion always already "in the everyday understanding of being," it is not that we have in an

ordinary fashion—nor extraordinary!—*the* meaning of being, nor *a* meaning of being, nor *the* meaning in order to be. It is that we are, we exist, in multiplying voices, and that this sharing is what we *are*: we give it, we share it, we announce it. "To be" already in the understanding of being is not to be already in the circulation, not in the circularity of meaning: it is "to be," and it is to be abandoned in this sharing, and to its difficult community, where being is that which we announce to ourselves one to another, unless being is only announcing ourselves to one another, in a "long" poetic, magnetic, and rhapsodic "chain." ("Sharing" 244; original emphasis)

This passage provides a glimpse of where Nancy will go in his later work in pursuit of the persistence of *Mitsein* in Heidegger's thought.[14] However, Nancy's primary concern in this part of his text is to begin tracing out the ways the voice, as the dialogic sharing of sense, proliferates throughout Heidegger's writings beyond *Being and Time*. Nancy's reference to "a 'long' poetic, magnetic, and rhapsodic 'chain' " at the end of the just cited passage is part of his reading of Heidegger's reading of the *Ion*, Plato's dialogue on poetic interpretation, which appears in "A Dialogue on Language" from *Unterwegs zur Sprache* (1959).[15] His interest in this text is part of his claim that the dialogic scene of the voice he identifies in Heidegger's conceptualization of logos appears repeatedly and is *performed* throughout Heidegger's work well into his later reflections on language.

As its full title states, "A Dialogue on Language" is a conversation Heidegger stages "between a Japanese and an Inquirer." Their theme is the meaning of *hermēneia*, and since the *Ion* is also a dialogue on *hermēneia*, the interlocutors take it up in the course of their exchange. The *Ion* itself stages a debate between Socrates and the dialogue's titular character on whether poetic interpretation depends on actual knowledge (*technē*) and understanding of the poetic word or is merely a form of mimetic repetition of it. To satisfy Ion, who insists that his ability to interpret Homer is an actual skill reliant on being able to understand the Homeric text, Socrates weaves a mythic image of the divine Muse who inspires the poets, who in turn inspire the rhapsodes such as Ion, who in turn inspire the spectator, etc., as if they were all members of a great magnetic chain. In convincing Ion of this chain of meaning, Socrates demonstrates that Ion really doesn't know that of which he speaks, and the *Ion* extends Plato's critique of mimesis by casting it as a kind of contagious madness.

By returning to Heidegger's return to Plato in the context of his argument about the sharing of logos, Nancy is more concerned with the levels of staging and restaging at work in these texts than with the content of each set of scenes depicted in them. For Nancy, the *Ion* stages a sharing of the voice, which Heidegger's "A Dialogue on Language" restages as a dialogue about a dialogue about the transference of meaning. In Nancy's view, there is something significant happening in this scenic *mise-en-abyme*: (1) they do not offer any closure on meaning but instead open onto more and more scenes, more and more figures; and (2) they present the theatricality of *hermēneia*, the way that *hermēneia* requires a scene of presentation (*Darstellung*) ("Sharing" 239, 247). This results in an exigency to rethink the relationship between logos and mimesis. The latter is not an imitation of the former; mimesis is the presentation, the appearance, of logos and its necessary link to appearance. Mimesis comes to name the presentation of the scene of the voice and the fact that there is no voice without a scene.

If Nancy is correct about this performative aspect of the voice in Heidegger, then it must be possible to discover more scenes of presentation in his writings. In chapter 3, I claim to do just that in Heidegger's treatments of Sophocles's *Antigone*, which are found in his *Introduction to Metaphysics* (1935) and *Hölderlin's Hymn "The Ister"* (1942). Approaching Heidegger's treatments of *Antigone* as presentations of the voice's figuration will help us appreciate Heidegger's turns to poetry as a way to access the constellation of language, finitude, figuration, and affect.

Without a proper appreciation for the role the figure plays in Heidegger's conceptualization of the voice, we will continue to think of language and affect as distinct from each other and consequently bar ourselves from a full understanding of either. Following my chapter on "Heidegger's Antigones," I proceed to follow two itineraries in Continental thought that I wish to argue respond to the Heideggerian conceptualization of the voice as a constellation of language, finitude, figuration, and affect.

One itinerary will express some hesitation in the face of this constellation, particularly in terms of the primacy of the figure and the ethical and political implications of that primacy for the relation to the other human being that Nancy's reading of the voice uncovers. This will be the set of engagements that I cover in chapter 4 on Nancy and Philippe Lacoue-Labarthe's debate on the Heideggerian voice and whether the necessary figuration the voice appears to signal is at the root of his fascination with fascist spectacularization. Chapter 5 will follow up on what we will see is Lacoue-Labarthe's call for the political task of defiguration by considering

Maurice Blanchot's severe recasting of the relation between language and human finitude in his conception of the narrative voice of literature.

By contrast, the other itinerary I will map out will acknowledge the impasse the primacy of the figure appears to pose for a philosophy of difference, but it will respond in a way that ends up embracing Heidegger's constellation. This is the path staked out by Gilles Deleuze in his writings on univocity, sense, and simulacra, which I will discuss in chapter 6. In addition to demonstrating how his conceptions of sense and simulacra resonate with Nancy's theorizations of the sharing of voices and figuration, I will also detail the ways Deleuze is in direct dialogue with Heidegger on the voice.

Chapter 3

A Finite Scene?

Heidegger's Antigones and the Returns of the Voice

polla ta deina kouden anthrôpou deinoteron pelei.
Wonders are many, and none is more wonderful than man.

—Sophocles, *Antigone*

What kind of knowledge and what kind of word is this? What voice, whose voice comes to word in the choral ode? What is the chorus in Greek tragedy?

—Heidegger, *Hölderlin's Hymn "The Ister"*

Chapter 2 introduced a number of important themes for our understanding of the voice in Heidegger. The first is that the extra-metaphysical image of language upon which he constructs the voice leads to, and is indeed the condition for, Heidegger's offering of it as a figure of human finitude. And as my reading of Jean-Luc Nancy's "Sharing Voices" showed, Heidegger's reappropriation of the philosophical logos in forging the voice's extra-metaphysical relation to language is not a liability to his attempt to destructure the history of metaphysics. Rather, by conceiving logos as an event of the sense of Being, Heidegger's reappropriation makes it possible to see the essential relation between human finitude—the human Dasein's thrown existence from an understanding of the sense/meaning of Being—and interpretation. To exist is to interpret one's existence *and* have this interpreting thrownness—one's facticity—appear to and before oneself. Our existence is one of bearing witness to our interpretation of our existence, which, as Nancy demonstrates, is imbricated with the existence of the other human Dasein, who is also interpreting their own respective thrownness. The voice (*die Stimme*) testifies to this fact: it calls us back as an affective, figurative echo of our fundamental relation to the sensibility (*die Stimmung*) of Being, which we always-already understand and always-already share in a relation (before relation) to the other human Dasein.

Since interpretation harbors this specular dimension,[1] Nancy's "Sharing Voices" also presented us with the idea that the multiplicity of interpretations in which we are always-already thrown yields a multiplicity of figures. Given that there is no single meaning of Being, only the interpretations arising from our thrown existence, there must not be any single or original figure either. Just as interpretation is always-already built upon existing interpretations, figuration simply gives way to more and more figures. These multiplicities of interpretations and figurations become even greater when we consider the fact, as Nancy attempts to bring forth, that our thrown existence is exactly that—composed of an "our," of a *dia-logos*, of a partitioning of meaning that is shared among different human Daseins. In light of this fact, "Sharing Voices" contends we must include Heidegger's own elaboration of the voice as participating in the sharing of meaning. Yet what sets Heidegger's reflections on the voice apart from other interpretations is that they restage the *dia-logos* of meaning. They thus show the becoming-figure of human finitude in the voice. Heidegger's reflections enact the scene of the voice.

This chapter carries forward these themes through a close analysis of Heidegger's readings of Sophocles's *Antigone*. My supposition at the conclusion of chapter 2 was that if Nancy is accurate in his characterization of the performative nature of Heidegger's text, then it must be possible to locate other moments of figuration, other attractions to the scene of the voice, in his writings. As I signal with my choice of epigraphs at the opening of this chapter, I wish to consider Heidegger's readings of *Antigone* as instances of the repetition and return of the voice in his text.

Beginning with his interpretation of the tragedy's First Choral Ode (the "Ode to Man"), which he undertakes in 1935 in *Introduction to Metaphysics*, and extending to his attention to Antigone (the character herself) seven years later in *Hölderlin's Hymn "The Ister"* (1942), Heidegger engages with *Antigone* the work on a number of levels: first as an artistic realization of the scene of human finitude and then as producing a figure of the voice in the character Antigone herself. While these engagements exemplify Heidegger's sustained thematization of the scene of the voice, to the extent that they open up for him questions about the differences between premodern and modern interpretations of Being, they also count as further examples of his text's enactment of the voice as advanced by Nancy in "Sharing Voices." For, as we will see, Heidegger's interpretations of *Antigone* are inflected through both the question of the degree to which it is possible to recover the Greek Dasein's interpretation of Being (which he posits as being more originary than the modern relation to Being) and an interpretation of Hölderlin's translations of the Greek scene of human finitude from ancient Greek to modern German. And, of course, harbored within this reception of interpretation and translation is also Nietzsche's legacy of reflecting on the tragic work of art. On the one hand, then, we can expect the themes of interpretation and an extra-metaphysical relation to language to persist as a question of translation. On the other hand, it seems Heidegger's readings of *Antigone* are predicated upon, and unfold as, a sharing of voices among the ancient Greek and modern German Daseins.

Heidegger's readings of *Antigone* also offer an opportunity to investigate connections between his reflections on the work of art, which he presents in "The Origin of the Work of Art" (1935–36), and the aesthetic character of the voice as figure. If the voice is an aesthetic, affective, and figurative echo of human finitude, then what connection, if any, does it have to the aesthetic and affective qualities of the work of art? Specifically, do Heidegger's reflections on *Antigone* bring together the voice and the work of art only coincidentally, or can Heidegger be seen as pursuing some essential relation between them?

The answer I offer in this chapter is that, for Heidegger, the "work" that the work of art performs is that of providing a frame for the scene of the voice. That is to say, the artwork is a scene *of the* scene of finitude and thus constitutes a space of the voice's return or echo (thus, an echo of an echo, a kind of *mise-en-abyme*). In addition, if the artwork is a return of the voice, this means it is also a return of the figure; it is a figure for finitude's figuration.[2] In what follows, I establish this set of claims by attending to Heidegger's reflections on the figure (*Gestalt*) in "The Origin of the Work of Art" and its connection to what Heidegger describes as the artwork's "en-framing" (*Ge-stell*) of the "strife" (*Streit*) between world and earth, which Heidegger contends constitutes the work of art's "truth" as an unconcealing event of Being (as *aletheia*). To the extent we can consider the strife between world and earth a dynamic and repetitive announcement of finitude, the work of art can be said to stage a scene of the voice's claim (*Anspruch*).[3] It is a scene for the scene of the voice.

Tragedy, furthermore, occupies a privileged position in Heidegger's conception of art's relation to finitude. For Heidegger, tragedy does not illustrate or reflect human finitude. Rather, human finitude is tragic in its essence. The tragic work of art is thus an originary presentation—a *saying*—of finitude as the scene of the human relation to Being. Therefore, after opening with an overview of Heidegger's remarks on the figure in "The Origin of the Work of Art" and how they connect to the facticity of finitude that I reviewed in my earlier chapters, I turn to a focused comparison of the different readings Heidegger conducts of *Antigone* in *Introduction to Metaphysics* and in *Hölderlin's Hymn "The Ister."* In the former, we find Heidegger regarding *Antigone* as a poeticized saying of the voice. In the latter, Heidegger alters his approach in a noteworthy fashion by thematizing "the singular figure of Antigone" (*die einzige Gestalt der Antigone*) as "the purest poem itself" *(das reinste Gedicht selbst).*[4] These extraordinary formulations, I wish to argue, announce his interpretations as attempts to hear and respond to the works' saying. In other words, they attest to the finitude of Heidegger's own text, to the fact of its (and therefore Heidegger's) interpreting thrownness, a claim I will seek to support through careful examination of the intricate deliberations Heidegger gives to the task of translating *Antigone*. This task brings with it the necessity to pay attention to the fact that Heidegger's translation of *Antigone* is very much a response to Hölderlin's translations of the play and is inflected by Nietzsche's theorization of the relation of tragedy to human existence. Together, Heidegger's interpretations of *Antigone* indicate not only returns of the voice in his thought; they also announce the emergence of a collective and historical inflection he gives to the voice in the form of the voice of a people, which has significance for evaluating the social and political implications of his corpus.

"The Origin of the Work of Art"

Heidegger's "The Origin of the Work of Art" (also commonly referred to as the "artwork essay") is well known for its realignment of art with truth, two areas (aesthetics and epistemology, respectively) that are typically considered separate philosophical categories. The key contribution the artwork essay makes is to force a vision of the work of art as an existential object in movement, one that serves as an opening for the appearance of Being.

This is the artwork's truth as *aletheia* (unconcealment)—it is a site for the unconcealment of Being.

The unconcealment of Being, however, is never an event that remains stable. Being always falls back into concealment, or forgetting, as we saw with the structure of Dasein's finite transcendence. Unlike most aesthetic theories, then, which take as their basic premise the idea that art is simply the joining of form and matter (thus subordinating the latter to the former, sedimenting them into a static object, and concealing the becoming of Being), Heidegger conceives the work of art as a fundamentally dynamic struggle between the becoming of Being and Being's concealment or forgetting. Heidegger tries to capture this struggle in his description of the work of art as figuring the relation of "world" and "earth" in what he calls the "rift-design" (*Riß*). Summarizing this configuration, Heidegger writes,

> Truth establishes itself in the work. Truth is present only as the strife [*Streit*] between clearing and concealing in the opposition between world and earth. As this strife of world and earth, truth wills its establishment in the work. The strife is not resolved in something brought forth specifically for that purpose, but neither is it merely housed there. The strife is, rather, opened up by the work. . . .
>
> This strife which is brought into the rift-design, and so set back into the earth and fixed in place, is the *figure* [**Gestalt**]. The createdness of the work means: the fixing in place of truth in the figure. Figure is the structure of the rift in its self-establishment. The structured rift is the jointure [*Fuge*] of the shining of truth. What we here call "figure" is always to be thought out of that *particular* placing [*stellen*] and placement [*Ge-stell*] as which the work comes to presence when it sets itself up and sets itself forth.[5]

Although by this time Heidegger has already begun to move away from a phenomenology of Dasein that formed the project of *Being and Time*, he has not abandoned that project's essential terms. In "The Origin of the Work of Art," "world" is to be heard in a manner consistent with Heidegger's thematization of that concept in *Being and Time*. Namely, "world" designates the horizon of Dasein's concerns, and since Dasein's concerns entail both an understanding of the sense/meaning of Being and Dasein's facticity (its interpretation of its existence from its understanding of the sense/meaning of Being), Heidegger is linking here the facticity of Dasein with the work of art.

If "world" is a manifestation of finitude (i.e., if there is no world without finitude), then "earth" is the brutal force of Being's becoming, which pushes back against Dasein's existential projects and ultimately ends up undoing them. It is because of this resistance, however, that our projects come into relief as projects. Heidegger writes, "Earth shatters every attempt to penetrate it. It turns every merely calculational intrusion into an act of destruction. Although such destruction may be accompanied by the appearance of mastery and progress in the form of the technological-scientific objectification of nature, this mastery remains, nonetheless, an impotence of the will" ("Origin" 25). This is the strife between world and earth. Yet Heidegger is clear that while it seems earth prevails over all attempts at constructing world, earth still needs world in order to appear as earth ("Origin" 24).

It is thus no coincidence that when describing the strife between world and earth, Heidegger appeals to the ruins of a Greek temple as an exemplar that makes visible "world-withdrawal and world-decay" ("Origin" 20).[6] The ruin reflects back the circular dimension of finitude in which human beings' relation to beings as objects or equipment, first enabled by an originary understanding of Being, leads to a forgetting of the fact of this understanding. The work of art's presentation of the strife between world and earth—and the enframing (*Ge-stell*) of this strife in and by the figure—underscores the difference between it and an object that simply serves as equipment. Through the presentation of this strife, the "work" that the work of art performs is one of unconcealment and concealment. Through this work, the work of art enacts the rhythm of human finitude, the to and fro between understanding the sense/meaning of Being and forgetting the fact of this understanding (the *hin und her* movement described in chapter 1). The work of art thus figures the relation between human being and Being that makes possible any relation to beings ("Origin" 39–40).

In the course of discussing the Greek temple, Heidegger briefly invokes tragedy. He states that, like the temple, tragedy is not a portrayal or theatrical staging of world; it is the appearance of world (and perhaps, world as that which appears) ("Origin" 22). Although Heidegger does not make the connection directly here in the artwork essay, there is much to suggest that tragedy is not just any other art form for him. Since the strife of world and earth the work of art figures conjures an image of human finitude as ruinous and tragic (it is not earth that destroys but those previously cited "calculational" drives "to penetrate it" that do), it would seem tragedy would occupy a privileged position vis-à-vis the other arts. While all art would figure the strife of world and earth, tragedy posits this strife as the matter proper to it and could thus be viewed as the art of art.

Such a view is supported by Heidegger's ultimate declaration in "The Origin of the Work of Art" that poetry and the poeticizing gesture constitute art's essence. "Truth," he says, "as the clearing and concealing of that which is, happens through being poeticized [*gedichtet*]. *All art*, as the letting happen of the advent of truth of beings, is, *in essence, poetry*" ("Origin" 44 / "*Ursprung*" 58; original emphasis). But just as crucial, I suspect, is the collective character that both the architecture of the Greek temple and tragedy share, a quality that allows Heidegger to then begin to theorize a collective voice sounded by the work of art. As we will see in the following sections dedicated to his readings of *Antigone*, this emphasis on the voice of a people, specifically that of the Greeks, reverberates in both his description of Antigone as "the purest poem itself" and also in his initial reading of the First Choral Ode, which he describes in *An Introduction to Metaphysics* as a "poetic outline" (*dichterischen Entwurf*) of the essence of being-human (*das Wesen des Menschseins*).[7] If all art is a poetic saying of human finitude, which is to say, a scene of the voice, then Heidegger's engagement with *Antigone* needs to be read as a kind of hearing and sharing of this voice, which he underscores as the singular saying of the Greeks' historical Dasein. For Heidegger, the task that confronts the modern historical Dasein is how to attune its hearing to the voice of the Greeks.

Antigone: From *An Introduction to Metaphysics* to *Hölderlin's Hymn "The Ister"*

AN INTRODUCTION TO METAPHYSICS

In *An Introduction to Metaphysics*, Heidegger takes up *Antigone*'s First Choral Ode as part of his engagement with the fragments of Heraclitus and Parmenides. Heidegger reads the three together on the way to crafting a "formula" for expressing the essence of being-human: "*physis = logos anthrōpon echōn*: being, overpowering appearing, necessitates the gathering that pervades and grounds being-human" (*das Sein, das überwältigende Erscheinen, ernötigt die Sammlung, die das Menschsein (acc.) innehat und gründet*) (IM 175 / EM 184, translation modified). All three aspects—the fragments of

Heraclitus, those of Parmenides, and the choral ode—aid Heidegger in deriving this formula. Heraclitus helps Heidegger elucidate the relationship between *physis* and *logos*, and Parmenides provides the connection between Being and thinking. But it is the ode that Heidegger regards as presenting explicitly the Greek understanding of the essence of being-human. Without the ode, Heidegger seems to go so far as to suggest, modern thought would lack the means to hear the essence of being-human he claims is expressed in the fragments of the two Presocratics.

Why is modern thought incapable of an authentic hearing, as Heidegger puts it, of the Greek Dasein? Because it conceives of existence not in terms of Da-sein, being-there, but as grounded in the subjectivity of "man," a being who is defined not by its understanding of the sense/meaning of Being (and hence a relation to Being) but as "the animal equipped with reason": "*zōion logon echōn*" (IM 175). It is precisely this modern definition of the human ("*anthrōpos = zōion logon echōn*") that Heidegger wishes to oppose with the formula he offers for the scene of finite transcendence: "*physis = logos anthrōpon echōn*" (IM 175).

Furthermore, because modern thought grounds thought itself in the rationality of man, this rationality then serves as the ground and image of all possible future thought. The rational, logical character of modern thought, or what Heidegger calls "the end," thus precludes an encounter with what Heidegger describes as the "beginning": the "poetic thinking" (*das dichterisch Denken*) of the Greeks (IM 175; 144/EM 184; 153). Greek thought is characterized as a poetic thinking, Heidegger holds, because it reflects the human's essential struggle (*Kampf*) or contestation (*Auseinandersetzung*) with beings (*Seienden*), an event Heidegger describes as an "originary poeticizing" (*ursprüngliches Dichten*) (EM 153).

At the specific moment in the text in which he considers the choral ode, Heidegger is attempting to read Parmenides's famous fragment *to gar auto noein estin te kai einai*. Traditionally rendered as "thinking and Being are the same," Heidegger retranslates the fragment as: "Reciprocally belonging-together are apprehension and Being" (*Zusammengehörig sind Vernehmung wechselweise und Sein*) (IM 145/EM 154, translation modified). Again, holding that the fragment contains an originary understanding of finite transcendence, Heidegger writes, "*What is expressed in Parmenides' maxim is a determination [Bestimmung] of the essence of [the human] from out of the essence of being itself*" (IM 144/EM 152, translation modified; original emphasis). However, modern thought's translation of the Parmenidean maxim obscures this fact (the eventful nature of finite transcendence, as well as its affective character as a form of *die Stimmung*) by treating both thinking and Being as things "present-at-hand" (*vorhanden*) and standing in a logical relation of equal measure to each other.

In an effort to bring the poetic thinking of Heraclitus and Parmenides to understanding, Heidegger enlists what he names "its contrary aspect" (*seine ihm zugehörige Gegenseite*)—tragedy, which he characterizes as the "thinking poetry" (*das denkerisch Dichten*) of the Greeks (IM 144–45/EM 153). "Because the definition of being-human effected by Parmenides is strange and hard to approach directly," explains Heidegger, "we shall first seek help and counsel by consulting the poetic project of being-human among the Greeks" (IM 146). It is at this point that Heidegger turns to *Antigone*. While this is the first direct naming of tragedy's role in the expression of the essence of being-human, it is not the first time tragedy appears in the text. Citing Karl Reinhardt's then recent 1933 interpretation of *Oedipus Rex* as exhibiting the "tragedy of appearance" (*Tragödie des Scheins*) in conjunction with Hölderlin's line from the poem "*In lieblicher Bläue blühet . . . ,*" "Perhaps King Oedipus has an eye too many," Heidegger presents Oedipus as the name or figure of the speculative drive underlying modern science. This drive treats beings in a derivative mode, not in the event of their appearance as beings but "en-visions" them, so to speak, as present-at-hand. In this way, the vision inherent to modern science is Oedipal; it is a blind sight. When Oedipus finally puts his eyes out and becomes physically blind, this then constitutes an originary sight, according to Heidegger, for it causes Oedipus to understand appearance as such as the struggle of Being itself to appear (IM 107–8/EM 114–15).[8]

For Heidegger, the elaboration of the tragic (in)sight is found in the choral ode's first line: *polla ta deina kouden anthropou deinoteron pelei*. Interestingly enough, despite his insistence on the authenticity of the Greek poetic word in its understanding of Being, Heidegger does not present the Greek at first, but his translation of the Greek text into German:

Vielfältig das Unheimliche, nichts doch
über den Menschen hinaus Unheimlicheres ragend sich regt. (EM 155)

There is much that is strange, but nothing
that surpasses the human in strangeness. (IM 146)

It is worth contrasting Heidegger's translation (including its English translation by Manheim) to a conventional English rendering of the ode. In Sir Richard Jebb's 1891 translation, the same lines appear as follows: "Wonders are many, and none is more wonderful than man." In typical fashion, the Jebb translation goes on to emphasize the "technicity" of "man," the capacity for "man" to employ *technē* to shape and overcome nature (*physis*).⁹ In its course of strophes and antistrophes, the ode speaks of man's taming of wild beasts, his faculties of thought and speech, his building of cities, and ability to construct protection from the weather. *Technē*, in this traditional reading, is of course conceived as ratio, reason, "skill" (l. 365), a faculty belonging to man so far as he is defined as *zōion logon echōn* (the rational animal). It is also, therefore, the result of a modern interpretation of the ode, Heidegger submits, that is then projected onto the ode's first line. According to the modern interpretation, "man" is the most wonderful of wonders because he possesses *technē*.

Heidegger's translation is thus aimed at wresting back the Greek definition of the human from the modern interpretation, or rather, projection. His strategy is to reverse this projection by focusing on the translation of the first line and inflecting the remainder of the ode (save, curiously, its final verse) through his retranslation.

Heidegger's entire interpretation proceeds from the confrontation/oppositional affinity (*Auseinandersetzung*) between *deinon* and *to deinotaton*.¹⁰ As Andrzej Warminski says, their relation constitutes a "riddle" for Heidegger.¹¹ The phrase "much that is strange" (*polla ta deina*) refers to "the essent as a whole" (*das Seiende im Ganzen*), beings in their totality, according to Heidegger. As a totality, beings comprise *deinon*, the "overpowering power." By contrast, as the "strangest of the strange," *to deinotaton*, human beings are the most powerful among the overpowering power of the totality of beings (IM 150/ EM 159).

The relation between *deinon* and *to deinotaton* constitutes a confrontation, Heidegger says, because it "cuts across the contending separations [*die gegenwendigen Aus-einander-setzungen*] of being" (IM 149/EM 158). *Deinon*, Heidegger continues, is powerful in the sense of one who not only "disposes" power (*Gewalt*) but who is fundamentally violent (*gewalt-tätig*) in their Dasein (IM 149–50/EM 159). But the human is *to deinotaton* because, fundamentally, it "uses power [*Gewalt*] against the overpowering [*das Überwältigende*]. Because [the human] is twice *deinon* in a sense that is originally one, he is *to deinotaton*, the most powerful: violent in the midst of the overpowering" (IM 150/EM 159).

However, Heidegger translates *deinon* as strange (*un-heimlich*) in order to accentuate its meaning "as the supreme limit and link of human being" (IM 150/EM 159–60). The human does not become strange or take on strange feelings or attributes because of its status as the most powerful. The strange is not an affect appended to a subject. Rather, as the most powerful, the human is essentially and perpetually cast out of the familiar, the "homely" (*das Heimische*). With this notion of the unhomely, Heidegger arrives at what he calls "the authentic Greek definition" of the human. "We shall fully appreciate this phenomenon of strangeness [*das Geschehnis der Un-heimlichkeit*]," Heidegger claims, "only if we experience the power [*Macht*] of appearance and the struggle [*Kampf*] with it as an essential part of being-there" (IM 151/EM 160). In this way, Heidegger appeals once again to the sense of uncanniness with which he describes both Dasein's thrownness as well as the call of conscience in *Being and Time*, which we touched on in chapter 1.

In the remaining parts of his interpretation of the ode, Heidegger emphasizes this essential event of strangeness. Thus, Heidegger reads line 360 in the middle of the second strophe, *pantaporos aporos ep' ouden erchetai*,[12] "Everywhere journeying, inexperienced and without issue, he comes to nothingness," as organized around the opposition between *pantoporos* and *aporos*. Everywhere without a path (*pantaporos aporos*), the human is forced to "make himself a path" (IM 151/EM 161). The human is essentially without a path, *ausweglos*, "without issue," issueless (IM 152/EM 161). Similarly, Heidegger reads the opposition in line 370 between *hypsipolis* and *apolis* as reiterations of the human Dasein's strangeness. Instead of translating *hypsipolis* as someone who follows the laws of the city (*polis*), and *apolis* as someone who does not, he renders them as "rising high above his place" and "losing his place," respectively (IM 147–48/EM 157). He then interprets this pairing as a juxtaposition between "the ground and scene" (*der Grund und Ort*) of the human Dasein and the "place and scene of history" (*die Geschichts-stätte*) itself (IM 152/EM 161). For Heidegger, line 370 opposes, yet also links, the human scene of finitude and the scene of history. The human Dasein's *Unheimlichkeit* is the condition of its historical acting.

What stands out at this moment in Heidegger's commentary, of course, is his invocation of the scenic in this description of the groundlessness of human finitude. These passages are remarkable in that they posit this fundamental groundlessness as the ground/foundation of history itself. But by history (*Geschichte*), Heidegger means the history of Being, so once more, we have a formulation of the human Dasein's destiny (*Geschick*) being connected to the sending (*schicken*) of Being. Human being *is* insofar as it is the nonground of the history of Being. In existing, the human is "the place and scene of history" (*die Geschichts-stätte*).[13]

Human finitude's groundlessness marks human existence as a creative, "poetic project," says Heidegger (IM 158/EM 167). But the radical exposure such an existence entails opens onto a tragic condition as well. According to Heidegger, all creation out of this fundamental scene of strangeness—all casting out into the unfamiliar of the overpowering—necessitates an exposure to "*atē*, ruin [*Verderb*], catastrophe," disaster (IM 152/EM 161). The irreducible immanence of human existence means that there is no longer any transcendence. The human Dasein's absolute freedom is conditioned by its absolute lack of ground. Which is to say, nothing lasts. In the terminology of "The Origin of the Work of Art," world crashes against earth.

As he continues with his interpretation, Heidegger stresses the encounter with disaster as Dasein's most basic experience following from its position as *to deinotaton*. This will lead him to state that the essential relation the human has to disaster results in it having an essential relation to death. "Insofar as the human *is*," Heidegger writes, "it stands in the issuelessness of death. Being-there is the taking-place of strangeness itself" (IM 158/EM 167, translation modified; original emphasis). Death is the ultimate limit of the possibilities the human creates through its violent strangeness.

Disaster thus rules over the human Dasein, and as such, it is the condition of possibility for all human action and knowledge (*technē*). Following this motif through, Heidegger interprets the conflict between *machanoen technē* and *dikē* in the final strophe as a further interpretation of the original confrontation in the opening line between *to deinotaton* and *deinon*, respectively. Here *dikē* is not justice in the juridical, moral sense, but the "governing order," and *technē* is human accomplishment, "a manifesting realization of Being *in* the essent" (IM 159/EM 168; original emphasis). Their confrontation brings both victory and defeat, simultaneous mastery of the overpowering and the overpowering's persistence through such mastery. "Both," Heidegger says, "are menaced by disaster":

> The *violent one*, the creative man, who sets forth into the un-said, who breaks into the un-thought, compels the unhappened to happen and makes the unseen appear—this violent one stands at all times in venture (*tolma*, line 371). In venturing to master being, he must risk the assault of the non-essent, *mē kalon*, he

must risk dispersion, in-stability, disorder, mischief. The higher the summit of historical being-there, the deeper will be the abyss, the more abrupt the fall into the unhistorical, which merely thrashes around in issueless and placeless confusion. (IM 161/ EM 170; original emphasis)

Yet, despite the disastrous risk of existence, Heidegger adds that, for the human, "disaster is the deepest and broadest affirmation of the overpowering [*Der Untergang ist ihm das tiefste und weiteste Ja zum Überwältigende*]" (IM 163/EM 172). With this statement, Heidegger clearly announces a dialogue with Nietzsche, combining the saying yes (*Ja-sagen*) to life Nietzsche identified in the ancient Greeks' invention of tragedy with the "going-under" (*Untergang*) his Zarathustra performs in order to win an overcoming (*Übergang*) of humanity.[14] For Nietzsche, the ancient Greeks invented tragedy in order to affirm the fact that the powers of reason and representation with which human beings are endowed, symbolized under the figure of Apollo, allow human beings to create meaning. But this creative act is also a violent one, installing separation and difference among beings and cutting them off from what Nietzsche called the "primordial unity (*das Ur-Eine*)" shared by all existing things, which he symbolized with the figure of Dionysus.[15] This inherent violence to human existence results in a tragic condition in which human beings' efforts to transcend suffering through representation and meaning end up ensuring that very same suffering through the perpetuation of individuality and difference. Without representation, human beings would not be able to make sense of life. Yet the reliance on representation results in the fact that this life will continue on as suffering. Tragedy, to invoke Heidegger's interpretation, amounts to an affirmation of existential violence insofar as it does not seek to escape representation but instead represents the human need for, dependence on, and investment in representation. As Nietzsche submits, tragedy produces images—scenes—of the suffering that results from the Apollinian embrace of representation.[16]

Heidegger reads the *Auseinandersetzung* between *deinon* (the power of Being) and *to deinotaton* (the power of human being) in the choral ode as a scene of tragic necessity. For him, the ode presents a scene of the disaster that inevitably—necessarily—follows from human finitude. Notice in the following passage the emphasis Heidegger places on the German term *Not*, which he deploys to mean alternately "need," "necessity," and "affliction" (it also carries meanings of distress and adversity). This emphasis also extends to those terms that have *Not* as their root:

> This necessity of disaster can only subsist insofar as what must shatter is driven into such a being-there. The human is forced [*genötigt*] into such a being-there, hurled [*geworfen*] into the affliction [*Not*] of such being, because the overpowering as such, in order to appear in its power, *requires* [*braucht*][17] a place, a scene of disclosure [*die Stätte der Offenheit*]. The essence of being-human opens up to us only when understood through this need compelled by Being itself [*von dieser durch das Sein selbst ernötigen Not*]. (IM 162–63/EM 171–72; original emphasis)

Nietzsche regards tragedy's affirmation of the necessity of disaster as a "pessimism of strength" (*The Birth of Tragedy* 4). Like Nietzsche, Heidegger questions whether the modern ear is capable of hearing tragedy's affirmation. And he consequently wonders whether modern culture is capable of matching the Greeks' "historical greatness," which they achieved through their artistic pessimism (IM 164/EM 173). For "in the unique need [*Not*] of their Dasein," writes Heidegger, "they alone responded solely with violence, thus not doing away with the need but only augmenting it" (IM 164/EM 173). By responding to their existential need with violence—that is to say, by not succumbing to existence but continuing to live and thus perpetuate the violence of acting—the Greeks affirmed their Dasein. The implication, which Heidegger shares with Nietzsche, is that modern existence exhibits a fear of life and reacts to life with a saying no, with a nihilism directed at denying one's own existence.[18]

Saying no to existential need is not just a negation of one's own existence, though. For Heidegger, it is also saying no to Being's claim on one's Dasein and therefore a turning away from one's finitude. *Antigone*'s choral ode is actually a reappearance of the concept of need (*chrē*) that Heidegger identifies earlier in the text in Parmenides's sixth fragment: *Chrē to legein te noein t'eon emmenai*. Conventionally translated as "That which [*eon*] can be spoken [*legein*] and thought [*noein*] needs must be [*chrē emmenai*],"[19] Heidegger retranslates it in the following way in order to recapture what he holds is its originary meaning: "Both are needful, the *legein* as well as the apprehension—of the essent in its being [*Not ist das* legein *sowohl als auch die Vernehmung, nämlich des Seiend in dessen Sein*]" (IM 140–41/EM 149).

By retranslating the fragment in this way, Heidegger wants to stress the relation between Being and human beings as an event in which Being gathers ("*legein*" in the sense we reviewed in chapter 2) and apprehends human beings. Together, these components from *Antigone* and Parmenides aid Heidegger in realizing his revision of the definition of the human from "*anthrōpos = zōion logon echōn*" to "*physis = logos anthrōpon echōn*" (IM 175). However, we can now hear Heidegger's emphasis on the relation of need between Being and human being: "Being, overpowering appearing, necessitates [*ernötigt*] the gathering which pervades and grounds being-human" (IM 175 / EM 184, translation modified). The human exists as part of the taking place of Being (and vice versa).

Furthermore, by having its essence defined in terms of this event of the gathering and apprehension of Being and human being, the human becomes a historical being (IM 141/EM 150). Thus, while Heidegger reads *Antigone*'s choral ode as a figuration of the scene of human finitude—that is, as scene of the voice—the fact that it echoes Parmenides's saying of existential need (*Not*) marks it as a historical scene of finitude. That is to say, as a scene of the Greeks' historical relation to Being.[20]

So the point of a modern hearing of this scene is not for moderns to repeat the Greeks' relation to Being but to relate to their own historical apprehension of Being in the same manner the Greeks did.[21] Their "historical greatness," as Heidegger put it, was not due to their particular relation to Being but to the fact that they reflected on the fact of their historical Dasein. For Heidegger, *Antigone*'s choral ode is just such a reflection. It is an example of the Greek depiction of the scene of their facticity. As a result, it is a scene of the scene of the (Greek) voice.

Moreover, as I underscored in my reading of Nancy's "Sharing Voices," it is important to remember that the scene of finitude is always-already a scene of interpretation. Thus when Heidegger says the Greeks responded to their essential experience of existential violence by "augmenting" it, he means they affirmed the violent creation of meaning by embracing the necessary (yet ultimately disastrous) act of interpretation. For the modern ear to hear *Antigone*'s "poetic outline" of human finitude, it must interpret the Greek interpretation of its historical Dasein (i.e., hear the Greek voice), while at same time interpreting its own historical Dasein. For Heidegger, this means a willing embrace—and a performance—of one's own interpretive violence, a conviction he appears to follow when he frames his presentation of *Antigone* in *An Introduction to Metaphysics* against the distinction between the violence of an authentic interpretation and the sober, superficial character of a scientific one: "The authentic interpretation [*eigentliche Auslegung*] must show what no longer stands in the words and yet is nonetheless said. Thus, the interpretation must necessarily use violence. The authentic is to be found where scientific interpretation [*wissenschaftliche Interpreta-*

tion], which brands as unscientific everything that transcends its limits, no longer finds anything" (IM 162/EM 171).[22] In the analysis of *Hölderlin's Hymn "The Ister"* to which I now turn, I will continue to trace this willful embrace of interpretive violence Heidegger says is required in attending to the ancient Greeks' poetic articulation of their historical Dasein. Except in the case of his interpretation of Hölderlin's poem "The Ister" another layer will present itself. For as we will see, Heidegger's own hearing of the Greek saying of finitude is shaped by the voice of Hölderlin's modern interpretations of Sophocles. In this next section, we will see how interpretation and translation—between Sophocles and Hölderlin, in one respect, and among Sophocles, Hölderlin, and Heidegger, in another respect—complicate the matrix of finite saying and hearing.

Hölderlin's Hymn "The Ister"

To exist is to interpret one's existence. As Heidegger shows, *Antigone* is the Greek poetic interpretation/affirmation of this fact of interpretation, the inherent relation to Being it holds, and the disastrous limit to which it leads. In *An Introduction to Metaphysics* Heidegger poses the question of whether modern ears are capable of hearing this poetic saying of the Greeks, marking a limit between modern "scientific interpretation" (*wissenschaftliche Interpretation*) and the Greeks' "authentic interpretation" (*eigentliche Auslegung*). In *Hölderlin's Hymn "The Ister,"* we find a slight change in emphasis. Heidegger relaxes the severity of his suspicion regarding the capability of modern hearing, at least as it concerns Hölderlin. In this reading, which takes place seven years after the reading offered in *An Introduction to Metaphysics*, Heidegger stresses the issue of translation between the Greeks and modern thought. Although this issue is present in *An Introduction to Metaphysics* and bears as much on the translatability of the fragments of Heraclitus and Parmenides as on Sophocles, in the 1942 lectures Heidegger's focus is on the extent to which Hölderlin successfully translates *Antigone*'s poetic saying. It is on this question of translation that we see Heidegger temper his condemnation of modern hearing.

Central to Heidegger's reading of Hölderlin is a distinction he maintains between translation as *Übersetzung* and translation as *Übertragung*. At stake in this distinction is the difference between a setting-over (*Übersetzung*), or transferal, of a specific set of meanings from one place to another and a carrying-over of meaning (*Über-tragung*) that preserves the fact of meaning and its singular differentiations. The former is translation understood from within the regime of modern hermeneutics, as Nancy describes it in "Sharing Voices." The latter honors what we saw Nancy call the sharing (*partage*) of the sense of Being and the multiplicity of the voice.[23] Heidegger's consideration of the speech of Antigone herself, the character, will only underscore the idea of Heidegger's regard for *Antigone* as a historicizing scene of the voice and its multiplications.

In *Hölderlin's Hymn "The Ister"* Heidegger returns to *Antigone*'s first choral ode while elaborating the link he asserts exists between the image of the river Hölderlin creates in the poem "The Ister" (*"Der Ister"* [1803]) and the historicality of the human essence.[24] Through the relation of "locality and journeying" (*Ortschaft und Wanderschaft*), Heidegger contends Hölderlin's poem tells the story of—indeed, poeticizes—the human being's "becoming-homely" (*Heimischwerden*) in "unhomeliness" (*Unheimlichkeit*) (HH 48/GA53 60). In its continuation of the theme of uncanniness, Heidegger argues, "The Ister" echoes the Greek reflection on the essence of being-human. However, he maintains that the poem not only echoes the poetic project of the Greeks, it also resonates with what he assesses to be *the* poetic document of the essence of being-human: *Antigone*'s choral ode and its casting of the human within the word "*deinon*."

The resonance Hölderlin's "The Ister" has with the Greek poetic project points to the existence of what Heidegger calls a "historical," "poetic dialogue" (*eine dichterische Zwiesprache*) among Hölderlin, Sophocles, and Pindar (HH 49, 55/GA53 61, 69). Although he acknowledges Hölderlin was also translating Sophocles during the writing of "The Ister" (most notably, his *Antigonä* [1800/01–04]), Heidegger dismisses such references as "historiographical." His concern is not with Hölderlin's "influences," he says, but with a historical dialogue (HH 49–50/GA53, 61–62). The historical, Heidegger holds, is marked by an "encounter" (*Auseinandersetzung*) between "one's own fundamental truth in history" and "the foreign"; the historical is a carrying-over (*Übertragung*) of one to the other (HH 49/GA 53, 61). But what grounds the historical in general, we will remember from *Being and Time* and more immediately from the reading of the choral ode in *An Introduction to Metaphysics*, is the scene of human finitude: the event of human beings' contestation with beings from out of an understanding of the sense/meaning of Being. Thus, what is historical about the dialogue Hölderlin maintains between himself and the Greeks is not a simple "carrying-over" of his modern moment to the ancient moment, or vice versa. What makes the dialogue historical is instead their shared thinking of the singular scene/appearance of the essence of being-human (HH 55–56/GA53 69–70). The

84 / The Scene of the Voice

"*zwie*" of *Zwiesprache* emphasizes the "split" nature of this sharing and recalls Nancy's concept of a divided-sharing in the voice's scenic communication of human finitude.[25] Nonetheless, it is this understanding of the historical that underlies Heidegger's employment of the term *Übertragung* to refer to Hölderlin's translations of the choral ode (GA53 70).[26]

Insofar as Hölderlin's translations are an engagement with the existential ground of human historicality that Heidegger says characterizes the choral ode, they constitute a "carrying-over"—a "trans-lation," an *Über-tragung*—of the historical as such. For Heidegger, Hölderlin's translations present the Greeks' presentation of their historical encounter with the presencing of Being. In translating the choral ode, Hölderlin repeats the Greek project of poetic thinking.

Yet curiously, despite the weight he gives to this historical *Übertragung* between Sophocles and Hölderlin, Heidegger begins a focused discussion of the resonance he says exists between "The Ister" and *Antigone*'s choral ode—not, however, with Hölderlin's translation of the ode but with his own translation from *An Introduction to Metaphysics*. Following a presentation of the ode's first lines in Greek (something he neglects to do in *An Introduction to Metaphysics*), *polla ta deina* . . . , Heidegger gives his own translation: "*Vielfältig das Unheimliche* [. . .]": "There is much that is strange [. . .]" (HH 52/GA53 64–65).[27] This will make for a number of contradictions in Heidegger's explication of Hölderlin's thought.

First, Heidegger explains this strategy by saying that his translation "paraphrases and emphasizes some things in a clearer manner" than Hölderlin's does, justifying his claim somewhat cryptically by appealing to his distinction between translation as *Übersetzung* and translation as *Übertragung*. According to Heidegger, Hölderlin's translation (*Übersetzung*) of Sophocles would not be understood without reference to "the whole of the Hölderlinian translation" (*das Ganze der Hölderlinischen Übertragung*) (HH 57/GA53 70).[28] It is not clear, however, whether Heidegger means the whole of Hölderlin's translations of Sophocles, the different translations of *Antigone*, or something else entirely. Perhaps a "carrying-over" of what he refers to further down in the same passage as "the Greek world"? (HH 57/GA53 70).

Yet, while Heidegger does end up turning to Hölderlin's translations later in his analysis, he presents nothing more than Hölderlin's renderings of the choral ode's first lines (thus presenting them, in contradiction to his own stated criteria, out of context):

From Hölderlin's 1804 translation:

> *Ungeheuer ist viel. Doch nichts*
> *Ungeheuerer, als der Mensch.*
>
> There is much that is extraordinary. Yet nothing
> More extraordinary than the human being. (HH 69)

From Hölderlin's 1800/01 translation:

> *Vieles gewaltige giebts. Doch nichts*
> *Ist gewaltiger, als der Mensch.*
>
> There is much that is powerful. Yet nothing
> Is more powerful than the human being. (HH 70)

This is the only place in the text where Heidegger considers Hölderlin's translations of the ode, and he reads them as supporting his own translation and interpretation of *deinon* as "*unheimlich.*" The meaning Heidegger gives *das Unheimliche* remains consistent from *An Introduction to Metaphysics*: it expresses primarily the unhomely (*das Unheimische*) but also, as in Hölderlin, the powerful, violent, and overpowering (*das Gewaltige*). In fact, Heidegger understands "the monstrous" (*das Ungeheuere*)[29] in terms of Hölderlin's earlier translation of *deinon* as "*gewaltig,*" reading the later translation through the earlier one and inflecting his own translation, it would seem, through the 1800–1801 rendering as well.

If, indeed, Hölderlin's translations of the ode inform in a decisive way Heidegger's translation and explication from 1935's *An Introduction to Metaphysics*, we may wonder why Heidegger did not indicate this fact then and resists indicating it now in the 1942 lectures on "The Ister." I do not believe this is a question of influence. By raising this issue of Hölderlin's presence in Heidegger's text, we do not need to depart from Heidegger's program of reading, for it remains consistent with his insistence on the intimate relation among reading, translation, and interpretation. As Warminski notes in the essay cited earlier, every translation is an interpretation, every interpretation is a translation, and every language, in order to be historical, stands in need of translation/interpretation or *Übertragung* ("Monstrous History" 203). "For translation," writes Heidegger, "moves not only between two different languages, but rather there is a translation within the same language. The interpretation of Hölderlin's hymns is a translation internal to our German language" (GA53 75, cited in "Monstrous History" 203).[30] Furthermore, Heidegger continues,

> Insofar as it is necessary for us to interpret works of thought and of poetry of our own language, this indicates that every historical language in itself and for itself is in need of translation and not only in relation to a foreign language. This in turn indicates that a historical people is at home in its own language not of itself, that is, not without its contribution [its act in addition, *Zutun*]. Hence it can happen that we indeed speak "German" and yet talk in nothing but "American." (GA53 79–80, cited in "Monstrous History" 203)

Warminski consequently claims "that it is no wonder Heidegger . . . does not (indeed cannot) use Hölderlin's 'own' translation but rather has to retranslate both Sophocles's Greek and Hölderlin's German. For Hölderlin's German is not his own, is not truly German, *is* not in an authentically historical sense, except in dialogue with Greek" ("Monstrous History" 203; original emphasis). According to Warminski, Heidegger is thus attempting to think "more Hölderlinian than Hölderlin himself," just as Heidegger claims that we have "to think more Greek than the Greeks themselves" (GA53 100, cited in "Monstrous History" 204).

Another possibility exists, though, in terms of what is taking place with this concept of translation as *Übertragung*, which would present a third alternative to the schema Warminski offers in his reading (and would not be opposed to it necessarily). The direction of translation, as Warminski reads it, goes from out of Hölderlin's German and Sophocles's Greek into Heidegger's German. What if the opposite was the case? In other words, what if the text Heidegger is translating into the language of Hölderlin and Sophocles was *his own*, thus creatively (and perhaps poetically) constituting their respective texts? What if Heidegger was performing a violent sharing of voices through his text?

As we see, Heidegger's injection of the historical into the question of translation expands the scope of how we are to think the scene of facticity. Yet, this added consideration of the historical also expands the figure of the dialogue as the sharing of voices. To be sure, the poetic dialogue Heidegger describes Hölderlin as having with Pindar and Sophocles is not limited to those three. In his reflections on translation, Heidegger also accounts for his own text/voice in this dialogue. Insofar as it reaches toward historicality,

Heidegger's voice is also one of finitude; it also speaks, or rather bears witness, to the scene of the essence of being-human. As such, the scene attended to and simultaneously depicted in Heidegger's interpretation, which *is* this interpretation, is also, in its "dialogicity," as Nancy demonstrates, that of *hermēneia*. This fact in turn accounts for the circularity we began to embark upon (and indeed threatened to become lost within) previously, with the attempts to determine *the* direction of interpretation/translation, or *the* origin of the text of translation/interpretation. As we have seen, Heidegger's instinct is to frustrate such a drive toward the determination of meaning and instead intensify or expand the movement of the circle. He does this on yet another level when he turns to a consideration of another voice in Sophocles's tragedy, the voice of Antigone herself, which he demonstrates always-already appears within the dialogic scene.

The Dia-logue That We Are? The Question of Antigone "Herself"

In *Hölderlin's Hymn "The Ister"* Heidegger notably extends his reading of *Antigone* beyond the choral ode and engages with its plot, which includes a focus on Antigone, the character herself.[31] He does so in order to frame "the introductory dialogue between Antigone and Ismene," in which the two sisters discuss the consequences of Antigone's decision to bury their disgraced brother Polyneices. Once again, the term Heidegger uses for the word "dialogue" is *Zwiesprache*, so there is an indication that he considers this dialogue between Antigone and Ismene a continuation of the form of dialogue he claims exists between Hölderlin and Sophocles—that is, as an enactment of the dialogical structure of the scene of finitude. "The words and counter-words of the two sisters," says Heidegger, "are like an encounter between two swords whose sharpness, gleam, and power we must experience in order to apprehend something of the lightning that flashes when they strike" (HH 98/GA53 122).

The dialogue concerns the degree of responsibility Ismene is supposed to share in Antigone's decision to go against Creon's edict. Near the end of the dialogue, Antigone at first admonishes Ismene for standing against her but then absolves her of any of responsibility in the act she is about to commit. It is this last part of their exchange that draws Heidegger's attention:

A: εἰ ταῦτα λέξεις, ἐκθαρῇ μὲν ἐξ ἐμοῦ,
ἐκθρὰ δὲ τῷ θανόντι προσκείσῃ δίκῃ.

ἀλλ' ἔα με καὶ τὴν ἐξ ἐμοῦ δυσβουλίαν
παθεῖν τὸ δεινὸν τοῦτο· πείσομαι γὰρ οὐ
τοσοῦτον οὐδὲν ὥστε μὴ οὐ καλῶς θανεῖν.

Wenn dies du sagst, im Haß stehst du, der mir entstammt,
im Haß auch trittst entgegen du dem Toten, wie sich's schickt.
Doch überlaß dies mir und jenem, was aus mir Gefährlich-Schweres rät:
ins eigne Wesen aufzunehmen das Unheimliche, das jetzt und hier erscheint.
Erfahren nämlich werd' ich allenthalben Solches nichts,
daß nicht zum Sein gehören muß mein Sterben.

If you say this, in hatred you stand, arising from me,
and the hatred of he who is dead will come to meet you, as is fitting.
Yet leave this to me, and to what within me that counsels the dangerous and difficult:
to take up into my own essence the uncanny that here and now appears.
For everywhere shall I experience nothing of the fact
that not to being my dying must belong.

I: ἀλλ' εἰ δοκεῖ σοι, στεῖχε· τοῦτο δ' ἴσθ', ὅτι
ἄνους μὲν ἔρχῃ, τοῖς φίλοις δ' ὀρθῶς φίλη.

Doch wenn's dir so erscheint, dann geh! Dies aber wisse, daß ohn Wahrheit bei dir selbst du gehst, den Freuden freilich wahrhaft Freundin bleibst.

If thus it appears to you, then go! Yet know this, that you go without truth besides you, though to your friends you truly a friend remain. (HH 98–99/GA53 123–24)

Heidegger chooses not to delve into Ismene's declaration to Antigone, which he refers to as a "rather cryptic word" (HH 103). Although others have read Ismene's invocation of *philia* in relation to what Heidegger describes as Antigone's essential relation to death and the uncanny (*deinon*).[32] Heidegger claims that it is instead Antigone who delivers the "decisive word" (*das entscheidende Wort*), "to deinon," when she says *pathein to deinon auto*: "to take up into my own essence the uncanny that here and now appears."

Translating *deinon* as the uncanny as he did before in his reading of the choral ode, Heidegger sets up Antigone's speech here as a mirror—or better said, echo—of the choral ode's saying of the human essence. *Pathein*, Heidegger writes, means "to suffer, to bear" (*erleiden, ertragen*) (HH 103/ GA53 127). It is an active "taking upon oneself" (*Aufsichnehmen*) of the *deinon*, not a passive acceptance or tolerance, he says, not only in this case regarding Antigone but in all cases of Greek tragedy. *Pathein* is the "fundamental trait" (*Grundzug*) of *to drama*, the dramatic as such (HH 103/GA 53 128). In uttering this phrase, Antigone not only takes the uncanny upon herself. She "inhabits" the uncanny, becoming its exemplar, occupying the "supreme" (*höchste*) instance of *deinon* (HH 102–03/GA53 127–28). Antigone is the figure of "becoming homely in being unhomely" (*das Heimischwerden im Unheimischsein*) (§20).

Heidegger goes on to find further evidence of Antigone's uncanniness, and especially of how her voice exemplifies a relation (before relation) to Being. Following the choral ode, Creon confronts Antigone with her act of defying his edict forbidding the burying of her brother Polyneices (ll. 449–57). In her response, Antigone says she cannot identify the origin of the impulse to transgress Creon's law; she acted without any command from the divinities above or below or in obedience to any human law (HH 116). According to Heidegger, prevailing interpretations of *Antigone* make a profound mistake when they try to read the tragedy for reasons that explain Antigone's actions, for "they are concerned only with finding some reference to beings, whether the prevailing or ancient cult of the dead, or the familial blood-relatedness" (HH 116). In other words, these interpretations reduce her actions to the ontic realm. (One cannot help but hear a rebuke of Hegel in these words.) What these interpretations refuse to see, Heidegger says, is "that she is not speaking of a being at all. This gives rise to the appearance that she speaks indeterminately—whereas she says quite unequivocally the singular thing that remains to be said here" (HH 116). That singular thing is the relation to Being as such (HH 118). I cite the decisive statement by Heidegger, because it is vital to hear the constellation of voice (*die Stimme*), determination (*das Bestimmen*) of Being, and attunement (*die Stimmung*) to Being that he constructs in it:

> *Das Bestimmende, das Antigone zu ihrem Sein bestimmt, ist über den oberen und den unteren Göttern [von dennen sie in ihrer Unterhaltung mit Kreon erzählt (Antigone, V. 449–457)]. Aber es*

> *ist zugleich doch Solches, was den Menschen als Menschen durchstimmt.* (GA53 145)

> That which is determinative, that which determines Antigone in her being, is beyond the upper and lower gods [of whom she speaks in her exchange with Creon (ll. 449–457)]. And yet it is something that pervasively attunes human beings as human beings. (HH 116)

For Heidegger, the point of the indeterminacy of Antigone's response to Creon is to indicate the indeterminacy of that which determines, namely Being. According to him, "she names being itself," and in so doing, she embodies *deinon*, the uncanny/unhomely (HH 118). Transgressing Creon's decree, Antigone stands in the contestation (*Auseinandersetzung*) between beings and Being. Her speech becomes the site upon which this contestation unfolds, the site of this contestation's disclosure. She *is* the scene of the voice.

From this act of embodying the scene for the appearance of the contestation of beings and Being, Heidegger draws a startling connection between Antigone *herself* and the choral ode. Whereas the ode poetizes the appearance of the human relation to Being, Antigone takes on the status of being "the purest poem itself" (*das reinste Gedicht selbst*) (HH 119/GA 53 149). In other words, Antigone herself becomes the work of art. She exists as a site of unconcealment (HH 119–20). Heidegger speculates that it is perhaps because of their status as poetizing sites of finitude that the choral ode and Antigone "came to speak ever anew to the poet Hölderlin" (HH 122). Heidegger implies that, as a poet, perhaps Hölderlin possessed the ability to become attuned to their poetizing events (HH 122).

Nonetheless, I think it is worth pausing over the prominence Heidegger reserves for Antigone. It is one the Western metaphysical tradition usually does not make available to feminine figures. The fact that Heidegger does not explicitly thematize Antigone's being as woman, however, indicates he either takes it for granted or fails to see that it has any significance. As we move on to evaluate the status of the scenic in Heidegger's thought, this labor that Antigone's figure performs for Heidegger's conception of the artwork's relationship to finitude raises questions concerning the work she does, as a figure, for his theorization of the voice, particularly in the ways she appears to provide a site around which a historical, communal voice is able to cohere. For Heidegger's identification of Antigone as *the* figure who "suffers the uncanny," and his emphasis on her intimacy with death, once again brings his thought of finitude within close proximity to the Western metaphysical tradition's use of the feminine for establishing its speculative project. This troubling fact will appear in a more pronounced fashion in our next chapter on Nancy and Lacoue-Labarthe's debate regarding the status of the figure in Heidegger and its social and political implications, specifically with respect to the shift we tracked in this chapter from the voice as a figuration of the individual Dasein's finitude to its appearance as the figuration of the historical, collective finitude of a people.[33] Their debate will provide a framework for viewing Blanchot's and Deleuze's respective theorizations of the voice as responses to Heidegger and also to the issues regarding figuration Nancy and Lacoue-Labarthe raise.

Appendix

The First Choral Ode from Antigone and Accompanying Translations

ΧΟ.[34] πολλὰ τὰ δεινὰ κοὐδὲν ἀνθρώπου δεινότερον πέλει·
τοῦτο καὶ πολιοῦ πέραν πόντου χειμερίῳ νότῳ   335
χωρεῖ, περιβρυχίοισιν
περῶν ὑπ' οἴδμασιν·
θεῶν τε τὰν ὑπερτάταν, Γᾶν
ἄφθιτον, ἀκαμάταν, ἀποτρύεται,
ἰλλομένων ἀρότρων ἔτος εἰς ἔτος,   340
ἱππείῳ γένει πολεύων.

κουφονόων τε φῦλον ὀρνίθων ἀμφιβαλὼν ἄγει
καὶ θηρῶν ἀγρίων ἔθνη πόντου τ' εἰναλίαν φύσιν   345
σπείραισι δικτυοκλώστοις,
περιφραδὴς ἀνήρ·
κρατεῖ δὲ μηχαναῖς ἀγραύλου
θηρὸς ὀρεσσιβάτα, λασιαύχενά θ'   350
ἵππον ὀχμάζεται ἀμφὶ λόφον ζυγῶν,
οὔρειόν τ' ἀκμῆτα ταῦρον.

καὶ φθέγμα καὶ ἀνεμόεν   354
φρόνημα καὶ ἀστυνόμους ὀργὰς ἐδιδάξατο καὶ δυσαύλων
πάγων ὑπαίθρεια καὶ δύσομβρα φεύγειν βέλη,

παντοπόρος· ἄπορος ἐπ' οὐδὲν ἔρχεται   360
τὸ μέλλον· Ἅιδα όνον φεῦξιν οὐκ ἐπάξεται·
νόσων δ' ἀμηχάνων φυγὰς ξυμπέφρασται.

σοφόν τι τὸ μηχανόεν   365
τέχνας ὑπὲρ ἐλπίδ' ἔχων τοτὲ μὲν κακόν, ἄλλοτ' ἐπ'
    ἐσθλὸν ἔρπει·
νόμους γεραίρων χθονὸς θεῶν τ' ἔνορκον δίκαν,
ὑψίπολις· ἄπολις ὅτῳ τὸ μὴ καλὸν   370
ξύνεστι τόλμας χάριν. μήτ' ἐμοὶ παρέστιος
γένοιτο μήτ' ἴσον φρονῶν ὃς τάδ' ἔρδει.   375

Cho. polla ta deina kouden anthrôpou deinoteron pelei·
touto kai poliou peran pontou cheimeriôi notôi   335
chôrei, peribruchioisin
perôn hup' oidmasin·
theôn te tan hupertatan, Gan
aphthiton, akamatan, apotruetai
illomenôn arotrôn etos eis etos,   340
hippeiôi genei poleuôn.

kouphonoôn te phulon ornithôn amphibalôn agei
kai thêrôn agriôn ethnê pontou t' einalian phusin 345
speiraisi diktuoklôstois,
periphradês anêr·
kratei de mêchanais agraulou
thêros oressibata, lasiauchena th'   350
hippon ochmazetai amphi lophon zugôn,
oureion t' akmêta tauron.

kai phthegma kai anemoen   354
phronêma kai astunomous orgas edidaxato kai dusaulôn
pagôn hupaithreia kai dusombra pheugein belê,
pantoporos: aporos ep' ouden erchetai   360
to mellon: Haida monon pheuxin ouk epaxetai·
nosôn d' amêchanôn phugas xumpephrastai.

sophon ti to mêchanoen   365
technas huper elpid' echôn tote men kakon, allot' ep' esthlon
    herpei·

nomous gerairôn chthonos theôn t' enorkon dikan,
hupsipolis: apolis hotôi to mê kalon 370
xunesti tolmas charin. mêt' emoi parestios
genoito mêt' ison phronôn hos tad' erdei. 375

Jebb's Translation (1891)

Chorus.

Wonders are many, and none is more wonderful than man; the power that crosses the white sea, driven by the stormy south-wind, making a path under surges that threaten to engulf him; and Earth, the eldest of the gods, the immortal, the unwearied, doth he wear, turning the soil with the offspring of horses, as the plows weave to and fro from year to year.

And the light-hearted race of birds, and the tribes of savage beasts, and the sea-brood of the deep, he snares in the meshes of his woven toils, he leads captive, man excellent in wit. And he masters by his arts the beast whose lair is in the wilds, and roams the hills; he tames the horse of shaggy mane, he puts the yoke upon its neck, he tames the tireless mountain bull.

And speech, and wind-swift thought, and all the moods that mould a state, hath taught himself, and how to flee the arrows of the frost, when 'tis hard lodging under the clear sky, and the arrows of the rushing rain; yea, he hathe resource for all; without resource he meets nothing that must come: only against Death shall he call for aid in vain; but from baffling maladies he hath devised escapes.

Cunning beyond fancy's dream is the fertile skill which brings him, now to evil, now to good. When he honours the laws of the land, and that justice which he hath sworn by the gods to uphold, proudly stands by his city: no city hath he who, for his rashness, dwells with sin. Never may he share my hearth, never think my thoughts, who doth these things!

Heidegger's Translation (1935)[35]

Vielfältig das Unheimliche, nichts doch
über den Menschen hinaus Unheimlicheres ragend sich regt.
Der fährt aus auf die schäumende Flut

beim Südsturm des Winters
und kreuzt im Gebirg
der wütiggeklüfteten Wogen.
Der Götter auch die erhabenste, die Erde,
abmüdet er die unzerstörlich Mühelose,
umstürzend sie von Jahr zu Jahr,
hintreibend und her mit den Rossen
die Pflüge.

Auch den leichtschwebenden Vogelschwarm
umgarnt der und jagt
das Tiervolk der Wildnis
und des Meeres einheimisch Gerege
der umher sinnende Mann.
Er überwältigt mit Listen das Tier,
das nächtigt auf Bergen und wandert,
den rauhmähnigen Nacken des Rosses
und den niebezwungenen Stier
mit dem Holze umhalsend
zwingt er ins Joch.

Auch in das Getöne des Wortes
und ins windeilige Allesvertehen
fand er sich, auch in den Mut
der Herrschaft über die Städte.
Auch wie er entfliehe, hat er bedacht,
der Aussetzung unter die Pfeile
der Wetter, der ungattigen auch der Fröste.

Überall hinausfahrend unterwegs, erfahrungslos ohne Ausweg
kommt er zum Nichts.
Dem einzigen Andrang vermag er, dem Tod,
durch keine Flucht je zu wehren,
sei ihm geglückt auch vor notvollem Siechtum
geschicktes Entweichen.

Gewitziges wohl, weil das Gemache
des Könnens, über Verhoffen bemeisternd,
verfällt er einmal auf Arges

gar, Wackeres zum anderen wieder gerät ihm.
Zwischen die Satzung der Erde und den
beschworenen Fug der Götter hindurch fährt er.
Hochübberragend die Stätte, verlustig der Stätte
ist er, dem immer das Unseiende seined
der Wagnis zugunsten.

Nicht werde dem Herde ein Trauter mir der,
nicht auch teile mit mir sein Wähnen mein Wissen,
der dieses führet ins Werk.

English translation of Heidegger's translation[36]

There is much that is strange, but nothing
that surpasses man in strangeness.
He sets sail on the frothing waters
amid the south winds of winter
tacking through the mountains
and furious chasms of the waves.
He wearies even the noblest
of the gods, the Earth,
indestructible and untiring,
overturning her from year to year,
driving the plows this way and that
with horses.

And man, pondering and plotting,
snares the light-gliding birds
and hunts the beasts of the wilderness
and the native creatures of the sea.
With guile he overpowers the beast
that roams the mountains by night as by day,
he yokes the hirsute neck of the stallion
and the undaunted bull.

And he has found his way
to the resonance of the word,
and to wind-swift all-understanding,
and to the courage of rule over cities.

He has considered also how to flee
from exposure to the arrows
of unpropitious weather and frost.

Everywhere journeying, inexperienced and without issue,
he comes to nothingness.
Through no flight can he resist
the one assault of death,
even if he has succeeded in cleverly evading
painful sickness.

Clever indeed, mastering
the ways of skill beyond all hope,
he sometimes accomplishes evil,
sometimes achieves brave deeds.
He wends his way between the laws of the earth
and the adjured justice of the gods.
Rising high above his place,
he for the sake of adventure takes
the nonessent for essent loses
his place in the end.

May such a man never frequent my hearth;
May my mind never share the presumption
of him who does this.

Hölderlin's Translation (ca 1800)[37]

Vieles gewaltge gibts. Doch nichts
Ist gewaltiger, als der Mensch.
Denn der schweifet im grauen
Meer' in stürmischer Südluft
Umher in wogenumrauschten
Geflügelten Wohnungen.
Der Götter heilige Erde, sie, die
Reine die mühelose,
Arbeitet er um, das Pferdegeschlecht
Am leichtbewegten Pflug von
Jahr zu Jahr umtreibend.

Leichtgeschaffener Vogelart
Legt er Schlingen, verfolget sie,
Und der Tiere wildes Volk,
Und des salzigen Meers Geschlecht
Mit listiggeschlungenen Seilen,
Der wohlerfahrne Mann.
Beherrscht mit seiner Kunst des Landes
Bergebewandelndes Wild.
Dem Nacken des Rosses wirft er das Joch
Um die Mähne und dem wilden
Ungezähmten Stiere.

(Published 1804 translation)[38]

Ungeheuer ist viel. Doch nichts
Ungeheuerer als der Mensch.
Denn der, über die Nacht
Des Meers, wenn gegen den Winter wehet
Der Südwind, fähret er aus
In geflügelten sausenden Häusern.
Und der Himmlischen erhabene Erde
Die unverderbliche, unermüdete
Reibet er auf; mit dem strebenden Pfluge
Von Jahr zu Jahr
Treibt sein Verkehr er mit dem Rossegeschlecht',
Und leichtträumender Vögel Welt
Bestrickt er und jagt sie;
Und wilder Tiere Zug,
Und des Pontos salzbelebte Natur
Mit gesponnenen Netzen,
Der kundige Mann.
Und fängt mit Künsten das Wild,
Das auf Bergen übernachtet und schweift.
Und dem rauhmähnigen Rosse wirft er um
Den Nacken das Joch, und dem Berge
Bewandelnden unbezähmten Stier.

Und die Red und den luftigen
Gedanken und städtebeherrschenden Stolz

Hat erlernet er, und übelwohnender
Hügel feuchte Lüfte und
Die unglücklichen zu fliehen, die Pfeile. Allbewandert,
Unbewandert. Zu nichts kommt er.
Der Toten künftigen Ort nur
Zu fliehen weiß er nicht,
Und die Flucht unbeholfener Seuchen
Zu überdenken.
Von Weisem etwas, und das Geschickte der Kunst
Mehr, als er hoffen kann, besitzend,
Kommt einmal er auf Schlimmes, das andre zu Gutem.
Die Gesetze kränkt er, der Erd und Naturgewalt'ger
Beschwornes Gewissen; Hochstädtisch kommt, unstädtisch
Zu nichts er, wo das Schöne
Mit ihm ist und mit Frechheit.
Nicht sei am Herde mit mir,
Noch gleichgesinnet,
Wer solches tut.

English translation of Hölderlin's 1804 translation[39]

Much is monstrous. But nothing
More monstrous than man.
For he, through the night
of the sea, when toward the winter
the south wind blows, he sets out
In winged and whispering houses.
And the heavenly sublime earth
The incorruptible, tireless earth
He erases; with the striving plough,
From year to year
He purses his dealings, with the race of stallions,
And the lightly dreaming world of birds
He ensnares, and hunts them;
And the train of wild animals,
And of Pontos's nature animated by salt
With spun nets
This knowing man.
And with arts he catches game

That spends the night and roams on mountains.
And over the neck of the rough-maned stallion
He throws a yoke, and over the untamable steer that
Wanders the mountains.

And the honest and airy
Thoughts and the pride ruling over the city,
He has learned, and slopes of damp air where ill dwell,
And misfortune, the arrows,
He has learned to flee. Wandering everywhere
Unwandered. To naught he arrives.
Death, the future place, alone
He does not know how to flee,
And the flood of temporary plagues
He thinks through.

Possessing more of wisdom, and the skill of art,
Than he can hope for,
He arrives at disaster, on account of something else.
He complains of the law, of the earth, of the power of nature
With the oath of his conscience.
High citied, uncitied,
He arrives at nothing,
Where the beautiful
Is with him and audacity.
One who does this
Should never be with me at the hearth
Never be of similar mind.

Part 2
Nancy and Lacoue-Labarthe

Chapter 4

Figuration and Finitude

Ontological Mimesis and Onto-typology between Nancy and Lacoue-Labarthe

Chapter 3 explored the ways in which the figure of the voice persists and returns in Heidegger's thought. This exploration tested a number of assertions that emerged from my analysis of Jean-Luc Nancy's "Sharing Voices" in chapter 2, namely: (1) that since the voice names an essential relation among finitude, interpretation, and figuration, there is never just one figure of the voice but a multiplicity of voices; and (2) that this multiplicity of voices is shared/divided (*partagé*) among a multiplicity of Daseins, who exist as part of one another's world. Thus, if we follow Nancy's assertions, Heidegger's reflections on the voice cannot be exempted from this relation but must be seen as enactments of it and therefore as interpretive events giving rise to more figures as part of the multiple sharing of voices. Using Nancy's image of the sharing of voices, it should be possible, as I hypothesized at the conclusion of chapter 2, to discern the ways the voice insists and returns in Heidegger's thought.

Indeed, as chapter 3 revealed, Heidegger's intimation of a relation between figuration and finitude in "The Origin of the Work of Art" already confirms Nancy's assertion of the necessity of figuration. But Heidegger's conceptualization of the work of art also adds another consideration to Nancy's interpretation. For if figuration implies a necessary scenic character to the voice, the work of art's unconcealing figuration of the rift structure of world and earth must then be understood as a presentation of the scene of finitude; that is to say, the artwork is a scene of the scene of the voice.

The work of art therefore does not so much add an aesthetic quality to the event of the voice as reveal the voice's essential aesthetic—as well as affective—character (which itself is revelatory of the affective character of Dasein's finitude). At the same time, this aesthetic and affective character of the voice would not have the force it does (it would not shock the human Dasein back to the fact of its finitude) were it not for the extra-metaphysical conception of language that structures the voice, or for the extra-metaphysical conception of work (the setting of world against earth) that structures the work of art. That is to say, the voice's aesthetic and affective power lies in its figuration of the human Dasein's experience (before experience) of being claimed by the sense/meaning of Being. Any instance of the voice's return in Heidegger must exhibit this joining of sense and figure—of finitude's figuration.

As I show in chapter 3, this joining appears and announces returns of the voice in the readings of Sophocles's *Antigone* that Heidegger undertakes in *An Introduction to Metaphysics* and *Hölderlin's Hymn "The Ister."* In the former, Heidegger attempts to attune the modern ear to the saying of the Greek Dasein (the Greek voice) as it is embodied in the poetic word of *Antigone*'s First Choral Ode. In the latter, Heidegger assesses whether such a hearing has been accomplished with Hölderlin's translation of the tragic work. However, in the process of interpreting Hölderlin's interpretive translation, he presents us with a stunning reconceptualization of the tragedy: the Greek voice moves from being embodied by the choral ode and comes to reside in the figure of Antigone herself, who Heidegger casts as "the purest poem itself" (HH 119). That Heidegger occupies himself in the later work with the problem of the modern hearing of the Greek Dasein, and especially with the question of translation as a mode in which this problem of hearing announces itself, displays a transformation of the voice from its depiction in *Being and Time* as an event primarily circumscribed by the phenomenology of the individual human Dasein to a collective, historical voice of a people. This transformation suggests that Heidegger was attuned to that dimension of finitude that Nancy brings forth as the sharing of voices. Yet, above all, it is also evidence of Heidegger participating in the finite sharing of voices to the extent that he works to attune the modern voice to the voice of the Greeks.

It is perhaps now that we are finally in a position to understand the full extent of the uncanny manner in which the voice calls the human Dasein aesthetically and affectively back to the fact of its finitude. As I demonstrated in chapter 1, Heidegger says the voice's claim on Dasein is an uncanny one insofar as it originates with Dasein yet appears as if it came from somewhere or someone else. Within that discussion, I pointed to the partial explanation offered in *Being and Time* for this uncanniness of the voice, which is that the voice mirrors Dasein's existential uncanniness—the fundamental way that Dasein's finitude throws it ecstatically ahead of itself toward its potentiality-for-Being—back to it. The voice reflects back to Dasein its essential, existential doubling.

However, it is with Nancy's intervention of the sharing of voices that one is able to take the full measure of both Dasein's uncanniness and the voice's uncanniness. With his conception of the voice as a shared/divided event with the other Dasein, Nancy draws out the experience of alterity that Heidegger's theorization of the voice implies yet leaves opaque. For Nancy, both Dasein's and the voice's uncanniness are primarily indices of the fact that the world into which Dasein is thrown (the world that Dasein's thrownness constitutes) is shared with many other voices—and therefore many figures—and therefore many worlds, or what Nancy, along with Aurélien Barrau, has called a "plurality" of worlds.[1] In this way, the voice is not only an echo of Dasein's ecstatic thrown existence; it also an event in which the plurality of worlds with which Dasein is always-already in relation touches Dasein's being, unsettles it. The voice is an antimimetic, anti-identitarian figure of dissimulation. This is the voice's power of uncanniness.

This chapter maps out the implications of this dissimulating, antimimetic gesture at the heart of Heidegger's theorization of the voice. While this gesture aligns with Heidegger's project of destructuring the metaphysics of presence by destabilizing the metaphysical subject's self-presence and self-mastery, the voice's apparent reliance on figuration has spurred worries among some of Heidegger's most dedicated readers. Derrida, as I noted in my introduction, is perhaps the most prominent of Heidegger's critics in this regard. In this chapter, I consider responses by Nancy and Philippe Lacoue-Labarthe and specifically the critical debate they engage in concerning Heidegger's reliance on the figure in his theorization of the voice and of human finitude generally.

Nancy and Lacoue-Labarthe regard the very character of the voice that Heidegger presents as a break with the metaphysics of presence—namely its figural/scenic aspect—as the site of metaphysical fascination. For them, the voice is a symptom of Heidegger's capture by metaphysical speculation and therefore constitutes another moment of metaphysical haunting, if not its return. In Nancy and Lacoue-Labarthe's reception of the Heideggerian voice, speculative capture takes on two related meanings: the capture of

Being in the form of spectacle and mesmerization by the spectacularization of Being. Yet, while both agree that the Heideggerian voice falls prey to speculative capture, they differ on how much it is possible for philosophical thought as such to escape such capture. In their debate, they deliberate over the possibility that the spectacularization of Being may be essential to the philosophical enterprise. If this is not the case, if philosophy does not depend on representation, then it may be possible for philosophical thought to open onto an experience of difference that the scene of the voice promises. If the spectacularization of Being is a condition of thinking, however, then the prospects for an authentic encounter with difference diminish greatly, for that puts into profound doubt the ability to escape from representation, and the critique of metaphysics finds itself right back where it started.

Nancy summarizes what he takes to be the basis of his and Lacoue-Labarthe's debate about the scenic in the first of a series of letters they exchanged and published under the title "*Scène*" in 1992.² Classifying the scenic under the notion of the figure, which he affirms "preoccupies [them] both," Nancy writes in the series' opening letter: "For you, it evokes suspicion toward what you have termed 'onto-typology,' that is to say toward a figural and fictional assignation of the presentation of being and/or of truth" ("Scene" 274). At stake, Nancy suggests, is the possibility of accomplishing the "interruption of myth," which Nancy thematizes explicitly in *The Inoperative Community* and which he and Lacoue-Labarthe schematize in their collaborative essay "The Nazi Myth."³ The social and political implications of the figure, as we learn in those texts, concern the question of its necessity for community's grounding, a question influenced in no small way by National Socialism's ideological grounding in and through the appropriation of myth. Does community require myth—and therefore, figuration—for its possibility? Or is community (or any identity at all) possible without figuration? Again, the answers to these questions determine whether the economy of representation governs the social, and if so, whether that means that no real relation to difference is possible through the social.

Nancy notes that while he and Lacoue-Labarthe may agree on the need to interrupt myth, it is not clear whether this means also interrupting the figure. Moreover, if an interruption of the figure is required, then what does this actually entail? As Nancy explains, their debate seems to have staked out two possible paths.

For his part, Nancy conceives interruption as "a cutting movement, which, in cutting, delineates another area of enunciation." He declares the act of interrupting the figure as "inseparable, then, from a voice" ("Scene"

274 / "*Scène*" 13). This view is consistent with his reconfiguration of Heidegger's conception of human finitude as the *partage* of the sense of Being and as a sharing of voices.

Lacoue-Labarthe, however, understands the interruption of the figure as a definite "cessation" or "de-figuration" [*dé-figuration*], a term Nancy recalls Lacoue-Labarthe invoking in his essay "*Il faut*" ("Scene" 274 / "*Scène*" 13).[4] For both, Heidegger's corpus serves as a touchstone for investigating both the figure and its interruption, not only because of his infamous affirmation of National Socialism's "inner truth and greatness."[5] For what grounds this affirmation, in their view, is his thinking of finitude's figuration through the voice, language, and the work of art. For Lacoue-Labarthe, Heidegger's engagement with tragedy, and what Lacoue-Labarthe considers as his misuse of Hölderlin in this engagement, reveals a theatrical/tragic dimension in which both philosophy and the political meet and that both philosophy and the political repress. Heidegger's employment of tragedy, which is exemplified, not coincidentally, in his readings of *Antigone,* and the hypostatization of a collective historical voice in those readings, as we saw in chapter 3, belong to what Lacoue-Labarthe describes as a drive underlying all speculative thought and is therefore a site of metaphysical reinscription in Heidegger's philosophy. This inspires not only the notion of de-figuration as *Entgestaltung* in Lacoue-Labarthe's work but also his linking of de-figuration with Walter Benjamin's call for the demythologization (*Entmythologisierung*) of modern thought ("*Il faut,*" 50–51; 54–55). De-figuration will be the movement Lacoue-Labarthe invokes in order to bring about a "(de)structuring" of the tragic in philosophy and realize what he calls, following his own counter-reading of Hölderlin, a "caesura of the speculative."[6]

While for Nancy the figure and its interruption involve what he seems to suggest is an inseparable relation to the voice, Lacoue-Labarthe reserves suspicion about such inseparability. For him, the voice, particularly the figure of the Heideggerian voice, is a perpetuation of metaphysical speculation operating under the guise of a break with metaphysics. In order to prove this, Lacoue-Labarthe leads us back through the metaphysical tradition. However, instead of viewing the tradition as a privileging of presence, he describes it as a single drive to master mimesis. Thus, rather than being an antimimetic, dissimulating event, the Heideggerian voice is a continuation of the Platonic project of mastering mimesis by first banishing it from so-called proper philosophical thinking and then appropriating it in a bid to claim a unique philosophical style of writing (the dialogue, for instance). According to Lacoue-Labarthe, Heidegger's effort to master mimesis is, like

Plato's, political at heart: by figuring the voice, Heidegger gains control of mimesis' threat to philosophy (its power to undo all identity and all ground). However, this also reifies the voice—mythologizes it—rendering the politics of fascist mythologization a site of attraction.

In what follows, I reconstruct how Nancy and Lacoue-Labarthe each read the figure of the voice as decisive for the image of the political in Heidegger's corpus. After reviewing their respective critical engagements with the Heideggerian voice, I return to the debate they undertake in their initial exchange of letters in "*Scène*," as well as in a dialogue dating some twelve years later in which they take up the problem of the scenic once more. An analysis of how Nancy and Lacoue-Labarthe formulate and deliberate over the question of the figure will be useful for us in a number of ways. First, it will demonstrate that what is at stake in the constellation of language, affect, finitude, and the figure is the question of mimesis, which will not only expose the opposition between language and affect as a false one but also, and more importantly, open up the ethical and political stakes of the question of the voice for Heidegger, post-Heideggerian thought, and the contemporary turns to affect and the aesthetic. Secondly, Nancy and Lacoue-Labarthe's debate will consequently provide a lens with which to view Blanchot's and Deleuze's respective inheritance of, intervention in, and reformulation of the Heideggerian voice as it is inflected through the question of mimesis and the challenge to thinking that results from their respective engagements.

Nancy and *Partage*'s Returns

With "Sharing Voices," Nancy gives us one of the first examples of what he understands by interrupting the figure. In that text, as I explicated in chapter 2, Nancy intervenes in the critical conception of the Heideggerian voice as a mere reinscription of the metaphysical logos and as a reappearance of the figure of metaphysical subjectivity. While he acknowledges the threat of these metaphysical repetitions and even recognizes instances of them in Heidegger's thought, he nevertheless labors to excavate the sites in Heidegger's writings where his text ultimately exceeds the metaphysics of presence. Nancy accomplishes this by recovering the relation to alterity—the alterity of Being and the alterity of the other Dasein—at the heart of the Heideggerian voice. In so doing, Nancy interrupts the figure of the voice as an extension of the logos and the metaphysical subject.

"Sharing Voices" is also a clear demonstration of what Nancy means by interruption as a cutting movement that gives rise to another voice. Once Nancy interrupts the figure of the voice by elucidating its plural nature, human finitude takes on the figure of a shared multiplicity of voices. But, as we will see Nancy acknowledge, this new figure, this new enunciation, can and typically does morph into the figure of community, with this figure taking on the characteristics of a metaphysical super subject. The figure—and the mythic writing—of community becomes the focus of Nancy's concerns following his intervention in "Sharing Voices." In *The Inoperative Community*, for example, Nancy explicitly ties the project of interrupting community to the task of interrupting myth.

The scholarship on Nancy's theorization of community focuses mainly on *The Inoperative Community* and attends primarily to two aspects surrounding that text: Nancy's use of Georges Bataille for placing the concept of community into question, and the "debate" Blanchot is said to have inaugurated in response to Nancy with his book *The Unavowable Community* (1988) (*La communauté inavouable* [1983]).[7] Commentators have also pursued connections between Nancy and others working on the question of community.[8] With a couple of exceptions, there has been little scholarship that maps connections between Nancy's intervention in the Heideggerian voice and his reflections on community.[9] There has been no work in that category that deals with the Heideggerian voice as a figure of finitude as I have interpreted it in the opening chapters and thus none that entertains Nancy's confrontation with the problem of community as a confrontation with the figure.

My aim in this section is thus twofold. First to show how Nancy's reflections on community emerge out of and are part of a continuous engagement with the Heideggerian voice and Heidegger's conception of the centrality of figuration to human finitude. They represent, that is to say, Nancy's sustained meditation on his concept of *partage* and how this concept insistently returns in the question of community in his thought. I then want to submit this background of Nancy's reflections on community as the basis of his debate with Lacoue-Labarthe regarding the figure.

Once the continuity of Nancy's engagement with Heidegger becomes visible, it will become clear how community becomes a concern for Nancy as a problem of the figure and why he regards the figure as an inescapable condition of social existence—yet one that nonetheless calls for consistent interruption. In this respect, Heidegger remains a critical interlocutor for Nancy. For while Nancy sees the figure and myth of community form a metaphysical threat in Heidegger's thought, it is Heidegger's theorization of the figure, particularly in terms of the relationship of *Gestalt* to the work of art that we studied in chapter 3, that nonetheless gives Nancy tools for addressing this threat and intervening in community's mythic "con-figuration."

After mapping the paths Nancy takes from his occupation with the voice and figure in Heidegger to the voice and figure of community more generally, I demonstrate how Nancy's use of Bataille in conceiving the interruption and rewriting of community—especially his employment of Bataille's concept of sacrifice in figuring the unworking of community—is a response to the trope of sacrifice in Heidegger. Once this critical assemblage is in place, it will be possible to see how Nancy's reflections on the work of art are not incidental but central to his concerns with Heidegger, Bataille, community, and the figure.

RE-PRESENTING THE BEING-WITH OF BEING-THERE

While Heidegger is a constant presence throughout Nancy's oeuvre, he is not the primary focus of *The Inoperative Community*. In fact, it is not until some years later that Nancy links the theme of *partage* that he pursues from his reading of Heidegger in "Sharing Voices" to the project he undertakes in *The Inoperative Community*. One of the first gestures he makes in this direction is his *Being Singular Plural* (1996), which expands his meditation on *hermēneia* from "Sharing Voices" to Heidegger's description in *Being and Time* of the roles *Mitsein* ("Being-with") and *Mitdasein* ("Being-there-with") play in the structure of human finitude.[10] However, it is really with his essay "The Being-with of Being-there" (2003) that Nancy conducts a sustained reading of those sections from *Being and Time*.[11] It is in that essay where Nancy explains that, though the structure of *Mitsein* and *Mitdasein* provides an opening for conceiving the shared/divided relation of voices at the heart of human finitude, Heidegger ultimately represses this fundamental relation to difference when he asserts that Dasein's destiny is to be realized in an act where it gives itself up (i.e., sacrifices itself) to the collective identity of *das Volk* (the people), which, of course, is not just any term when Heidegger's corpus is concerned.

In "The Being-with of Being-there," Nancy opens with the observation that Heidegger's accounts of *Mitsein* and *Mitdasein* in *Being and Time* form a contradictory moment in the project of fundamental ontology. As Nancy summarizes, Heidegger asserts that *Mitsein* and *Mitdasein* are "equiprimordial" (*gleich ursprünglich*) with Dasein's Being-in-the-world (MR 149/SZ 114). When Dasein is in the world (which is always, since Dasein's being is to be projected ahead of itself in a concern with its being from out of a fundamental understanding of the sense/meaning of Being), Dasein "encounters" (*begegnet*) the being of other Daseins who, by definition, are also in-the-world in virtue of their respective understandings of the sense/meaning of Being (SZ 118, §26). Since to "have a world" means encountering other Daseins, Dasein's Being-in-the-world is constituted by both *Mitsein* and *Mitdasein*. As he rehearses this constellation of Dasein, *Mitsein*, *Mitdasein*, and the multiple sharings in the sense/meaning of Being among Daseins, Nancy's summary echoes the atmosphere of *partage* that he evokes in "Sharing Voices."

Yet despite being "co-essential to Dasein's essence," *Mitsein* and *Mitdasein* do not receive the relentless critical exegesis for which Heidegger is known, notes Nancy ("The Being-with" 2, 4). Instead, Nancy says, as he delves further into "the economy of *Being and Time*," Heidegger quickly directs the Being-with of Dasein into two possible directions: an inauthentic (*uneigentlich*) mode in which Dasein falls prey to the whims and demands of an anonymous "Anyone" (the *they*, Nancy's translation of *das Man*) and an authentic (*eigentlich*) mode in which Dasein's being is realized through alignment with the destiny of "the people" (*das Volk*) ("Being-with" 6–8). As we recall from our overview of the voice in chapter 1 above, when Dasein is subject to the Anyone (the *they*), Dasein is lost to itself, giving itself over to such devices as rumor and idle talk (*die Gerede*) (*Being and Time*, §35). This is a Dasein who has relinquished its being to others, a Dasein who has abdicated its claim to its ownmost possibility, especially that ultimate possibility that is Dasein's alone, namely its death (*Being and Time*, §27).

Nancy continues in his analysis of the difference Heidegger draws between the Anyone and *das Volk*, focusing specifically on how Heidegger associates Dasein's ability to become authentically historical exclusively with the latter ("Being-with" 8–10):

As Nancy recounts from §74 of *Being and Time*, Dasein recovers from being lost in the Anyone and becomes a "Self" by becoming resolute in its being as possibility. Becoming resolute means that Dasein chooses its fate as a being who is thrown "futurally" toward death as its ownmost possibility. Dasein no longer lets its existence be determined by the Anyone but embraces its existence as thrown and therefore as temporal. As temporality, Dasein is also historical, and in becoming resolute, Dasein "historizes" its existence. However, because Dasein's Being-in-the-world means being with other Daseins, Dasein can only historize itself and thereby exist authentically when it aligns its futurity with the destiny of a people (*Being and Time*, §73–74). In its authentic relation to *Mitsein*, Dasein aligns its being with the destiny of *das Volk* through an act Heidegger characterizes with the term *Aufgeben*, which prevailing English translations of *Being and Time* render as a "giving up" (SZ 391/MR 443).

To Nancy's ears, however, *Aufgeben* implies more than a simple giving up; it carries the imperative of a "self-sacrifice" ("Being-with" 11n10). Thus, in Nancy's view, as soon as Heidegger introduces the radical dimension of *Mitsein* and *Mitdasein* as coessential to Dasein's existence, a dimension that upsets the isolation of the metaphysical subject that forms the basis of the modern Western philosophical tradition, Heidegger excludes this dimension from having any further purchase on the project of fundamental ontology ("Being-with" 5). In place of a real thought of "the with" and its implications for the thrown existence of Dasein, Heidegger presents two possibilities for Dasein's relation to "the with" that, in Nancy's estimation, are equally impoverished: in one respect, the "pure exteriority" of the Anyone, in which Dasein is simply a person alongside other people ("Being-with" 4). In another respect, there is the "pure interiority" of "the people," in which Dasein's singular existence (and any thought of singularity, which, as Nancy defines it, is Dasein's exposure to the other Dasein in their shared finitude) is assimilated to a "single communal *Dasein*" ("Being-with" 4). While the Anyone is a metaphysical notion that works within the logic of "the simple contiguity of things," "the people" is just as metaphysical insofar as it exchanges the subjectivity of "the person" for a group subject. Nancy writes: "Between two subjects, the first being 'the person' and the second 'the community,' there is no place left for the 'with,' nor in a more general way for that which would neither be a 'subject' (in the sense of self-constitution) nor a simple thing (in the sense of the things put simply beside one another, or a sense of the *with* which Heidegger precisely wants to dismiss)" ("Being-with" 5). It is between these two subjects that Nancy says that "the *with* has been hidden, lost or suppressed in the economy of *Being and Time*" ("Being-with" 5).

As Nancy stresses, the repression of "the *with*" in *Being and Time* is not a simple oversight on Heidegger's part. It serves as part of the foundation for Heidegger's political itinerary in the 1930s, not only for his initial commitment to Nazism but also for his eventual argument with it ("Being-with" 3). And philosophically, Nancy notes, "the people" will persist as a figure in Heidegger's work following his self-pronounced turn (*die Kehre*) away from the existential analytic of *Being and Time* to the appropriating event of Being (*das Ereignis*) that becomes the focus of his later thought ("Being-with" 5).

Yet, Nancy is also careful to specify that what persists in Heidegger's thought is not simply the figure of metaphysical subjectivity; it is the figure of the metaphysical subject as embodied by a voice, some evidence of which we have already encountered in the form of the historical Greek voice in his interpretations of *Antigone* treated in chapter 3. He thus draws our attention to Heidegger's 1936–38 *Beiträge zur Philosophie (Vom Ereignis)* (*Contributions to Philosophy [of the Event]*), which is largely considered Heidegger's second major work following *Being and Time*, and the idea he says Heidegger advances in that text that "the people is one voice" ("Being-with" 5).[12]

According to Nancy, then, as soon as Heidegger posits the multiple imbrications of Daseins and worlds with his concepts of *Mitsein* and *Mitdasein*, testifying, in Nancy's terminology, to the shared/divided character of human finitude, he exchanges one figure of the voice for another. He abandons the voice as a dissimulating/disappropriating figure (the voice as that which calls Dasein back to the fact of its ecstatic existence and that opens it to an originary relation to the other Dasein) for a voice that is the property of an individualized metaphysical subject, one that returns to its familiar home in representation. As Nancy argues in *The Inoperative Community*, it is this voice that persistently threatens metaphysical reinscription, not only in Heidegger's thought, but in the entire Western philosophical tradition. It is this voice that stands in perpetual need of interruption.

THE INOPERATIVE COMMUNITY: CONCEIVING VOICE AND COMMUNITY AS INTERRUPTION

In *The Inoperative Community*, Nancy actually pursues a radical reversal: he not only argues for the need to interrupt any subjectivized form of community and community voice; he also calls for a concept of community and for a concept of the voice as forms of interruption. He wants "community" and "voice" to name—to sound—the interruption of community and voice. To arrive at this conception, Nancy first reconstructs the way the figure of community is founded and maintained in myth, that is to say, as a mode of fiction or "fictioning" (*The Inoperative Community* 56). He then utilizes Bataille's conceptions of communication and sacrifice in order to conceive of community as a process of perpetual writing and "unworking" (*désoeuvrement*), for sounding community as a voice of interruption.

In "Myth Interrupted," the first chapter of *The Inoperative Community*, Nancy charts the dialectical unfolding of myth and community. "Mythic thought," he writes, "is in effect nothing other than *the thought of a founding fiction, or a foundation by fiction*" (*The Inoperative Community* 53; original emphasis). He will go on to read Schelling in analyzing the figurative dimension of myth, which Nancy thinks in an active sense: myth figures through a movement he calls alternatively an "auto-fictioning" (*auto-fictionnement*) and "autofiguration" (*auto-figuration*) (*The Inoperative Community*, 53–54; *La communauté désoeuvrée*, 134–38). In one respect, he continually reemphasizes the idea that "myth is essential to community" (62), that all community is founded in myth, or, to say it more strongly, that there is no community without myth. In another respect, Nancy shows that myth harbors its own interruption, a "self-knowledge" that is aware of its function as community's fictive-figural ground but that, once having caught a glimpse of itself, nonetheless gives way once again to myth's perpetuation. If this dialectical tension between myth and community becomes sublated, it is through the fact that "community" is simultaneously the name of a mythic founding and an active unworking (*désoeuvrement*) of any final communal determination or accomplishment. Nancy describes this unassimilable resistance within community as "community against community" (*The Inoperative Community* 60). This unassimilable of community within community is what he calls a "passion of and for community" that undoes the reification of Being-with into a collective Subject, such as *das Volk* (*The Inoperative Community* 61).

What is this unassimilable of community within community, precisely? What is the destabilizing force that necessarily ruins in advance community's closure? According to Nancy, the unassimilable of community is the singular communication of human finitude that inheres in the sharing of the sense/meaning of Being in *Mitsein*. The ecstasis of Dasein's existence (its being thrown ahead of itself from its understanding of the sense/meaning of Being), and the fact that its facticity (its self-interpretation) is addressed at once to itself as well as to other Daseins, means that Dasein's finitude is fundamentally that of exposure. Dasein does not appear simply to itself; rather, Dasein "compears" with other Daseins, and this "compearance," Nancy tells us, "puts them in communication with one another" (*The Inoperative Community* 60–61). But this "being-communication" (*The Inoperative Community* 24) is not a transmission of information or an exchange of meaning between individuals. That would follow the metaphysics of subjectivity—that is, the structure of a "subject-representing" (*The Inoperative*

Community 24)—that conceives community as a collection of self-contained individuals with mastery over their respective representations.

It is here that Nancy invokes Bataille's concept of communication. In Batallean communication, what is communicated is nothing other than the radical exposure that is human finitude. Referring to the human being's existence as an experience of fundamental exposure and vulnerability, Bataille writes, "A being that isn't cracked isn't possible. But we go from enduring the cracks (from decline) to glory (we seek out the cracks)."[13] What Daseins communicate to one another are not simply their respective self-interpretations of their finitude. As each Dasein's self-interpretation is an interpretation of its possibility—and ultimately, to refer to Heidegger's terminology, that "ownmost" possibility that is Dasein's impossibility or death—what Daseins communicate to one another is a sharing in Being-towards-death. Bataille's concept of communication "seek[s] out the cracks" of Being-towards-death that constitute human existence and expresses this fact—of being-cracked, of being-exposed, of exposure as being—as its message.

This is to say that Being-with is at the same time dying-with, and in pursuing this thought, Nancy follows Bataille in conceiving community as the work/share (*part*) of death (*The Inoperative Community* 17–18).[14] It is this working/sharing (*part*) of death in the sharing/division (*partage*) of sense that makes community inevitable and that is also the unassimilable of community within community. The *partage* of sense as the work/share (*part*) of death (and vice versa) unwork community even as they are the basis of *Mitsein*. Belief in community as a collection of subjects, and in community itself as some "super Subject," conceives existence as individuated and enclosed. Even more fantastical, such belief posits death as something that can be mastered. However, because it is turned toward possibility, the communication of finitude that calls for and constitutes community is necessarily open to difference, exposed to that which is other than itself. As with Dasein's "ek-sistence," community is "ek-static"; it is always-already standing outside itself, other to itself. Community denies the proper and refuses completion. Community's work is its unworking.

If community does not avail itself of consolidation into a Subject, if it "resists" this fundamentally, as Nancy states (*The Inoperative Community* 58), then Heidegger's description of Dasein's *Selbstaufgabe* (self-sacrifice, "giving up of oneself") to *das Volk* is an instance of community's mythic reinscription. It amounts to a repetition of that Hegelian fictioning in which the individual "dies" to the collective, but in so doing, "lives on" by becoming universalized through the constitution of the communal Subject. However, Nancy suggests that if community's work/share is death, if "community" "is" not, then in order to accord with community's (un)working, Dasein must instead undergo an act of sacrifice on a Bataillean, not a Hegelian-Heideggerian, register.

In the Hegelian dialectic, the individual has one destiny: to participate in the universal realization of Spirit (*Geist*). Thus, in Hegel, the individual sacrifices him/herself for the (fictive, imaginary) life of the collective Subject. The individual is negated, but its negation is preserved and transcended (i.e., put to work) for the life of the collective.

Bataillean sacrifice, by contrast, refuses this appropriation of the individual by the collective. In Bataille, the individual undergoes a movement of self-effacement that cannot be capitalized upon, profited from, or recuperated.[15] This act of self-effacement resists recuperation absolutely because it gives itself over to the dispossessing ecstasis of existence that is the ground of *Mitsein*. It is sacrifice thematized as a condition of subjectivity, as a kind of "absenting" that takes place prior to the "giving up of oneself" (*Selbstaufgabe*) required of the subject's participation in the collective. Or, to say more figuratively, it is a "dying" that is the condition for the possibility of being born as a subject.[16] For Bataille, self-effacement is a sacrifice that submits to the communicative exposure and radical becoming-other of existence—that *is* existence.[17] Only through Bataille's conception of sacrifice as self-effacement, Nancy submits, does Dasein accord itself with the exposure that is community (*The Inoperative Community* 17).

By drawing on Bataille's concepts of sacrifice and communication to recover the Being-(and dying-)with of Dasein's finitude, Nancy corrects the image of history projected by Heidegger's mythic prescription of Dasein's *Selbstaufgabe* to *das Volk*. Dasein's *Selbstaufgabe* not only repeats the Hegelian subsumption of the individual to the collective; Heidegger's description of Dasein historicizing itself through *das Volk* via this *Selbsaufgabe* also echoes strongly the Hegelian schema in which History unfolds through the realization of Spirit. In interrupting the coherence of the metaphysical subject, Bataillean sacrifice also interrupts the metaphysical conception of History as the work of a collective Subject, such as *Geist* or *das Volk*.[18]

It is here that Nancy theorizes an "other" voice. Myth carries its own interruption, according to Nancy, and since community is founded in mythic fictioning/figuration, community also interrupts itself. As the fictioning (and fictive) voice of myth invokes community, an "other" voice interrupts the fictive call:

> This voice is the voice of community, or of the community's passion. If it must be affirmed that myth is essential to community—but only in the sense that it completes it and gives it closure and the destiny of an individual, of a completed totality—it is equally necessary to affirm that in the interruption of myth is heard the voice of the interrupted community, the voice of the incomplete, exposed community speaking as myth without being in any respect mythic speech. (*The Inoperative Community* 62)

This is the cutting movement to which Nancy refers in the first letter of his exchange with Lacoue-Labarthe on the scene. Nancy describes this other voice that "says" the interruption of myth/community as a rustling or murmuring that persists beneath the overtures of the mythic voice that invokes community (*The Inoperative Community* 62).

Nancy proceeds to describe the interruptive saying of community that lies within community as a voice that is shared out (*partagé*) (*The Inoperative Community* 25). As the voice of *Mitsein*, community cannot *not* be heard. Thus, community's voice is a demand—an exigency—addressed to thought, requiring a response, where not responding (or even a failure to respond) nonetheless counts as having registered community's call. As Nancy declares, "An ethics and a politics of discourse and writing are evidently implied here. . . . This is nothing other than the question of *literary communism* . . . something that would be the sharing of community in and by its writing, its literature" (*The Inoperative Community* 26; original emphasis). What Nancy means by "its writing, its literature" is not a writing or literature that is proper to or written by a certain community. He means "literature" as the "exposition" of community, a writing that touches on the exposure that is community and is therefore a writing that is an experience of community's exposure (*The Inoperative Community* 26). According to Nancy, "literature" itself is nothing other than the writing of community to the extent that it would not exist without community's unworking force: "It is because there is this, this unworking that shares out our being-in-common, that there is 'literature.' That is to say, the indefinitely repeated and indefinitely suspended gesture of touching the limit, of indicating it and inscribing it, but without crossing it, without abolishing it in the fiction of a common body. To write for others means in reality to write because of others" (*The Inoperative Community* 67). The fact that there is literature testifies to the fact of community as the unassimilable force of Being-(and dying-)with. "Literature" is the voice that "sounds" community's interruption, and literary communism is that writing that responds to the exigency of community.

With the concept of literary communism, Nancy invokes an image of literature that exceeds the economy of representation and therefore the economy of metaphysics. It is a conception of literature practiced not only by Bataille but also, as we will see, by Blanchot. And there is an extensive history of thinkers in the Western philosophical tradition who have looked to literature, poetry, and the work of art in general as lying outside the philosophical and as being "purer" than philosophy, including Kant, Schopenhauer, Nietzsche and, not coincidentally, Heidegger.

In fact, in his writings on the question of the work of art, which follow upon his call for a literary communism in *The Inoperative Community*, Nancy reengages with Heidegger in order to investigate how the sharing of the sense/meaning of Being plays out with respect to artistic practice. This trajectory in Nancy's writings displays an interest in connecting the work of community to the "work" performed by the work of art and is thus a clear echo of Heidegger's questioning in "The Origin of the Work of Art."

Yet, at the same time, this reengagement with Heidegger also proves to be a noteworthy redirection in Nancy's thought. Whereas *The Inoperative Community* reads Bataille in order to recover the sharing of voices that, as Nancy argues, Heidegger discovers yet represses of human finitude, Nancy's writings on the work of art go back to Heidegger as a way to address a metaphysical conundrum that emerges out of (or, I should say, vexingly returns) in Bataille's conception of sacrifice: namely, a return of the problem of the figure. In the next section, I retrace Nancy's interreading of Heidegger and Bataille, particularly how he draws on Heidegger's reflections on the work of art to intervene in the metaphysics of figuration—specifically, mimesis—into which Bataille's sacrificial logic inadvertently tips. As we will see, though, this employment of Heidegger to address the problem of mimesis in Bataille will set Nancy on the way to his debate with Lacoue-Labarthe concerning the figure, its interruption, and the revelation of mimesis as *the* problem of the voice.

MIMESIS, ART, AND SACRIFICE

It should be no surprise that Bataille would lead Nancy to the work of art. In addition to his thematization of literature and writing, Bataille looks to art generally as a sacrificial practice that imitates and acts out the desire for the world's destruction.[19] Art, for Bataille, is both a theatrical reproduction of the sacrificial drive that is existence (a presentation, perhaps even a scene, of Being-towards-death) and an expression of what all sacrifice aims at—namely, the experience of finitude that Bataille names "sovereignty," the unworking of all that exists.[20] For Bataille, art is an enactment of finitude's radical exposure.

Yet the problem with this model of sacrifice, Nancy notes, or with what he calls this "sacrificial logic," is that it rests upon a structure of mimesis ("The Unsacrificeable" 59). Art imitates/theatricalizes the sacrificial drive. It therefore participates in the economy of representation that it aims at unworking.

This is a problem of which Bataille himself was aware. In "Hegel, Death, and Sacrifice" (1955), Bataille attends to a series of paradoxes surrounding sacrifice as a mode through which the human being comes to acknowledge its finitude: in representing death and finitude, sacrificial logic gains control and masters them, which makes sacrifice a form of false consciousness or bad faith. Yet there is no not representing death and finitude. For being human means having consciousness of death, becoming aware of it, and knowing that one will die. On this, Bataille is no different from Hegel and Heidegger and many others in the Western philosophical tradition. But the only way to really know death is to die, at which point the human cannot *be* human because one has ceased to be at all.

Accordingly, says Bataille, "This difficulty proclaims the necessity of *spectacle*, or of *representation* in general, without the practice [*repetition*] of which it would be possible for us to remain alien and ignorant in respect to death, just as beasts apparently are. Indeed, nothing is less animal than fiction, which is more or less separated from the real, from death."[21] Bataille describes spectacle as a "subterfuge" ("Hegel, Death, and Sacrifice," 287), one that is necessary to overcome the paradox finitude presents. In order to be human, the human being must fool itself into having a relation to death through that which is not death, through a simulacrum that gives "an impression of really dying" ("Hegel, Death, and Sacrifice," 287). Representation (of death) is thus a means by which the human becomes what it is and at the same time remains in suspended alienation from itself.

The problem consequently becomes one of distinguishing Bataille's conception of art, and the sacrificial labor it supposedly performs, from representation employed as subterfuge for the human relation to death. As Nancy implies in his treatment of this problem, Bataille does not provide clear means for resolving this issue, which Nancy credits Bataille with helping make visible but which Nancy also says Bataille exacerbates. However, in this same treatment, Nancy makes a parenthetical, yet provocative, observation linking Bataille's efforts to think art as a form of sacrifice and Heidegger's remark in "The Origin of the Work of Art" that associates the event of truth in the work of art with what Heidegger refers to as "the essential sacrifice" (*das wesentliche Opfer*).[22] It seems, then, that Heidegger's artwork essay could point a way out of the problem of determining art's status in relation to the configuration of representation, death, and sacrifice. However, that would only be possible if Heidegger's reflections on art yield a simultaneous revision of both sacrifice and mimesis as movements of appropriation.[23]

As we might recall from the treatment of "The Origin of the Work of Art" in chapter 3, one of Heidegger's chief objectives in the artwork essay is to dislodge the categories of truth, mimesis, and art from their conceptions within the history of aesthetics. He recasts truth as "*aletheia*," unconcealment, and the work that the artwork performs as the dynamic play and struggle of world and earth. By implication, Heidegger recasts the artwork's mimetic character as breaking with the metaphysics of representation. Mimesis is a movement of *aletheia*; it is not an image that re-presents beings but an event of the relation between the human Dasein and Being's coming-to-appear. The artwork, then, is not a simulation of Being; it dissimulates, for in the relation between the human Dasein and Being, the human is radically exposed to the groundless fact of its understanding of the sense/meaning of Being. Insofar, then, as the artwork can be understood as a scene presenting this relation between Dasein and Being, it is a scene of human finitude.

But as I also explain in my discussion in chapter 3, Heidegger does not say that the work of art constitutes Dasein's world. Instead, he says it figures world ("the fixing in place of truth in the figure") ("The Origin of the Work of Art" 38). The work of art, in other words, presents the facticity of Dasein's finitude and is as a result a figuring of the figuration that inheres in human finitude. As I argue in my treatment of the artwork essay, insofar as the voice is a figure of human finitude and insofar as human finitude carries with it a scene of the voice, the voice returns in the rhythmic play of world and earth that the artwork stages. But it is a return of a return, of course, or an echo of an echo, since the voice is already an affective figural echo of Dasein's understanding of the sense/meaning of Being.

What we see in Heidegger's conception of the work of art, then, is a meditation on the necessity of the figure, and it is this aspect of Heidegger's conception that I believe grounds both Nancy's theorization of the relation between myth and community and his reflections on art. Heidegger's conception of the work of art tells us that there is no getting behind the fact of facticity, that the human Dasein is always-already interpreting its existence from out of an understanding of the sense/meaning of Being. This is why there is no a-figural or nonmythic grounding of community. Figuration is inevitable, which is why interrupting the voice of community can only give way to other voices, other figures.

At the same time, Heidegger's casting of the work of art as affirming the inevitability of figuration allows Nancy to approach the question of art as a question of the plurality of worlds. This plurality, and Heidegger's revision of the artwork as a dissimulating event, will help Nancy in his efforts to see artistic practice as a mode of community's sacrificial unworking.

In his work *The Muses*, Nancy relates the singular plurality of human finitude to the fact of the singular plurality of art: there is no art "in general," but instead only the irreducible plurality of the arts, which nonetheless allows itself to be collected under the name "art." For Nancy, the fact of the multiple arts and their irreducibility serves as evidence of the multiplicity of worlds, and communicates the singular plurality of human facticity. Just as there is a division of the sense/meaning of Being and our understanding of this sense/meaning in and through multiple worlds, there are multiple arts. If they meet together in "art," it is because all the arts "touch" on the sensibility of sense.[24] Art "touches" on the fact of sense, according to Nancy; it gives sensibility to the fact *that there is sense*. As Nancy asks,

> But what does art do if not finally touch upon and touch by means of the principal heterogeneity of "sensing"? In this heterogeneity in principle that resolves itself into a heterogeneity *of the* principle, art touches on the sense of touch itself: in other words, it touches at once on the "self-touching" inherent in touch and on the "interruption" that is no less inherent in it. In another lexicon, one might say: it touches on the immanence and the transcendence of touch. Or in still other terms: it touches on the trans-immanence of being-in-the-world. Art does not deal with the "world" understood as simple exteriority, milieu, or nature. It deals with being-in-the-world in its very springing forth. (*The Muses* 18; original emphasis)

Art, for Nancy, is consequently an affective site of the excess of sensibility that cannot be recuperated fully by the logic of representation. Art makes sensible the fact that there is sense. He understands art as communicating (in the sense of Battaillean communication) the shared/division (*partage*) of sense. It communicates the sharing of voices. Thus, the fact of the plurality of art not only points to the fact of the plurality of worlds but also affectively presents the fact of sense's excess.

In another work on aesthetics, *The Ground of the Image*, Nancy intensifies this set of claims. The singular plurality of art becomes the basis for an exploration of the singular plurality of sense as such via the image. In the volume's opening chapter, "The Image—the Distinct," Nancy charts how the image retraces (in the sense of *retrait*—as a "drawing and withdrawing"[25]) many of the themes from his earlier reflection on art, this time relating the image to the concepts of mimesis, sacrifice, *partage*, touch, etc. In so doing, Nancy joins a discursive tradition that elevates the image to a status above that of mere representation and casts the image as encompassing more than simply the visual (*Ground* 4).[26] However, a couple of nuanced gestures are introduced by Nancy this time around: first, a notion of "force" appears in these reflections, and secondly, a thought of mimesis as a form of collective sharing or *methexis*.

Of the image's act of retracing, which he suggests communicates the sharing/dividing of *partage*, Nancy writes:

> If it is possible for the same line, the same distinction, to separate and to communicate or connect (communicating also separation itself . . .), that is because the traits and lines of the image (its outline, its form) are themselves (something from) its intimate force: for this intimate force is not "represented" by the image, but the image is it, the image activates it, draws it and withdraws it, extracts it by withdrawing it, and it is with this force that the image touches us. (*Ground* 5)

The force Nancy ascribes to the image has both a Kantian as well as a Nietzschean-Battaillean connotation. In one sense, the image obeys the structure of Kant's conception of the transcendental schematism (*Ground* 23); in another sense, it stands for a separation in Being. From Kant (and then from Heidegger's reading of the schematism), Nancy seems to understand force here as the force of presentation (*Darstellung*), in which "what is presents itself. . . . Therefore being is torn away from being; and it is the image that tears itself away" (*Ground* 24). Through the image, "what is" assembles itself as some *thing* that is but does so through a dis-semblance. This would be the sharing/dividing communication of the sense/meaning of Being and therefore also the Nietzschean-Bataillean inflection of sacrifice. Such is what Nancy calls the image's "distinctness": the image is "distinct," he says, because it brings out "the dissimilarity that inhabits resemblance, that agitates it and troubles it with the presence of spacing and of passion" (*Ground* 9). Rather than consolidate identity, the image introduces alterity into the heart of resemblance.

Here we meet again the recasting of mimesis as sacrificial movement, as a dissembling, rather than resembling, force that both exceeds the economy of representation and, through this excess, claims the spectator in its sharing/dividing communication. Because the image does not resemble, neither does it reflect the subject back to itself in order for the subject to affirm its self-presence. The image's communication therefore remains "faithful" to the Bataillean inflection where the integrity of both addresser and addressee is compromised and fragmented. "We" are not intact but are rather a "we" insofar as we are prevented from cohering into a group subject. For Nancy, the image, we might say, "is" the unworking—and therefore inscription—of community par excellence.

It is in virtue of this shared sacrificial communication (again, a shared Being-[and dying-]with) that Nancy describes the image's mimesis as a *methexis*: invoking the theatrical, as opposed to the Platonic, definition of *methexis*, Nancy characterizes this experience as "a participation or a contagion through which the image seizes us" (*Ground* 9).[27] Like the voice, or rather, *as the voice*, the image interpellates "us," calls us to (our shared) "ek-sistence" in the shared/division (*partage*) of the sense/meaning of Being. As we are about to see, this conception of mimesis Nancy shapes through his interreading of Heidegger and Bataille will come close to the conception Lacoue-Labarthe pursues in his critical assessment of Heidegger. Together, they will move us closer to an understanding of how mimesis is *the* problem around which the question of language, affect, and finitude revolves. Nonetheless, Nancy and Lacoue-Labarthe will differ on their conception of mimesis in important ways; in fact, the problem of how to conceptualize mimesis—and more precisely, the problem of the figure's relation to mimesis—will be one of the main sites of contention between them. Nancy gives us an image of the voice as inevitable and yet standing in need of perpetual interruption, so that we might retain access to the dissimulating force of the Being-with that inheres in it, and so that we may guard against its reification into a property of a metaphysical Subject writ large. Much more skeptical, and much less forgiving of Heidegger's entrapment by the voice of National Socialism, Lacoue-Labarthe argues for the necessity of de-figuring the voice, for the exigency of effacing it entirely. It is to his critique of Heidegger's complicity in the metaphysics of the figure, in what he calls "onto-typology," that I now turn.

Lacoue-Labarthe: This Figure Which Is Not One

As we just saw, Nancy charts a course through Heidegger's text that begins with the voice and arrives at the work of art. The shared/divided communication of the sense/meaning of Being that Nancy recovers in Heidegger's figuration of the voice is then thought by Nancy through Heidegger's recasting of mimesis in "The Origin of the Work of Art." Nancy "imparts" the two poles of this trajectory with Bataille's conception of sacrifice, but Heidegger's text remains the touchstone of Nancy's theorizations. With Lacoue-Labarthe, however, Heidegger occupies less the position of interlocutor than antagonist. Working from the opposite trajectory—in the direction from the artwork to the voice—Lacoue-Labarthe departs decisively from Nancy on the status of Heidegger's text: for him, it is not Being-with that is suppressed in Heidegger but rather mimesis. What Nancy identifies as Heidegger's revision of mimesis in "The Origin of the Work of Art" is actually another moment in philosophy's long history of suppressing mimesis, according to Lacoue-Labarthe. And the mechanism by which Heidegger suppresses mimesis, yet also entangles himself further with it, Lacoue-Labarthe submits, is that of the figure.

Like Nancy, Lacoue-Labarthe shows the act of suppression gives way to a reinscription of metaphysical subjectivity in Heidegger's thought. Unlike Nancy, however, he does not locate within Heidegger's revision of mimesis an opening in which Heidegger's text resists the return of metaphysics and enables the thought of a postmetaphysical Being-with, as Nancy does through community and the work of art. Lacoue-Labarthe is much more severe and unyielding in his assessment of Heidegger. For him, Heidegger's suppression of mimesis places his text firmly within the history of the figure, which from Lacoue-Labarthe's perspective *is* the history of metaphysics (*including* the history of its overcoming). By suppressing mimesis, Lacoue-Labarthe sees Heidegger aligning himself with the entire metaphysical tradition that works to master mimesis' dissimulating/dissembling force, from the Platonism Heidegger sought to overcome to the Hegelian technique of putting the negative (i.e., death) to work for speculative thought. According to Lacoue-Labarthe, the consequences of Heidegger's participation in the tradition of mimesis' suppression are contradictory, if not altogether paradoxical: the effort to contain mimesis leads to its return in the figure, which Lacoue-Labarthe characterizes as a form of specular capture, exactly that which the containment of mimesis was originally intended (again, since Plato) to guard against.

The problem thus becomes one of determining whether and to what extent the sharing of voices Nancy recovers in Heidegger is able to reach a level that amounts to the "caesura of the speculative" that Lacoue-Labarthe calls for in response to Heidegger's text. Such a caesura is necessary for overcoming what he observes is the narcissistic doubling of the subject that takes place through the figure of the voice.

Perhaps the simplest way to capture the nature of Nancy and Lacoue-Labarthe's disagreement concerning the figure is to say that where Nancy holds the figure (in Heidegger and following him) as an opening of difference, inseparable from a thought of mimesis as the presentation (*Darstellung*) of Being, Lacoue-Labarthe regards the figure as the object of a bait and switch: the figure being installed as that which only masquerades (i.e., is merely a figure) of difference, the product of a long con perpetrated by metaphysical thought in order to secure its authority, especially in the moment when its standing seemed most threatened.

Lacoue-Labarthe initiates his interrogation of this speculative sleight of hand—or "trick," as he comes to call it—in the essay "Obliteration" (1973), which attends to Heidegger's reception of Nietzsche.[28] And he reserves his most pointed and well-known critical assessment of Heidegger's place in this discursive history for his *La Fiction du politique* (1987), in which he draws a direct link between Heidegger's perpetuation of speculative thought and his specular capture in National Socialism.[29] However, it is in his 1975 essay "Typography" ("Typographie"), which appears as the first chapter of the English edition *Typography*,[30] that Lacoue-Labarthe sustains his most detailed analysis of mimesis' fate at the hands of metaphysics, as well as the specific steps in which Heidegger "contributes" to the metaphysical appropriation of mimesis. As Lacoue-Labarthe will argue, it is Heidegger's deployment of the concept of *Ge-stell* and its series of cognates in his reflections on art and technology that leads Lacoue-Labarthe to suspect Heidegger's complicity in the Western philosophical tradition's treatment of mimesis.

According to Lacoue-Labarthe, there is a pattern to how the tradition has handled mimesis, which is repeated in Heidegger's critique of the metaphysical tradition: first, the tradition's subjugation of mimesis to theorization, which attempts to fix mimesis' essence in specularity, and;

secondly, its appropriation via the figure. Once Lacoue-Labarthe charts this constellation within metaphysical thought, and also between Heidegger and the metaphysical tradition, he then asks about the possibilities of realizing a "caesura of the speculative" and, just as importantly, what such an interruption of speculative thought might look like. (To ask about what *form* a caesura of the speculative might take on, however, would be contradictory and therefore may already be to come up against the limit of its possibility, or at least, its intelligibility.)

In order to touch on each of these main areas of Lacoue-Labarthe's critique—the metaphysical tradition's assimilation of mimesis' dissimulating force, Heidegger's repetition of this assimilation, and the possibility of a caesura of the speculative—my discussion in this section will focus mainly on the texts "Typography" and "The Echo of the Subject,"[31] and make connections when called for to Lacoue-Labarthe's other writings, such as *Musica Ficta* and "The Scene is Primal."[32] Although I will not be able to be comprehensive in my treatment of Lacoue-Labarthe's corpus, I do analyze what I take to be essential to Lacoue-Labarthe's *explication* (as in *Auseinandersetzung*) with Heidegger while also mapping as clearly as possible the trajectories Lacoue-Labarthe and Nancy each take on the way to their exchange on the "Scene." For that final discussion, I will seek to situate their exchange within Lacoue-Labarthe's reflections on the caesura of the speculative, as well as within the context of what he and Nancy have called "the retreat [*retrait*] of the political."

Philosophy and Its Double

Lacoue-Labarthe's "Typography" opens elliptically, with interwoven epigraphs from Nietzsche's *Daybreak* and Plato's *Republic*. Each of these epigraphs refers to madness. Nietzsche's describes a madness that he implies the philosopher of the future must inhabit in order to break with existing forms of morality. Plato's likens the mimetic artist to the madman. Following upon these, Lacoue-Labarthe makes a provocation concerning philosophy's relation to madness, or rather one imputing a madness proper to philosophy: "In the long run," he declares, "the question posed here is that of 'philosophical madness'. . . . Is it possible, *for example*, that there is some philosophical predestination to madness?" ("Typography" 44–45; original emphasis). With this provocation, Lacoue-Labarthe extends Foucault's and Derrida's earlier examinations of philosophy's "othering" of madness toward a question of philosophy's desire. He is evoking something on the order of philosophy's mad desire, as well as philosophy's desire for madness, as that which is most proper to philosophy's self-identification as "Philosophy."

For Lacoue-Labarthe, one glaring symptom of philosophy's mad desire/desire for madness can be gleaned from the proclivity that Western thought's major thinkers exhibit for the philosophical figure or type who stands in these thinkers' writings as an exemplar of philosophical thought. In this respect, we see that Lacoue-Labarthe's selection of Nietzsche and Plato for the essay's epigraphs is not random. Both feature a narcissistic self-mirroring—a mimetic doubling—as an essential component of their texts. For Nietzsche, it is "Zarathustra," and for Plato, it is "Socrates" who serve as surrogates for the thinkers themselves.

Both Nietzsche's and Plato's narcissistic indulgence and desire for mimetic madness become exposed in one fell swoop, according to Lacoue-Labarthe, when Erwin Rhode, having read the first draft of Nietzsche's *Thus Spoke Zarathustra*, comments in a letter on the book's "typography." Zarathustra, Rohde observes, serves as a philosophical "type" or "figure" for Nietzsche the same way that Socrates did for Plato ("Typography" 48). However, Nietzsche vehemently rejects this characterization, insisting both in a reply to Rohde and in *Ecce Homo* that Zarathustra is "without model, comparison, or precursor" (quoted in "Typography" 49). Thus, instead of realizing his own mimetic indulgence, Nietzsche intensifies his narcissistic misrecognition by declaring Zarathustra's exemplarity.

Lacoue-Labarthe proceeds to trace how this theatre of typographical doubling expands throughout the Western philosophical tradition. He sees it repeated in Heidegger's reception of Nietzsche, and specifically in his equivocation regarding the status of Zarathustra as figure. Particularly salient are the moments in Heidegger's writings where he first acknowledges Zarathustra as a figure (*Gestalt*), denies any affinity between Zarathustra and Socrates, and then attempts to distance himself from the apparent endorsement of figuration through the critique of the figure in Ernst Jünger's work.[33]

The second and third moments of Heidegger's equivocation—concerning the status of Zarathustra and Socrates as figures and his self-distancing vis-à-vis figuration through his critique of Jünger—deserve our critical attention, Lacoue-Labarthe suggests. For according to him, it is in these moments that Heidegger can be seen to be taking steps to assimilate mimesis in order to be able to "mimic" its power of dissimulation and appropriate this power for philosophy without exposing philosophical thought to the threat of its own dissimulation and "dissembly." This is the theater of doubling Lacoue-Labarthe contends speculative thought constructs in its self-constitution, the madness interior to philosophy that is speculative thought.

According to Lacoue-Labarthe, the moments in Heidegger's reception of Nietzsche where he is taking steps to assimilate mimesis involve instances where he seems somewhat overly invested in determining Zarathustra's status as figure. One such moment Lacoue-Labarthe identifies is from Heidegger's 1953 "Who Is Nietzsche's Zarathustra?," in which Heidegger presents Zarathustra in a contradictory light. In one respect, he recognizes Zarathustra as a figure (*Gestalt*) "who appears within metaphysics at the stage of its completion" (77; quoted in "Typography" 51); in another respect, he refuses to acknowledge any continuity between Zarathustra and any other figure in the history of metaphysics (Parmenides being an interesting exception). As Lacoue-Labarthe recounts, what sets Nietzsche's Zarathustra apart so decisively for Heidegger is the fact that he is the only figure to have been "poeticized [*gedichtet*] . . . or, more precisely and literally, thought out: fictionally thought out [*er-dacht*]" ("Who Is Nietzsche's Zarathustra?" 77; quoted in "Typography" 51). As we will see, Lacoue-Labarthe will attend specifically to this connection between Nietzsche and this notion of fictioning as a major critical development in Heidegger's relation to and appropriation of mimesis.[34]

However, before he moves on to the connection Heidegger makes between Nietzsche and fictioning, another moment Lacoue-Labarthe identifies as a step Heidegger takes to assimilate mimesis involves his evaluation of Socrates as figure. According to Lacoue-Labarthe, this moment appears in the 1951–52 lecture course *What Is Called Thinking?* It is there that Heidegger claims that Socrates stands alone in Western thought for the fact that he never wrote, referring of course to the historical Socrates rather than the literary Socrates (the "Socrates" of Plato's dialogues) (*What Is Called Thinking?* 17; "Typography" 52–53). How it is that Heidegger can ignore the literary Socrates is puzzling, in Lacoue-Labarthe's view. But he nonetheless sees in Heidegger's oversight a desire to mark off a space between philosophy and literature, which may or may not correspond to the advent and closure of metaphysics, as well as an apparent need to deny any affinity between Socrates and Zarathustra (including any affinity one might draw between Plato and Nietzsche). By insisting on these demarcations—the one between philosophy and literature, the other between metaphysics and its closure, and finally the one between Plato and Nietzsche—Heidegger can press the singularity of Zarathustra (and therefore Nietzsche) ("Typography"

53). And in favoring Nietzsche, Heidegger lays claim to the fictioning/figurative movement that he, at least in Heidegger's estimation, represents.

It would seem, then, that it is by pressing the singularity of Zarathustra/Nietzsche that Heidegger further embraces figuration and thereby appropriates mimesis. But Heidegger takes another step, which appears counterintuitive: he critiques Jünger's deployment of the figure, basically describing it as a turn to Platonism, and therefore, metaphysics. However, how can that be if fictioning/figuration belongs to the closure of metaphysics?

The text at issue is Heidegger's 1955 essay "On the Question of Being," his contribution to Jünger's Festschrift on the occasion of Jünger's sixtieth birthday. The essay takes the form of a letter and offers a critical interpretation of, among other writings, *The Worker: Dominion and Form* (1932), Jünger's famous reflection on modernity and technology and their embodiment in the figure of "the Worker."[35] As Lacoue-Labarthe makes clear, Heidegger's critique serves two purposes: first, to identify Jünger's employment of the figure—*Gestalt*—as an example of his philosophy's participation in and perpetuation of the history of metaphysics; and second, to set up Jünger as a contrast to his own theorization of *Ge-stell* (enframing) as a more originary, nonmetaphysical—and nonfigural—conception of Being. It is not necessarily the case, then, that Heidegger's critique of *Gestalt* in Jünger is an abandonment of his embrace of figuration. Rather, Heidegger's critique of Jünger on his conception of *Gestalt* sets up a path for the appearance of what Heidegger argues is a more originary relation: that of *Ge-stell*. It will be the appearance of *Ge-stell* that solidifies Heidegger's appropriation of mimesis.

In his review of Heidegger's argument in "On the Question of Being," Lacoue-Labarthe says that Heidegger reads Jünger's figure of the worker as an example of "the Platonic determination of Being as *eidos/idea*" ("Typography" 54). Lacoue-Labarthe quotes Heidegger directly in his characterization of Jünger's worker as an artifact of Platonic "*seeing* 'which the Greeks call *idein*, a word that Plato uses for a look that views not that changeable thing that is perceivable through the senses but that immutable thing, Being, the *idea*.'"[36] Jünger's other operative concepts, such as "mastery" and "work," Lacoue-Labarthe summarizes from Heidegger's critique, imply not only the presence of a metaphysical subject but also a metaphysical ideation/figuration of Being. Lacoue-Labarthe translates Heidegger's critique into his own terminology: according to him, Heidegger sees Jünger promoting an "onto-ideo-logy"—an "onto-typo-logy"—that unreflectively posits the figure as stamping/making an impression (*Stempel/Prägung*) upon Being as a basis for identifying the meaning of a given historical epoch, in this case, modernity ("Typography" 54–55).

As we can recall from the discussion of Nancy's reading of Heidegger's artwork essay in the first part of this chapter, at one point in his thought Heidegger embraces an idea of the necessity of figuration (*Gestaltung*) as part of his theorization of the artwork as an extension of human facticity. Yet with his critical questioning of Jünger, he seems to display a turn away or distancing from *Gestalt*. As his critique of Jünger's *The Worker* attests, Heidegger recognizes in the concept of *Gestalt* an onto-typological drive and regards it as "the final name of the Idea, the last word designating Being as 'theorized' in its difference from beginnings—that is to say, transcendence, or the meta-physical as such."[37] He thus identifies a metaphysics of *Gestalt* in Jünger so that he may contrast this metaphysics with his own extrametaphysical formulation of *Ge-stell*. In order to hold fast to this distinction, though, Heidegger must conveniently forget his own prior investments in *Gestalt*. Either that or he must explain the relationship between *Gestalt* and *Ge-stell*.

As Lacoue-Labarthe continues to explain in his summary, Heidegger thus poses the question of whether *Gestalt* follows from (i.e., can be derived from) *Ge-stell*, or vice versa. For Heidegger, the difference in direction dictates the degree to which it is possible to think beyond the metaphysical imprint that the Platonic idea or form (*eidos*) makes on Being. If *Gestalt* is primary, then *Ge-stell*, what Heidegger deems as "*the word for the forgotten/ withdrawn/concealed essence of Being*" ("Typography" 59; original emphasis), offers us no chance to think beyond the history of metaphysics; instead, it is only another means of perpetuating this history. Lacoue-Labarthe proceeds to claim, however, that the choice between the primacy of *Gestalt* or *Ge-stell* is a false one ("Typography" 54–59).[38] For Heidegger's arrival at *Ge-stell*, as Lacoue-Labarthe views it, is less than transparent or even consistent, in fact quite the opposite on both counts. As a result, Lacoue-Labarthe proposes investigating "what, *exactly*, happens, then, with the word *Ge-stell*" in Heidegger's thought ("Typography" 59; original emphasis). At stake in answering this question is nothing less than determining Heidegger's relationship to figuration, which is to say his relationship to the metaphysical tradition he seeks to deconstruct.

As it turns out, a great deal happens with the word *Ge-stell* in Heidegger's thought. As Lacoue-Labarthe will seek to show, it is Heidegger's formulation of *Ge-stell* that reveals an ambition to appropriate mimesis and the dissimulating force mimesis names. To be more precise, Heidegger's theorization of *Ge-stell*, as Lacoue-Labarthe will show, opens onto the scene of his appropriation of mimesis. As for how Heidegger conceives *Ge-stell*, Lacoue-Labarthe's reading proceeds to locate this less often in the works where *Ge-stell* is explicitly thematized—"The Origin of the Work of Art" (1935–36) and "The Question Concerning Technology" (1953)— than in the *Nietzsche* lectures (1936–40), which take place between those texts.[39] This means that sorting out "what, *exactly*, happens" with "*Ge-stell*" involves reconstructing the way Heidegger formulates the term as part of his interpretation of—and his own identification with—Nietzsche's "inversion" (*Umdrehung*) of Platonism. As the previous set of moments Lacoue-Labarthe surveys indicates, Lacoue-Labarthe believes something is afoot with Heidegger's relationship to Nietzsche and Plato: his identification with Nietzsche's project of inverting Platonism requires Heidegger to concern himself deeply with Plato's opposition between art and truth, while keeping Plato and Nietzsche distinct. At the same time, since, according to Heidegger, Nietzsche's Zarathustra is a "figure who appears within metaphysics at its stage of completion" ("Who Is Nietzsche's Zarathustra?" 77; cited in "Typography" 51), Nietzsche cannot help but repeat (or Heidegger cannot help but see Nietzsche repeating) Platonism's metaphysical constructions.

Lacoue-Labarthe thus holds that in order to discover the fate of the term *Ge-stell* in Heidegger's thought (and assess the fate of Heidegger's thought itself), it is essential to inhabit the drama between Plato and Nietzsche into which Heidegger inserts himself. Lacoue-Labarthe thus proceeds to read Heidegger's reading of Nietzsche's reading of Plato.

According to Lacoue-Labarthe, one instance in which Heidegger views Nietzsche as repeating Plato is in the way Nietzsche's writing resists poetic mimesis in favor of philosophical *poiesis* (making, producing). Responding to a common charge that Nietzsche's work is more poetry than philosophy, Heidegger writes, in a passage from the 1939 summer semester *Nietzsche* lecture "The Will to Power as Knowledge," that such a view mistakes as poetic what is actually Nietzsche's conception of "the poetizing essence of reason" (*das dichtende Wesen der Vernunft*).[40] This passage from the *Nietzsche* lectures, which grounds Heidegger's aforementioned contention that Zarathustra represents Nietzsche's fictional thinking-out (*Er-denken*) of the figure, is Heidegger's elaboration of what names the "Nietzschean schematism." The Nietzschean schematism, according to Heidegger, is Nietzsche's critical description of the human animal's necessary imposition of a form or schema on "chaos" in order to make knowledge possible.[41] With this description, Nietzsche revises similar conceptions in Kant and

Plato. For them, the schematizing impulse is a rational one. For Nietzsche, it stems instead from a "biological compulsion [*Nötigung*]," an animal "instinct."[42] Heidegger then ties this instinct to "the poetizing essence of reason," which he says Nietzsche does not abandon, despite—or perhaps because of—the fact that this power of reason to shape intelligible form from chaos fulfills a utilitarian function for life (*Nietzsche* 3–4:97). This is to say that, according to Heidegger, Nietzsche conceives "the poetizing essence of reason" as a compulsion proper to the human animal and essential to human existence. "The poetizing essence of reason" is Nietzsche's way of conceptualizing facticity.

As Lacoue-Labarthe notes, Heidegger is quick to distinguish reason's "poietic," "poetizing" power from the "poetic" ("Typography" 71; *Nietzsche*, vols. 3 and 4, 96). A *dichtende Wesen* (a poietic, poetizing essence) precedes, indeed is higher than, a *dichterische* (poetic) one, "for no more is all thought thinking [*denkerisch*] than all poetization, all fictioning [*Ausdichten*], is poetical," contends Heidegger.[43] In this distinction between the poietic and the poetic, in which Heidegger posits the latter as derivative of the former, we recognize his typical gesture distinguishing the authentic from the inauthentic, the ontological from the ontic. As Lacoue-Labarthe proceeds to show, it is this valorization of *poiesis* over mimesis, inherited and repeated from Plato and Nietzsche, onto which Heidegger maps his elevation of *Ge-stell* over *Gestalt*. From this positioning of *Ge-stell*, Heidegger unfolds a constellation of concepts, each standing for different degrees of originariness in relation to the experience of Being.

THE *GE-STELL* OF "*GE-STELL*"

In a subsection of "Typography" entitled "The Stele," Lacoue-Labarthe proceeds to reconstruct the labor *Ge-stell* performs for Heidegger, both generally and particularly in his reading of Nietzsche reading Plato. It is in this part of the essay, which constitutes the core of his critique, where Lacoue-Labarthe demonstrates how it is through the theorization of *Ge-stell* that mimesis is lost/suppressed by Heidegger and then, through this loss and suppression, appropriated/assimilated/mastered by him. A host of displacements, suppressions, and replacements—most notably, that of the metaphysical subject—follow from this, asserts Lacoue-Labarthe. As a result, Heidegger's theorization of *Ge-stell* is, according to Lacoue-Labarthe, indicative of Heidegger having fallen for—and repeating—a speculative trick/trap set first by Plato.

In addition to *Gestalt*, Lacoue-Labarthe notes that a "long chain" of "some of the major concepts of metaphysics . . . can be derived from

Ge-stell" ("Typography" 64). Lacoue-Labarthe lists some of these concepts in this chain. But as we shall see, this is not a list of just random concepts but rather those Heidegger treats in his interpretation of the relationship among Nietzsche and Plato on art and truth: "There is *stellen* (to summon, to challenge verbally, 'to stop someone in the street in order to call him to account, in order to force him to *rationem reddere*'), there is *bestellen* (to cultivate or appoint), *vorstellen* (to represent), *verstellen* (to dissimulate), *darstellen* (to portray, to (re)present), *herstellen* (to produce), *nachstellen* (to track or be after, to avenge), etc."[44] Lacoue-Labarthe proceeds to describe this chain as alternately a "lacework" and a "network," and then slightly more critically as "a sort of vegetal labyrinth proliferating around (or out of) a single root" ("Typography" 64). In such a labyrinth, he asserts, it is easy to get lost among the derivations and also just as easy to lose a term here and there. Just such a fate, Lacoue-Labarthe claims, befalls *Darstellung* in relation to *Ge-stell*. Lacoue-Labarthe reconstructs *Darstellung*'s loss by focusing first on the moment Heidegger introduces *Ge-stell* in "The Question Concerning Technology." There, "in the beginning," Lacoue-Labarthe says, "everything goes rather well."[45] Although *Herstellen* and *Darstellen* are distinguished by Heidegger as producing and (re)presentating, respectively, he nonetheless thinks them together as rooted in the *stellen* of *Ge-stell*.[46] What they and the various forms of *stellen* share is "the sense of *poiesis*," of "let[ing] what presences come forth into unconcealment [unveiling, *die Unverborgenheit*]" ("The Question Concerning Technology" 21; quoted in "Typography" 65). In being poietic, *Herstellen* and *Darstellen* are part of the movement of *aletheia* ("The Question Concerning Technology" 21; "Typography" 65).

Ge-stell "gathers" the *stele*'s multiple conjugations and, in Lacoue-Labarthe's reading, serves as a word for presence ("Typography" 69). However, *Ge-stell* also announces a hierarchy among the varieties of unconcealment; this is precisely what Heidegger himself was calling Jünger's attention to when he prompts Jünger to reconsider *Gestalt* as something derivative of *Ge-stell*. As forms of *poiesis*, both *Herstellen* and *Darstellen* install/set-up Being ("Typography" 67). They therefore also underwrite the fictioning essence of reason, or enable reason's theorizing act to be seen as poietic in nature ("Typography" 71). However, reason's theorizing enacts a secondary installation, so to speak, that is the idea or *Gestalt*, which fixes the installation of Being, stabilizes it for the concept, shores it up, and renders it static through a kind of "onto-steleo-logy" ("Typography" 71).

The Nietzschean schematism, which describes the drive at the basis of the fictioning essence of reason, helps Heidegger place *Gestalt* within a hierarchy that runs from the most originary event of Being to the least:

from *aletheia* and *Ge-stell* to *poiesis*, *Herstellen*, *Gestalt*, and finally *Darstellen*. However, as a result, Heidegger is presented with a new problem: does categorizing *Ge-stell* as more originary than *Gestalt* not reinscribe a metaphysical hierarchy between Being and appearance? Even if one could argue that the traditional hierarchy is reversed in this case, placing presencing above presence, would this not be a reproduction of the Platonic primacy of Being over appearance but simply flipped upside-down?[47] How does this "new" hierarchy, then, of *Ge-stell* over *Gestalt* advance the overcoming of metaphysics? How does it not simply rearrange terms?

Lacoue-Labarthe sees Heidegger attempt to resolve this problem in the *Nietzsche* lectures, but he also notes that in the process of doing so, Heidegger changes the onto-steleo-logical hierarchy he establishes in "The Question Concerning Technology." Focusing on the way Nietzsche overturns the opposition Plato instates between art and truth, Heidegger shows how Nietzsche's inversion of Platonism is more than a mere mechanical reorganization of the sensuous above the supersensuous, of appearance above (true) Being. Instead of a simple reversal, then, Heidegger claims Nietzsche will abolish the opposition of appearance to truth entirely and recover a more authentic relation to Being as *aletheia*, as unconcealment (*Nietzsche* 1:201). Yet, while this reinterpretation of Plato by Nietzsche helps Heidegger ground his derivation of *Gestalt* from *Ge-stell*, Lacoue-Labarthe notices that something gets lost in this grounding exercise. As he reconstructs Heidegger's reading of Nietzsche's reinterpretation of Plato, Lacoue-Labarthe depicts *Darstellung* as being lost from the onto-steleo-logical hierarchy altogether. As a result, *Darstellung*—i.e., mimesis—becomes barred from having a relation to Being's appearance.

The fate of mimesis in the *Nietzsche* lectures provokes some real questions about Heidegger's relationship to the metaphysical tradition. The fact that mimesis becomes effectively exiled by Heidegger prompts Lacoue-Labarthe to suggest that we have seen this before—in Plato. So does Heidegger exile mimesis again due to oversight? Or is he quite conscious that he reissues the judgment that the history of speculative thought has already rendered upon mimesis? And if he is aware of this repetition, does he do so in order to repeat metaphysics' speculative trick with regard to mimesis (i.e., cast mimesis as philosophy's "other" so as to appropriate its power)? Or does Heidegger himself fall for this trick? To address these questions, Lacoue-Labarthe delves into the passages from the *Nietzsche* lectures in which Heidegger translates the central components of Plato's conceptualization of mimesis as he reconstructs Nietzsche's overturning of Platonism.

The Speculative Trick

The trick is Plato's. Lacoue-Labarthe is clear on this. Nonetheless, he is also clear in maintaining that Heidegger, in following Nietzsche in trying to correct or "outdo" Plato regarding the relation of mimesis to *aletheia*, cannot help but fall for Plato's trick, and in so doing, repeat it ("Typography" 89). According to Lacoue-Labarthe, Heidegger rereads the "decisive" account of mimesis in *Republic* X in order to show "that Plato (already) no longer understands the essence and meaning of *aletheia* . . . but instead begins to interpret it in terms of *homoiosis*, adequation" ("Typography" 81). Yet, Heidegger and Lacoue-Labarthe will differ fundamentally on why exactly Plato's critique of mimesis in *Republic* X is decisive. For Heidegger, Plato's critique in *Republic* X establishes the metaphysical (mis)interpretation of *aletheia* as *homoiosis* (i.e., as adequation—correspondence or likeness—instead of unconcealment). However, Lacoue-Labarthe regards Plato's critique of mimesis in *Republic* X as decisive because that is where metaphysics renders its first and final verdict on mimesis. It is there that the metaphysical "theorization" of mimesis as degraded imitation is inaugurated and yet also solidified, a theorization that Lacoue-Labarthe sees Heidegger repeating. According to Lacoue-Labarthe, Heidegger is so eager to prove that Plato has misinterpreted *aletheia* that he oversells it by injecting "the *stele*" into his translation of Book X, specifically the section where Socrates[48] likens the work of the mimetic artist to simply holding up a mirror to the world.

While Books II and III of the *Republic* present Plato's criticism of mimetic poetry and argue for the poet's exclusion from the just state (*politeia*), respectively, Plato returns in Book X, after establishing the structure of the soul and his epistemology of the Forms, to the question of mimesis in order to explain its nature. Plato's critique of mimesis is typically one of the first lessons that students learn in the history of Western philosophy, yet curiously, the odd sequence in which mimesis appears in the *Republic* is not often analyzed. For instance, why is part of the critique of mimesis concentrated early in the *Republic* and then taken up again in its last book, almost like an afterthought? After banishing the mimetic poet in Book III, why consider admitting him back into the *politeia*?

Heidegger's analysis of the *Republic* in the *Nietzsche* lectures is significant in that it scrutinizes Plato's thematization of mimesis. By arguing that Plato mistranslates mimesis as imitation instead of as presentation (*Darstellung*) in order to establish an essential difference between Being (what is) and appearance or becoming (what is not), Heidegger troubles this supposed essential difference and clears the path for Nietzsche's overturning of Platonism. However, in his reconstruction of Heidegger's retranslation and reconceptualization of mimesis as *Darstellung* in the *Republic*, Lacoue-Labarthe uncovers the ways Heidegger falls for and repeats Plato's exclusion and appropriation of mimesis. According to Lacoue-Labarthe, Heidegger performs this repetition through a "twisting of *Darstellung* into *Herstellung*," turning *Darstellung* (mimesis) into *Herstellung* (installation/production [*poiesis*]), and causing mimesis to disappear from the scene of philosophy altogether ("Typography" 78).

Lacoue-Labarthe sees Heidegger begin to twist *Darstellung* into *Herstellung* with his summary of Plato's critique of mimesis in *Republic* III. Here is Lacoue-Labarthe quoting from the *Nietzsche* lecture "The Will to Power as Art":

> In the pursuit of such inquiry [*concerning the essence of the State, of communal existence [Gemeinwesen], of the education required for such communal existence*], the following question emerges, among others: does art too, especially the art of poetry, belong to communal existence; and, if so, how? In Book III (1–18) that question becomes the object of the discussion. Here Plato shows in a preliminary way [*aber erst vordeutend*], that what art conveys and provides is always a *Darstellung* of beings; although it is not inactive [*untätig*], its installing [*Herstellen*] and making [*Machen*], *poiein*, remain *mimesis*, counterfeiting [*Nachmachen*], copying and transforming [*ein Ab und Um-bilden*], poetizing [*Dichten*] in the sense of fictioning [*Erdichten*]. Thus art in itself is exposed to the danger of continual deception and falsehood. In accord with the essence of its activity [*Tun*], art has no direct, definitive relation to the true and to true being. (*Nietzsche* 1:168; quoted in "Typography" 75; original emphasis)

In including and attending to the original German text, Lacoue-Labarthe retraces how Heidegger's translation of mimesis as *Darstellung* and *poiesis* as *Herstellung* subsumes the former to the latter. This classification of *Darstellung* as a mode of *Herstellung* sets the stage for *Darstellung*'s disappearance in Heidegger's retranslation of Book X.

Lacoue-Labarthe focuses specifically on Heidegger's intricate treatment of *Republic* X (596b–c). This is the passage at the beginning of Book X in which Socrates proposes the wondrous figure of the *dēmiourgos* (the demiurge) who "is not only able to make [*poiesai*] all implements, but he produces all plants and animals, including himself, and thereto earth and heaven and the gods and all the things in heaven and in Hades under the earth."[49] After Socrates's interlocutor Glaucon expresses incredulity at the existence of such a "craftsman," Socrates states that such a person can accomplish such an act by taking a mirror and turning all around him (596d). Once Glaucon asserts that doing so would only make things *appear*, not bring them into being "as they truly are" (596e), Socrates greets this distinction with excitement and declares that that is how the work of the painter should be regarded: as a creation of appearance, not of things as they truly are.

As part of his effort to undo the opposition between Being and appearance, Heidegger narrows his focus on the term *dēmiourgos*, the "maker [*Macher*] of something for the sake of the *demos*," the people. "In our language," Heidegger continues, "we have a word for such a person, although, it is true, we seldom use it and its meaning is restricted to a particular realm: the *Stellmacher* (the wheelwright), who constructs frames [*Gestelle*], meaning wagon chassis [*Wagengestelle*]" (*Nietzsche* 1:174–75; cited in "Typography" 80–81). Heidegger states that "the everyday state of affairs by which the framemaker frames and produces gave a thinker like Plato something to think about—for one thing, this: in the production of tables the tablemaker proceeds *pros tēn idean blepōn poiei*, making this or that table 'while at the same time looking to the Idea'" (*Nietzsche* 1:175). What, then, of the mimetician? According to Heidegger, he is still a producer; only he would be "a man, *hos panta poie, hosaper heis hekatos tōn cheirotechnōn* (596c), 'who produced everything that every single craftsman' is able to make" (*Nietzsche* 1: 176). However, the mimetician's wondrous ability—his "uncanniness"—would not be due to his being a different kind of being ("each of us is capable of achieving such production," says Heidegger [*Nietzsche*, 1:176]), but is due rather to the "way" (*tropos*) he produces (*Nietzsche* 1:176).

The common translation of *tropos* as "way" or "manner," though, inadequately conveys the notion of turning harbored within the term, says Heidegger (*Nietzsche*, 1:176–77). Here Heidegger emphasizes the mimetician's turning of the mirror as a mode of production, of *poiesis*, production "in the Greek sense," as Heidegger repeatedly states (*Nietzsche* 1:178). Since the *dēmiourgos* produces with an *eye* toward the Idea, the *dēmiourgos' poiesis* attends to appearance. Thus, the mimetician produces as well with his turning of the mirror by attending to beings in their "self-showing" (*Nietzsche* 1:178).

In Glaucon's response to Socrates's description of the *dēmiourgos*, he makes a distinction between appearances (*on phainomenon*) and things as they are (*tēi alētheia*). Now that he has established the *dēmiourgos*' turning of the mirror, and relatedly, the mimetician's art, as modes of *poiesis*, Heidegger revises the translations of *on phainomenon* and *tēi alētheia* to "being as self-showing" and "being as undistorted." They come together, however, as "ways of presencing" (*Nietzsche* 1:178). Summarizing his reconstruction of Heidegger's treatment of Book X, Lacoue-Labarthe says that inasmuch as mimesis "is linked to a certain turning of *Herstellung*, of installation," it is nonetheless a "*diversion* of (demiurgic) *poiesis*. That is to say, it is a *displacement*, a '*disinstallation*'" ("Typography" 85). Instead of mimesis being essentially opposed to *poiesis*, it is simply a diverted *poiesis*. Mimesis is a derivative, "fallen" form of *Herstellung*. Lost or misplaced—or subsumed (perhaps even exiled?)—in the revised series of derivations, however, is *Darstellung*, which no longer has a place. Mimesis, if it "is" anything, is a "bad" *poiesis* ("Typography" 86).

Something still puzzles Lacoue-Labarthe, however, and that is Heidegger's translation of *aletheia* as "*Unverstelltheit*," "non-distortion" (or "non-dissimulation") ("Typography" 79). Near the conclusion of his commentary on the *Republic*, Heidegger writes: "*The interpretation of Being as* eidos, *presencing in outward appearance, presupposes the interpretation of truth as* aletheia, *nondistortion*" (*Nietzsche* 1:182; original emphasis). As Lacoue-Labarthe sees it, by translating *aletheia* as *Unverstelltheit*, Heidegger reasserts the centrality of the *stele* in his interpretation. Doing so, however, also exposes the contortions Heidegger is willing to enact in order to maintain his reading of Plato (in the service of his reading of Nietzsche). For, as Lacoue-Labarthe holds, *Unverstelltheit* "does not translate *aletheia*." "If it translates anything," he says, "it would be rather *non-displacement, remaining-standing*, or *not-falling, non-instability*" ("Typography" 79; original emphasis). In a footnote to this correction, Lacoue-Labarthe adds "that *verstellen* ('to disinstall,' 'to displace,' 'to disarrange,' 'to mix up,' etc.) can also mean 'to counterfeit' or 'to disguise' (one's voice, one's gestures, one's writing)" ("Typography" 79n56). Nevertheless, Lacoue-Labarthe finds it curious—and telling—that Heidegger appears to appeal only to this translation of *aletheia* in relation to mimesis, whereas elsewhere (most famously in the artwork essay) he characterizes *aletheia* as unconcealment or unveiling (*Unverborgenheit*) ("Typography" 79–80). With this idiosyncratic act, Heidegger "submit[s] the *stele* to the law of unveiling," writes Lacoue-Labarthe. This, he asserts, is significant because, first, this means "it is not the erection [(the *stele*)] that unveils, but the unveiling that erects" ("Typography" 80). What this then means is "that all *Stellung*, in whatever form (beginning with *Darstellung*), can be interpreted only in terms of the initial (always prior) determination of the essence of truth as *aletheia*" ("Typography" 80). By subordinating the *stele* to *aletheia*, mimesis falls under the economy of truth by default. Heidegger thereby confirms to himself Plato's misinterpretation of *aletheia* as *homoiosis* but also sets himself up to mirror Plato ("Typography" 81).

In addition, Heidegger's translation of *aletheia* as *Unverstelltheit*, as the negation of dissimulation and disinstallation, has the odd effect of "installing" mimesis' "essence" as the originary condition that demiurgic *poiesis* "corrects." In this installation, then, we find a further oddity or even paradox: mimesis disappears as soon as its essence is determined, in other words, as soon as it is subject to judgment. With the characterization of *aletheia* as *Unverstelltheit*, the notion of mimesis as *verstellen* is emphasized, and its threat to truth is underscored, even as it is brought under control theoretically as a diversion of *Herstellung*. We thus are presented with the speculative trick, at least its first moment. The *stele* provides a means to fix mimesis, to stabilize that which is cast as instability as such, by submitting mimesis to the theoretical (i.e., speculative) gaze. Theory renders a decision regarding mimesis by telling us its essence. Fixing mimesis by establishing its essence—as *unheimlich*, as unstable—accomplishes its suppression and brings it under speculative control.

Except the theoretical can't do this, technically speaking. For if mimesis is dissimulation and disinstallation as such, then it must, by definition, frustrate all attempts to establish its essence. Mimesis will always escape any attempt to fix it in place because its essence is to masquerade as that which is other than it. Mimesis "is" always-already otherwise. Mimesis "is" not. This is mimesis' threat—both to knowledge and to the *politeia*—which is why it must be controlled.

Therefore, Heidegger's insertion of the *stele* into Plato's "mimetology," as Lacoue-Labarthe calls it ("Typography" 77, 81), is an indication of Heidegger having fallen for "a trap consisting of an artfully masked hole" designed, by Plato, to hide from view the mimetic *mise-en-abyme*, the fact of its essential inessentiality, its fundamental "undecideability." The shell game is fully underway once Plato gives legitimacy to the pretension, at the beginning of Book X, to be able to determine "what" mimesis is ("Typography" 89). But then as soon as he does so, the shells begin to be shuffled: where is mimesis actually to be located? What is its actual act? Is it the *tropos* of the mimetician who turns the mirror, or is it the mirror itself? And what of the painter? How is the painter equivalent to either the mimetician who turns the mirror or to the mirror itself? ("Typography"

87–88). The "what" becomes a "who," which in turn becomes a "what" again and a "who" once more.

Saying that mimesis "is" either the act of turning the mirror or the act of reflecting "performed" by the mirror preserves the Platonic contention that mimesis is nothing other than "pure passivity" (it doesn't "do" anything, thus its danger) ("Typography" 89), but then "what" actually is installed through mimesis? Where is the "work" of mimesis? In the metamorphoses of "whats" and "whos," "we discover here, after the fact, that the trick has consisted in speaking of the producing 'subject' (of the producer) in terms of the product. It has consisted in *displacing* the emphasis from the producer to the product, in minimizing this product . . . in order to be done with the producer" ("Typography" 90; original emphasis). Such had been Plato's aim all along, as Lacoue-Labarthe notes, in the "ancient discord, [the] long-standing difference (*palaia diaphora*—607b) between" philosophy and the tragic author ("Typography" 90). But why should Heidegger aid and abet Plato in this con to the degree that he does by injecting the *stele* and all its derivations (to the exclusion of *Darstellung*) into Plato's mimetology? In fact, declares Lacoue-Labarthe, Heidegger's failure to pick up on the ruse causes him to miss "a certain *fictioning* of the text (of the dialogue, if it is one), a certain *Erdichtung* which is its *Darstellung*" ("Typography" 91).

The conflation of the author with his work, perpetuated by Plato, is repeated by Heidegger and results in his failure to pose the question of the presentation of Plato's text. Heidegger's repetition here results in his failure to investigate the *Darstellung* of Plato's text, or rather, in a failure to investigate it *as Darstellung*. Nowhere do we find Heidegger pausing over *Republic* X as the presentation of a scene of the scenic's expulsion, as a spectacularization of mimesis ("Typography" 115). This spectacularization enacts a reversal. It is not mimesis that exercises the uncanny ability to change one thing into another and cause one to take one thing for another, including and especially the voice. Instead, theory is the magician. If Heidegger (not [only] Nietzsche) never overcomes metaphysics, it is because he never leaves theory, which itself has never escaped—can never escape—the threat of mimetic instability. We thus learn that the problem of mimesis has never been a problem of representation. It is not a problem of "properly" representing the object or the anxiety that representation never captures the object properly. It is not mimesis as representation that has been a problem for philosophy. Rather, mimesis has always been a problem *for* representation. It is that which undoes representation and gives the lie to the desire for the proper itself. Mimesis never allows the subject (of representation) to coincide, or align, "properly" with itself ("Typography" 133, 136). In his reading of Plato, then, Heidegger misses an opportunity to think the voice as mimesis and forge a true dissimulating experience of finitude.

THE VOICE OF THEORY

Following his critique of Heidegger's appropriation of mimesis in "Typography," Lacoue-Labarthe extends this critique to the ways the Western philosophical tradition has sought to master mimesis through its theorizations of music, particularly in the case of modern German thought. In taking music seriously, modern German thought appears to take mimesis seriously, as opposed to its dismissal by Plato. However, once again, Nietzsche and Heidegger play prominent roles in Lacoue-Labarthe's effort to demonstrate that the opposite is the case, where once again, a kind of "success" in theorizing music, in subjecting music to philosophical speculation, constitutes a success in mastering mimesis yet a failure to think it (and thus a failure to think the voice).

As Lacoue-Labarthe argues in his work *Musica Ficta*, Heidegger's repetition of Plato's mimetology—and thus, his repetition of speculative thought's project of suppressing mimesis—is not accidental but rather programmed into Heidegger's critique of aesthetics and metaphysics in general. The *Nietzsche* lecture "The Will to Power as Art" is central to Lacoue-Labarthe's analysis in *Musica Ficta* as well. Lacoue-Labarthe draws a line of continuity, first, between the *Republic* and Nietzsche's break with Richard Wagner, and then another line from Nietzsche to Heidegger and back to Plato. In short, according to Lacoue-Labarthe, Nietzsche follows Plato's critique of mimesis when he rejects Wagner's pursuit of a formless, affectively disappropriating, and *feminizing* Dionysian art in favour of a sobering Apollinian "style." Heidegger, in turn, will again follow Nietzsche (and thus also Plato once more) when he proceeds to *theorize* the artwork's essence as *Ge-stell*—a "properly virile" one that gives form (*Gestalt*) as opposed to the passive malleability of Wagnerian formlessness (*Musica Ficta* 105–7).

"It is thus an onto-typology," declares Lacoue-Labarthe, "that organizes the deconstruction of the aesthetic and forges Heidegger's complicity with Nietzsche contra Wagner—in all its political consequences" (*Musica Ficta* 109). This complicity includes adopting Nietzsche's position that Wagner's work constituted "a floundering devoid of measure and pace" (*Nietzsche* 1:88–89), that is to say, adds Lacoue-Labarthe, a lack of rhythm that figuration makes up for and corrects (*Musica Ficta* 109). Thus, what might appear to be an actual embrace of the musical and of mimesis—and which might exceed the economy of representation—in our previous review of Heidegger's conception of the work of art (the rift-design of world and earth, or the temporality of concealment and unconcealment [*aletheia*]) is actually anything but: such instances, according to Lacoue-Labarthe, are actually simulacra of mimesis.

Lacoue-Labarthe's claim becomes more convincing when we consider his essay "The Echo of the Subject," which deals specifically with music, rhythm, the voice, and their returns or haunting in Theodor Reik. There Lacoue-Labarthe demonstrates that rhythm and voice are invoked as prostheses to secure the stability of the subject of representation, where music (as a stand-in for mimesis in general) provokes a feeling of the subject's dissolution, and hence its death.[50] This is bad news for an idea of the voice (whether of conscience or of Being) as *unheimlich* and as a rupture to metaphysical subjectivity. Seen from this perspective, voice and rhythm are merely figures—simulacra—of mimesis. As Lacoue-Labarthe claims in the concluding section to "Typography," suppressing mimesis through the shell game of the *stele* is only one part of Heidegger's perpetuation of speculative (i.e., metaphysical) thought. What should take on the characteristics of mimesis once it has been theorized, spectacularized, and brought under control but *aletheia* itself as the figure of an "anonymous voice" ("Typography" 119). What Heidegger's text suffers from is an affliction inherited from Plato: "It is . . . the moment . . . wherein *aletheia* and mimesis resemble each other and are, literally, in *homoiosis*" ("Typography" 121).

Aletheia thus represents an attempt to install a pure voice that would not be subject to mimesis' instability (137, 139). In a subsection of "Typography" named "The Unstable," Lacoue-Labarthe pushes forward with a reading of René Girard in order to show how Plato casts mimesis as a "scapegoat" for the instability of language itself. In so doing, Plato can install the philosophical logos in mimesis' place and thereby secure the logos' authority. Although Lacoue-Labarthe does not return to Heidegger again in the essay, Heidegger's repetition of Plato's speculative capture—the speculative capture of mimesis but also the theory of mimesis as a result of being captured by the specular, which is to say, by theory—suggests strongly that the voice in Heidegger is only an apparent escape from the economy of representation. Instead, the voice offers structural reinforcement for this economy; it is the "voice" as theory.[51]

The reinforcement of theory through the voice is thus a symptom of what Lacoue-Labarthe describes in his essay "Transcendence Ends in

Politics" as "Heidegger's constant refusal . . . to take seriously the concept of *mimesis*."⁵² As a consequence of this refusal, argues Lacoue-Labarthe, Heidegger prevents himself from seeing the political gesture that grounds his privileging of the philosophical, or what Lacoue-Labarthe says is his "overvalorization" of the philosophical ("Transcendence" 288). The political in this respect is the "fundamental *mimetology*" that governs Heidegger's adjudication of essence ("Transcendence" 297–98). The possibility of breaking free of this fundamental mimetology, and of thinking what Lacoue-Labarthe and Nancy will name the *retrait* (retreat/retrace/withdrawal) of the political, is what animates their debate on the scenic.

THE RETREAT OF THE SCENE

"*Scène*" (1972) and "*Dialogue sur le dialogue*" (2005), the two sets of letter exchanges in which Nancy and Lacoue-Labarthe hold their debate on the status of the scenic and the figure, promise to bring into focus their long-standing opposition regarding the possibility of breaking free from the specular. Of course, such focus never comes into view; the exchanges instead intensify the distinction between Lacoue-Labarthe's insistence on the necessity of "de-figuration"⁵³ and Nancy's pursuit of the "interruption of myth" ("Scene" 274). In fact, even the question of whether the scene and the figure are different or the same is a matter of disagreement. Nevertheless, the two exchanges rehearse the main points of contention sustained between the two, and as a result, offer a kind of map for reading their respective bodies of work. However, while the letters convincingly convey the fact of their disagreement on the figure, they distract from another fact: their collaborative writings strive to theorize the figure's *retrait*.⁵⁴ So while reading their exchanges on the scenic and the figure is instructive, it will be even more prudent to ask how their respective positions may be reconciled with their demonstrated shared interest in realizing the *retrait* of the figure. For it is specifically through their formulation of a "*retrait* of the political" that they imagine an other practice of writing, one that we will see Blanchot take up as a project.

After summarizing their opposing positions in his opening letter of "Scene," Nancy attempts to "re-stage" their debate according to their respective takes on Aristotle's conception of the *opsis* (stage) in the *Poetics*. There, Nancy recounts, Aristotle presents two contradicting descriptions of the *opsis* and the nature of its participation in the tragic effect of catharsis. In one respect, Aristotle says the *opsis* is a prerequisite for catharsis; no catharsis can be achieved without there being a scene presented to the spectator. Implied in this claim is the idea that there is no presentation without a stage. Yet in another respect, Aristotle also describes the tragic effect as being achievable through the act of reading alone, "even without enactment and without actors (50b18)" ("Scene" 273). These opposing accounts come to stand for Lacoue-Labarthe's and Nancy's respective positions regarding the figure; the question of the *opsis'* necessity for the tragic presentation seems here to signal the larger question of whether Being requires figuration in order to come to presence. Thus, Nancy claims he "always take[s] the side of the *opsis*" to the extent he finds no issue with the necessity of the stage. This necessity, he goes on to say, can be referred to as Being's "archi-necessity," as an *"ontological mimēsis"* ("Scene" 285; original emphasis). Mimesis in this sense is not representation but *Darstellung*, presentation, as well as enunciation. In this way, Nancy is not far from the meaning of mimesis Lacoue-Labarthe appears to want to recover in "Typography." Furthermore, in arguing for this archi-necessity, Nancy critically revises Lacoue-Labarthe's charge of onto-typology against the speculative tradition. For, Nancy asserts, a stage is requisite for figures to appear, but it does not follow that figures must appear on a stage. When figuration does take place in the form of myth, then it becomes imperative to interrupt myth, cutting the figure, in order to "[delineate] another area of enunciation" ("Scene" 274).

By contrast, according to Nancy, Lacoue-Labarthe falls on the side of the "solitary reading," for Aristotle's apparent devalorization of the *opsis* in his description of the tragic effect as being achievable through the text alone implies a nonrepresentational appearance of Being. The solitary reading therefore aligns with Lacoue-Labarthe's call for "de-figuration" ("Scene" 274). In sum, Nancy suggests, their debate concerns the status of the figure; it is either a mode of enunciation or one of representation. Conceiving the figure as a site of enunciation, as Nancy advocates, leaves open the possibility of it exceeding the onto-typological order of representation.

Nancy implies it is possible to acknowledge the necessity of the stage without having to commit to figuration, but Lacoue-Labarthe is not so certain. He responds with a correction to Nancy's translation; *opsis* does not mean "stage" but rather "performance" (*spectacle*) ("Scene" 277). Rereading the *Poetics* with *opsis* translated in this manner reveals no inconsistency or contradiction, says Lacoue-Labarthe. More to the point, what has primacy, he states, is not the *opsis*; rather, it is the enunciation upon which any performance is based. Such primacy of enunciation, Lacoue-Labarthe suggests, "defines a sort of *archi-theater*" ("Scene" 279; original emphasis). So, in a way, Lacoue-Labarthe does not see himself disagreeing with Nancy on the necessity of enunciation. The question for him is, instead, "how to break the performance" ("Scene" 280).

What does "breaking the performance" mean? Lacoue-Labarthe proceeds to clarify that Nancy is right to raise questions about Lacoue-Labarthe's "suspicion" toward onto-typology. However, Lacoue-Labarthe qualifies that when he speaks of "de-figuration," he is repeating Benjamin's notion of the "*Verlagerung des Mythologischen,* deposition of the mythological" ("Scene" 281). This deposition, Lacoue-Labarthe says, needs to be realized along two slopes: one concerns "the figural petrification" of the enunciation and the other the petrification of the poet into a figure that stands "between gods and men (the people)" ("Scene" 281). This is to say that Lacoue-Labarthe is calling less for the avoidance of figurality in his call for de-figuration than the disruption of figuration, which he actually conceives as a "broadening" of the figure. "The freedom of a new enunciation," he writes, "implies the deconstruction (*déconstruction*) of a previous figure" ("Scene" 281).

How to proceed, then, if the matter is one of embracing the inevitable fact of ontological mimesis or figurality while at the same time guarding against the "petrification of the figure" into figuration or onto-typology? Nancy suggests a need to confront a tension "between spectacularity and effacement" as a way to view the problem ("Scene" 285). But how much guidance such a view provides remains a question, for although "this ontological figurality would not come under what you have christened 'onto-typology,'" writes Nancy, "it would resemble it" ("Scene" 285–86).[55]

In many respects, it seems Nancy and Lacoue-Labarthe are in agreement, especially given Lacoue-Labarthe's distinction between figurality and figuration. Nonetheless, Lacoue-Labarthe persists in questioning "the necessity of the figure" ("Scene" 295). He repeats observations we saw in "Typography," as well as elsewhere,[56] in which he takes note of metaphysical thought's peculiar drive to imagine itself through the figure, even at the moment of its closure or so-called overcoming: these include the figures of Plato's Socrates, Christ, Nietzsche's Zarathustra, Freud's Oedipus, Marx's proletariat, Jung's working class, and Bataille's Acephalus ("Scene" 296).[57] The "modern" set of figures is especially instructive. They present themselves as transcending the religious, yet they nonetheless retain mythological status and consequently reveal the failure of modern thought to break free from onto-theology. Thus, Lacoue-Labarthe is convinced that "our task . . . is to be resolutely *atheist,* even—or first of all—in our writing, that is in our manner of speaking" ("Scene" 292).

In "*Dialogue sur le dialogue*," Lacoue-Labarthe returns to the theme of atheism, this time emphasizing it more strongly as a needed response to the theoretical impulse as such. To the extent that "theory" names a certain desire for presence and drive to re-present, it embodies, and is embodied by, the *theos* in a mode similar to the theater's ("*Dialogue*" 79). But instead of following Heidegger, who, as Lacoue-Labarthe notes, recovers the *theos* and the *thea* from theory for a thought of aletheia in his critique of science, Lacoue-Labarthe calls for an "*atheo-logic*," an "atheology" ("*Dialogue*" 79, 85). However, is such an atheological writing possible? And what would it look like? Could it still go by the name of "theory"? Once again, we are brought back to the problem of how to realize a practice of de-figuration that would reliably destabilize, or dissimulate, the "archi-theater" to which Lacoue-Labarthe insists all thinking is subject. Nancy's proposal to oppose the "theo-logical" character of theory with the "dia-logical" character of *partage* is not enough to overcome this fate of thought, claims Lacoue-Labarthe. As an example, Lacoue-Labarthe points to Plato's dialogues as a theatricalization of *sophia*, which, he says, constructs the mythologization of philosophy ("*Dialogue*" 81).

Elsewhere in their exchange, Nancy describes his figure to counter the "theo-logical" as an "archi-dialogue," and he compares it against Lacoue-Labarthe's notion of archi-theater ("*Dialogue*"104–5). Nancy appeals to the linkages he has made in his work between *partage* and the plurality of the arts, while Lacoue-Labarthe responds by pulling this supposed plurality back under the primacy of an archi-theater: "all art begins by 'making a scene' [*faire une scène*]," he says ("*Dialogue*" 92). This "onto-theo-logical" *différend*, as Lacoue-Labarthe refers to it, between him and Nancy continues much in the way we saw in the debate in "Scene" until Nancy makes a very interesting remark, not on the question of theater's relation to the other arts or on the difference between theater and dialogue but on the notion of the "archi-" as such. Why, Nancy asks, the prefix—and "pre-fixation" on—"archi-"? Is Lacoue-Labarthe's invocation of the "archi-" an allusion to Derrida's notion of "*archi-écriture*"? If so, then Nancy suggests it is a misinterpretation ("*Dialogue*" 88, 105).

Nancy does not pursue this charge of misinterpretation much further, but his question regarding Lacoue-Labarthe's repeated appeal to an "archi-event" nonetheless touches on an essential difference between Derrida's formulation of *archi-écriture* and Lacoue-Labarthe's delineation of archi-theater. As Rodolphe Gasché has outlined, *archi-écriture* is Derrida's reconfiguration of Heidegger's conception of the withdrawal of Being as *Entziehung/Entzug* into the notion of the *retrait* (retrace/retreat/withdrawal) of "the text."[58] Even though the *retrait* repeats Heidegger's casting of the question of Being as a self-effacing movement,[59] the primary distinction between the question of Being and the "being" of the text is that there is, "properly speaking," no phenomenology of the latter ("Joining the Text" 168–70). By not appearing, or by only appearing in its retreat, the text opens onto an experience of the closure of metaphysics, in a way, more fully than the question of Being, which remains subject to a phenomenology of Being and therefore within the region of metaphysics ("Joining the Text" 173). Insofar as *there is* the text, the text is *not* ("Joining the Text" 170).

Derrida's notion of the text leaves open as a possibility a thought of writing that would not—indeed could not—be recuperated completely by onto-typology. It is thus the Derridean concept of the text that seems to underwrite Nancy's call for the interruption of myth (as opposed to Lacoue-Labarthe's call for de-figuration/demythologization). While an atheistic writing may not be possible within philosophy, it may be possible from a writing that engages the writing of philosophy, just as Derrida's "text" re-marks the word "Being" ("Joining the Text" 173). However, as we have seen, the metaphysical worry Lacoue-Labarthe harbors about philosophy as speculative thought finds its stakes in a worry about the political following Heidegger's *Destruktion* of the history of ontology (from which, not coincidentally, at least according to one account, the name "deconstruction" draws its development[60]). Philosophy's onto-theological reliance on the figure, on onto-typology, passes into a reliance on a political mode of appearance, the appearance of philosophy as the appearance of the political, or, as Lacoue-Labarthe and Nancy write in their "Opening Address to the Centre for Philosophical Research on the Political," "the philosophical *as* the political" (*Retreating the Political* 110). What unites the philosophical and the political in their schema seems to have less to do with the fact that they both appear and concerns instead the matter of how they comport to appearance as such. Their respective reliance on onto-typology indicates an unthought and unconscious relation to appearance.[61]

To the extent that Heidegger's attempts to think the closure of metaphysics stand also as the completion of metaphysics, they are at once the closure of the political and its completion (*Retreating the Political* 110). Lacoue-Labarthe and Nancy agree that at the limit of both philosophy and the political stands the figure, as well as the question of writing. What they seek to engage with through the concept of the *retrait* is the retrace, retreat, and withdrawal of the political, insofar as it fails to appear as a question, as well as the exigency of re-marking/re-tracing the political, insofar as it appears in its withdrawal (*Retreating the Political* 112). This re-marking or re-tracing is writing in the Derridean sense, not a positive installation of a program to be executed but a disinstallation—a mimesis—of any metaphysical ground of the political and of the social (*Retreating the Political* 120). The *retrait* is a writing in the "form" of dis-identification—with and through the figure but also with and through the subject, the people, and what Lacoue-Labarthe and Nancy refer to, in a reading of Freud, the Father (*Retreating the Political* 118–19). The *retrait* is a writing of the excess of the political—its trace, the political *as* trace—whose movement Lacoue-Labarthe and Nancy thus identify with "the mother" (*Retreating the Political* 119; 133–34), or, as they introduce it elsewhere, "a more obscure maternal instance."[62] As Lacoue-Labarthe and Nancy quickly acknowledge, this "mother" can easily slip back into the figure of the Father as soon as one opposes the two. Thus, they advance an image of the de-figuring "maternal instance" as the opening of the "*outre-mère*" (beyond-mother), "an identification with the withdrawal of identity" ("The Unconscious" 203).

Is the "identification with the withdrawal of identification," with the *retrait*, the same as effacement?[63] Or mimesis? Is such a strategy sufficient to "dis-articulate" the coreinforcing rhythms of philosophy and the political and bring about a caesura of the speculative like the one Lacoue-Labarthe uncovers in Hölderlin's theorization of the tragic transport? ("Caesura" 234–35). And yet, why (still) an invocation of the figure of "the mother," or the feminine? As we have seen Lacoue-Labarthe remark throughout his critique of figuration and the scenic character of the speculative, the identification of mimesis, death, and the feminine with one another belongs to the process by which theory establishes itself as foundational against an outside that is posited as threatening all foundation.[64] What, then, does it mean for Lacoue-Labarthe and Nancy to repeat this process—to put the feminine to "use" as a figure—even as they acknowledge it critically?

Since these questions concern theory's use of the feminine not only to found but also to reproduce itself (appropriating the reproductive essence that theory, as Father, assigns the feminine[65]), Lacoue-Labarthe and Nancy's invocation of the figure of "the mother" (even in lowercase) raises the problem of how their practice of writing can be exempt from theory's speculative, appropriating gaze. This is a problem that haunts the question of what it means to write following Heidegger, for, as Luce Irigaray and Avital Ronell have shown,[66] Heidegger, too, repeats philosophy's appropriation of the feminine in his theorizations of human finitude. In the following chapters, we will further chart these various vectors of haunting and the extent to which Blanchot and Deleuze are able to confront them as questions of writing in their respective inheritances of the Heideggerian voice and the problem of speculative thought's drive to master mimesis as a drive to master difference.

Part 3
Blanchot

Chapter 5

The Other Night of the Voice

Désoeuvrement, Effacement,
and the Limit-Experience of the Outside

The previous chapter on Nancy and Lacoue-Labarthe raised questions about the status of the voice in Heidegger's thought, specifically his use of the voice as a figure both for the relation between language and human finitude, and for recovering the question of Being as an affective experience of difference. As the debate between Nancy and Lacoue-Labarthe demonstrates, Heidegger's reliance on figuration for capturing the human Dasein's affective relation, in language, to Being—from the voice of conscience in the analytic of Dasein in *Being and Time* to the movement of *aletheia* in the reflections on the work of art—appears to replicate the metaphysics of presence that Heidegger sought to undo with his invocation of the voice. Although the ecstatic structure of the voice of conscience dissimulates the self-presence presupposed by the notion of the metaphysical subject, and although the voice's return in the rhythmic appearance and withdrawal of *aletheia* in the artwork denies the objectification of Being, Heidegger nevertheless insists that the experiences of difference that these two events of the voice designate must appear through some form (*Gestalt*). As we saw, in "The Origin of the Work of Art," Heidegger actually employs the language of figuration (*Gestaltung*) to describe the process by which truth as *aletheia* is enacted in the work. While we saw that Nancy and Lacoue-Labarthe differ on how exactly to respond to this metaphysical repetition in Heidegger's thought, they nonetheless agree on a number of points: that the repetition is a continuation of philosophy's speculative drive to master mimesis, and therefore, the becoming of Being; that Heidegger's perpetuation of metaphysical speculation is tied to his attraction to National Socialism's specular economy, thereby exposing an inextricable link between the philosophical and the political; and that what is consequently called for is a practice of writing that brings about the *retrait* (retreat/retrace/withdrawal) of the figure.

Where we saw Nancy and Lacoue-Labarthe disagree, however, was on the nature of this other mode of writing. Should it embrace the necessity of what Nancy calls "ontological mimesis" (the idea that figuration is inevitable) and treat itself as always provisional, always needing to be rewritten under a new set of figures? Or should it refuse figuration and the drive to onto-typology altogether, as Lacoue-Labarthe maintains, by submitting to a logic of self-effacement? By embracing figuration, Nancy's approach can be seen as soliciting the dissimulating force of mimesis, even celebrating it as a force of becoming that ultimately undoes—or rather, "unworks"—philosophy's various attempts to master it. By contrast, Lacoue-Labarthe's posture is one of refusal and lament, teetering almost on melancholia, as he appears to regard mimesis as an ever-receding, ungraspable event of difference. In our review of his writings, we encountered a number of limit-concepts that Lacoue-Labarthe employs to evoke the effacement of the figure, deflect the penetrating gaze of metaphysical speculation, and inhabit a space outside the economy of representation: caesura, de-figuration, demythologization, *retrait*. In fact, later, toward the end of his life, he gravitates toward a term that appears twenty-five years in the making—*phrase*—which also sounds another affective register that connects directly to the thought of Maurice Blanchot, the subject of our present chapter. As we will see, that register, which Lacoue-Labarthe names *l'émoi*—dismay, turmoil—indicates just how close his attraction to the exigency of effacement approximates that of Blanchot's.[1]

Beyond Lacoue-Labarthe's immediate connection to Blanchot, though, and rather than a simple critique of Heidegger, the debate between Nancy and Lacoue-Labarthe on the metaphysics of the figure offers a useful schema for viewing contemporary Continental thought as inheriting, responding to, and transforming Heidegger's conceptualization of the voice. It is a schema that will aid us in situating Blanchot's relation to Heidegger's thought.

In one respect, Heidegger's conceptualization of the voice as a figure of the human Dasein's affective relation to language and finitude sets contemporary Continental thought on a course focusing on the question of language (commonly referred to as the "linguistic turn"), as well as the question of the boundaries between philosophy and literature. In another respect, Heidegger's positing of the voice as part of his project of the destructuring (*Destruktion*) of metaphysics, including his self-acknowledged struggle to realize this project at the limit of (but nonetheless still from within) the discourse of metaphysics, has exposed his thought to the very destructuring he inaugurated. The critical movement known as deconstruction, as we noted in the conclusion to chapter 4, can be understood both as part of Continental thought's inheritance of Heidegger's project of *Destruktion* and also as a critique that identifies Heidegger's work as a discourse in need of deconstructive reading itself, particularly as it concerns the social-political implications of his work's unavoidable repetition of the metaphysics of presence. While the reflections Nancy and Lacoue-Labarthe undertake follow both of these critical vectors, it is the latter that informs their interrogation of the figure and the problem of how to write "after Heidegger" in ways that honor the affective relation between language and human finitude without perpetuating metaphysics' speculative economy of presence and becoming entranced by what Walter Benjamin, as part of his own reflection on the work of art, famously referred to as the "aestheticization" of the political.

However, as I indicate in my previous chapter's opening remarks, and as I also reiterate in its concluding section, Nancy's and Lacoue-Labarthe's respective approaches to the question of writing after Heidegger can also be seen as delineating two distinct paths pursued by Continental thinkers that specifically elaborate the Heideggerian problematic of the voice but in a decisively critical way. Of the Continental thinkers whose writings reflect this engagement with Heidegger, Maurice Blanchot and Gilles Deleuze exemplify sustained commitments both to Heidegger's theorization of the voice as a figure of the affective relation between language and human finitude and to the exigency of writing otherwise in response to the closure of metaphysics that Heidegger's corpus at once inaugurates and yet also extends. My closing chapters in this study attend to Blanchot and Deleuze as inheritors of the Heideggerian voice who also enact critical transformations of Heidegger's conception of the voice in ways that realize the modes of writing for which Nancy and Lacoue-Labarthe each call in their respective critiques of the figure. Deleuze, who is the focus of my concluding chapter, promotes an image of the voice in writing as an "eternal return" of the figure and thus, in his view, as a solicitation of Being's becoming. His conception of the voice, I will show, therefore resonates with Nancy's embrace of the inevitability of figuration. By contrast, Blanchot pursues both a conception and a practice of writing as an event of the voice's effacement—that is to say, of the voice *as* effacement—that brings forth the encounter with language as a most severe experience of finitude, as an experience of the limit of experience. The image of the voice Blanchot elicits is one of absolute disquiet, of absolute refusal; it is one that, as we will see, he casts as atheistic, approaching in many ways the atheism called for by Lacoue-Labarthe in his desire to escape figuration's speculative economy.[2]

The aim of the present chapter is to dwell in the disquiet of Blanchot's voice—what I call its "other night"—and to do so by showing how Blanchot forges this disquiet through a specific inversion (as in *Umkehrung*) of the trajectory Heidegger follows in his conception of the voice. Where Heidegger begins with the voice of conscience in order to arrive at the voice's return in the work of art, Blanchot begins with "the Work" (*l'Oeuvre*) of literature in order to arrive at what he names "the narrative voice." Yet, I read Blanchot's critical inversion as less a rejection of the Heideggerian voice than an intensification of it, especially in terms of Heidegger's emphasis on the experience with language as a condition of an affective encounter with the sense/meaning of Being, as in Dasein's understanding of the sense/meaning of Being as a condition for Being-in-the-world and for being able to hear and be touched by the call of conscience. As I will show, with Blanchot, this emphasis becomes intensified in his description of the writer's experience with the Work and with the event of writing, which he characterizes in terms of an affective alteration among states of passivity, fatigue, *malheur* (affliction, distress, pain), and *impouvoir* (nonpower, impotence), all of which perhaps inspire Lacoue-Labarthe's meditation on dismay/turmoil. This existential affectivity arises from the event of unworking (*désoeuvrement*) (a connection he shares with Nancy) that Blanchot characterizes as the passage from Work to voice and that ultimately results in the writer's dispropriating alienation from themselves, the Work, and language itself. Denied the shelter of interior subjectivity by this event of the Work, the writer is exposed to what Blanchot calls the limit-experience of "the outside" (*le dehors*) and "the neuter."

Taken together, these unfolding connections in the movement from Work to voice constitute a scene of ecstasis, and thus a scene of finitude, much more extreme than any offered by Heidegger. So although the scenes of finitude given by Heidegger destabilize the unity of the metaphysical subject, they nonetheless rest on an image of finitude as a relation to the possibility of Dasein's impossibility, its death; in so doing, Heidegger also preserves an idea of a relation between Being and human being. Blanchot's scenes, however, overturn that conception of finitude by casting finitude as the impossibility of possibility. They refuse any relation whatsoever: they stage a nonrelation beyond the economy of Being and nonbeing. Thus, we will be presented with the possibility of a scene beyond the figure. Where figuration and the scenic seem to collapse in the debate between Nancy and Lacoue-Labarthe, Blanchot appears to say that the scene is not the figure.

Given the sheer breadth and complexity of Blanchot's oeuvre, which extends over multiple forms—including literature, philosophy, theory, as well as journalism—this chapter will not attempt a comprehensive presentation of his work. Instead, it will focus on moments in his theoretical writings that I consider foundational for his project of reconceptualizing the concept of the voice from a reconceptualization of the work of art. My analysis will concentrate on these "steps" Blanchot takes realizing the passage from the Work to the voice,[3] specifically in *The Work of Fire* (1949), *The Space of Literature* (1955), and *The Infinite Conversation* (1969). But I will also give sustained attention to his short essay "Artaud" (1956), which not only plots many of the concepts just named through the scene of Artaud's anguished alienation from his own work but does so through one of Blanchot's more explicit engagements with Heidegger, specifically, Heidegger's *What Is Called Thinking?* (1954). (As we will see in chapter 6, this is a connection that attracted a great deal of interest from Deleuze as well.)

The approach I am taking to Blanchot's work in this chapter is limited to his inheritance and critical transformation of the Heideggerian voice. In so doing, my aim is to avoid giving his corpus an appearance of philosophical systematicity. It is precisely because his oeuvre unfolds as an assemblage of ever-returning scenes that troubles the boundaries between philosophy, theory, and literature that it is invaluable for appreciating its intervention in what we have learned is at stake in the question of the voice—namely, an experience of finitude, in language, free of mimetic mastery. As we saw from Nancy's and Lacoue-Labarthe's respective critiques of the figure, the ability for mimesis to appear as mimesis and not under the concept through which philosophy has historically tried to master it is not incidental to the question of finitude; it is instead a condition for the possibility of recovering an experience of finitude as an experience of radical difference—difference *as* difference and not difference in relation to the identity of "the Same" (as we will see Blanchot refer to it). Which is to say that despite the resistances to Heidegger documented in this study's final chapters, the essential connection between the question of finitude and the question of language that Heidegger establishes with his conception of the voice continues as a project that his readers nonetheless seek to carry forth.

My plan is to reconstruct the constellation of scenes through which Blanchot elaborates the Work as an event that clears the space for the experience of finitude and difference that mimesis names, pausing in particular on the Work's power to dissimulate the metaphysical subject and consign the human to a state of radical passivity—and thus radical finitude. In the wake of the Work, Blanchot tells us, there is a voice; however, what speaks is neither Dasein nor Being but language as neither Being nor nonbeing. By leading us through an experience of the Work as a fundamental unworking, Blanchot "en-scenes" us within the unfolding of mimesis itself, of which his own work is necessarily a part, not merely a description. The challenge Blanchot's enactment of the voice presents, then, which this chapter takes up, is to offer a logic of Blanchot's presentation of mimesis while preserving an appreciation of his work as an enactment of "the Work." This is to say, the exigency of Blanchot's oeuvre, its demand, is not to approach it as offering a theory of the voice but to experience it as the voice of *désoeuvrement*.

The Voice of Writing: An Atheistic Interruption

Blanchot's essay "Atheism and Writing. Humanism and the Cry" from *The Infinite Conversation* constitutes an instructive point of departure for studying his reconfiguration of the voice.[4] In addition to developing many of the themes that Blanchot unfolds in *The Infinite Conversation* overall, it also elaborates ones he had begun to theorize in earlier writings. These include writing, the Work, *désoeuvrement*, the outside, and the neuter. Blanchot identifies these themes as crucial to the possibility of realizing a nonmetaphysical conception of the voice distinct from what he describes as Heidegger's "faithful belonging to the ontological logos" (IC 261). In this way, "Atheism and Writing" signals its intersection with the general critique of the persistence of onto-theology in Heidegger's thought; yet, in stating through its title a focus on the relationship between atheism and writing, it also suggests a connection to the problem of an atheistic writing that we saw Lacoue-Labarthe evoke in the concluding sections of chapter 4.

As Blanchot conveys in the essay's opening, he had been motivated to take up the theme of atheism by Foucault's *The Order of Things* (*Les Mots et les choses* [1966]), which had then just been published. He was inspired specifically by the critical reaction generated by Foucault's controversial declaration in the book's conclusion that "man" is a "recent" (i.e., modern) invention that came about with the very disciplines designed to analyze "him" (IC 246–47).[5] Blanchot characterizes the critical reaction as a form of paranoid panic around the implications of Foucault's claim, namely, that by exposing man as an invention of modern thought, man will cease to exist along with the humanism that elevates the figure of man as a replacement for the theological worldview of previous epochs (IC 247).

However, Blanchot is surprised by these critics' attachment to humanism. Who among serious thinkers, he wonders, ever really took humanism seriously? (IC 247). Had it not, ever since its championing by those such as Feuerbach, "been constantly knocked about and rejected by all important research"? (IC 247). For that matter, what does it even mean to "believe" in humanism in the first place? What is there in humanism to believe in?

These last two questions prompt Blanchot to revisit the event of the death of God as proclaimed by Nietzsche and the way that proclamation appears to announce the advent of humanism. But he finds in Feuerbach's humanism, which centers man as "truth" and "absolute being" (IC 247), a curious insistence of the theological. With humanism, Blanchot observes, not only has "religious man . . . taken his own nature as object" (IC 247); he has simultaneously transferred onto that object qualities that were previously attributed to God (IC 253). This is one reason why Nietzsche, according to Blanchot, lists the death of man as part of the sequence following from the death of God: God's death leads to man's death, which then allows for the arrival of "the overman" (*der Übermensch*). However, Blanchot notes that throughout this sequence in Nietzsche, the figure of man persists. Man is preserved "as future, a future that always returns" (IC 247). If, as Nietzsche holds, God is a creation of man, and if God's death permits man to take God's place, then God's death is nothing more than a direct reappearance of man to himself. As Blanchot argues, the death of God is the eternal return of man—man as eternal return.

Yet Feuerbach's brand of humanism shows something more. Beyond man as eternal (narcissistic) return, what also returns in humanism is the theological. But not in the sense that man simply takes up the place opened by God's death and assumes God's powers. Rather, instead of regarding the theological as solely a mythic creation of man, Blanchot argues that "humanism is a theological myth," a myth that serves the purpose of distracting us from the fact that "man is but the pseudonym of a God who dies in order to be reborn in his creature" (IC 248). "Hence," Blanchot writes, humanism's "attraction and usefulness (God is in turn called up in human form so he may work at constructing the world: compensation for the long while man lived in working for the other world) but also its weighty simplicity. To meddle with man is to meddle with God" (IC 248). Humanism is nothing more than the continuation of the theological by other means—and vice versa. Together, they form an entrenched ideological mimetic economy.

By exposing the opposition between the theological and humanism as a false one, Blanchot reveals the investments informing the paranoid attachments of humanism's adherents. But if the aim of critical thought is still that of ridding itself of onto-theology, then it now becomes even more urgent to bring about humanism's eclipse—and therefore onto-theology's as well—through a critique of the onto-theological structures upon which humanism has built and maintains itself. As Blanchot notes, the divine attributes transferred onto man by humanism after the death of God are transferred onto his "tools" as well, most immediately in the form of "a speech that sees and says meaning, [and] a speaking gaze that reads it" (IC 253). Here, Blanchot reads Foucault's intervention in *The Order of Things* for the way it exposes the human sciences as being constructed through a discourse that positions man as the object and subject of knowledge simultaneously, while also masking its status as discourse in order to give the appearance of direct empirical access to the object it claims to be able to know (i.e., "Man"). This discursive operation results in a curious contradiction, says Blanchot, where scientific discourse not only disavows its role in humanism's narcissistic economy and its existence as discourse; it also denies the reality of language. For in elevating itself to "a univocal language," to "a single voice that says the Same and represents it identically" with the objects it aspires to grasp (IC 254), scientific discourse takes on an orderly character that is the opposite of language, which, as Blanchot establishes at the outset of *The Infinite Conversation*, is one of difference and discontinuity (IC 3–10). By reifying language into a monolithic voice (as in the voice of "Science," for example), scientific discourse obscures the voice of difference in language and obediently serves as a vehicle for humanism's onto-theological self-mirroring.

By now, it should be clear that the relationship between writing and atheism that Blanchot is pursuing is not accidental. It is rather an essential one. Given the way that language is made to carry out an onto-theological project under humanism, the question of writing *is* the question of atheism. Is an atheistic writing possible at all? Under what conditions would it be able to appear? Or rather—is writing atheistic in its essence? In which case it would not only be necessary to oppose language and writing but also to contend that the task of writing is to dissemble the onto-theological dimension of language.

Blanchot argues the latter of these alternatives, proposing writing as an interruption of the onto-theological and of the humanist speculative discourse through which it disguises itself. "Let us now," he says,

> attempt to ask of discourse what would happen to it if it were possible for it to break free of the domination exercised by the theological, be it in the humanized form of atheism. It may well come down to asking whether *to write* is not, from the start and before anything else, to interrupt what has not ceased to reach us as *light*; to ask as well if *writing* is not, always from the start and before all else, to hold oneself, by way of this interruption, in relation with the *Neutral* [*le* Neutre] (or in a neutral relation): without reference to the Same, without reference to the One, outside everything visible and everything invisible. (IC 256/EI 384; original emphasis)

With this brief, deceptively simple proposal, Blanchot imbues writing with the power (which we will see him call elsewhere a "non-power" or *impouvoir*) "to interrupt what has not ceased to reach us as *light*," and to operate in a realm "outside everything visible and everything invisible." Of course, it is onto-theological discourse, such as the discourse of scientific rationality, that trades in light in its pretensions to conjure Being to appear as an immediate presence via a "speech that sees and says meaning, [and] a speaking gaze that reads it" (IC 253). So that which writing interrupts is none other than the speculative economy of presence—of Being *and* nonbeing, of visibility *and* invisibility—at the heart of the metaphysical enterprise that constitutes Western thought. Writing, Blanchot submits, is "outside" this economy. Writing occupies the space of the neuter.

But the reason why this statement on writing remains deceptively simple is twofold. It is composed of extensive formulations that emerge from long conceptual meditations that Blanchot conducts across two of his earlier theoretical works, *The Work of Fire* and *The Space of Literature*, two texts that we will need to consider if we are to approach the full measure of the power he ascribes to writing. At the same time, and more crucial to the question of the possibility of an atheistic writing he explores in the present piece, Blanchot's statement only hints at one of the most devastating implications of the conceptualization he outlines. If, as he goes on to state, this conceptualization is "fraught with writing" (IC 257)—that is, if it is in tension with the very writing that allows its articulation—then this is because, by lying outside the economy of Being and nonbeing, writing, "properly" speaking, neither *is* nor *is not*, "is" neither present nor absent. It is perhaps and not coincidentally like mimesis, the improper par excellence, the name for impossibility as such, and as such, that which resists any writing that attempts to capture it, including the very conceptualization Blanchot proffers in this statement on writing's interruptive force.

The impossibility that writing names serves as the nonground of what Blanchot posits as an other voice that dissembles the onto-theological voice of scientific discourse and its fantasy of univocity. This other voice of writing is what Blanchot will call "the narrative voice" (IC 379–87), and because it "speaks" from outside the onto-theological economy, it is a speech that neither sees (i.e., trades in light and exercises a speculative gaze) nor emits a sound that can be heard. It is a speech that does not speak (IC 261).

This formulation of the narrative voice as a speech that does not speak is reminiscent of Heidegger's conception of the voice of conscience as a silent voice that communicates nothing.[6] However, Blanchot is careful to mark a distinction between himself and Heidegger here. In one of the rare instances where Blanchot makes direct reference to Heidegger by name, he writes, "Writing conceives itself on the basis neither of vocal nor of visible manifestation, these being merely opposed through a complicitous opposition that is roused where Appearing [*l'Apparaître*] reigns as meaning, and light as presence: the pure visibility that is also pure audibility. And this is why Heidegger, in his faithful belonging to the ontological logos, can still affirm that thought is a seizing by hearing that seizes by way of the gaze" (IC 261). Like Lacoue-Labarthe, Blanchot regards Heidegger as maintaining allegiance to the metaphysics of presence and remaining committed to the logic of appearance, which Blanchot reminds us encompasses not just the specular but also the aural.[7] For this reason, the conception of writing he puts forth extends the disruptive power he ascribes to speech elsewhere in *The Infinite Conversation* in a chapter titled "Speaking Is Not Seeing" (IC 25–32).[8] Composed as a conversation of anonymous voices in a form reminiscent of Wittgenstein's *Philosophical Investigations*, this chapter performs the declaration announced in its title by debating speech's subservience to "the optical imperative [of] the Western tradition" and laying out irreconcilable claims about this historical subservience, thereby provoking the very "disorientation" and boundless "wandering" that one of the chapter's voices claims animates speech (IC 27). The chapter sketches multiple paths about the character of speech, while refusing to reveal a unifying, perspicuous view of speech. It appears as speech about speech that neither brings speech to visibility nor consigns it to invisibility but rather, through the *written* form of the dialogue, oscillates incessantly in between the two outside what one of the voices describes, this time quoting and paraphrasing Heidegger (though without citing him), as the "'region where there is a place for unveiling and veiling'" (IC 27):[9]

> "—Words are suspended; this suspense is a very delicate oscillation, a trembling that never leaves them still.
>
> —And yet, they are immobile.
>
> —Yes, of an immobility that moves more than anything moving. Disorientation is at work in speech through a passion for wandering that has no bounds. Thus it happens that, in speaking, we depart from all direction and all path, as though we had crossed the line.
>
> —But speech has its own way, it provides a path. We are not led astray in it, or at most only in relation to the regularly traveled routes.
>
> —Even more than that perhaps: it is though we were turned away from the visible, without being turned back round toward the invisible. I don't know whether what I am saying here says anything. But nevertheless it is simple. Speaking is not seeing. Speaking frees thought from the optical imperative that in the Western tradition, for thousands of years, has subjugated our approach to things, and induced us to think under the guaranty of light or under the threat of its absence. I'll let you count all the words through which it is suggested that, to speak truly, one must think according to the measure of the eye.
>
> —You don't wish to oppose one sense to another, hearing to sight?
>
> —I would not want to fall into that trap." (IC 27)

One who falls into that trap, of course, is Heidegger with his appeal to the call of conscience and therefore to hearing (or "hearkening," *Hörchen*) as destabilizing the metaphysical subject's theater of specular self-presence. Yet by casting the call as an affective event that shocks the human Dasein back to the fact of its understanding of Being (the fact of its finitude), Heidegger fails to break free completely from the logic of appearance—and he also makes language an accessory to that logic. In order to avoid being ensnared in that same trap, then, Blanchot will not stop at proposing a speech that refuses the speculative metaphysics of revelation; the conception of writing he proposes in the chapter on atheism refuses hearing as well. Mirroring his formulation from the outset of *The Infinite Conversation* that "speaking is not seeing," Blanchot proceeds to proclaim in the chapter on atheism that "writing is not speaking" (IC 261). In fact, he says, "Writing begins only when language, turned back upon itself, designates itself, seizes itself, and disappears" (IC 260–61). Writing is the effacement of language.

Nonetheless, Blanchot insists, this atheistic writing he describes constitutes a voice—not in spite of its work of effacement, its "worklessness [*désoeuvrement*]" (IC 259/EI 388) but because of it. "Writing ceases to be a mirror," he tells us. "It will constitute itself, strangely, as an absolute of writing and of voice" (IC 259). Against the work of scientific knowledge, which follows a "simple and homogenous line" of progress expanding out from a localizable origin whose voice is an empty image of the objects it claims to represent, the voice of writing moves in the torsions of "the origin's retreat [*retrait*]" (IC 260/EI 388). This "twisting movement" constitutes instead "the Work [*l'Oeuvre*]" as "interruptive becoming," a "lacunary interlacing" that "is neither figurable nor unfigurable," lying "always entirely outside [*toujours tout au dehors*]" (IC 260/EI 388). For Blanchot, the voice is the voice of effacement, where effacement notably means being "neither figurable nor unfigurable." Effacement's movement—as *retrait*, as *désoeuvrement*—constitutes the Work as an exposure of the outside.

But the outside of what exactly? All we know for the moment is that, by the outside, Blanchot means outside the onto-theological economy of presence. But since that economy constitutes the boundaries of sense, meaning, and knowledge, how are we to make sense of this outside that the Work, as *désoeuvrement*, designates, and from which the voice of writing issues forth?

Ultimately, if we accept the conditions Blanchot outlines for an atheistic writing, there is no making sense of these terms—the outside, the Work, *désoeuvrement*, voice, the neuter, and even writing itself. There is no systematizing them into a philosophical theory. In fact, the community of the "we" that would ostensibly make sense of such terms would not exist, for it would be effaced in its exposure to and by their very operation in writing. Along with the "I" from which it would be an extrapolation, the "we" (like *das Volk* in Heidegger) would be dissembled through writing's unworking of the onto-theology of presence. So there can be no subject either, singular or plural, that can be the originator of such writing.[10]

If atheistic writing "is" neither an object within a system of knowledge nor the product of a subjective will, then under what conditions can it appear, especially if its appearance must refuse the economy of visibility and invisibility altogether? As suggested by Blanchot's focus in his earlier critical writings in *The Work of Fire*, particularly its essay "Literature and the Right to Death," and in *The Space of Literature*, the answer calls for an engagement with literature—but not literature as merely an aesthetic object. What is required is an engagement with the ways the existence of literature poses a question to thought, with how the fact of literature constitutes an *affective* provocation to think.

One place this provocation appears is in the "Note" with which Blanchot opens *The Infinite Conversation*. Referring to the "labor [*travail*]" it performs, Blanchot says literature's aim is to "formulate" the following question: "What would be at stake in the fact that something like art or literature exists?" (IC xi/EI vi). Blanchot gives an answer a few pages later that signals what he will say about the dissemblance atheistic writing brings about; it is language itself that is at stake in the fact of literature's existence (IC 6), in the fact that there exists this form of writing named "literature." And the implication is that the question of the existence of literature, in questioning language itself, places existence as such into question. To encounter literature as literature would mean being touched by this question, to have one's existence affected by the question of the existence of literature. To confront the fact of literature is to pose the question of finitude.

By joining the question of literature to the question of finitude, Blanchot hews closely to the path staked out by Heidegger in his reflections on the work of art. But by portraying literature as performing a kind of labor, he is also alluding to Hegel and particularly Hegel's famous invocations of the labors constituting the movement of the dialectic—"the labor [*Arbeit*] of the negative"[11]; "the labor of world history" (PS 19); "the labor of the concept" (PS 44). This allusion to the Hegelian trope of labor or work (*Arbeit*) points to Blanchot's reading of Hegel (via Hyppolite and Kojève) in "Literature and the Right to Death" and the role this reading plays in Blanchot's formulation of the Work of literature, as well as the concepts we previously surveyed that correlate closely with this formulation: *désoeuvrement*, the outside, the neuter, and; the limit-experience of writing. As we now move on to examine the arguments of "Literature and the Right to Death" and *The Space of Literature* to understand in more detail Blanchot's theorization of these terms and how they intone the voice's affective register, we will see how Blanchot uses Hegel further to revise Heidegger's conception of finitude. Understanding this revision will be critical for distinguishing Blanchot's conceptualization of the voice from Heidegger's but also for appreciating Blanchot's incorporation of Artaud in describing the voice's affective claim on thinking.

Literature, Death, and the Immemorial Loss of Finitude

Before Blanchot actually leverages Hegel to revise Heidegger's conception of finitude, however, he introduces the question of literature to intervene in that speculative metaphysical economy known as Hegel's System. "Literature and the Right to Death" is the chief text where Blanchot sustains this intervention, contrasting the work of literature to the work of the dialectic, deliberately playing on both senses of the term—work as an aesthetic object (*oeuvre*) and work as labor (*travaille*). For Blanchot, the literary work constitutes the outside to the work of the dialectic, which, from the Hegelian perspective, is not possible. For Hegel, there is no outside to the dialectic; the very idea of an outside relies on the logic of negation and opposition, which is precisely what the dialectic puts to work as part of its operation. As a result, Blanchot recognizes it is senseless to oppose the dialectic and that he must find a way to disrupt it by inhabiting its space of negation.

Literature's relationship to negation is thus a central theme in "Literature and the Right to Death," and Blanchot approaches this relationship in two ways: first, in terms of literature's self-negation—the way he says it calls itself into question—and then in terms of literature's negation of language's use of negation. The former enables Blanchot to claim that literature's relation to negation differs starkly from the role of negation in language, which, consistent with its ostensible role as a medium of signification and representation, works according to negation in order to construct meaning. By opposing literary writing to language, particularly everyday language, Blanchot anticipates what he says in "Atheism and Writing" about writing's ability to disrupt scientific language and the onto-theological economy of presence upon which language, as signification and representation, relies. It is an opposition that very much resonates with the antagonism of language in Heidegger's thought that I elaborated in chapter 2. However, through situating literature in a space outside the negative movement of language, Blanchot also discovers in literature a power to interrupt the movement of the dialectic, to "be" the outside of the dialectic and to unwork its work, which he will describe as the power to bring forth the exposure of finitude that he names, following Lévinas, the *il y a*. The *il y a*, in turn, will be the opening Blanchot leverages to formulate the narrative voice as a response to Heidegger's *es gibt*—the event (*Ereignis*) of Being that claims the human Dasein in its experience of finitude and to which the voice of conscience affectively testifies.

Blanchot opens "Literature and the Right to Death" by denying the idea that one would need to know anything about oneself in order to write, questioning presumptions about authorial self-knowledge, as well as the possibility that a writer could be fully present to themselves. To emphasize this, he illustrates a somewhat uncanny scene of a writer observing himself writing: "As a writer watches his pen form the letters, does he even have the right [*le droit*] to lift it and say to it: 'Stop! What do you know about yourself? Why are you moving forward?'"[12] In this authorial self-interrogation, Blanchot seems to portray at a minimum a splitting between the writer and himself (or his "self") as he writes, calling into question the very act of writing and therefore his identity as a writer. "Why can't you see that your ink isn't making any marks," the writer asks himself, "that although you may be moving ahead freely, you're moving through a void, that the reason you never encounter any obstacles is that you never left your starting place?" (WF 300). The "right" Blanchot seems to be implying is at stake in this scenario goes beyond a claim to the marks on the page. It seems to extend to the right to self-possession, to self-propriety, to what is proper to the (writing) self.

This self-negating, alienating relation Blanchot posits in the experience of writing becomes the basis for his conceptualization of literature. Blanchot proposes that literature as such unfolds as a movement of self-negation and that it proceeds in blithe indifference to the writer's subjective concerns:

> Let us suppose that literature begins at the moment when literature becomes a question. This question is not the same as a writer's doubts or scruples. If he happens to ask himself questions as he writes, that is his concern; if he is absorbed by what he is writing and indifferent to the possibility of writing it, if he is not even thinking about anything, that is his right and his good luck. But one thing is still true: as soon as the page has

> been written, the question which kept interrogating the writer while he was writing—though he may not have been aware of it—is now present on the page; and now the same question lies silent within the work, waiting for a reader to approach—any kind of reader, shallow or profound; this question is addressed to language, behind the person who is writing and the person who is reading, by language which has become literature. (WF 300–301)

What marks literature as literature is that it realizes itself by placing its very possibility into question, regarding with severe skepticism both the process of writing that brought it into existence as well as the act of reading that recognizes and sustains it. Literature monumentalizes this absolute, self-negating questioning, confirming suspicion of its own impossibility, in and through its writing as literature.

However, when it comes to the relation to language harbored in the literary work, the questioning literature poses takes on an interesting inflection. If literature's interrogation of the writer and reader ultimately results in their displacement, then to whom or what is literature's questioning addressed? The address, Blanchot states, is directed to language by language itself. Literature is the name for an event of language in which language ceases to serve as a vehicle for a human voice; instead of being spoken by and exchanged between subjects, language speaks to itself alone.

The image of language addressing itself evokes immediately Heidegger's engagement with the question of language in his later thought, specifically the provocation he issues about the speaking of language ("*Die Sprache spricht*" ["language speaks"]) and the effort he adopts "*to bring language as language to language*."[13] Yet while it might be tempting to assume here that Blanchot is alluding to these expressions in Heidegger and is critically responding to them with his own variation on the theme, a couple of facts urge against making such an assumption. For one, Blanchot's conception of language's self-address in literature in "Literature and the Right to Death" actually predates Heidegger's.[14] Secondly, the image of language's self-relation as a basis for conceptualizing the purity of language, uncontaminated by the vulgarities of communication, is an identifiable modernist trope, as Heidegger himself shows with his reflection on Novalis's *Monologue* in *On the Way to Language* (OW 111). So, while we cannot accurately claim that Blanchot is responding to Heidegger in his own deployment of this modernist image of language addressing itself, their common attention to it nonetheless demarcates a shared attraction to the scene of the human subject being set aside by the event of language. Each will interpret this scene differently, and it is in their contrasting interpretations that we can see Blanchot take a "step" toward a critical revision of the Heideggerian conception of the relation between language and human finitude, specifically as this conception entails an essential relation to nothingness. The key site to view Blanchot taking this step is in "Literature and the Right to Death," and it is noteworthy that he recruits Hegel, and specifically Hegel's theorization of the negative, as part of his approach in doing so.

Blanchot begins with an extended interpretation of the writer's self-negation (one influenced by Kojève's reading of Hegel) via some of the more well-known themes in the *Phenomenology of Spirit*, charting a path from the stages of self-consciousness Hegel labels stoicism, skepticism, and the unhappy consciousness to Hegel's reading of the French Revolution and the Reign of Terror, which for Kojève stages the individual's confrontation with death[15] and that Blanchot extrapolates to theorize literature's revolutionary impulse and the writer's relation to death. Quoting repeatedly Hegel's famous characterization of Spirit in the *Phenomenology*'s preface as "the life that bears death and maintains itself in it" (WF 322, 327, 336; translation modified),[16] Blanchot connects the writer's relation to death with the negations language enacts in order to give the impression that it can bring beings (and hence, Being) to presence in signification. He reads these negations as perpetrating a kind of death: "For me to be able to say, 'This woman,' I must somehow take her flesh-and-blood reality away from her, cause her to be absent, annihilate her. The word gives me the being, but it gives it to me deprived of being. The word is the absence of that being, its nothingness, what is left of it when it has lost being—the very fact that it does not exist. Considered in this light, speaking is a curious right" (WF 322). Considered in such a light, to employ language is to exercise a right to death.[17] But it is also a right to possibility.[18] Death, Blanchot goes on to say, proves to be a paradoxical condition of meaning: a being's death to language allows me to have access to that being but not to its being. A being's death to language makes it possible for that being to appear in signification but impossible for its being to appear, since what appears as that being is not that being; it is a representation of it. Each time one exercises, via language, the "curious right" to death, they enclose themselves all the more decidedly in the enabling prison of representation, which Blanchot characterizes, both here and throughout his corpus, as a day without end (WF 323). By making it possible for beings to appear, language as representation is a form of light. But because what it enlightens is not the being of those beings, language is also what makes access to the presence of those beings impossible. All that language gives access to are beings in their absence. As Blanchot writes, "I do not speak in order to say something; rather, a nothing demands to speak, nothing speaks, nothing finds its being in speech, and the being of speech is nothing" (WF 324). The essence of language is nonexistence, nothingness.

He does not announce it explicitly at this moment in "Literature and the Right to Death," but Blanchot's discussion of the negation of language is highly reminiscent of the passages on sense certainty from the first chapter of the *Phenomenology of Spirit*, which describe the development of consciousness in its most "primitive" formations. In those passages, Hegel famously discusses the "This," as well as the "Here" and "Now," as instances where human consciousness believes it has immediate access to the object of cognition through sense experience, only to find that in referring to "this" object "here," or "this" moment "now," it has been dealing all along in the abstraction of language. Ultimately, Hegel states, those who believe their words actually reach the objects they refer to mean the opposite of what they say, since what they actually say is an abstraction of the object to which they mean to refer. What they say is not what they mean (PS, para 110, 67).

For Hegel, this contradiction between saying and meaning does not call into question Spirit's development; it only propels it further to develop more sophisticated modes of cognition. Similarly, Blanchot observes that everyday language remains remarkably unbothered by its paradoxical conditions and even takes advantage of representation's abstractions in order to make it seem that language yields certainty of the things of which it speaks (WF 325). If everyday language were ever to admit of the absences that constitute it, then it would admit the impossibility of communication, which is to say, its own impossibility. As a result, for the sake of "peace," everyday language represses the fact of its impossibility and provides an appearance of stability between words and things (WF 325).

Not so with literature, however. In stark contrast to everyday language, literature eschews peace. "Literary language," Blanchot asserts, "is made of uneasiness"; unlike everyday language, literature does not seek refuge from the discovery that there is something inherently impotent about language, from the realization that, as Blanchot puts it, "words . . . are sick" (WF 325). Literary language instead embraces this realization by embracing the absence constituting language as this absence becomes present—becomes reality—in and through the word (WF 325). In fact, according to Blanchot, "literature's ideal" is "to say nothing, to speak in order to say nothing," to let the nothing of language speak (WF 324).

It is in this moment, with his conception of literature's embrace of the nothingness communicated in language, that Blanchot marks a decisive break with both the negativity of the Hegelian dialectic and "the nothing" that Heidegger famously claims "makes possible in advance the manifestness of beings in general."[19] Confronting Hegel with the truth of the movement of negation constituting representation, which Hegel acknowledges yet disavows, Blanchot suspends the dialectic by conceiving literature as refusing to indulge in the denials and self-deceptions of everyday language. Literature, for Blanchot, says the absence at the heart of all language, the absence that language makes present, the absence that makes language possible. Yet, at the same time, Blanchot uses Hegel's discovery of the nothingness at the heart of all language, of the impossibility that is the condition of the possibility of representation, to present literature as inhabiting an origin more originary than the event of Being as Heidegger depicts it. Among other names, such as the appropriating event (*Ereignis*) and the clearing of Being (*die Lichtung des Seins*), Heidegger focuses on the phrase "*es gibt*" ("there is"/"it gives") as announcing, in language, the appearance of Being.[20] But for Blanchot, literature's origin is more originary than the *es gibt* precisely because it lays bare the relation to existence that denies absolutely any phenomenological or conceptual revelation. Against the "there is" of Heidegger's *es gibt*, Blanchot, in dialogue with Lévinas, opposes the "there is" of the *il y a*, which, as Blanchot says, "names" "the anonymous and impersonal flow of being" (WF 332 note), and from which, Lévinas adds, there is "no exit."[21]

While the *il y a* is taken to be a critical revision of the Heideggerian *es gibt*, neither Blanchot nor Lévinas wage a direct attack on that specific formulation as it appears in Heidegger.[22] Instead, both Blanchot and Lévinas introduce the *il y a* as a response to Heidegger's reflections on the relationship between anxiety and nothingness, which he conducts in *Being and Time* and "What Is Metaphysics?"[23] As just noted, Heidegger thematizes the nothing as revelatory of Being, and he submits that the encounter with the nothing takes place through the affective experience of anxiety. In contrast to fear, which is always directed at an object, anxiety is always anxiety before existence as such; there is no thing before which one has anxiety but everything at once, Being as such. "In the clear night of the nothing of anxiety," Heidegger writes, "the original openness of beings as such arises: that there are beings—and not nothing" (PM 90).

Through anxiety, Heidegger demonstrates that Being and nothingness are intrinsically connected.

Both Blanchot and Lévinas pick up on this image of the night Heidegger invokes. However, for them the night of the *il y a* is not the affective experience of the night of anxiety that Heidegger describes but rather the much more radical nothingness inhabited by literature. The nothingness that speaks in literature is the failure of language to make Being present; the nothingness of literature exposes language's attempt to proffer the absence of Being as Being's presence.

Yet, it is only literature, and not language, that embodies the *il y a* because while language masquerades as having the power to make Being present, literature rejects that pretense; it proceeds as the knowledge, which haunts all of language, that despite language's attempts to negate Being in order to bring it to presence, language fails (a failure that is the condition of its "success"), and Being persists untouched by representation, exceeding it. The *il y a* is therefore not "the clear night of the nothingness of anxiety" that Heidegger describes but rather the night of Being that will never have come to presence. It is both the impossibility of bringing Being to presence and "the very impossibility of emerging from existence" (WF 332). It is nothingness absolutely divorced from presence; it is an interminable night, the night of horror, according to Lévinas, which is much more radical than anxiety because it bars the appearance of beings and Being and denies the possibility of experience altogether (EE 55–57). In addition to characterizing the *il y a* as a night that haunts all language and thought (EE 56–57; WF 336), Lévinas and Blanchot also identify it as the restless wakefulness of language and thought, an insomnia from which they are destined never to attain any respite, precisely because it is the condition for the possibility of their existence as language and thought (EE 61–64; WF 328; 338).[24]

We are now getting closer to the right to death that Blanchot holds is proper to literature and that conditions literature's impropriety. It is a right that is also a drive, a death drive, in fact. If death gives rise to language, language keeps death alive in order that it may live as language. While language denies this truth about itself and tries to keep (its knowledge of) the death/negation/excess of the *il y a* at bay, literature is drawn to it. This is how, for Blanchot, literature gives new meaning to "the life" that Hegel says "endures death and maintains itself in it"; in this respect, literature's insomnia is an endless search for the moment that precedes it, for the existence that literature, through its existence as language, obliterates and that literature can only capture as always-already lost (WF 327). (As "melancholia" is the name Freud gives for the pathological mourning of an anonymous, unknown object, perhaps it was not at all inappropriate to suspect that what we detected as Lacoue-Labarthe's melancholia possesses a link to Blanchot's pursuit of writing as effacement.)

At this moment, Blanchot appeals to another figure to convey this immemorial loss proper to language and thought that is the *il y a*: Lazarus. But not the Lazarus who Jesus resurrects from the dead and who serves as a figure of the dialectic. It is rather the dead Lazarus Blanchot invokes, Lazarus the cadaver: "Lazarus in the tomb and not Lazarus brought back into the daylight, the one who already smells bad, who is Evil, Lazarus lost and not Lazarus saved and brought back to life" (WF 327).[25] It is the dead Lazarus that makes the dialectic possible but whose death therefore can never appear in representation, which is to say, can never appear as possibility. Lazarus is the impossible death that registers the true measure of death as alterity,[26] as that which exceeds representation—language and thought—radically and absolutely. It is simultaneously the dying that must persist ad infinitum in order for representation to take place and the spectral flow of existence that representation negates yet that returns in every negation (EE 56–57), since in representation existence can only appear as "existence without being" (WF 328). By attempting to present the *il y a*, literature thus exists as that attempt "to become the revelation of what revelation destroys" (WF 328). And because the gaze by which it attempts to reveal the *il y a* only guarantees the *il y a*'s effacement, literature ceaselessly invites figures for theorizing the desire that both animates it and dooms it to failure, as evinced by Lazarus here in "Literature and the Right to Death," and aptly, by the figure of Orpheus in *The Space of Literature*. It is Orpheus, as we will see, who Blanchot conjures to embody the Work's movement of unworking and the radical exposure to the outside to which it constitutes a passage.

As we will also see, Blanchot's conceptualizations of the Work and the outside emerge from literature's paradoxical ontology—an ontology of presence and absence that he has shown disrupts ontology as such, disrupting not only the economy of presence upon which the Hegelian dialectic trades but also that of the Western metaphysical tradition generally. As Blanchot's and Lévinas's respective castings of the *il y a* imply, Heidegger's conception of finitude—particularly the affective valence of anxiety through which Heidegger theorizes it—belongs to this metaphysics of presence. Not only does the *il y a* designate an affective experience that challenges experience as such (what Blanchot will later call the "limit-experience"), it inverts the relation between possibility and impossibility that Heidegger asserts forms the temporal horizon of human finitude. Where Heidegger defines human finitude in terms of Dasein's thrownness toward its death as the possibility of its impossibility, Blanchot and Lévinas redefine that conception and radically overturn it, especially the propriety Heidegger assigns it (the "mineness" [*Jemeinigkeit*] that makes the human Dasein's death theirs alone). As we have just reconstructed, the *il y a* names a relation to death as the impossibility of possibility. Its excess beyond and underlying all language and thought names an alterity so other that it will never have appeared as such and can only appear as an immemorial loss: as an absolute dispossession and depersonalization that is the condition of possibility for any world (and self) whatsoever.[27]

In bringing forth the alienating anonymity of the *il y a*, literature realizes the antihumanism Blanchot argues should be embodied by atheistic writing. Literature is the event in which language ceases to be an instrument of human speech and becomes a pure self-relation. Literature is the event in which language addresses itself (WF 301), declaring " 'I no longer represent, I am; I do not signify, I present' " (WF 328). The literary work's unworking thus dissembles simultaneously both language as representation and the subject of representation, the subject that would express itself—as well as be present to itself—via a voice. Together, these two acts of dissemblance disavow the metaphysics of presence and form the contours of an atheism that delineates the space of the outside, consigning both writer and reader to what Blanchot describes as a radical passivity figured under the name of the neuter, which Blanchot will say speaks in the mode of what he calls the "narrative voice" (it is precisely such passivity that is intimated in the aforementioned trope of insomnia).[28] And while this limit-experience of radical passivity is so severe that it denies any attempt by the subject to claim that passage of alienation as an experience proper to it, Blanchot nonetheless describes the subject's dissemblance from its exposure to the outside and to the narrative voice in affective terms: as fatigue, weariness, *impouvoir* (powerlessness, impotence), and *malheur* (pain, affliction, distress).

In the next and final section of this chapter, I reconstruct the way Blanchot develops the outside and connects it to the narrative voice, beginning with the outside's initial appearance in "Literature and the Right to Death," to its elaboration in *The Space of Literature*, and to its role in the conception of the narrative voice in *The Infinite Conversation*. As the voice of literature, the narrative voice is in one sense not unlike the event of *aletheia* in Heidegger's conception of the work of art, which we analyzed in chapter 3 as the return of the voice in Heidegger's later work and that we encountered again in Lacoue-Labarthe's critique of Heidegger in chapter 4. Yet it is very much *not aletheia* to the extent that, as the movement of the *il y a*, the narrative voice neither reveals nor conceals but refuses the economy of concealment-unconcealment altogether, refuses figuration (*Gestaltung*) altogether. As we will see, the narrative voice effaces itself as any kind of voice at all. If it is thus able to avoid any recourse to the figure and thus able to approximate the moment of mimesis more "accurately" than Heideggerian *aletheia*, it is only because the narrative voice refuses whatsoever any return to an origin, whether that be Dasein or Being as such. It is the improper par excellence. It "is" not.

Throughout his work, Blanchot looks to specific writers to study their relationship to writing and the outside. Mallarmé, Kafka, and Rilke are featured prominently in *The Space of Literature*, for example. My discussion in the next section will extend this analysis to Blanchot's treatment of Artaud, whose personal torment Blanchot takes up as a scene of the *impouvoir* of writing and thinking—that is to say, the experience of powerlessness (at the limit of experience) that Blanchot submits writing and thinking constitute. This scene, I contend, announces yet one more inversion of Heidegger's thought by Blanchot: instead of defining the experience of finitude as the affective realization that we are not yet thinking, as Heidegger does in *What Is Called Thinking?* (1954), Blanchot redefines it as "the impossibility of thinking which is thought" through Artaud's afflicted, anguished passivity before the narrative voice of the outside.

The Writing of the Outside and the Affliction of the *Impouvoir* of Thinking in Artaud

In "Literature and the Right to Death," Blanchot makes only a brief mention of the outside, but it intimates how he will develop it further in subsequent work. Perhaps anticipating his later appeal to the geometric concept of the Riemann surface in *The Infinite Conversation*, Blanchot describes the outside in "Literature and the Right to Death" as emerging from literature's discovery that its landscape is not one of meaning and the interiority of consciousness that meaning is presupposed to transmit but is instead "the outside which has been changed from the outlet it once was into the impossibility of going out" (WF 331). "Literature," he continues, "is that experience through which the consciousness discovers its being in its inability to lose consciousness" (WF 331). In what we might consider then another revision of the Heideggerian conception of finitude, this time in terms of an essential involution of the ek-static character of Dasein's Being-in-the-world, literature is consciousness no longer intended phenomenologically toward an object but rather that from which consciousness can find "no exit," as Lévinas says. Literature is the outside insofar as it refuses to provide the sanctuary of a navigable division between the interiority of consciousness and the exteriority of things.

In *The Space of Literature*, Blanchot conceives the relationship between the literary work and the outside in a more intense (even more essential) way. In this text, the literary does not simply open onto the outside; now, literature reveals how the experience of the work of art in general constitutes an experience of the outside as such. As he does in "Literature and the Right to Death," Blanchot establishes this identification between art and the outside by leveraging Hegel in a revision of Heidegger, although this time in terms of their respective theorizations of art. The central point of departure for Blanchot is Hegel's famous declaration in his *Lectures on Aesthetics* that, as Blanchot paraphrases it, "art for us is a thing of the past," a declaration that, not coincidentally, also attracted Heidegger's attention in "The Origin of the Work of Art."[29] However, where Heidegger questions the finality of Hegel's judgment concerning art and suggests it reflects a failure to ask about the essence of the working of the artwork—specifically, its act of disclosing the truth of Being as *aletheia* and the relation of Being and human being in the strife between world and earth—Blanchot appropriates Hegel's claim in order to emphasize art's absolute separation from both the work of history (in terms of contributing to the unfolding of Spirit) and the constellation of world and truth (i.e., as a site of the unconcealment of Being).[30]

For Blanchot, Hegel's claim of art having been transcended in the history of Spirit serves as an unconscious acknowledgment of its opening onto the outside. As such, the work of art performs no work whatsoever, not for the unfolding of history and certainly not for the dialectic. It unworks instead. It remains idle (*désoeuvrée*), a presentation of the powerlessness that results from the encounter with the *il y a*, with Being's absolute resistance to appearing. It "is" (the) outside, which means it refuses to appear within the economy of Being and nonbeing altogether. As Blanchot writes in *The Space of Literature*, echoing formulations we encounter in "Literature and the Right to Death":

> Art—as images, as words, and as rhythm—indicates the menacing proximity of a vague and vacant outside, a neutral existence, nil

and limitless; art points into a sordid absence, a suffocating condensation where being ceaselessly perpetuates itself as nothingness.

Art is originally linked to this fund of impotence [*impuissance*] where everything falls back when the possible is attenuated. (SL 242–43/EL 255)

Similar to "Literature and the Right to Death," which inverts the Heideggerian conception of finitude, here Blanchot undertakes another inversion of the Heideggerian schema, however, this time in terms of Heidegger's contention regarding art's truth (and origin) as *aletheia*, as the unconcealing event of Being. Where "Literature and the Right to Death" shows how literature inhabits the space of the *il y a*, overturning the Heideggerian image of finitude from the possibility of impossibility and laying bare instead the impossibility of possibility that conditions and haunts all language, *The Space of Literature* does something similar with Heidegger's conception of the work of art. In this work, Blanchot exposes the unconcealing movement of *aletheia* Heidegger contends the artwork realizes as yet another layer of concealment. Just as literature presents the failure of signification, of making present the thing being represented, the work of art for Blanchot discloses the inevitable failure of unconcealment and suggests that any claim to unconcealment is merely a mask of this fact of inevitable failure: unconcealment as concealment's masquerade. By recasting the work of art in this way, Blanchot both anticipates Lacoue-Labarthe's critique, studied in our previous chapter, of Heidegger's conception of *aletheia* as an appropriation of mimesis but also recovers the sense of mimesis as absolute dissimulation that ruins in advance all efforts to conceptualize and master it.

As we saw in "Literature and the Right to Death," one prominent figure to which Blanchot appeals to evoke the work's ruinous power is Lazarus. In *The Space of Literature*, he calls on the tragic myth of Orpheus and Eurydice in order to emphasize repeatedly both the work's self-effacing movement as well as the artist's effacement, which the artist visits upon themselves through the very act of creation. Like Orpheus, the artist is drawn to that "*other* night" (another name Blanchot gives the outside) (SL 163–70; original emphasis), that night of Being that thought seeks to bring to the day of appearance, experience, and knowledge—in other words, to be mastered. But once the artist does so, once they turn their gaze upon the night, Being, like Eurydice, withdraws from sight and from the artist's grasp, from their prehension. The work is the emblem of the artist's *in-com-prehension*. But, for Blanchot, the outside's in-com-prehensibility, which consigns the artist to a state of radical passivity, also and at the same time attracts the artist all the more irrevocably toward it, in a relation Blanchot describes alternately as fascination and "tyrannical prehension [*la préhension persécutrice*]" (SL 25/EL 15), a persecuting, tormenting hold. It is because the artist cannot grasp, cannot (com)prehend, the outside, that they are drawn all the more to it and are incapable of releasing themselves from its gravitational pull. All the while, the Work works (which is to say, unworks) independent of them.

In the brief section where Blanchot introduces the idea of tyrannical prehension, he presents the image of a "sick hand" that cannot stop writing, despite the artist's desire to do so (SL 25). This malady, which suggests not only the artist's self-alienation, but also a shattering diremption between thought and action, is a symptom of the affective ordeal to which the artist is subjected in their creative encounter with the event of the Work. As noted at the outset of this chapter, Blanchot evokes repeatedly this affective state throughout his writings in order to underscore the severity of the dispropriating passivity to which the artist is consigned. Those evocations, as noted earlier, appear under various names, including fatigue, *malheur*, and, as we have already seen, *impouvoir*.

At this point, one thing must be said about this affective state to which Blanchot continually returns in his thought, especially as we prepare to attend to his reading of Artaud. While the scholarship on the centrality of this affect of affliction in Blanchot's writings is extensive, there is interestingly little that appears to consider it critically as the perpetuation of the modernist mythic image of the heroic, suffering male artist.[31] Yet, Blanchot's emphasis on this experience (at the limit of experience) seems to do just that, and, as we have seen intimated, it is an image whose coherence relies upon the equally traditional (and equally suspect) appropriation of the feminine.[32] These aspects of Blanchot's appeal to affect thus raise questions about the extent to which Blanchot's conceptualization of the subject's desistance in language is free of a metaphysics of presence, and they also raise questions about the so-called newness of affect that we have seen recent proponents of the affective turn claim it announces for thinking.

What if, then, the contemporary turn to affect that we surveyed at the opening of this study does not signal the arrival of a new organization of the social, as is claimed, but rather the continuation, or at least reappearance, of a thoroughly modernist sensibility, one to which we must also include Heidegger's conception of affect as *Stimmung*?[33] As I have been arguing, such lack of novelty regarding affect not only casts suspicion on related claims about the ability to separate affect from language (or sensibility from sense/

meaning). Their inextricability indicates strongly that they share a more fundamental relation, which I am pursuing in the second half of the present study as the question of mimesis—the question, that is to say, not only of how language and affect meet in mimesis, but more vitally, the question of how contemporary thought ("Philosophy," "Theory") responds to the threat mimesis announces to thinking. As we move into Blanchot's reading of Artaud, I want to suggest that Blanchot is working from this question of mimesis and the claim or demand it makes—not to decide between affect and language but to weigh the possibility of whether thinking is willing to expose itself to the dissembling encounter with difference mimesis names or prefers instead to flee from it by theorizing (i.e., mastering) it.

In 1956, a year after the publication of *The Space of Literature*, Blanchot published a short essay on Artaud in the *Nouvelle Revue Française*.[34] In it, we see Blanchot identifying in Artaud's account of his experience with writing a convergence of the themes of powerlessness, passivity, and the diremption between thought and action. Yet this convergence also allows Blanchot to demonstrate how the encounter with literature enacts one more reversal of Heidegger's text, this time as it concerns the affective provocation that Heidegger says opens onto the event of thinking: "*Most thought-provoking*," he declares throughout *What Is Called Thinking?*, "*is that we are still not thinking. . . .*"[35] However, rather than this idea that "we are still not thinking" as being the "most thought-provoking," Blanchot insists that Artaud's experience of writing reveals thought to be "the impossibility of thinking" as such ("Artaud," 130).[36] It is in fact Artaud, we discover, who inspires Blanchot's thematization of the *impouvoir* in speech and writing.[37]

Blanchot's point of departure is a series of letters exchanged between a young Artaud and the then editor of the *Nouvelle Revue Française*, Jacques Rivière, after the latter rejected Artaud's poems for publication. It is a correspondence that, at least on Artaud's part, constitutes not so much a dissatisfaction with the unacceptability of his poems than a "confession" concerning their "absolute acceptability," that is to say, "their literary existence."[38] Their exchange is predicated upon a fundamental misunderstanding: In his first letter to Rivière, Artaud writes,

> I suffer from a horrible sickness of the mind. My thought abandons me at every level. From the simple fact of thought to the external fact of its materialization in words. Words, shapes of sentences, internal directions of thought, simple reactions of the mind—I am in constant pursuit of my intellectual being.

> Thus as soon as *I can grasp a form*, however imperfect, I pin it down, for fear of losing the whole thought. I lower myself, I know, and I suffer from it, I consent to it for fear of dying altogether. ("Correspondence" 31; original emphasis)

Rivière, in turn, interprets this to be a description of the conditions that resulted in the "awkwardnesses and . . . oddities" of Artaud's poetry, "a *lack of control*," Rivière writes to him, "over your ideas" that "with a little patience" will result in the writing of "poems that are perfectly coherent and harmonious" ("Correspondence" 33; emphasis added).

Almost half a year later, Artaud writes back to Rivière to say that the latter's interest in responding with a "literary judgment" to the presentation of what Artaud describes as "the rarity of certain mental phenomena which actually made it impossible for these verses to be any different" distracted from the actual matter at hand, namely, the "fragility" of a "mind which exists *literarily*, as T. exists, or E., or S., or M," strikingly likening his mind's being, it seems, to the being of the letters on a page ("Correspondence" 35; original emphasis). Artaud emphasizes the fact that, as he stated in his first letter to Rivière, nothing less than the "whole problem of [his] thinking is at stake," that it is the matter of whether or not "from the point of view of *literature*" his thought succeeded in existing at all or as such, and that his concern is whether or not he any longer has "the right to continue to think, in verse or in prose" ("Correspondence" 32; original emphasis). The fault in his poetry lies not in inexperience, nor in a simple absence of self-mastery. His poetry's "failure," he says, has to do with his relationship to thinking itself, which he can only experience as an absolute absence, absence as such.

Replying again, Rivière does not make the same mistake twice. Rather than try to reassure Artaud or assuage his anxieties, he responds this time by finding evidence in Artaud's writing—both his letters and his poetry—to validate Artaud's suspicions about the integrity of his thought. Yes, confirms Rivière, despite the "extraordinary precision of your self-diagnosis," the "vagueness, or at least *formlessness*, of your creative efforts" is matched by "your *handwriting*—tormented, wavering, collapsing, as if sucked in here and there by secret whirlpools" ("Correspondence" 38–39; emphasis added). With this, Rivière betrays his allegiance to the metaphysics of subjectivity and its attendant investment in the unity of thought and action. Rivière's suggestion here of a sick hand falls disastrously short of Blanchot's figure of "tyrannical prehension" because, in contradistinction to Blanchot, Rivière is appealing to a mimetic correspondence between hand and mind, if not also a hierarchical relation of mind to body. As Blanchot insists later throughout *The Infinite Conversation*, writing is not at odds with the madness or sickness Artaud describes in his letters to Rivière; writing *is* a sickness. *Writing is madness.*

Given all this, Blanchot asks, "Why then does he write poems?" ("Artaud" 131). The answer to this question gives us a glimpse of what precisely is at stake for Artaud in the fact of literature (in the fact that it exists). As if the question had been actually put to him, Artaud asks Rivière, "Do you believe that in a well-organized mind apprehension is accompanied by extreme weakness, and that one can simultaneously astonish and disappoint?" ("Correspondence" 35). That is to say, is it possible to see that the poems he submitted are not failed or inchoate forms of expression, the result of a certain dysfunction of his creative capacities, but rather the *fully formed* expressions of a fundamental and "central collapse of the soul, . . . a kind of erosion" of thought as such? ("Correspondence" 34–35). "Everything suggests," Blanchot asserts, quoting from this same letter from Artaud to Rivière, "that poetry, linked for him 'to this sort of erosion, at once essential and ephemeral, of thought,' thus essentially involved in this central loss, at the same time gives him the certainty that it alone can be the expression of this loss, and promises, to a certain extent, to save this loss itself, to save his thought in so far as it is lost" ("Artaud" 131). The loss of thought—the experience of the loss of thought that is thinking—is not opposed to literature, but is rather essential to it, is rather the condition of literature.

In an allusion to Heidegger, Blanchot writes that Artaud "knows, with the profundity afforded by the experience of suffering, that thinking is not simply having thoughts, and that the thoughts he has only make him feel that he has not 'yet *begun* to think'" ("Artaud" 131; original emphasis). This is why Artaud, still referring to himself, speaks in his penultimate letter to Rivière of "a sickness which deprives you of speech, memory, which uproots your thought," a soul that "is not damaged *outside of thought*," but, as he suggests, within thought, and, as Blanchot would add, is exposed to the outside ("Correspondence" 44; original emphasis). Only within the interiority of thought does the suffering Artaud describes take place, yet it is an experience of interiority that immediately exiles one to an outside, to *the* outside, an experience of thought as the impossibility of thinking. It is on such grounds that the aphasia his work performs breaks with the conception of the voice as an expression of subjective interiority and intentionality and testifies to a state in which Artaud experiences an "'absence of a voice to cry out'" ("Artaud" 131).[39]

From this speech bereft of voice, Blanchot contends that "poetry is linked to the impossibility of thinking which is thought" and to the solitude of the outside of thought to which the impossibility of thinking gives one over ("Artaud" 131). Exiled from both thought and language, Artaud inhabits the "essential solitude" that Blanchot describes in *The Space of Literature* as constituting the "impersonality" that is proper to the artist's being (and which contradicts Heidegger's conception of the human Dasein's claim to its death) (SL 149–50). But this solitude to which Artaud bears witness is not that of someone alone in the world; as Artaud declares, he is not "in the world" at all ("Correspondence" 44). It is an essential solitude to the extent that his writing is not the expression of having been "set aside" by thought but is the very movement of being "set aside" by the Work as an essential part of the Work's realization, as part of the Work's "essencing" (SL 21–22). The Work's appearance, outside the economy of appearance, is predicated upon the writer's disappearance or effacement.

For Blanchot, the "worldlessness" and effacing movement of Artaud's writing are confirmed in a letter identifies as being written by Artaud "some twenty years later," in which Artaud declares, "All my work has been and can only ever be built on nothingness" ("Artaud" 131–32).[40] By nothingness, Blanchot understands Artaud to be articulating not a lack of having anything to say but rather "a radical nullity" that compels him to write ("Artaud" 132). Paradoxically, this nothingness upon which Artaud claims his work is built, which leaves him without a voice, also grounds his "*right* to speak" ("Artaud" 132; "Correspondence" 36; original emphasis). Clearly echoing themes from "Literature and the Right to Death," Blanchot reads Artaud's right to speak as a claim to the right to death that not only conditions all language and representation but also results in his own "death" in the form of his disappearance as a writer and origin of the Work. The Work speaks as the voice that survives the effacement of the voice and the suffering of thought—the suffering that Blanchot says *is* thinking ("Artaud" 135).

Above all, though, Blanchot regards the affective interruption between thought and language that Artaud's epistolary testimony evinces as not something accidental to writing. Interruption is instead the essence of writing. In an essay included in *The Infinite Conversation* titled "Interruption: As on a Riemann Surface" (taken in part from another essay published originally in 1964 titled "Interruption"), Blanchot distinguishes between two types of interruption, the kind that is simply an interval between words that is necessary for the continuity of sense and meaning, and the kind that suspends itself within the "infinite gap between beings" (IC 78). Blanchot classifies all speech that is emitted "out of fatigue, out of pain or affliction [*malheur*]" as giving rise to the latter type, and he describes that form of interruption as an encounter with the neuter, by which he also means the outside (IC 78). Such speech, by occupying the "infinite gap between beings" and eschewing the temptation to close this gap through a unifying and universalizing dialectical gesture that would negate and appropriate difference, attempts instead "to involve the outside of any language in language itself, that is to say, speaking within this Outside [*Dehors*], speaking according to the measure of this 'outside,' which, being in all speech, may very well risk turning speech back into what is excluded from all speaking" (IC 78–79; EI 111). This speech—as with Artaud's speech—is a speech of "impossible interruption," says Blanchot, a speech of the "exigency of speech," a "wait[ing]"—a patience, perhaps—"that measures infinite distance" (IC 79).

Rather than wonder why Artaud writes, then, perhaps it would be more apt to ask, What is Artaud waiting for in his writing? What does he stand vigilant over? As Blanchot has already suggested, perhaps what Artaud is waiting for, what prevents him from resting and requires that he writes, is what every writer attends to and that also conditions the very possibility of writing as impossibility: the limit-experience of the neuter, the outside. Which is to say their own desistance to the self-address of language—language's narrative voice. Such writing speaks via the neuter, in the neutral, as an anonymous "it" (*il*) that we should not be surprised to learn also evokes the *il y a* (IC 379–87). As such, however, we must remember that this narrative voice is not the voice of presence. But nor is it an absent voice. It is rather a voice that withdraws from both presence and absence, visibility and invisibility, revelation and concealment (IC 385–86). The narrative voice is thus "spectral, ghostlike," Blanchot says, because it speaks not from the center but from the limit of the Work that is the outside, denying any privileged perspective or any focus (IC 386). "Afocal," decentered, aphonic, the improper par excellence, the narrative voice addresses "no one" and as such cannot, properly speaking, be heard, although its demand to be heard cannot be denied (IC 385–86). It instead addresses language itself, delivering it over to the limit of sense/meaning, refusing the labor of making Being appear (as representation, which is to say, as nonbeing), which is why it tends to be confused "with the oblique voice of misfortune, or of madness" (IC 387).[41] In a passage that will eventually draw Foucault's attention, Blanchot characterizes this voice as "barely a murmur":

> I listen to this. To whom is it addressed? of whom does it speak? who speaks? who listens? who could respond at such a distance? that which comes from so far and does not even come, why is

> it unaware of me? why is this ignorance within my reach? why does it make itself heard? Speech? Not speech, barely a murmur, barely a tremor, less than silence, less than the abyss of the void; the fullness of the void, something one cannot silence, occupying all of space, the uninterrupted, the incessant, a tremor and already a murmur, not a murmur but speech, and not just any speech, distinct speech, precise speech, within my reach.[42]

In fact, though Artaud reports being so deprived of voice that he cannot even cry out, Blanchot goes on to interpret this suffering to which he testifies as a passage to an other voice that he thinks alternately under the figures of the cry and the murmur. It is in the form of both, he says at the conclusion of "Atheism and Writing," that this other voice announces the "passing" of "man" (IC 262). Such passing is so extreme, so past, that it is no longer man who cries out; the cry is instead "the murmur of this cry," the reverberations of man's death (IC 262).

Blanchot ultimately leaves us with a paradoxical imperative: "to think the humanity in man," but without "man" (IC 262). And, he adds, the ability to follow this imperative rests on the ability to follow another one that is equally paradoxical: to write without language (IC 262). Writing as the effacement of language. The scene—not figure—of human finitude in Blanchot, then, is one of exposure to the effacement of the human and the disruption of any claim to language as belonging—as proper—to human being. It is an exposure that the human undergoes affectively "through what will most distance it from language: the cry—that is to say, the murmur" (IC 262). Yet, it is not that the human cries out; rather, it is the cry that testifies to the human's effacement, to which the human bears witness. Through the cry, the human witnesses its effacement and encounters itself as mere murmur. Through the cry, the voice of language as that which can never appear—the neuter, the outside, the *il y a*—resounds as writing. With Blanchot, then, if the voice names the constellation of affect, language, and human finitude, it does so by shattering that very constellation, by shattering the received meanings upon which they rest. In Blanchot, the voice is a writing of the disaster, as in *dés-astre*, a "break with the star," a break with the cosmic order, "the night delivered of stars, multiple night."[43] The voice: an other night.

As we will see in the next chapter, Deleuze will also seize on the figure of the cry in Artaud as part of his reflections on the limit of sense/meaning. But there we will discover that he interprets this convergence of

Heidegger, Blanchot, and Artaud on the (im)possibility of thinking in ways counter to Blanchot's image of the voice as a writing of effacement. Instead of a *retrait* of the voice corresponding to Lacoue-Labarthe's call for de-figuration, Deleuze will capitalize on the affective shock of the impossibility of thinking that arises from Blanchot's encounter with Artaud and claim this shock opens onto a new image of thought. Such an image, he will contend, must always be provisional, much in the same way that Nancy, in his debate with Lacoue-Labarthe, argues for the inevitability of myth. With Deleuze, we will see him argue that there will always be a need to create new images of thought, new figures, which at times he refers to as simulacra (and at other times also as myth) in order to clear a space for the becoming of difference. Strikingly, however, Deleuze theorizes this becoming as a voice and places himself in dialogue with the Heideggerian voice as part of doing so, thus constituting another—and as we shall see, unexpected—site of reception of Heidegger's conceptualization of language, affect, and human finitude.

Part 4
Deleuze

Chapter 6

Deleuze and the Voice of Simulacra

The work of Gilles Deleuze may seem an unexpected note upon which to conclude this study of the voice, especially as I have been analyzing it as it is first theorized in Heidegger's thought and then as it is received by Nancy, Lacoue-Labarthe, and Blanchot. As Deleuze himself observed, he was never associated with the intellectual lineage of post-Heideggerian French thinkers, and he never regarded himself as part of the Heideggerian legacy. He surmises that this was because he never embraced formulations like the closure of metaphysics or the death of philosophy, "and [he] never made a big thing about giving up Totality, Unity, the Subject."[1] Furthermore, very few of Deleuze's commentators have ever entertained the idea that he has any connection to Heidegger, much less that he may be counted as one of Heidegger's readers.[2]

Yet as I contend in the concluding section of chapter 5, there are indications that Deleuze is not only a reader of Heidegger but that he is engaged in his own elaboration of the Heideggerian voice. One significant moment occurs in *The Time-Image* (1985), the second volume of Deleuze's *Cinema* books, specifically in the chapter titled "Thought and Cinema," where he takes up the same constellation of Heidegger, Blanchot, and Artaud that we studied in chapter 5 in order to argue that cinema enacts Blanchot's revision of Heidegger's description of the provocation of thinking. Citing both Heidegger's *What Is Called Thinking?* and Blanchot's essay on Artaud, Deleuze writes,

> A being of thought which is always to come [*toujours à venir*] is what Heidegger discovered in a universal form, but it is what

Artaud lived as the most singular problem, his own problem. Between Heidegger and Artaud, Maurice Blanchot was able to give the fundamental question of what makes us think, what forces us to think, back to Artaud: what forces us to think is "the inpower [*impouvoir*] of thought," the figure of nothingness, the inexistence of a whole which could be thought. What Blanchot diagnoses everywhere in literature is particularly clear in cinema: on the one hand the presence of an unthinkable in thought, which would be both its source and barrier; on the other hand the presence to infinity of another thinker in the thinker, who shatters every monologue of a thinking self.[3]

By "shatter[ing] every monologue of a thinking self," cinema refuses to furnish a ground for subjective interiority. The cinematic subject, if you will, is one that is precisely *not one* (i.e., not unified) but multiple, always-already exposed to—and composed of—a multiplicitous alterity. Instead of the shelter of a self-reflecting monologue that shores up and affirms the subject's coherence as subject, the cinematic subject (as Deleuze describes it citing Blanchot on Artaud) is one who is subjected to the "dissociative force" of cinema and the "figure of nothingness" it introduces. In a way that resonates provocatively with Nancy's image of the sharing of voices, Deleuze conceives the cinematic subject as one delivered over to the dispossession of "multiple voices, internal dialogues, always a voice in another voice" (TI 167).

In his appeal to Blanchot and Artaud, Deleuze implies that cinema (post-WWII, that is) possesses the power of *impouvoir* on the same order of that which Blanchot names literature. At the same time, he enlists the assemblage of Heidegger, Blanchot, and Artaud to argue that cinema presents an "image of thought" that upends all previous conceptions of what thinking is, which is to say it upends philosophy itself. Although readers of Deleuze will recognize the image of thought as a problem that occupies Deleuze throughout his work, neither Heidegger's influence in this project nor the fact that Deleuze considers the problem as involving the voice is typically acknowledged. Nonetheless, not only do we receive confirmation that Heidegger and the voice are present in *The Time-Image*, but this passage from the *Cinema* project bringing together Heidegger, Blanchot, and Artaud invites us to read Deleuze's work with a new set of questions: Is Heidegger's appearance here a mere fleeting occurrence? Or is it an indication of a more substantial presence? Relatedly, to what extent can Deleuze be regarded as making the voice—and therefore, language—part of his central concerns? And while it is clear, given not only his well-known preoccupation with Spinoza and Nietzsche but also his interest in Artaud, that Deleuze's philosophical commitment is centered on affect—and crucially, the affective character of thought—to what extent does his attention to affect involve a reflection on the relationship between language and finitude?

One site where we receive answers to these questions, I want to claim, is *Difference and Repetition* (1968), Deleuze's doctoral thesis and what he considered to be his first mature philosophical work ("the first book in which I tried to 'do philosophy,'" as he says[4]). As we will see, it is thus noteworthy that his first philosophical work is devoted to the concept of the voice in the form of the problem of univocity, and, as we will also see, that it is Heidegger that is the first philosophical source he invokes at the work's outset. Together—the voice and Heidegger, but also, Heidegger's theorization of the voice—point the way, so Deleuze implies, to realizing the task *Difference and Repetition* sets before philosophy: to craft an authentic thought of difference and, anticipating the gesture he makes in *The Time-Image*, give itself a new image of thought.

As I noted in my introduction to this study, this chapter is the most experimental of all those that I present in the book to the extent that it pushes against received conceptions of Deleuze's work and especially Deleuze's relationship to Heideggerian thought. This entails not only staging an *Auseinandersetzung* or *explication* between Deleuze and Heidegger; it also means reading Deleuze against himself at turns. Nonetheless, in terms of interpretive claims I want to put forth in this chapter, I mainly want to read Deleuze as harboring and seeking to bring about ambitions that align with the imperatives Nancy delineates in his debate with Lacoue-Labarthe concerning the primacy of the scenic in and to philosophical thought, specifically with respect to trying to realize a form of writing that embraces the dissimulating and dissembling force of mimesis that stands in contrast to what I trace is the desire for a writing of effacement in Lacoue-Labarthe and Blanchot.

In order to accomplish this, I focus on the role Heidegger plays in Deleuze's recovery of univocity, through which Deleuze establishes a line of inheritance from the Heideggerian voice to his own philosophical project incorporating the thought of Spinoza and Nietzsche. What Deleuze seeks to recover with univocity is the being of Becoming, which Deleuze figures under the name "simulacra." "Simulacra" invoke for Deleuze the affective force of mimesis but also ground that force in the sense/meaning of existence. Univocity thus constitutes the intersection of affect and language in Deleuze, for whom I show language means a fundamental relation to the sense/meaning of existence and affect means a sharing of that sense/meaning in a manner that resonates with Nancy's figure of a sharing of voices. The concern for writing that I argue Deleuze demonstrates (and that I hold extends to his collaborations with Félix Guattari) is an affirmation of this connection between language and affect, but it is also linked to the exigency he sounds for a new image of thought that responds to the dissembling voice of simulacra: "That form of writing," as Deleuze puts it, "which is nothing but the question 'what is writing?,' or that sensibility which is nothing but the question 'what is it to sense?,' or that thought which asks 'what does it mean to think?'" (DR 195). I hasten to add that as I work to assemble these resonances between Deleuze and Heidegger, I want to emphasize them as resonances and not wholesale alignments or reproductions; I believe this is possible to maintain while also being alert to Deleuze's transformations of the concepts of voice, language, finitude, and affect, as well as thinking itself.

In what follows, I begin with a brief recapitulation of Heidegger's appearance in *Difference and Repetition* as Deleuze relates him and his thought to the book's overall thematization of the problem of univocity. I then reconstruct the conception of univocity that Deleuze formulates in the work, particularly as it connects to his writings on Spinoza and Nietzsche. From there, I move on to examine his critique of the false conceptual difference he claims philosophy has inherited from Aristotle and his recovery of the reality of simulacra that he submits is to be found in Plato but is glossed over by what he argues is Aristotle's Platonism. I then connect this "voice of simulacra," as I refer to it, to Deleuze's analyses of expressionism in Spinoza and the "scene of the voice" that I see Deleuze take Nietzsche's eternal return to present.

The final sections of this chapter analyze Heidegger's role as a bridge between the conception of univocity Deleuze formulates in *Difference and Repetition* and its further development in *The Logic of Sense*, particularly as it informs what he views, via a reading of Artaud, to be the "theater of cruelty" that literature enacts for the saying of difference. With *The Logic of Sense*, then, we will see how Deleuze demarcates both the writing that responds to univocity, as well as the path for his later engagement with Heidegger, Blanchot, and Artaud on the idea of "the image of thought" in *The Time-Image*. My closing discussion traces the connections Deleuze makes between the image of thought and the relation to language in the form of the concept of "minor literature" he develops in his collaborations with Guattari. This final section will emphasize the interest Deleuze shares with Heidegger and Blanchot on the power of art to open onto—and provide a scene of—an encounter with difference.

Heidegger and the Path from the Reality of Simulacra to the Exigency of Univocity

In *Difference and Repetition*, Deleuze calls for a return to or recovery of the problem of univocity, but he frames this exigency of a return as a response to another problem: that of simulacra, which he asserts confronts modern thought and challenges philosophy's historical dependence on representation and identity. Heidegger will play an important role in the arrival of both problems for Deleuze.

According to Deleuze, the history of philosophy has been dominated by "conceptual difference," reducing difference "to the identity of the concept," which is to say, the identity of the Same (DR xv). It is therefore a false thought of difference that limits the possibilities for thinking itself. Hegel obviously epitomizes this false conception of difference in the history of philosophy, but what Deleuze also notices at the time of his diagnosis is a kind of atmospheric change taking place in contemporary philosophy, art, and culture, starting with "Heidegger's more and more pronounced orientation towards a philosophy of ontological Difference," which, in Deleuze's view, indicates the advent of "a generalized anti-Hegelianism" that registers the upheavals of modern thought and the modern's challenge to the regime of representation (DR xix). For what characterizes the modern, he says, is not representation but simulacra. In the modern, "All identities are only simulated, produced as an optical 'effect' by the more profound game of difference and repetition" (DR xix).

For someone who claims that he was never attracted to ideas like the end of philosophy, Deleuze does seem to subscribe at this moment to the critique of the metaphysics of presence that phrase announces. And with his description of simulacra as revealing "the more profound game of difference and repetition" beneath the mask of identity, Deleuze appears to echo efforts by Heidegger and others to solicit the dissimulating power of mimesis in order to recover an authentic experience of Being. His characterization of modern life as inaugurating the return of simulacra is consequently not a mourning of the loss of identity but a call to recognize the opportunity to recover the reality of simulacra as the reality of difference.[5] From the outset of *Difference and Repetition*, then, Deleuze appears to be signaling a need to return to the question of simulacra and the ways it has been cast as unreal or a form of degraded reality in the history of Western thought. What we can be certain of so far is that for him simulacra are not copies and therefore do not belong to the order of representation. He seems instead to be referring to a conception of simulacra that also reaches back to the more originary meaning of mimesis that we encountered in chapter 4—namely, mimesis as *Darstellung* (presentation).

Despite the Western philosophical tradition's allegiance to identity and representation, Deleuze does discover (or, as he would say, "rediscovers") moments in the history of philosophy when the thought or "concept of difference" (DR xv) for which he calls makes an appearance, if only to be overlooked or suppressed. Not coincidentally, these moments appear in the works of those thinkers who make up the set of historical studies Deleuze writes that precedes and prepares the way for *Difference and Repetition*. These include Hume, Nietzsche, Bergson, and Spinoza. Also not coincidentally, these are thinkers who had been marginalized in (or, in the case of Nietzsche, excluded altogether from) the history of philosophy. But for Deleuze, their exclusion is a sign of the radical potential—or indeed, threat—their thinking poses to philosophy proper (i.e., philosophy's image of itself as "Philosophy," the queen of the disciplines). He is therefore eager to mine their writings for concepts that he can deploy against philosophy's fealty to the regime of representation and gain access to the encounter with difference that to his mind modern thought's opening up of the space of simulacra announces.

To get at the reality of simulacra (and the "simulacral" nature of identity), Deleuze draws heavily from Nietzsche's conception of the work of art (yet another way that he is in league with his predecessors, including Heidegger, who treat Nietzsche as a guiding figure). Deleuze not only adopts Nietzsche's conception of art as that which exposes the ascetic nihilism of the will to truth to which Western culture unquestioningly submits; he also follows Nietzsche's appeal to art as embodying a "will to falsehood" that opposes the metaphysics of "being, the true and the real," which deny life, say no to it, and arrest it in a mutilated death mask.[6] Summarizing Nietzsche's thought, Deleuze writes in *Nietzsche and Philosophy* (1962), "The world is neither true nor real but living. And the living world is will to power, *will to falsehood*, which is actualised in many different powers" (184; original emphasis). In *Difference and Repetition*, and again in the *Cinema* project, Deleuze will name these powers the "powers of the false" (DR 128; TI 126–55), and he will say that art is singular in its ability to pierce the false promise of fixed presence made by representation and present the repetition (i.e., becoming) of difference (DR 1). For this reason, Deleuze mirrors Nietzsche's elevation of tragedy as the art form par excellence by saying that all art is "a veritable *theatre* of metamorphoses and permutations. A theatre where nothing is fixed, a labyrinth without a thread (Ariadne has hung herself). The work of art leaves the domain of representation in order to become 'experience,' a transcendental empiricism or science of the sensible" (DR 56).

Leaving aside for the moment the (violent) image of feminine death that is once again put to work to illustrate the transgression of representation, for Deleuze only theater realizes Nietzsche's eternal return, which Deleuze interprets as a figure for the repeated and unending becoming of difference (and difference of becoming), against which Western metaphysics has conjured a host of essences—Being, truth, reality—in order to protect itself. And the reason theater is able to realize the eternal return is because it alone runs toward becoming, not from it, opening a space that solicits the proliferation of simulacra and not their prohibition, as seen in Plato onward. In this way, Nietzsche's Dionysus is the figure for simulacra in the theater: "Here too, for Nietzsche," writes Deleuze, "it is a matter of filling the superimposed masks and inscribing the omnipresence of Dionysus in that superimposition, by inserting both the infinity of real movement and the form of the absolute difference given in the repetition of eternal return" (DR 9). But the relation between theater and the eternal return is not just one of the former providing a stage for the presentation of the latter; there is also a *mise-en-abyme* at work between them. If theater is singular in its ability to present the eternal return, it is because the eternal return is essentially theatrical: "With Nietzsche," Deleuze contends, the eternal return "is a theatre of unbelief, of movement as *Physis*, already a theatre of cruelty" (DR 11).

This allusion to Artaud's theater of cruelty not only anticipates his later appearance with Blanchot and Heidegger in the *Cinema* books but also indicates that Deleuze views Artaud as being among the inheritors of Nietzsche's reflections on tragedy and cruelty.[7] But recalling the debate between Nancy and Lacoue-Labarthe on the necessity of the figure, particularly the turn their debate took toward the scenic and Lacoue-Labarthe's contention of an inevitable "archi-theater" as the condition for the possibility of any enunciation whatsoever, we can see Deleuze's privileging of theater as taking up a specific position vis-à-vis the question of the figure. By endorsing the proliferation of simulacra, it is clear that Deleuze is interested in retrieving the power of mimesis from its suppression in the history of

Western metaphysics. This endorsement corresponds to Nancy's embrace of mimesis through fictioning, places Deleuze at odds with Lacoue-Labarthe's call for de-figuration, and stands as a counter-example to Blanchot's pursuit of the writing of effacement. In soliciting the differentiating, dissimulating force of simulacra, which modern thought, in spite of itself, has awoken through its very attempts to master life, Deleuze seeks to retrieve the force of existence itself. For Deleuze, "simulacra" is the name for a thought of Being that challenges thought itself. This is why he follows Nietzsche in saying it is because of the threat simulacra represent that Western metaphysics has worked so tirelessly to silence their force.

It is against this background that Deleuze turns to the question of the voice. Yet it is not just because the force of existence has been silenced by the Western philosophical tradition that Deleuze holds the stakes of the experience of difference to be a matter of the voice. Difference is at stake in the voice because one of the first sites upon which Deleuze says the age-old contestation between identity and difference takes place is with the problem of the voice of Being itself. Specifically, it is with the question concerning the sense of Being—originating with Aristotle (and reaching its height with the Scholastics) of whether the same meaning of Being applies univocally (in the same sense) or equivocally (in different senses) to all the various modes in which something is "said" to exist—that Deleuze says an actual concept of difference is forsaken in favor of the metaphysical masquerade that is conceptual difference (difference subordinated to the identity of the concept, to the identity of the Same [DR xv]). As Deleuze will recount, Aristotle's concept of the analogy of Being—later taken up fully by Aquinas and one we will analyze in detail in this chapter, in which all senses of being are related proportionately to one another—provides an apparent solution to the problem of conceiving difference while not reducing it to sameness. In Deleuze's view, however, this "solution" allows a simple, degraded ontology to masquerade as a true statement about Being while suppressing the much more difficult concept of the univocity of Being, which, as Deleuze explains, thinks Being in its self-differentiation. Thus, in opposition to the Aristotelian legacy, Deleuze declares:

> There has only ever been one ontological proposition: Being is univocal. There has only ever been one ontology, that of Duns Scotus, which gave being a single voice. We say Duns Scotus because he was the one who elevated univocal being to the highest point of subtlety, albeit at the price of abstraction. However, from

Parmenides to Heidegger it is the same voice which is taken up, in an echo which itself forms the whole development of the univocal. A single voice raises the clamour of being. (DR 35)

With this declaration, we see that Heidegger serves as a bookend in a couple of ways in the opening of *Difference and Repetition*. His thought both introduces the possibility of clearing a space for an encounter with difference and also constitutes part of the history of univocity that Deleuze will claim Western thought has kept suppressed in an effort to offer only representations of difference. Noteworthy, then, is the accompanying implication that the project of recovering the thought of univocity for both philosophy and for an encounter with difference (*as* difference) necessitates an engagement with Heidegger's thought. Once we reconstruct Deleuze's recovery of univocity from the philosophical tradition and how he conceives it as opening onto the voice of simulacra in *Difference and Repetition*, we will see how Heidegger returns in the text to serve as a bridge to Deleuze's elaboration of univocity in *The Logic of Sense* and in particular to the conception of writing as an affirmation, as well as proliferation, of the voice of simulacra.

From Aristotle to Plato: Conceptual Difference versus the Reality of Simulacra

As previously stated, Deleuze views the Western philosophical tradition as one that, instead of producing a real concept of difference, has settled for forms of conceptual difference that present the appearance of an encounter with difference but actually just allow philosophy to master difference and render it less threatening to thought. It is a claim very reminiscent to the one we saw in Lacoue-Labarthe's critique of onto-typology. One key difference is that Deleuze does not include Plato among those who have sought to master mimesis. He instead makes a distinction between a Platonism that has furnished false concepts of difference and Plato's insight about the reality of simulacra.

For Deleuze, the forms of conceptual difference upon which philosophy has relied conceive difference differentially (i.e., always in relation to some other term), which thus subordinates difference to a relation between identities: this ultimately amounts to a grand failure to think difference in itself. Such a failure is most evident to Deleuze in the texts that have come to dominate Western metaphysics, namely, those of

Aristotle and Hegel. In his focus on their legacy, Deleuze brackets Plato off from Western metaphysics' history of failing to think difference. Although he invokes a Platonic terminology when he characterizes both Aristotle and Hegel as following a logic that subsumes the Many to the One, it is Aristotle, not Plato, who Deleuze describes as promoting—and indeed, completing—a misguided interpretation of Plato that he calls Platonism and lists Hegel as someone who perpetuates this Platonist itinerary. As a result, at the beginning of *Difference and Repetition*, Deleuze identifies Aristotle's conception of the analogy of Being as one of the earliest instances of the metaphysical reduction of difference to the identity of the concept. Once he demonstrates how the analogy of Being promotes a form of Platonism, Deleuze then rereads Plato to show what Aristotle misses in Plato's treatment of simulacra and how the figure of simulacra makes possible a thought of the univocity of Being as a thought of difference.

As with many of the doctrines attributed to Aristotle, that of the analogy of Being is nowhere stated as such in his writings. Rather, his commentators have assembled it from their interpretations of his work, finding various parts of the doctrine in the *Metaphysics*, the *Categories*, and the *Posterior Analytics*. However, one statement Aristotle makes in *Metaphysics* IV is commonly held to capture the doctrine's essence: " 'Being' is said in many ways [*legetai pollakos*], but related to one [*pros hen*], that is, to some one nature, and not equivocally" (1003a33–34).

Yet Being is not said univocally either, for that would merely repeat the premise of the Platonic theory of Forms and reduce the particular to the universal, erasing, in Aristotle's view, any meaningful notion of difference. Nonetheless, Aristotle's insistence on the irreducibility of particular things draws him into the very difficulties he sought to avoid in the critique of Plato's Forms: In the *Posterior Analytics*, the concept of the "subject-genus" that establishes the unity of individual sciences and their objects gives rise to the problem of the unity of the sciences in general, and especially the unity of that science called metaphysics.[8] Since metaphysics is a science of Being qua Being, this must mean there is a unity called Being that encompasses all that exists. The *Metaphysics* elaborates this problem in the form of the question of Being as the highest genus. If things in the world are grouped together and subdivided according to shared characteristics (human beings form one species, as do dogs, but both are members of the genus "animal"), then at some point we must get to the highest genus, the genus of all genera, namely Being. For in order to be classifiable, all things we classify must share the common trait of existence, no? Relatedly, in the *Categories*,

Aristotle confronts the problem of how multiple senses of Being employed in predication are related if not by an ultimate, univocal sense of Being.[9]

Aristotle is thus faced with two alternatives, both of which, from his perspective, are unsatisfactory: (1) Being is univocal and thus unites all things insofar as they all share existence; or (2) Being is equivocal, with individual things related in terms of shared characteristics but not in terms of existence. The former denies difference; the latter gives way to an anarchic distribution. The analogy of Being—Being as a relational (*pros hen*), "focal" point of meaning—offers a standpoint between univocity and equivocity.[10] It is not Being that unites; rather, all the many ways Being is said are united in that they "make reference or point" to Being as a single substance (*ousia*).[11]

Deleuze follows Aristotle's deliberations closely, including the argument he makes in the *Metaphysics* in support of the claim that Being is not a genus and that therefore it cannot serve as the highest genus.[12] The reasons why that is the case, Aristotle tells us, is that the differentia (*diaphora*) that distinguishes a species within a genus must be of a different kind than that genus.[13] "Man" is a species within the genus "animal." What makes a human being "man" and not, say, "dog," however, is that man is differentiated from dog by being a rational animal. "Rational" cannot be of the same kind as "animal," because if it were, then to call someone a rational animal would be the same thing as calling them an "animal animal," which would be redundant and therefore constitute a meaningless difference.[14] At the same time, we think that differentiae *are* (i.e., that they exist). Thus, if Being were a genus, and all differentiae, as existing things, were of the same kind as the genus that contains them, this would amount to saying that there is nothing besides Being (Blachowicz, *Essential Difference* 70). In order for Being to be differentiated, differentiae would have to be of a different kind, which is to say, they would have to be nonbeing, which would be an absurdity (*Metaphysics* 998b22–27; see Halper, *One and Many* 397). Therefore, there cannot be any highest genus, Being, that could be the genus of all genera.

For Deleuze, however, the appeal to analogy reveals that Aristotelian division obeys two different "Logoi" simultaneously: univocity of Being within species, and equivocity of Being among genera (DR 32–33). Consequently, Deleuze declares that Aristotle's distribution of difference, his "*diaphora* of the *diaphora*," is only a "false transport," one in which genera and species are "tied together by their complicity," he says, "in representation" (DR 32, 34). It is not a true thought of difference, but difference thought through the opposing identities of concepts—conceptual difference. Such an act of division is "a point of accommodation," Deleuze writes, "for the Greek eye—in particular for the Greek eye which sees the mean, and has lost the sense of Dionysian transports and metamorphoses" (32). The Greek eye has lost sight of mimesis.

According to Deleuze, although he is most famously identified with banishing mimesis from philosophy, Plato is not the one to whom this Greek eye belongs; it is held instead by Platonism, a very specific misinterpretation of Plato's work that subordinates "difference to the powers of the One, the Analogous, the Similar and even the Negative" (DR 59). Aristotle's conception of the analogy of Being is for Deleuze not only exemplary of Platonism but also one of the first misinterpretations of the Platonic conception of division, of the relation between the Many and the One. In Deleuze's view, Aristotle's doctrine interprets the dialectic of the Many and the One as a problem of demarcating species within genera, as opposed to what Deleuze says Platonic dialectic really is, namely, attending to the problem of how to select among difference(s) (DR 59–61). In missing this fact, Aristotle carries out a speculative "sleight of hand" that surreptitiously swaps a false image of difference—the conceptual difference of analogy—for a true thought of difference (univocity) that Deleuze asserts would constitute "a kind of fracture introduced into thought" (DR 32–33). It is precisely here that the history of metaphysics takes a wrong turn. "Our mistake," Deleuze thus proclaims, "lies in trying to understand Platonic division on the basis of Aristotelian requirements" (DR 59), and a distinction must be made between Plato and the Platonism that follows from the Aristotelian interpretation of the division between the Many and the One.[15]

What is significant for Deleuze is that myth makes an appearance in many of Plato's dialogues just as Plato is deep in the act of division, of determining the identity and difference among kinds of things. It is a moment in *Difference and Repetition* that echoes both Nancy's interest in myth, as well as Lacoue-Labarthe's remarks in "Typography" about Plato's employment of mimesis within his critique of mimesis. In the *Phaedrus*, Deleuze observes, the myth of the circulation of souls appears right at the moment in which Socrates and Phaedrus attempt to distinguish between the different kinds of madness, as if to suggest that the attempt at division is a kind of madness in itself (DR 61). In the *Statesman*, Plato has the Stranger invoke the cosmic myth of the "ancient shepherd-God" when the young Socrates asks how to distinguish part from kind (*Statesman* 268d–274e; cited in DR 61). For Deleuze, these appearances of myth support the conviction that the Dionysian could still have been found in Plato were it not for Aristotle's conflation of the Idea with the concept. "Myth," writes Deleuze, "tells us that it always involves a further task to be performed, an enigma to be resolved. The oracle is questioned, but the oracle's response is itself a problem" (DR 63). The appeal to myth reveals the irony of trying to arrive at fixed divisions of the Idea (the Idea as Being or the thing itself) (DR 64, 66). This is something Deleuze contends Aristotle misses, causing Aristotle (and not Plato) to beg the question regarding the principle governing the act of division. The irony is that it is not myth that is the flight from the question of Being. The flight is what Nietzsche called the "will to origins." As Deleuze writes in *The Logic of Sense*:

> This flight, this appearance of flight or renunciation, is the second snare of division, its second irony. In fact, myth interrupts nothing. On the contrary, it is an integral element of division. The characteristic of division is to surmount the duality of myth and dialectic, and to reunite in itself dialectical and mythic power. Myth, with its always circular structure, is indeed the story of foundation. It permits the construction of a model according to which the different pretenders can be judged. What needs foundation, in fact, is always a pretension or a claim. It is the pretender who appeals to a foundation, whose claim may be judged well-founded, ill-founded, or unfounded.[16]

The invocation of myth thus points to this: It is a matter, Deleuze says, not of distinguishing between "'the thing itself' and the simulacra," as it is in Platonism (DR 66). Rather, it is a matter of seeing simulacra as "the thing itself," the becoming of simulacra as the becoming of Being itself (or, as Deleuze will insist, the being of Becoming). This is why Deleuze thinks of the circle of myth in Plato in terms of the eternal return. For "taken in its strict sense, eternal return means that each thing exists in returning, copy of an infinity of copies which allows neither original nor origin to subsist" (DR 67). As copies of a copy, simulacra lack a proper relation to an original object, which is why Platonism rejects them, and mimesis generally, and sees their impropriety as a threat to the proper itself. Deleuze, however, regards this lack of a relation to either "origin [or] original" as a virtue of simulacra. Far from being merely degraded copies, simulacra are instead figures of nonresemblance as such; embodying the dissembling force of mimesis, simulacra are figures of difference-in-itself.

While Deleuze's treatment of simulacra in *Difference and Repetition* remains cursory, he develops his analysis more thoroughly in *The Logic of*

Sense (253–74). It is also in *The Logic of Sense* that Deleuze will wonder whether Plato's ironic deployment of myth and simulacra anticipated and originally set out the path for the overturning of Platonism for which Nietzsche would later call (LS 256). Most interesting for us, however, is Deleuze's embrace of myth in his recovery of simulacra. He does not call for its interruption or caesura, as we saw in Nancy and Lacoue-Labarthe, respectively. If anything, Deleuze's relation to myth is similar to Nancy's insofar as he implies in his conception of myth that it interrupts itself. For Deleuze, simulacra, and the mythic saying to which the play of simulacra gives rise, is not representation. It neither mediates nor is mediated. It is difference as such—the thinking of difference-in-itself (difference as the movement of thinking)—and an event of difference that results in the "radical destruction" of all identity (DR 66).

We will see how Deleuze relates the play of simulacra to Artaud (as well as Heidegger and Blanchot) in order to craft a practice of writing that undergoes this event of difference. But the identification of the reality of simulacra is only one part of Deleuze's recovery of univocity. According to Deleuze, it is not until the arrival of Duns Scotus that a rejection of the analogy of Being is achieved by philosophy. For it is Scotus, Deleuze says, who rejects the "solution" of analogy as a mediating term between the univocity and equivocity of Being and works out an ontology of univocity as the only ontology. Deleuze finds in Scotus's conception of univocity the possibility of viewing simulacra as embodying both the power of difference-in-itself as well as difference's perpetual repetition. Deleuze will then find this "potentiality of simulacra," as we might call it, realized further in Spinoza and in Nietzsche's eternal return.

Univocity and the Potentiality of Simulacra: From Duns Scotus to Spinoza

In Deleuze's view, Aristotle's conception of the analogy of Being proves to be only a superficial remedy to the two-headed threat of univocity and equivocity. In fact, as the history of Western philosophy shows, the analogy of Being gave way to additional problems once it was inherited by Aristotle's medieval interpreters. The threat the univocity of Being originally represented in Aristotle's thought, namely, the obliteration of any real ontological difference, mutates into a profound worry about the relationship between the human and the divine. For if both God and human beings are said to exist, does this mean they are commensurable in terms of Being? If so, then the ontological difference between human beings and God would be one of degree rather than kind and admit of a homogenizing likeness between the human and the divine. Yet to insist on a difference in kind between human being and the being of God would pose epistemological problems concerning the ability to have knowledge of God's nature and whether human beings can ever say anything meaningful about God. The analogy of Being carries little explanatory force in this conundrum; instead, it merely begs the question of the relation between the human and divine by implying it is still a matter of moving between the finite and the infinite but without explaining how this is accomplished.

In an interesting twist, Deleuze casts Scotus's conception of univocity as a solution to these problems posed by analogy, rather than the other way around (analogy supposedly resolving the original problem of choosing between the univocity and equivocity of Being).[17] Scotus bypasses the problems of analogy, Deleuze explains, with a conception of univocity that maintains that "*being is predicated in the same sense* of everything that is, whether infinite or finite, albeit not in the same 'modality.'"[18] Here we are presented with Scotus's radical solution, what Deleuze elsewhere calls elsewhere Scotus's "mad thought" (*une pensée démente*):[19] the introduction of modes of Being. Being is intrinsically modal, which is to say intrinsically differentiating, differing only from itself. With the introduction of modes of Being, Scotus is able to retain the unity of Being while also accounting for differences among and, more importantly, between individual beings within the same species. It is precisely this that analogy was unable to do: account for how the man Socrates differed or was individuated from the man Plato. With the notion of modes of Being, Scotus provides a true principle of individuation and differentiation from within Being itself (DR 38): there are only modes (i.e., modifications) of Being, which itself does not change. More importantly, the modifications of Being emerge from out of Being itself, not from any cause outside Being. "In effect," writes Deleuze, "the essential in univocity is not that Being is said in a single and same sense, but that it is said, in a single and same sense, *of* all its individuating differences or intrinsic modalities. Being is the same for all these modalities, but these modalities are not the same. It is 'equal' for all, but they themselves are not equal. It is said of all in a single sense, but they themselves do not have the same sense" (DR 36).

A similar passage appears in *The Logic of Sense*, but there, Deleuze identifies univocity as a literal voice:

> The univocity of Being does not mean that there is one and the same Being; on the contrary, beings are multiple and different, they are always produced by disjunctive synthesis, and they themselves are disjointed and divergent, *membra disjuncta*. The univocity of Being signifies that Being is Voice that is said, and that it is said in one and the same "sense" of everything about which it is said. That of which it is said is not at all the same, but Being is the same for everything about which it is said. It occurs, therefore, as a unique event for everything that happens to the most diverse things, *Eventum tantum* for all events, the ultimate form for all of the forms which remain disjointed in it, but which bring about the resonance and the ramification of their disjunction. (179)

Three things are thus implied by univocity: (1) Being's intrinsic differentiation "*precedes* matter and form, species and parts" (DR 38); it is a differentiation prior to differentiation into genera and species; (2) it is a matter not of the being of differences but Being as "Difference" (in-itself or as such) (DR 39); and (3) Being is infinite but not indeterminate (EP 28).[20]

Because Scotus is constrained by the theological implications of univocity, specifically by the fact that univocity in the strong sense would lead to pantheism and an uncomfortable equivalency between God and creatures, Deleuze says Scotus has to maintain a conception of univocal Being that is neutral and indifferent with respect to "the distinction between the finite and the infinite, the singular and the universal, the created and the uncreated" (DR 39). All Scotus's conception of univocity allows is that the same sense of existence is shared by God and creatures alike; univocity refrains from rendering any positive judgment about the differentia that might distinguish God and creatures from each other. Whether God is infinite or finite, created or uncreated, etc., in order to debate such questions, one assumes the existence of that about which one is debating. The same (i.e., univocal) sense of Being applies across these differences.[21] This means, however, that Scotus's conception of univocity does not penetrate to the level of differentiation among beings, and as a result, Deleuze asserts that Scotus "only *thought* univocal being"; for him, univocity did not go beyond being "an abstract concept" (DR 39).

For what he considers a truly positive conception of univocity, Deleuze turns to Spinoza, who Deleuze says represents a second moment in the history of the thought of univocal Being following Scotus. With Spinoza, Deleuze asserts, Being breaks out of the abstraction and passivity under which it had been cast by Scotus and becomes expressive and productive for the first time. According to Deleuze, Spinoza forges this conception of Being in three ways: (1) he theorizes univocal Being and God as identical through the notion of substance; (2) defines substance as singular (i.e., *causa sui*, self-caused); and (3) defines substance as expressive.

Deleuze frames his reading of Spinoza's conception of univocity with Spinoza's formula "*Deus sive Natura*"—"God, or Nature"—from the preface to Book IV of the *Ethics*, which in Deleuze's view captures Spinoza's equation of substance with univocal Being (DR 40). Deleuze describes Spinoza as revising both Scotus's understanding of attributes, as well as the distinctions Descartes draws between substances, attributes, and modes. The key element Deleuze focuses on in Spinoza's revision is his insistence on the singularity of substance—that there is no outside of substance and that substance is absolutely independent, self-caused (*causa sui*), and differing only from itself.[22] While Descartes defines substance similarly to Spinoza, he ends up contradicting this definition when he thinks it is possible for there to be multiple substances: the two chief ones being mind and body.[23] Were that the case, it would mean that substance could be limited by something outside itself and be dependent on something other than itself, which would be absurd. As Deleuze explains, this contradiction is the result of Descartes confusing a numerical distinction with a formal distinction: "From the opening pages of the *Ethics*," writes Deleuze, "[Spinoza] shows that real distinctions are never numerical but only formal—that is, qualitative or essential (essential attributes of the unique substance); and conversely, that numerical distinctions are never real, but only modal (intrinsic modes of the unique substance and its attributes)" (DR 40; see EP 27–39). Where Descartes notes a real distinction between thinking and extension and then takes this differentiation of the two attributes as evidence of two numerically distinct substances (mind and body, respectively), Spinoza says instead that thought and extension are two of the infinite number of attributes expressed by "God, or Nature."

This univocity of the attributes establishes substance as immanent and "everywhere fully expressed, without any transcendental and ineffable reserve" (Hardt 72). The attributes thus reveal substance—Being, God, Nature—*as expression*. In other words, God is expression. As for the problem of individuation—namely, the differentiation between substance and existing things (i.e., modes), as well as the differentiation between modes themselves—this is not yet accounted for by the doctrine of substance's expressivity. The difference between substance and modes is affirmed by the attributes; they point to the "fact" of difference between substance and its modes. (For example, ideas, as modes of thought, differ from bodies, which are modes of extension.) But as to "what" distinguishes substance and modes, this is not addressed in terms of expression. For this, Spinoza turns to a theory of power.

For it is the power (*potentia*) of substance to express itself; its self-expression is the means by which it causes itself. As we have been reviewing, the attributes are the expression of substance. What they express is the essence of substance. The essence of substance, Spinoza tells us, is the power (*potentia*) to exist, and so far as substance exists, it expresses. That is to say, it produces. Spinoza thereby identifies power with essence. Reading Spinoza's *Short Treatise* and the *Ethics* at once,[24] Deleuze writes:

> To say that the essence of God is power, is to say that God produces an infinity of things by virtue of the same power by which he exists. *He thus produces them by existing*. Cause of all things "in the same sense" as cause of himself, he produces all things in his attributes, since his attributes constitute at once his essence and his existence. It is not enough, then, to say that God's power is actual: it is necessarily active, it is act. God's essence cannot be his power without an infinity of things proceeding from it, and this precisely in the attributes that constitute it. So that modes are also the affections of God, but God never suffers the activity of his modes; his only affections are active. (EP 94; original emphasis)

The essential difference between substance and modes is a difference of power, or as Deleuze says elsewhere, a difference in degrees of power ("Lecture on *Anti-Oedipe* and *Milles Plateux*"). It is a question of degrees of power, because, as Deleuze explains, "in Spinozism all power bears with it a corresponding and inseparable capacity to be affected" (EP 93). God's capacity to be affected is infinite and positive. It (God) is not touched by affections external to it, which Spinoza calls "passive affections," since those affections are part of and caused by God. Modes, however, suffer passive affections and produce active affections. This is the essential difference that is at the same time a difference in degrees of power. "Tell me the affections of which you are capable," says Deleuze, "and I'll tell you who you are [*dis-moi les affections dont tu es capable et je te dirai qui tu es*]" ("Lecture on *Anti-Oedipe* and *Milles Plateaux*").

One question that often emerges in response to Spinoza's *Ethics*, however, is what exactly makes it an ethics. Concerned primarily with the nature of substance, it is more apt to call it an ontology. Although it describes the workings of nature, including the place of human beings in substance's expressive univocity, the *Ethics* does not make normative prescriptions regarding action. The text speaks neither of responsibility nor obligation but simply of what is, and in this description of what is, human reason, upon which most every ethical theory in the history of Western thought is established, enjoys no central role.[25]

Yet it is actually because Spinoza's text does not form a traditional morality—and that it decenters the rational subject—that Deleuze insists on speaking of the *Ethics* as an "ethology," a concept Deleuze appropriates from biologist Jakob von Uexküll's work on the continuity between the animal and its environment. Deleuze combines this with Spinoza's ideas on the body and the power to affect and be affected.[26] We are capable of being affected both positively—by what Spinoza calls "joyful passions," in ways and by other bodies that increase our power—and negatively, by "sad passions," in ways and by other bodies that subtract and compromise our power: this is why Spinoza's *Ethics* is an ethics (SPP 27–28).[27] It is a matter of selecting among those affections that increase our power and rejecting those that subtract from it. The upshot for a philosophy of difference, then, is that by defining essence as the power to be affected, Spinoza affirms existence—finitude—in terms of the becoming and return of difference.

Often overlooked, however, by existing commentaries on Deleuze's interpretation of Spinoza, especially those that use Deleuze in support of the affective turn, is his situating of Spinoza's ethology within the lineage of univocity. By keeping this fact in view, we can discern two important implications from Deleuze's engagement with Spinoza's thought: First, ethics is inseparable from finitude. If ethics means selecting among joyful and sad passions, then this selection presupposes having a sense of existence—a sense of existence as the expression of sense. Secondly, this means that ethics presupposes the voice. To affirm the power-to-be-affected means to affirm the univocity of Being (which is said in the same sense of all its differentiations)—not, however, as the becoming of Being but as the being of Becoming. For Deleuze, Nietzsche's eternal return will come to serve as a figure of univocity—as a scene of the voice—that affirms the becoming of difference.

Nietzsche and the Eternal Return: The Voice as Return

Nietzsche's eternal return plays an important role in Deleuze's project, not only because it provides the movement of repetition that Deleuze posits as central to the event of difference but also because it is a figure that affectively performs what he holds is the relation between univocity and simulacra. In so doing, the eternal return, so Deleuze argues, furnishes philosophy with a new image of thought that dislodges it from its nihilistic, metaphysical attempts at avoiding the reality of Becoming. However, as a figure, it also indicates the direction that philosophical thought and writing ought to take in order to affirm the reality of simulacra as the being of Becoming. Thus, in one instance, the eternal return serves as a pivot point from the affective experience of finitude Deleuze sees Nietzsche describing to the affective call of thinking we will soon see him take up in Heidegger. In another instance, it stakes out the site, in language, where the call of thinking—which is to say, the call of finitude—is answered.

In order to follow Deleuze's interpretation of the eternal return, a basic overview of the figure as it appears in Nietzsche's text is needed. Yet, as with any concept associated with Nietzsche's thought, the idea (or "doctrine," as it is sometimes referred to) of the eternal return is elusive. He invokes this idea in a number of prominent places, most notably in *Thus Spoke Zarathustra* (1885), which he himself casts as not only teaching the lesson of the eternal return but as being born from the idea.[28] Yet there is no one moment in Nietzsche's work that explains the eternal return explicitly. In *Zarathustra*, the eternal return is conveyed in pieces, through figures, and through disparate, dissonant voices, such as those of Zarathustra's animals. Notably, it is *they* who teach *him* the eternal return, telling him: "Everything goes, everything comes back; eternally rolls the wheel of being. Everything dies, everything blossoms again; eternally runs the year of being. Everything breaks, everything is joined anew; eternally the same house of being is built."[29] In *The Gay Science* (1887), instead of a traditional philosophical argument, we are given an affective *scene* that many commentators take to encompass the meaning of the eternal return but that, at most, intimates its appearance as a figure:

> —What if some day or night a demon were to steal into your loneliest loneliness and say to you: "This life as you now live it and have lived it, you will have to live once more and innumerable times more; and there will be nothing new in it, but every pain and every joy and every thought and sigh and everything unutterably small or great in your life must return to you, all in the same succession and sequence—even this spider and this moonlight between the trees, and even this moment

and I myself. The eternal hourglass of existence is turned upside down again and again, and you with it, speck of dust!"

Would you not throw yourself down and gnash your teeth and curse the demon who spoke thus? Or have you once experienced a tremendous moment when you would have answered him: "You are a god, and never have I heard anything more divine." If this thought gained possession of you, it would change you as you are or perhaps crush you. The question in each and every thing, "Do you desire this once more and innumerable times more?" would lie on your actions as the greatest weight. Or how well disposed would you have to become to yourself and to life *to crave nothing more fervently* than this ultimate eternal confirmation and seal?[30]

Together, these two moments from Nietzsche's texts outline the two main conceptions of the eternal return as commentators have understood it. In one respect, the eternal return seems to be a theory of the universe and of time, constituting Nietzsche's cosmology; in another respect, it appears to be a thought-experiment or test that forms the basis of Nietzsche's existentialism.[31] They are related, of course, and intimately so, insofar as the circularity of time is what the artificial, metaphysical conception of linearity covers over and denies, and insofar as that nihilistic conception of linear time, which wants to say no to the reality of existence as eternal repetition, informs the attitude of *ressentiment*, whose futile desire is above all to exact vengeance against the past.[32]

For Nietzsche, the chief characteristic belonging to the one of *ressentiment* is the inability to forget, and it is this inability that gives rise to modern morality's system of guilt, (bad) conscience, and ascetic ideals.[33] But *ressentiment* is in the first instance an Apollonian impulse, not merely in its saying no to existence but also in its drive to control existence—that is, in its drive to control Becoming—through reason and the concept. This is why whenever Nietzsche contrasts the nihilistic drive of *ressentiment* to the possibility of saying yes to existence, he evokes Dionysus, who, since *The Birth of Tragedy* has figured throughout Nietzsche's work not simply as the will to affirm existence but as existence as such. As the god of theater and masks, Dionysus figures the procession of appearances—which is to say, of simulacra—and the ephemeral nature of existence.[34] This is also the reason why Nietzsche invokes that version of Dionysus's mythic origin that tells of the infant Dionysus being torn apart by the Titans. He equates that primal scene of suffering and cruelty with both the experience of coming to appearance as phenomena (i.e., becoming individuated as a subject) and the experience of having any and all attempts at constructing foundations, metaphysical or otherwise, being exposed as mere phenomena and coming undone as a result.[35]

As we will soon see, Deleuze will pick up on this theme of cruelty and becoming in his reading of Nietzsche, and he will also link it to Artaud's image of a theater of cruelty on the way to imagining a form of writing that solicits the proliferation of simulacra. We note, however, that what enables this move on Deleuze's part is the literary character of Nietzsche's writing, which embodies his embrace of Dionysus as the dissimulating force of mimesis and which, like Plato, provides a space for this movement through its multiplicity of voices and personae. As an admixture of figures—Dionysus and the eternal return—Nietzsche's text performs the affirmation of simulacra through its affective, elliptical style and proliferation of voices.

In fact, it is as a choice between affective forces that Deleuze interprets the eternal return: to say yes to existence is to align oneself affectively with the forces of "becoming-active" in a way that corresponds to Spinoza's selection of active passions, whereas to say no to existence, as nihilism does, is to align oneself (still affectively) with the forces of "becoming-reactive" in a way that corresponds to Spinoza's selection of sad passions.[36] Will one become-active and affirm the being of Becoming, or will one become-reactive and try to master Becoming by imposing representation upon it, thus masking and denying its dissimulating force? Against references to the eternal return as "the eternal return of the Same," Deleuze insists this is a mischaracterization of Nietzsche's concept. "We misinterpret the expression 'eternal return' if we understand it as 'return of the same,'" writes Deleuze. "It is not being that returns but rather the returning itself that constitutes being insofar as it is affirmed of becoming and of that which passes" (NP 48). What returns is not the identity of Being, but the being of Becoming, Becoming as the eternally returning expression of the sense/meaning of existence, always-already there, as Heidegger would say.

However, Deleuze also attempts to bring out the complexity of the choice the eternal return confronts us with, showing that the alternative between becoming-active and becoming-reactive is not simply a choice between affirmation and denial. Often, what appears as affirmation is actually a form of denial; such a posture is the basis of nihilism, and according to Deleuze, one can see this at work in the character of the Ass from Nietzsche's *Zarathustra*. The Ass undertakes a faux affirmation; it says yes to difference but only to the extent it considers difference a burden that must be borne. "This Ass and the dialectical ox leave a moral aftertaste," writes Deleuze:

> They have a terrifying taste for responsibility, as though one could affirm only by expiating, as though it were necessary to pass through the misfortunes of rift and division in order to be able to say yes. It is as though Difference were evil and already negative, so that it could produce affirmation only by expiation—that is, by assuming at once both the weight of that which is denied and negation itself. Always the same old malediction which resounds from the heights of the principle of identity: alone will be saved not that which is simply represented, but the infinite representation (the concept) which conserves all the negative finally to deliver difference up to the identical. (DR 53)

One reason the Ass's yes is a faux affirmation is that it thinks difference only negatively, not as a source of action but as that which must be reacted to in the sense that it requires and awaits sublimation to the Same. The Ass seeks to represent difference and thereby transcend and master it. Representation here is a will-to-power. It is this instantiation of the will-to-power that Deleuze sees Nietzsche identify as the true source of nihilism, a no that masquerades as a yes but that is actually a becoming-reactive that leads to a turning-away from existence and the being of Becoming (NP 68).

In order to become-active, one must will only the affirmative forces and turn away from the turning-away that constitutes becoming-reactive. Unlike the Ass who arrives at affirmation via negation, and who we also note is the one of *ressentiment*—one who hurts, and has been hurt too much, the Dionysian yes-sayer, the *Übermensch*—arrives at negation after starting with affirmation (NP 116). The Dionysian denies *"everything which can be denied,"* says Deleuze, *"everything which cannot pass the test of eternal return,"* which is to say everything that says no to Becoming (DR 55; original emphasis). The yes-sayer actively forgets that which prompts the saying no that marks the attitude of the one of *ressentiment* (DR 55). Not only, then, does the Dionysian yes-sayer will the affirmative forces; it is only through active forgetting that they will their return. It is in this way that the eternal return, as a principle of selection, is also an ethical principle. In fact, it is *the* ethical principle, because it—specifically, the being of Becoming for which it stands—guides our actions by becoming the ultimate object of our will, thereby replacing Kant's categorical imperative, which is informed by a fear of existence and rooted in *ressentiment* (NP 68).

Yet, as a figure of univocity, the eternal return also speaks as an ontological lesson. What it teaches, Deleuze argues, is that becoming-reactive has no being. Because they are nihilistic, it would be contradictory if reactive forces returned (NP 71–72). It follows then that only a thought of the eternal return is a thought of Being (as becoming). Any thought not of the eternal return is thus not a thought of Being and thus not a thought. With the eternal return, Becoming does not imply lack, but rather the opposite: "The world is neither finite nor unlimited as representation would have it. It is completed and unlimited. Eternal return is the unlimited of the finished itself, the univocal being which is said of difference" (DR 57). "Everything returns" in, through, and as the same sense of Being (as becoming), but "what" returns is not the same. This is what the eternal return as a figure for the univocity of Being, as a scene of the voice, speaks: like Heidegger's voice of conscience, the eternal return calls to us in a way that we cannot not hear. We can only act or react, hearing the call of the eternal return and its affective claim, say yes, and affirm the being of Becoming; or we can pretend not to hear it, pretending not to be seized by it, say no, and deny Becoming through the artifice—that we refuse to acknowledge as artifice—of representation.

Should we choose to say yes, then the artifice of representation can be seen as (and affirmed for) the artifice it is, and, as Deleuze argues, we can see that the "everything" that returns is nothing other than simulacra.[37] "Taken in its strict sense," Deleuze writes, "eternal return means that each thing exists only in returning, copy of an infinity of copies which allows neither original nor origin to subsist" (DR 67). Under the eternal return, then, difference is a "*differing*," in which "every object, every thing, must see its own identity swallowed up in difference, each being no more than a difference between differences" (DR 56). Under the mimetic force of the eternal return, no thing serves as a model, no thing serves as a form or type, and no myth serves as an origin or foundation, since everything is fated to return in becoming. As a thought of mimesis, simulacra name the event of the presentation of difference.

As Deleuze goes on to assert, the eternal return implies the formlessness of Being, a state in which representation does not just come undone but does not ever "take shape." Deleuze calls this "chao-errancy": "With the eternal return, chao-errancy [*chao-errance*] is opposed to the coherence of representation; it excludes both the coherence of a subject which represents itself and that of an object represented. *Re*-petition opposes *re*-presentation: the prefix changes its meaning, since in the one case difference is said only in relation to the identical, while in the other it is the univocal which is said of the different" (DR 57; original emphasis).[38] This is actually the second time in *Difference and Repetition* that Deleuze invokes errancy in relation to univocity. Earlier in the text, he describes univocity as "a distribution of errancy and even 'delirium' [*une distribution d'errance et même de 'délire'*]" (DR 36; *Différence* 54, translation modified). Taken together, these passages underscore the fact that by errancy, Deleuze does not mean error but a wandering, its primary meaning in French that is obscured in its translation into English. The eternal return of simulacra, then, is not a falling into error but the perpetual movement that is Becoming.

Still, it's precisely because of its repetitive errancy that the eternal return threatens philosophy and the narcissistic image it has of itself (its image of thought), which, as we know, philosophy tries to maintain by denunciating becoming in all its forms. Chief among these, as we have seen, is mimesis, which philosophy casts as the source of deception and error. But because the eternal return of simulacra dissimulates all identity, this includes not only the identity of objects philosophy claims to be able to know, and not only the identity of the philosopher who would lay claim to such objects, but first and foremost the image philosophy has of itself as "Philosophy": as the subject whose proper object is thought itself, which it then simply assumes to be naturally aligned with "Truth" as such. "According to this image," writes Deleuze,

> thought has an affinity with the true; it formally possesses the true and materially wants the true. It is *in terms of* this image that everybody knows and is presumed to know what it means to think. Thereafter it matters little whether philosophy begins with the object or the subject, with Being or with beings, as long as thought remains subject to this Image which already prejudges everything; the distribution of the object and the subject as well as that of Being and beings. (DR 131; original emphasis)

As a thought of the being of Becoming, the eternal return is a restless image of thought. Deleuze describes it (in an echo of Blanchot) as an "insomnia of thought" (DR 29). The eternal return does not portray the cool, composed, and antiseptic image that finds the height of its expression in modern Cartesianism and Kantianism. With the eternal return, it no longer becomes a question of how to think difference but a question of conceiving thinking itself as a site of difference, where "thought 'makes' difference, but difference is monstrous" (DR 29). As a consequence of this image of thought-to-come, Deleuze tells us, "We should not be surprised that difference should appear accursed, that it should be error, sin or the figure of evil for which there must be expiation" (DR 29). In order to affirm the monstrosity of difference and errancy as the measure of thinking, however, we must denaturalize the dominant image of thought transmitted through the history of philosophy. "It cannot be regarded as a *fact*," Deleuze insists, "that thinking is the natural exercise of a faculty, and that this faculty is possessed of a good nature and a good will. 'Everybody' knows very well that in fact men think rarely, and more often under the impulse of a shock than in the excitement of a taste for thinking" (DR 132; original emphasis). This means that what has passed for thinking in the history of philosophy has been nothing but its opposite—a flight from thought and a flight from difference. Therefore, above all, we must denaturalize ourselves from our aversion to thinking for the possibility of experiencing difference. It is at this point that Deleuze turns to Heidegger, drawing from the conception of difference in what he understands to be Heidegger's formulation of univocity and in the shock to thought that constitutes Heidegger's image of thought. In so doing, Deleuze connects the affective call of the eternal return to the affective claim Heidegger asserts constitutes the call of thinking.

Heidegger, Univocity, and the Call of Thinking

Although Deleuze clearly includes Heidegger among the select few who is able to think the univocity of Being and thematize it as the matter of philosophy, he does not explicate in detail how he understands Heidegger to do so. Instead, Deleuze offers schematic gestures pointing to Heidegger's contribution to a thought of the univocity of Being. And although he ultimately declares that Heidegger appears not to have been able to conceive difference without subordinating it to the identity of the Same,[39] Deleuze nonetheless relies heavily on Heidegger's call of thinking as he assembles the new image of thought he sees Nietzsche inaugurating with the figure of the eternal return. It is notably the same call from *What Is Called Thinking?* that Blanchot reinterprets through the limit-experience of *impouvoir* in Artaud on the way to redefining thought as the impossibility of thinking. As we saw in the passage from *The Time-Image* with which we opened this chapter,

Deleuze is drawn not only to this arresting call but particularly to how it is received in the constellation of Heidegger, Blanchot, and Artaud. As we will see, Deleuze, like Blanchot, also pursues a mode of writing that responds to what he calls this "shock to thought." But unlike the self-effacing narrative voice that reverberates throughout the space Blanchot calls "literature," the voice that appears in Deleuze's conception of literature is that of simulacra. For Deleuze, this new mode of writing that makes a space for the saying of simulacra is a way to provoke a new image of thought that proceeds from out of the event of human finitude. Similar to Heidegger, who conceives human finitude as the affective exposure to and claim by the question of the sense/meaning of Being, Deleuze thinks human finitude as a response to the affective sense of expression/Becoming.

Given his remarks on the errancy of thinking in relationship to the eternal return, we might expect Deleuze to appeal to Heidegger's own reflections on errancy *(die Irre)* and thought, which Heidegger develops in relation to his recovery of truth as *aletheia*.[40] Deleuze does not do this, though. Instead, in a "Note on Heidegger's Philosophy of Difference" placed in the midst of his discussion of myth in Plato in *Difference and Repetition* (64–66), he focuses on the concept of the "Not" in Heidegger's early formulations of Dasein's experience of finitude—the nothing *(das Nichts)* that expresses the abyssal ground of Dasein's thrownness from out of its understanding of the sense/meaning of Being. From this concept of the Not, Deleuze draws out the connection between Heidegger's emphasis on the fundamental nature of questioning—as in the question of the sense/meaning of Being and Heidegger's definition of Dasein as that being for whom its being is a question—and the experience of difference.

Deleuze primarily engages with the Not as it appears in Heidegger's "On the Essence of Ground" (*Vom Wesen des Grundes* [1929]), published the same year as "What Is Metaphysics?," which also thematizes the nothing and that Deleuze also points to in his note. As Heidegger writes, together those two works provide two different perspectives on the Not as a condition of relation. In "What Is Metaphysics?," the Not is the experience of the nothing that names the ecstatic, abyssal ground of existence, of Dasein's finite transcendence; in "On the Essence of Ground," the Not names the ontological difference, the relation between Being and beings.[41] Heidegger stresses that the two appearances of the Not in the texts are not "identical [*einerlei*], yet they are the Same [*das Selbe*]"—they identify the Same as the matter *(die Sache)* of thinking, as that which provokes or calls for thinking.[42] (Of course, these formulations of the Not recall our discussion in chapter

1 of the nothing that is communicated by the voice of conscience and that the voice of conscience confronts the human Dasein with.)

What specifically catches Deleuze's attention here is Heidegger's invocation of the Same, not only in terms of its resonances with the portrayal of Nietzsche's eternal return as the return of the same but also for how they have both been misread, according to Deleuze. The distinction Heidegger makes between the identical (*das Gleiche*) and the Same (*das Selbe*) is a consistent theme throughout his thought, with the former signifying the homogeneity of representation and the latter the fundamental belonging-together (*Zusammengehörigkeit*) of Being and thinking as expressed in Parmenides's third fragment on which Heidegger meditates: *to gar auto noein estin te kai einai*—"For thinking and Being are the same."[43] For Heidegger, Parmenides's fragment is not a proposition about identity; it is rather an enigma positing the Same as an event that gathers together thinking and Being (*Identity and Difference* 27). Most importantly, the enigma that Parmenides confronts us with does not define thinking or Being but rather the opposite; it presents them as the fundamental questions that Heidegger takes them to be and that, as fundamental questions, constitute thinking and Being as affective existential encounters.

In "On the Essence of Ground," Heidegger tells us that the thought of the Same leads to an encounter with the Not—the difference between Being and beings that also expresses their belonging-together (97). This is the relation Heidegger names the "ontological difference," which the human Dasein is startled with anytime it pauses over the fundamental question of existence. Across "What Is Metaphysics?" and "On the Essence of Ground" (as well as *Introduction to Metaphysics*), that question takes on variations of the following: "Why something at all and not nothing?" ("On the Essence of Ground" 130).[44] As Heidegger argues, "But this 'and not nothing' . . . is not some kind of appended clarification. Rather, it makes possible in advance the manifestedness of beings in general."[45] The "and not nothing" is nothing other than the sense/meaning of Being by which the human Dasein is always-already claimed.

Deleuze thus reads the Not in Heidegger as the affirmation of univocity and as a concept of difference. As the Same, this sense/meaning of Being is an event of Being differentiating itself; Being gives itself in "differing itself." Deleuze describes the refusal of representation in Heidegger's conception of the ontological difference as a "stubborn differenciation [*une obstination dans la différenciation*]" that resists any and all attempts to synthesize, mediate, or reconcile—which is to say, master—difference (DR 65, *Différence* 90).

Unfortunately, according to Deleuze, the Same in Heidegger has been misread, and as a result, the sense of difference in the ontological difference has been missed. He writes: "It seems that the principal misunderstandings which Heidegger denounced as misreadings of his philosophy after *Being and Time* and 'What is Metaphysics?' have to do with the following: the Heideggerian *Not* refers not to the negative in Being but to Being as difference; it refers not to negation but to questioning" (DR 64). Furthermore, writes Deleuze, "Ontological Difference corresponds to questioning. It is the being of questions, which become problems, marking out the determinant fields of existence" (DR 65). In affirming "the being of the question" from out of the question of Being, Heidegger affirms the univocity of Being as the being of Becoming (DR 66).

As remarked upon earlier, Deleuze's "Note" on Heidegger appears somewhat awkwardly in his text, situated between his discussion of myth and simulacra in Plato. While we might expect the constellation we saw Lacoue-Labarthe attend to in chapter 4 involving Heidegger, Nietzsche, and Plato on the "proper" place of mimesis to also play a role in Deleuze's effort to distinguish between Plato and Platonism, it is nonetheless curious as to why the note on Heidegger appears in this particular moment of Deleuze's study. Even if we regard with Deleuze Heidegger's theorization of the Not as a concept of difference that affirms the univocity of Being, how, exactly, should we understand it as helping Deleuze set up the turn to simulacra?

The answer, I suggest, lies in Deleuze's stress on the relationship between questioning and difference in Heidegger. As we reviewed, the fundamental mode of questioning Heidegger urges eschews representation and the metaphysics of presence that subtends it. As Deleuze explains in his Note, because "representation subordinates difference to identity," difference cannot be an object of representation and still be a thought/experience of difference (DR 65). Implied, then, with his turn to simulacra following his discussion of Heidegger is that only simulacra can express the relation to difference that the originary questioning Heidegger calls for impels. Simulacra encompass the "being" of that which questioning encounters, which is not the self-same identity of the copy (as philosophy has historically viewed simulacra and mimesis generally) but is instead the dissembling power mimesis really names and threatens. "When the identity of things dissolves," writes Deleuze, "being escapes to attain univocity, and begins to revolve around the different" (DR 67). Heideggerian questioning, as a solicitation of univocity, gives itself over to the becoming named by simulacra and to a thought of simulacra as indices of the being of Becoming.

Deleuze thus extends Heidegger's conception of the voice to Heidegger's thematization of questioning, helping us see Heideggerian questioning as an affective scene of the voice, as answering to the call of thinking and the claim of finitude.

As Deleuze repeats throughout *Difference and Repetition*, though, the dissolution of identity is not only threatening but cruel. It is in such moments that Deleuze invokes Nietzsche in reference to the theme of cruelty in *The Birth of Tragedy*; yet, in tandem with this theme in Nietzsche and Nietzsche's appeals to Dionysian theater, Deleuze also conjures Artaud's image of a theater of cruelty (DR 11; 29; 219). In these moments, Deleuze interprets cruelty not only in terms of the dissolution of identity of the objects of thought. Recalling the passage previously cited where Deleuze describes this theater as a labyrinth haunted by the figure of an Ariadne who has died by her own hand, this experience of cruelty (at the limit of experience, we might say) takes place for Deleuze within an affective register that dissolves the identity of thought itself, shooting through and rupturing the subject presumed to have mastery over their thought and denying thought its image as a shelter for the subject of knowledge and experience. Referring to the same correspondence between Artaud and Rivière through which we saw Blanchot theorize the *impouvoir* of thinking (a theorization that, as the passage previously cited from *The Time-Image* suggests, served as a guiding text for Deleuze for much of his thought), Deleuze says, "Artaud pursues in all this the terrible revelation of a thought without image, and the conquest of a new principle which does not allow itself to be represented" (DR 147). Again, this is an affective passage of extreme exposure. As Deleuze explicates, Artaud's theater of cruelty is a "wounding gravitation capable of directly affecting the organism, a pure staging without author, without actors and without subjects. Spaces are hollowed out, time is accelerated or decelerated, only at the cost of strains and displacements which mobilise and compromise the whole body" (DR 219).

Like Blanchot, Deleuze will follow the path Artaud takes in conceiving the impossibility of thinking not as an impediment to art but as art's condition, specifically as a condition of writing. Unlike Blanchot, however, Deleuze will not pursue a writing of effacement; he will instead embrace a practice of writing that solicits the procession of simulacra and invites the cruel events of becoming. The next and final section of this chapter maps moments where Deleuze elaborates the concept of univocity through the questions of affect, language, and writing, specifically in *The Logic of Sense*, published just a year after *Difference and Repetition*, but also in his later collaborations with Félix Guattari. This next section will not be a detailed analysis of these moments, however, which deserve their own separate and sustained treatment. Instead, my aim is to offer a kind of coda that reflects on Deleuze's conceptualization of the voice in *Difference and Repetition* and that also illustrates the continued insistence of the voice throughout Deleuze's corpus. Where the present section sought to establish Deleuze's status as a reader of Heidegger and as an inheritor not only of the Heideggerian voice but also the question of the sense/meaning of Being to which it exposes thinking, the chapter's coda will suggest ways that Deleuze's conception of the voice invites a consideration of him as a philosopher of language, albeit one who thinks language inseparable from affect (and vice versa). While Deleuze has been celebrated by affect theorists, his relation to the question of language has failed to attract much critical attention by them even though it is an essential aspect of his occupation with affect. To be sure, there are studies that examine Deleuze's theorization of literature in terms of its affective casting of language; however, that is different from approaching him as a philosopher of language.[46] Recovering the connection between language and affect in Deleuze's thought consequently has much to teach affect studies and much to contribute to an idea of a contemporary Continental philosophy of language.

Voice, Language, and the Cruelty of Sense

Although *The Logic of Sense* elaborates many of the concepts Deleuze puts forth in *Difference and Repetition*, it remains one of his most challenging texts. In terms of content alone, it makes for an unorthodox study by further elaborating Deleuze's reading of Artaud from *Difference and Repetition* and extending it to Artaud's encounter with Lewis Carroll, with the Stoics and Melanie Klein mixed in along the way. Additionally, Deleuze assembles the actual text of the work in a way that goes against the paths that philosophical argumentation traditionally follows.

As we explained earlier, in *Difference and Repetition* Deleuze is critical of representation for the way it subsumes difference to abstraction. In its place, and as part of his overturning of Platonism, Deleuze installs the Idea, which Deleuze appropriates from Plato as a name for the reality of simulacra. Ideas, Deleuze asserts, are opposed to representation; instead of representing things, Ideas are formed by an assemblage of what Deleuze calls "structure-event-sense" (DR 191). By "event," Deleuze implies becomings of the sense of Becoming, and he describes "structure" as a kind of theater of events (DR 191–92). In *The Logic of Sense*, he elaborates the relation among structure, event, and sense with the term "series," which he intimates in *Difference and Repetition*, but which he conceptualizes more fully in *The Logic of Sense* as linkages of events, contained in turn by structures (LS 36–41; 48–51). In addition to putting forth this new image of thought to oppose representation, *The Logic of Sense* attempts to enact it in the form of its writing. Deleuze composes the work as a series of events, in the form of brief, elliptical vignettes that develop multiple lines of thinking in nonlinear fashion and read as almost fabulistic in nature. Populating these vignettes are an assortment of characters, including Carroll's Alice, Klein's Mother, and Artaud's *schizo*—all figures that readers of Deleuze and Guattari's collaborative works should recognize as playing vital roles in their thought. *The Logic of Sense* is thus one site where we witness their initial generation.

Deleuze pursues this form of writing both to oppose representation as well as solicit—or, in the terminology of *Difference and Repetition* that he develops from his reading of Bergson, "actualize"—"the difference of Being by taking its own difference as object—in other words, by posing the question of its own difference. Hence that form of writing which is nothing but the question 'what is writing?,' or that sensibility which is nothing but the question 'what is it to sense?,' or that thought which asks 'what does it mean to think?'" (DR 195). This writing, in other words, is a response to the challenge presented by the eternal return and an attempt to affirm the reality of univocity. Deleuze characterizes this reality in *The Logic of Sense* not only in terms of simulacra, behind which there are only more simulacra, more events of Becoming, but as a "disjunctive synthesis" of events (LS 178). If all events are events of the becoming of sense, then they all belong to the being of Becoming; they are not incompatible, but "'inter-expressive' (*s'entr' expriment*)," Deleuze contends (LS 177). In a formulation reminiscent of Schopenhauer's conception of the Will, events only appear incompatible when the individual fails to recognize that they, too, are events of Becoming (LS 178). So the challenge becomes one of how the individual is to affirm not their identity but the univocity of Being, in effect affirming the alterity that one always-already is (LS 178–79).

Once again, Deleuze turns to art, and specifically to literature, for evidence of, and as a path to, such affirmation. As mentioned, two literary figures he primarily focuses on in *The Logic of Sense* are Carroll and Artaud, each practicing a different way of affirming univocity through their respective occupations of the border between sense and nonsense. For

Deleuze, Carroll's famous employment of the portmanteau is an instance of the disjunctive synthesis in action. Quoting from Carroll's Preface to *The Hunting of the Snark* (1876), Deleuze presents Carroll's understanding of what the portmanteau accomplishes. Regarding his invention "frumious," which famously appears in "Jabberwocky" (1871), Carroll writes: "If your thoughts incline ever so little towards 'fuming,' you will say 'fuming-furious'; if they turn, even by a hair's breadth, towards 'furious,' you will say 'furious-fuming'; but if you have that rarest of gifts, a perfectly balanced mind, you will say 'frumious'" (cited in LS 46). As Deleuze interprets Carroll's account, the difference being expressed and affirmed is not between furious and fuming, but between "fuming-furious" and "furious-fuming." Each name for Deleuze a series of events that does not close off difference but rather calls "to other portmanteau words which precede or follow it, and which show that every series is already ramified in principle and still further ramifiable" (LS 47). As disjunctive syntheses, Carroll's portmanteaus indicate the movement of difference, the becoming of sense, as well as the sense of Becoming.

As valuable as Carroll's explorations of sense are for Deleuze, though (to say nothing of his figure of the little girl that Deleuze also finds useful),[47] he still regards him as surveying the surface of sense, not plumbing its depths and registering its affective dimensions the ways Artaud's writing does. As Deleuze argues, Artaud himself reveals Carroll's superficiality in his abandoned attempt to translate "Jabberwocky" as part of his therapy while institutionalized in the mental asylum in Rodez.[48] In a well-known letter that Deleuze cites, in which Artaud shares his assessment of "Jabberwocky" with his friend and established French translator of Carroll, Henri Parisot, Artaud describes the poem "as an affected infantilism," associating it with other "*poems or languages of the surface* which smell of happy leisures and of intellectual success."[49] "'Jabberwocky,' he inveighs, "is the work of a profiteer who, satiated after a fine meal, seeks to indulge himself in the pain of others" (Letter to Henri Parisot., cited in LS 84). What disgusts Artaud about Carroll is that there is no evidence that he ever created anything "from torment [*d'affre*]" or "suffering [*la souffrance*]" (Letter to Henri Parisot., cited in LS 84; *Logique du Sens* 103).

Despite his protestations against Carroll, Artaud nonetheless publishes the first stanza of his abandoned translation of "Jabberwocky" in 1947. Yet, because Carroll's original is composed almost entirely of portmanteau words, it is difficult to translate Artaud's rendering back into English or to assess its accuracy. (It is a simulacrum of a simulacrum, so to speak):

Jabberwocky

'Twas brillig, and the slithy toves
Did gyre and gimble in the wabe:
All mimsy were the borogoves,
And the mome raths outgrabe.[50]

L'Arve et l'Aume, tentative antigrammaticale contre Lewis Carroll

Il était roparant, et les vliqueux tarands
Allaient en gibroyant et en brimbulkdriquant
Jusque là lò la rourghe est à rouarghe a rangmbde
et rangmbde a rouarghambde:
Tous les falomitards étaient les chats-huants
Et les Ghoré Uk'hatis dans Grabugeument.[51]

Nonetheless, after comparing Artaud's rendering with those of Carroll's "other French translators" (whom he names but whose translations he does not present[52]), Deleuze says, "beginning with the last word of the second line, from the third line onward, a sliding is produced, and even a creative, central collapse, causing us to be in another world and in an entirely different language" (LS 83–84). Based on this, Deleuze apparently feels confident in offering the following declaration: "With horror, we recognize it easily: it is the language of schizophrenia" (LS 84). How Deleuze draws this conclusion (or arrives at this diagnosis) from the formal elements he describes is not at all clear. What is clear, though, is that for Deleuze Artaud becomes the *schizo* par excellence, a heroic figure that Deleuze will bring to his collaborations with Guattari.[53]

Until this moment in the text, Carroll has served as the exemplar of the affirmation of univocity through the disjunctive synthesis of the portmanteau. So if Carroll already responds to the call of univocity, what is to be made of Artaud's dismissal of him? Deleuze reconciles their apparent opposition by saying that their works designate two types of nonsense: a "surface series" in Carroll and "poles of depth" in Artaud (LS 91). Carroll's employment of portmanteau plays at the surface of sense, remaining incorporeal, according to Deleuze. Artaud's nonsense, in contrast, is exclusively corporeal, and although it also deals with a surface, that surface is that of the body that "absorbs and engulfs all sense" (LS 91), thus simultaneously "refer[ring] to two theaters, the theater of terror or passion and the theater of cruelty" (LS 90). These two theaters comprise schizophrenic language's dissolution of phonetic and tonic elements of sense, says Deleuze, dragging language itself into the subterranean regions of "sub-sense, a-sense, *Untersinn*" (LS 90). While Carroll's nonsense constitutes a fundamental stuttering, a fundamental "break (*coupure*)," Artaud's form of nonsense, Deleuze submits, demarcates a "deep *Spaltung*," an untraversable divide in sense itself (LS 91). Together, they have the effect of remarking on the fact of sense, the sense of sense, with Artaud's nonsense being more severe to the extent it carves out the space—the scene—of sense's disappearance, of a swallowing of the voice. This swallowing of voice (this swallowing *that is* voice) can be seen as the basis from which Deleuze approaches the figure of the "*cris-souffles*" or "howls-breaths" in Artaud (LS 83; 193), as well as for his attraction to the motif of the scream which he later comes to reflect upon in the art of Francis Bacon.[54]

Here we might observe that Deleuze's engagement with Carroll and Artaud in *The Logic of Sense* is an instance of the antagonism of language that I mapped out in Heidegger in chapter 2. In *The Logic of Sense*, Deleuze is still thinking through this antagonism through the terminology of linguistics; however, as he refines his approach to the question of language in his collaborations with Guattari, we see them resist what they take to be the ossifying image of language presupposed by linguistics, thereby resembling more closely Heidegger's critique of the technocratic conception of language as mere instrument of communication. Together, in such works as *Kafka: Toward a Minor Literature* (1975) and *A Thousand Plateaus* (1980), the concept of a "minor literature" that they develop constitutes an other language within language. It is so other, in fact, that it scarcely registers or is recognized as language. For this reason, we see such themes as stuttering and the experience of not being at home in one's language (an *Unheimlichkeit*, perhaps) recurring in their theorizations of the limit of language, as well as the appearance/question of the voice of the nonhuman animal.[55]

In their collaborations, Deleuze and Guattari are attracted to Kafka, who, like Artaud, is both a writer and figure often identified with the themes just noted. Unlike Deleuze's treatment of Artaud, however, their treatment of Kafka resists appealing to his personal history or background. In *Kafka: Toward a Minor Literature*, Deleuze and Guattari replace what they characterize as the psychoanalytically based interpretations of Kafka's work with an image of his writings as a "machinic assemblage," which they insist is precisely not an interpretation. Interpretation, by which they mean of the hermeneutic kind, assumes, they say, a stable, symbolic structure, a belief in a behind-the-statement, in a signified behind the signifier, in the representation of meaning. As Kafka demonstrates with the Parable of the Law in *The Trial*, there is nothing behind the door to the Law (of meaning) except another door, and another door behind that one, ad infinitum. Instead of an original meaning, there are only simulacra.

According to Deleuze and Guattari, the defining quality of Kafka's work is ignored by what they consider the prevailing readings of him. "The three worst themes in many interpretations of Kafka," they write, "are the transcendence of the law, the interiority of guilt, the subjectivity of enunciation."[56] But what is remarkable about Kafka's writings, they say, is that they enact a "dismantling (*démontage*)" of the speaking subject (*sujet d'énonciation*) and therefore a dissolution of the interiority of subjectivity. Echoing Deleuze's remarks on Carroll in *The Logic of Sense*, they argue that in Kafka the drive to meaning or for the origin is replaced by the pure surface of language itself. With Kafka, they write, "*language stops being representative in order to now move toward its extremities or its limits*" (K 23; original emphasis). He presents everything "as it is, it is as it is" (K 20), tearing language from sense, "bringing about [its] active neutralization" (K 21). Kafka's stories simply unfold a network of connections among statements, a machinic assemblage through which only language speaks.

How does Kafka bring about this dismantling of language's representative order? According to Deleuze and Guattari, it is by producing a minor language within a major one—a Prague Jew writing in German, creating "lines of escape" within an existing structure of language, "becoming-nomad" within "one's own language" (K 19)—which results in a "deterritorialization" of the meanings that have become sedimented in the major language. Like Artaud's voice, or more specifically, the voice in the form of "howls-breaths" (*cris souffes*) previously noted, Kafka's voice resides on the edge of sense, which is why Deleuze and Guattari give so much weight to the frequency with which nonhuman animal voices appear in Kafka's stories. They hear them as events of becoming: the becoming-insect of "The Metamorphosis," the ape's becoming-human in "A Report to an Academy," the singing of Josephine the mouse. "The animal does not speak 'like' a man," Deleuze and Guattari write, "but pulls from the language tonalities lacking in signification; the words themselves are not 'like' the animals but in their own way climb about, bark and roam around, being properly linguistic dogs, insects, or mice. To make the sequences vibrate, to open the word unto unexpected internal intensities—in short, an asignifying *intensive utilization* [*un* usage intensif *asignifiant*] of language" (K 22; original emphasis).[57] By "utilization" (*usage*), Deleuze and Guattari do not mean a literary effect Kafka intentionally brings about. They are referring to what comes about unintentionally due to Kafka having been forced to write in a language from which he was alienated. Here again is the theme of errancy encountered earlier in *Difference and Repetition*: "A withered vocabulary, an incorrect syntax" give rise to a misuse and a strangeness that dismantles German from within (K 22). Kafka's intentions and subjectivity have nothing to do with it. Furthermore, in their eschewing of the terminology of resemblance, Deleuze and Guattari offer a conception of writing—minor literature—that solicits the destabilizing force of becoming, that is to say, of mimesis as dissimulating force. Through his alien utilization, Kafka introduced an other language—an other voice, a plural speech—within language.

In *A Thousand Plateaus*, Deleuze and Guattari insert their reading of Kafka into a more expansive critique of linguistics and the homogenizing unity of "language" it assumes. "The unity of language is fundamentally political," they declare, for it dictates in advance normative bounds of what counts as sense and what is deemed nonsense.[58] The concept of Kafka's minor literature appears following a section that develops the notion of the minor from out of the relation between music and voice. Deleuze and Guattari express a kind of lament that linguistics did not learn more from music regarding the voice, particularly its power of differentiation among instruments and the way it invites experimentation, occupying a space between language and sound (TP 96–97). As with its other theorizations, the voice in *A Thousand Plateaus* names an experience of difference.

Connected to the sustained reflection on the voice in music is an interesting elaboration of a remark Deleuze and Guattari first make in the *Kafka* book regarding Jean-Luc Godard. When speaking of Kafka's utilization of German as a Prague Jew, they offer a brief aside about Godard's utilization of French. They suggest that, like Kafka, Godard also engages in a minor utilization of language, making "French a minor language within French" in his films. With Godard, this leads to a "generalized intensification . . . making the image vibrate" (K 23). In the elaboration of this description in *A Thousand Plateaus*, the relation between word and image that they merely touch on in *Kafka* becomes much more interesting. Deleuze and Guattari describe Godard as introducing a "stammering" into the cinematic image that results in a stammering of language itself: "It's easy to stammer," they write, "but making language itself stammer is a different affair; it involves placing all linguistic, and even nonlinguistic, elements in variation, both variables of expression and variables of content. A new form of redundancy. AND . . . AND . . . AND . . ." (TP 98). With this "AND . . . AND . . . AND," Deleuze and Guattari propose that Godard produces a nondialectical cinema, where the progression of images does not contribute to any economy of meaning and does not advance any narrative progression. Accordingly, Godard enacts a new ontology of the image. His images are not representational; they are not "images of" objects or events and thus perform no epistemological labor. As such, Godard's images open onto difference rather than identity, onto repetition without resemblance: the IS (*est*) gives way to the AND (*et*) (TP 98).[59] Godard's cinema, that is to say, rejects the metaphysics of identity and affirms the eternal return of simulacra. But insofar as it undertakes a becoming-minor of language, Godard's cinema accomplishes this return as an event of the voice, as an event of sense. What Deleuze and Guattari go on to call "style" is the assemblage of this heterogeneous, affective event of sense (TP 97–98).[60]

It is no coincidence, then, that when Deleuze later returns to Godard in the *Cinema* books, it is as part of the same discussion where he reconstructs the vectors of inheritance and responses among Heidegger, Blanchot, and Artaud on the image of thought (TI 156–88). As he describes Godard's method as that of "BETWEEN" and "AND"—"between two images"; "this and then that"—he again invokes Blanchot, specifically the figures of the outside and of interruption from *The Infinite Conversation* (TI 180), in order to argue that Godard realizes a cinema composed of the "irrational cut" (TI 181), a technique of discontinuity that gives rise to a profound and decisive separation between sound and image such that they no longer serve the object of producing narrative progression from which a coherent internal monologue can be discerned (TI 188). Instead, there is simply a continuous and anonymous differentiation of voices and images, which, resonant with Blanchot's narrative voice, Deleuze names "free indirect discourse" (TI 188; 242). With Godard, we are given a scene of the voice in which nothing is seen, "an unthought in thought" (TI 181).

As we arrive back to Deleuze's *Cinema* books, and to the configuration of concepts and thinkers (Heidegger, Blanchot, and Artaud) that for Deleuze help reveal cinema's power to forge a new image of thought, we might now see how central and persistent the voice and language are in his work. Although most critical commentaries treat these later writings on cinema almost exclusively as the culmination of Deleuze's elaboration of his Bergsonian-informed engagement with the materiality of the image and its affective dimensions, I would submit that the *Cinema* project, if not

Deleuze's corpus as a whole, remains undervalued if his engagements with voice and language are excluded from its consideration.[61] As I have also sought to show, Deleuze realizes this project from within a very particular constellation of language, affect, and the voice, one that situates Heidegger and Blanchot as central, if albeit subterranean, interlocutors.

At the same time, we should note that Deleuze also adds to the debate regarding the necessity of the figure and the scenic dimension of the voice in his theorization of simulacra and in affirming their eternal return. With the *Cinema* project, Deleuze contributes an additional inflection to this act of affirmation by casting cinema as the return not only of the voice but of the scene itself. The image of thought cinema presents is one populated not only with multiple voices but also with multiple stagings of the scene of the voice. Looking back, we can see that cinema is not alone in doing so; for Deleuze, but also for all the thinkers we have read in this study, this is the work that the work of art alone is able to accomplish for a thought of difference. So, although there is disagreement in post-Heideggerian thought (within which I include Deleuze) concerning the inevitability of the figure and whether it participates in speculation or names a space outside of it, there is a shared assumption that the debate must take place on the terrain of the question of art.

That ancient quarrel once again.

Epilogue

Thinking and Language after Affect

> One can see which solutions will prove inappropriate to such a problem: a language of assertion and answer, for example, or a linear language of simple development, that is to say, *a language where language itself would not be at stake.*
>
> —Blanchot, "Thought and the Exigency of Discontinuity"

The readings I have conducted of the voice in Heidegger and post-Heideggerian philosophy have had the express purpose of keeping in view for critical thought the relationship between language and finitude for which the voice figures as an affective echo. While not intended as a sustained critique of either the affective turn or the return to the aesthetic in contemporary theory, the present study nonetheless emerged from a concern that these turns' claim to have transcended the problem of language has resulted in a moving on from the question of language and a loss of the fact that Heidegger's posing of this question—his posing of language as a question that seizes hold of human beings and confronts us with the question of (our) existence—harbors a fundamental relation to human finitude that is the condition for the possibility of any thought of either affect or sensibility whatsoever. Consequently, so far as the theoretical turns of contemporary thought are predicated on a disregard for the question of language, they both fail to attend to the question of human existence and also block themselves off from the very thing—affect, sensibility—that they take as their ostensible objects of study.

As I sought to make clear in my readings, the matter of figuration is not incidental to the question of language but central to it, a fact that we saw Heidegger simultaneously acknowledge with his conceptualization of the voice and facticity and yet disavow with his suturing of the voice to the figure of truth as *aletheia*. This moment of occlusion, which, as I showed, marks a limit in Heidegger's thought, reinstates the occlusion or limit that appears in the Western metaphysical tradition's efforts to master the dissimulating power of mimesis through the figure. It also subjects Heidegger's thought to an amnesia regarding the figure's speculative dimension that, as the debate between Nancy and Lacoue-Labarthe revealed, gives us pause with respect to the question of the susceptibility of Heidegger's thought to the ideology of National Socialism. Yet, this very limit nonetheless also marks for Heidegger's readers a site of engagement with his text that generates competing attempts to think human finitude as a relation to difference in, through, and sometimes against the figure of the voice. And while these attempts were divided in terms of whether to embrace the figure, as in the case of Nancy and Deleuze, or to provoke its effacement, as exemplified in Lacoue-Labarthe's and Blanchot's reflections, we saw that they all shared an attention to the affective relation harbored within the question of language.

Thus, while some of my reservations about the affective turn and the return to the aesthetic lie in their claimed abilities to proceed untouched by the question of language, another has to do with these turns' apparent presumption that their writings are somehow neutral and devoid of figuration, especially in the case of the affective turn. As I surveyed in this study's introduction, given the affective turn's frequent recourse to such (Heideggerian) figures as "world" and "dwelling," this inattention to the medium of its "thinking" is curious, if not also seemingly expressive of a kind of magical thinking that believes it can, by simply wishing or asserting it, unlearn the implications of the linguistic turn and will itself to inhabit a realm outside of representation. As I hope became clear as my analyses throughout this study unfolded—but especially with my concluding chapters on Blanchot and Deleuze—what is at stake in a thought of the voice is not only the relation among human finitude, language, and affect but also the possibility of thinking itself. My placing of "thinking" in quotation marks just now when referring to the scholarship of the affective turn is therefore meant to underscore its dismissal of language as not only a failure to think affect but a failure to be provoked by the fact that it is not yet thinking.

Institutionally, the scholarly success of the turns to affect and the aesthetic is also troubling because, aside from what it reveals about the status of thinking in the industry we call academia, it demonstrates what often passes as a voice in this industry. That is, it testifies to the kind of speech that is, in many instances, unreflectively valued, promoted, reproduced, and exchanged as intellectual research: in other words, it does not qualify as speech at all but is rather a simulacrum that exists for the sole purpose of reproducing the institution and its recognized subjects.[1]

Among the thinkers whom we have engaged in this study, there is one, Blanchot, who offers a particularly compelling statement on the language of research. It is a statement that has been a companion of mine throughout my work, influencing from the very beginning my thoughts on the question of language following Heidegger, as well as my more recent concerns with the possibility of speech within the institutions of philosophy and the contemporary neoliberal University. Since this statement combines a reflection on institutional speech as it concerns the relation among language, human finitude, and the figure, and since it also raises questions about our affective attachments and identifications with such speech, I want to take it up as an opportunity to bring out the social, political, and ethical implications of the figure of the voice that I signaled at the outset of this study but in the context of the site of production in which this study participates and to which it contributes, namely research as part of the contemporary neoliberal University.

Titled "Thought and the Exigency of Discontinuity," and appearing as the first essay in *The Infinite Conversation*, Blanchot's statement discusses the types under which the language of research has appeared in the West, as well as the subjects (i.e., figures) who are ideally associated with its apparently different languages but that Blanchot maintains are really variations on the same language of progress and linear development. The exigency of discontinuity for which he argues is therefore an imperative to interrupt the reproductive economy of institutional speech with what he calls a "plural speech" (IC 8). At stake in such a speech is the possibility of a language of research that says the alterity of human finitude, that is to say, the exposure to/that is otherness that constitutes human finitude such that it bears on the very possibility of its speaking and carries within it the question of this possibility.

Notable in connection to the attention this study has given to the question of the relationship between *Gestaltung* (figuration) and *Gestalt* (figure or form), Blanchot opens the essay with a reflection on language and form. "Poetry has a form," he writes, "the novel has a form; research, the research in which the movement of all research is in play, seems unaware that it does not have a form or, worse still, refuses to question the form that it borrows from tradition" (IC 3). Blanchot is not speaking about any specific kind of research but about an idea of research that encompasses "the movement of all research." Moreover, in a note immediately following his observation about the forms of poetry and the novel, he corrects himself, declaring, "Or let us say rather: poetry, the novel, *are form*—a word that, far from clarifying anything, now carries the whole of the interrogation" (IC 437n1; emphasis added). So, in addition to raising a question about the relation between research and form, we are led to infer that, like poetry and the novel, research is also form. What this means is unclear. As Blanchot says, the term "form" does not clarify anything; instead it "carries the whole of the interrogation." Which interrogation, exactly? The one pursued in this brief essay or that of *The Infinite Conversation* as a whole?

Blanchot does not specify. But he does state that as long as research does not ask the question of its form (or question itself as form), it "would be the same as speaking without knowing in which language one speaks"; as a result, its "thinking" would always carry the designation of having failed to achieve anything that could be counted as thought (IC 3). In many ways, he suggests, the disciplinary structures that determine what counts as research—for example, the creation and employment of technical terms and concepts, exposition as the primary mode under which research is carried out, the genre of the academic dissertation—all conspire to suppress the fundamental question that animates research and to which research (the fact of research) testifies (IC 3). What appears in place of this fundamental question, Blanchot insinuates, are pseudo-questions, false in the sense that, in one respect, they are questions masquerading as questions and false in another sense to the extent that, in another respect, they appear within a language that is unconcerned about what authorizes it to speak.

For Blanchot, what the scholarly expository form obscures—or rather prevents—from appearing, is the encounter with the question that impels all research. It does this in a number of ways, first, by presenting itself as the natural language of research, never inviting an investigation into the historical formations that allowed it to become natural. Secondly, by in turn naturalizing the method of exposition, where scholarly work responds to, corrects, and builds on work conducted previously, the scholarly expository form also never questions either the set of questions or the mode of questioning it inherits; as a consequence, it encourages research to view itself as participating in a linear process leading to progress—a progress narrative. Not least, the scholarly expository form also promotes an image of the *subject* of research as a solitary thinker working in isolation, an image that Blanchot will show gets increasingly solidified in its travels through the institutions in which research has evolved. Since, as Blanchot argues, recovering the question that impels all research requires questioning the language of research and bringing research to question the language it speaks, he retraces the ways by which the originary site of questioning becomes obscured through its institutionalization and catalogues the various figures that have emblematized research's different institutional identities in the history of Western thought.

Perhaps most significant in the genealogy of research that Blanchot goes on to offer in the essay is his identification of the scene of teaching as the originary site of the research relation. According to Blanchot, "The form in which thought moves to encounter what it is seeking is often tied to teaching," and insofar as this form is exemplified in the figures of Socrates, Plato, and Aristotle, research and teaching are identified with philosophy (IC 4). As philosophy becomes institutionalized (or, as Blanchot states, "institutionalizes itself"), it assimilates itself to the forms of those institutions—namely, the "Church and State"—that permit its appearance (IC 4). In so doing, however, the relation to speech that teaching embodies becomes overridden by writing, with the figures of writer and philosopher becoming sutured together. At this moment, states Blanchot, "to write is to philosophize" (IC 4). With philosophy's self-identification with the institution, not only does teaching/philosophy become writing, but writing itself becomes institutionalized as philosophy and becomes the dominant form of teaching. For Blanchot, Rousseau comes to embody this figure of the philosopher as writer (and vice versa), for it is with him that the pedagogical relation becomes transformed from a relation of self and other to one of writing, with nature as teacher (IC 4).

It is with the University, however, that Blanchot says that philosophy's institutionalization reaches its epitome, and not surprisingly, Kant and Hegel are this form's ideal subjects. "From Kant onward," Blanchot writes, "the philosopher is primarily a professor. Hegel, in whom philosophy comes together and accomplishes itself, is a man whose occupation is to speak from the height of a university chair, to prepare courses, and to think in conformity with the demands of this magisterial form" (IC 4). Although Blanchot is quick to acknowledge Kierkegaard and Nietzsche (as well as Sade) as exceptions, he subtly suggests they never actually register as philosophers in the proper sense due to their writings' resistance to the protocols of academic speech. Less subtly, he gestures to Heidegger's appropriation of

Kierkegaard and Nietzsche along the path of his ascension to the rectorship of the University of Freiburg (IC 4–5).

Summarizing his genealogy of the forms of research using language that echoes Nietzsche's three metamorphoses of the spirit in *Thus Spoke Zarathustra*, Blanchot writes,

> One could reduce to four the formal possibilities that are available to the man of research: (1) he teaches; (2) he is a man of science and his knowledge is bound to the always collective forms of specialized research: psychoanalysis (a science of non-knowing), the social sciences, and basic scientific research; (3) he combines his research with the affirmation of political action; (4) he writes. Professor; man of the laboratory; man of praxis; writer. Such are his metamorphoses. Hegel, Freud and Einstein, Marx and Lenin, Nietzsche and Sade. (IC 5)

Beyond the mechanical nature of this progression, which is neat and orderly but something he clearly regards as unremarkable, Blanchot is not interested in assessing these different forms, as to him they are mere variations on a theme. He is instead interested in how they are permutations of the way philosophy and teaching are bound to each other, and he is concerned that, though various forms maintain some connection between philosophy and teaching, they also obscure the essential relation at stake in teaching.

"Teaching is speaking," Blanchot affirms, but what is essential about this speech is that it harbors a relation between master and disciple (IC 5). "We should understand," he writes, "that the philosopher is not merely one who teaches what he knows; and we should not be content with attributing to the master the role of example, or with defining his bond with the student as an existential one. The master represents a region of space and time that is absolutely other" (IC 5). That Blanchot does not doubt the identification of the teacher as philosopher—or, for that matter, the philosopher as master—is noteworthy if not curious, given the general ambivalence he displays in his writings, including in this particular essay. Nonetheless, what he refers to as "the master/disciple relation" allows him to emphasize that what is most essential in the speech of teaching is that this speech arises in relation to the question of relation itself, in relation to the discontinuity that is the measure of the relation between the "master" and "disciple" in the scene of teaching. It is not the master but "the region of space and time" the master represents that is "other": an "unknown" that Blanchot says at once marks the incommensurable, "*infinite distance*" between master and disciple and also draws them together (IC 6; original emphasis). Anticipating what he, in dialogue with Lévinas, will describe further along in *The Infinite Conversation* as a relation of nonrelation between Self and Other, Blanchot says that the unknown at stake in the speech of teaching interrupts relation as such (IC 6; 70–71).

Through its institutionalization, the relation of discontinuity and incommensurability that Blanchot suggests gives rise to and is the essential in research—the unknown that is also always-already a shared relation—is more than suppressed. It is disavowed altogether. Taking its place is an image of research as continuous, linear, and a contributor to cultural progress. This image unites both the objects of knowledge and, as Foucault would say, those installed as the ideal subjects of knowledge—that is to say, the proper names making up the Western philosophical tradition's heroic, patrilineal heritage. Ultimately, Blanchot levels a devastating critique of what has come to stand as research in the West. For him, the entire Western intellectual tradition has satisfied itself with a simulacrum of research that avoids research's fundamental question. So far as this simulacrum sustains the belief that thinking is based on establishing continuity among things, it fails to answer to the radical disruption of what Heidegger names the "call of thinking."

In order to take the measure of the incommensurable of research, Blanchot submits that a radical revision of the existing language of research is needed. "One can see which solutions will prove inappropriate to such a problem," he writes, "a language of assertion and answer, for example, or a linear language of simple development, that is to say, *a language where language itself would not be at stake*" (IC 6; original emphasis). Blanchot thus calls for "a plural speech" that would be able to speak the essential discontinuity of relation that inspires research but also for a mode of writing that embodies a language of questioning (IC 8). "Any language where it is a mode of questioning rather than responding," Blanchot states, "is a language already interrupted—even more, a language wherein everything begins with the decision (or the distraction) of an initial void" (IC 8). Such a writing must break with forms that amount to nothing more than "a pleasant interlacing of upstrokes and downstrokes" (IC 8), but it also must penetrate the fantasy/defense that the image of research as continuity holds.

What is this fantasy, exactly, and what does it defend against? According to Blanchot, it is the fantasy of the unity and continuity of things themselves. "This is the great Parmenidean sphere of Being, it is

Einstein's model of the universe," he says, which Blanchot argues falls prey to "the seductions of the immediate," which he claims even Hegel, so far as he postulated the absolute continuity of reality, was also entranced by (IC 9). And yet the defense is not against the necessity of mediation, which consigns us to representation and that philosophers since Kant have identified as the mark of our human finitude. Rather, it is a defense against the possibility "that the *ground of things*—to which [the human] surely in some way belong[s]—has as much to do with the demand of discontinuity as it does with that of unity" (IC 9; original emphasis). This discontinuity exists not in spite of speech and writing, Blanchot submits, but is instead announced by speech and writing (IC 10).

As I have said, this essay from Blanchot has been with me for many years, at least since the time that I was concluding my graduate coursework in philosophy and comparative literature and preparing to enter into my doctoral candidacy. At the time, what spoke to me in the essay was the way that Blanchot thematizes the problem of language while simultaneously extending that problem to encompass the very language that philosophy makes available to name language as a problem in the first place. Although that may seem an extreme form of metacritique, I frankly found it quite generative, if not exhilarating, because it enabled me to envision an idea of philosophy of language coming from out of the Continental tradition that, unlike philosophy of language conventionally conceived, did not take the object "language" as a given. Less clear to me at that time, though no doubt just as present, the ambivalence toward the philosophical tradition evinced by the essay resonated with my own growing ambivalence regarding the possibility of forging and attaining my own voice in philosophy, of being able to recognize myself in the heroic (and it must be added, white) patrilineal heritage Blanchot catalogues in his text. This ambivalence was (is?) perhaps some worry about my own affective ties to both the "pleasant interlacing of upstrokes and downstrokes" that I would mistake for actual thinking and the "community" of those who have assembled solely to share in—and be captured by—that same affect.

Today, as I strive to sound this concluding note to the present study, those previous reasons for why I was drawn to Blanchot's essay have not dissipated; on the contrary, they have consolidated into a sustained concern with voice and language along the horizons of disciplinarity, institutionality, and what I have come to refer to as the aesthetics of subjectivization. This might suggest that my commitments actually align with those of the affective turn and the return to the aesthetic rather than oppose them, a suggestion with which I would not necessarily disagree. In fact, many of the writings associated with these current movements have both informed other work I have pursued in the aesthetics of race, gender, and disability and also inspired me to reassess my engagement with the question of language: could the insights being offered by contemporary research on affect and the aesthetic reveal something missing in my approach to the question of language?

Certainly, one thing I was prompted to investigate from my encounter with the scholarship of the affective turn and the return to the aesthetic was the question of the relation between language and affect, particularly their supposed separability. (The relation between language and aesthetics was perhaps something I felt as less pressing an issue given their more obvious connection in literature and poetry.) As I describe in the introduction to this study, I found any claim separating language and affect to be dubious, but I was especially suspicious of the affective turn's self-proclaimed novelty, and I was frankly astonished that the turn, despite all evidence to the contrary, seemingly regards itself as being able to make claims about the nature of affect in a way unmediated (uncontaminated, perhaps?) by language. Yet, it was precisely this disregard that prompted me to delve into the figure of the voice in Heidegger and post-Heideggerian thought in order to reconstruct the ways language and affect not only cannot be thought in separation from each other, but more importantly, how Heidegger's conception of the voice reveals the sense/meaning presupposed by those championing the superiority of affect's sensibility over language, the assumption, that is to say, that affect "makes sense" to and is understood as meaningful by the one who experiences it.

Returning to Blanchot's essay in the present context has helped me see that, in addition to perpetuating an image of research as a single, linear, and continuous path of development, the affective turn is particularly guilty of both upholding a progress narrative that *needs* to denigrate and dismiss prior works of research and also promoting this image of continuity in order to delude itself into the belief that it has direct access to the immediate.[2] If we follow Blanchot's analysis in "Thought and the Exigency of Discontinuity," the affective turn's reluctance to attend to its own language—and thus its reluctance to being confronted with the discontinuity that impels thinking—is less a lament of the fact of human finitude conventionally understood as simple limitation and more a defense against human finitude as a relation of exposure to the fact of discontinuity, which is to say, the fact of difference. The affective turn's resistance to language is accordingly a defense against its own desire—which in my view it unquestioningly obeys—to write in such a way that it may forever avoid a confrontation with this fact. It is in this sense that the affective turn's resistance to language actually constitutes a resistance to its own object.

The language of desire, resistance, and defense of course conjures the conceptual apparatus of psychoanalysis, which I have not engaged with directly in this study but that is at the same time inseparable from the critical landscape of post-Heideggerian thought, including that of Blanchot's. My choice not to pursue that path notwithstanding,[3] it is worth taking note of how contemporary psychoanalytically informed theories conceptualize the voice as an "excess of speech and meaning" and as a lost object of desire simultaneously.[4] Since the voice in psychoanalysis names an untraversable "gap" and "limping causality" that is precisely what the affective turn claims to have finally ameliorated, it is no wonder that it is anathema to theorists of affect.[5]

Not coincidentally, this lost object of desire, famously given the name of *objet petit a* by Lacan, is exemplified by the mother's voice. What Kaja Silverman refers to as "the fantasy of the maternal voice" is what I have hinted at throughout the book as the trace of the figure of the feminine—specifically, the feminine figured as originary loss or figured as death—that persists in Heidegger and post-Heideggerian thought.[6] As I have suggested, there is a consistent, if tacit, avowal of this need/desire for the figure of the lost/dead feminine throughout the works we have studied in this book that predicates and pervades the entirety of their meditations on the limits of thinking. This "oedipedagogy," as Avital Ronell calls it, referring to the primal scene of the mother's call in *What Is Called Thinking?*, which Heidegger uses to evoke the seizure of the human Dasein by the call (*Anruf*) of thinking, is a fantasy that still requires deconstruction.[7]

Curiously, in their speculative drive toward an immediate reunion with the really Real that affect and the aesthetic name, the affective turn and the return of the aesthetic commit their own appropriation of the feminine via an appropriation of mimesis. However, in their efforts to transcend language (and ignore figuration altogether), they distance themselves even further than post-Heideggerian thought from the chance to become aware of this fantastical appropriation. That they might all share the same (masculinist) fantasy premised on the appropriation, transcendence, and denigration of the feminine is a critique that remains to be written.

Such, I anticipate, are the directions that future elaborations of this project may take. For now, although the philosophies of the voice examined in this study may differ from the writings of the affective turn—in that the latter refuse to recognize the fact that their speculative enterprise is founded upon a desire for a lost origin—the writings of the affective turn and its adjuncts remain largely grounded in the work of white European male philosophers and theorists.[8] From the standpoint of the business of research, then, what the objects known as "language" and "affect" may be said to cohere around is a persistent fascination and desire to identify with the masculine voice, or what we may understand as the fantasy named "Philosophy." To fulfill the task of thinking language after affect, we need to dismantle this fantasy, its pleasures, and especially the structures and practices in place that sustain both.

Notes

Introduction

1. See Quentin Meillassoux, *After Finitude: An Essay on the Necessity of Contingency*, trans. Ray Brassier (London: Continuum, 2008).

2. See *New Materialisms: Ontology, Agency, and Politics*, edited by Diana Coole and Samantha Frost (Durham, NC: Duke University Press, 2010).

3. See *The Affective Turn*, ed. Patricia Ticento Clough (Durham, NC: Duke University Press, 2007); *The Affect Theory Reader*, edited by Melissa Gregg and Gregory J. Seigworth (Durham, NC: Duke University Press, 2011); *Communities of Sense: Rethinking Aesthetics and Politics*, edited by Beth Hinderliter, William Kaizen, Vered Maimon, Jaleh Mansoor, and Seth McCormick (Durham, NC: Duke University Press, 2009); *The Aesthetic Turn in Political Thought*, ed. Nikolas Kompridis (New York: Bloomsbury, 2014); Michael Feola, *The Powers of Sensibility: Aesthetic Politics through Adorno, Foucault, and Rancière* (Evanston, IL: Northwestern University Press, 2018), and; *Aesthetics Equals Politics: New Discourses across Art, Architecture, and Philosophy*, ed. Mark Foster Gage (Cambridge, MA: MIT Press, 2019).

4. Jacques Derrida, *Of Grammatology*, 40th anniversary ed., trans. Gayatri Chakravorty Spivak (Baltimore: Johns Hopkins University Press, 2016), 172.

5. See Christopher Fynsk, *Language and Relation . . . that there is language* (Stanford, CA: Stanford University Press, 1996).

6. This of course remains an urgent question surrounding Heidegger's thought, reinvigorated by the recent publication and translation of his "*Schwarze Hefte*" ("Black Notebooks") and the renewed commentaries they have inspired. See Martin Heidegger, *Ponderings II–IV: Black Notebooks 1931–1938* (Bloomington and Indianapolis: Indiana University Press, 2016) (*Überlegungen II–VI [Schwarze Hefte 1931–1938]*, vol. 94 of *Gesamtausgabe* [Frankfurt am Main: Vittorio Klostermann, 2014]); *Ponderings VII–XI: Black Notebooks 1938–1939* (Bloomington and Indianapolis: Indiana University Press, 2017) (*Überlegungen VII–XI [Schwarze Hefte 1938–1939]*, vol. 95 of *Gesamtausgabe* [Frankfurt am Main: Vittorio Klostermann, 2014]); *Ponderings: XII–XV: Black Notebooks 1939–1941* (Bloomington and Indianapolis: Indiana University Press,

2017) (*Überlegungen XII–XV [Schwarze Hefte 1939–1941]*, vol. 96 of *Gesamtausgabe* [Frankfurt am Main: Vittorio Klostermann, 2014]).

7. See Peter Hallward, "Anything is Possible." *Radical Philosophy* 152 (November/December 2008): 51–57.

8. For a recent response to the new materialist turn that argues for the materiality of language, see Karmen MacKendrick, *The Matter of Voice: Sensual Soundings* (New York: Fordham University Press, 2016).

9. Michael Hardt, "Foreword: What are Affects Good For?," in *The Affective Turn*, ed. Patricia Ticento Clough with Jean Halley (Durham, NC: Duke University Press, 2007), ix.

10. Keith Ansell Pearson, *Germinal Life: The Difference and Repetition of Gilles Deleuze* (London and New York: Routledge, 1999), 170.

11. Book III, Proposition II, Scholium. Quoted in *The Affect Theory Reader*, ed. Melissa Gregg and Gregory J. Seigworth (Durham, NC: Duke University Press, 2011), 3. See Brian Massumi, *Parables for the Virtual: Movement, Affect, Sensation* (Durham, NC: Duke University Press, 2002), which is cited prominently in both *The Affective Turn* and *The Affect Theory Reader*.

12. *Disagreement: Politics and Philosophy*, trans. Julie Rose (Minneapolis: University of Minnesota Press, 1999) (*La Mésentente. Politique et philosophie* [Paris: Éditions Galilée, 1995]); *The Politics of Aesthetics: The Distribution of the Sensible*, trans. Gabriel Rockhill (New York: Continuum, 2004) (*Le Partage du sensible. Esthétique et politique* [Paris: La Fabrique-éditions, 2000]). Interestingly enough, Rancière's appearance on the aesthetic scene (he had been a figure in social-political philosophy since the 1970s, of course) more or less coincides with the 1995 publications of Eve Kosofsky Sedgwick and Adam Frank's essay "Shame in the Cybernetic Fold" and Brian Massumi's "The Autonomy of Affect," which Gregg and Seigworth note as "the watershed moment" for the turn to affect (*The Affect Theory Reader*, 5).

13. Max Blechman, Anita Chari, and Rafeeq Hasan, "Democracy, Dissensus, and the Aesthetics of Class Struggle: An Exchange with Jacques Rancière." *Historical Materialism* 13, no. 4: 292.

14. See, for example, Beth Hinderliter et al., eds., *Communities of Sense: Rethinking Aesthetics and Politics* (Durham, NC: Duke University Press, 2009) and Nikolas Kompridis, ed. *The Aesthetic Turn in Political Thought* (New York: Bloomsbury, 2014).

15. Clare Hemmings, "Invoking Affect: Cultural Theory and the Ontological Turn," *Cultural Studies* 19, no. 5 (September 2005): 548–67. The specific texts Hemmings takes up include: Sedgwick, *Touching Feeling: Affect, Pedagogy, and Performativity* (Durham, NC: Duke University Press, 2003); Sedgwick and Adam Frank, "Shame in the Cybernetic Fold: Reading Silvan Tomkins," in *Shame and Its Sisters: A Silvan Tomkins Reader*, ed. Eve Kosofsky Sedgwick and Adam Frank (Durham, NC: Duke University Press, 1995), 1–28; Massumi, "The Autonomy of

Affect," in *Deleuze: A Critical Reader*, ed. Paul Patton (Oxford: Blackwell, 1996), 217–39, and; Massumi, *Parables for the Virtual: Movement, Affect, Sensation* (Durham, NC: Duke University Press, 2002).

16. Ruth Leys, "The Turn to Affect: A Critique." *Cultural Inquiry* 37 (Spring 2011): 457, 443, 455.

17. See Hemmings, 550–51; Clough, 16–17.

18. *Disagreement*, 17.

19. "Art and the Heideggerian Repression: Rancière, Nancy, and a Communism of the Image." *Comparative & Continental Philosophy* 5, no. 1 (May 2013): 19–35.

20. Hemmings, 556–57.

21. In addition to the frequent appeals to "world" one encounters in Gregg and Seigworth's introduction to *The Affect Theory Reader*, just as many can be found in Nigel Thrift's contribution to the same volume. See his "Understanding the Material Practices of Glamour" (289–308). For examples of the same phenomenon regarding the notion of "dwelling," see Elizabeth Povinelli, *Economies of Abandonment: Social Belonging and Endurance in Late Liberalism* (Durham, NC: Duke University Press, 2011) and José Esteban Muñoz, "Feeling Brown, Feeling Down: Latina Affect, the Performativity of Race, and the Depressive Position." *Signs* 31, no. 3, New Feminist Theories of Visual Culture (Spring 2006): 675–88. (Although Povinelli does cite Heidegger, there does not seem to be an awareness on her part of the connection between her employment of the term "dwelling" and Heidegger's thought, especially as it concerns what she describes as "endurance.") For similar invocations of "dwelling" in the Heideggerian vein, see Marisol de la Cadena, *Earth Beings: Ecologies of Practice Across Andean Worlds* (Durham, NC: Duke University Press, 2015) and Gayatri Gopinath, *Unruly Visions: The Aesthetic Practices of Queer Diaspora* (Durham, NC: Duke University Press, 2018).

22. See Maurice Blanchot, *The Unavowable Community*, trans. Pierre Joris (Barrytown: Station Hill, 1988), 57 n.5 (*La Communauté inavouable* [Paris: Éditions de Minuit, 1983], 26 n.1). I include more details of Nancy's debate with Blanchot in chapter 4 and in chapter 5.

23. See, for example, *Memoires for Paul de Man*, rev. ed., trans. Cecile Lindsay, Jonathan Culler, Eduardo Cadava, and Peggy Kamuf (New York: Columbia University Press, 1989), 40 n.3.

24. Michel Foucault, Jacques Lacan, Jean-François Lyotard, and Emmanuel Lévinas are others who can also be included among those dealing with the problematics of the voice. In addition to *Of Grammatology*, Foucault's *The Archaeology of Knowledge* (1969), particularly his theorization of the *énoncé*, Lyotard's *The Differend* (1983), and Lévinas's *Otherwise than Being* (1974), with its distinction between the saying and the said, belong to a constellation involving figuration, finitude, and the voice. I address Lacan's thought more directly in the epilogue.

Chapter 1

1. This is a claim Heidegger himself makes at one point in his writings, most famously in his "Letter on 'Humanism'" (in *Pathmarks*, ed. William McNeill [New York: Cambridge University Press, 1998], 249–50).

2. For a very recent discussion, see Dermot Moran, "What Does Heidegger Mean by the Transcendence of Dasein?" *International Journal of Philosophical Studies*, 22, no. 4 (2014): 491–514. William J. Richardson's *Heidegger: Through Phenomenology to Thought* (The Hague: Martinus Nijhoff, 1963) was one of the first commentaries in English to focus on the concept of finite transcendence. See Christopher Fynsk, *Heidegger: Thought and Historicity*, expanded edition (Ithaca, NY: Cornell University Press, 1993), 107 for an explicit thematization of finite transcendence.

3. Fynsk draws specific attention to Heidegger's 1956 Addendum to "The Origin of the Work of Art." See Fynsk, *Heidegger: Thought and Historicity*, 17–18, and Heidegger, "The Origin of the Work of Art," in *Off the Beaten Track*, ed. and trans. Julian Young and Kenneth Haynes (Cambridge: Cambridge University Press, 2002), 55.

4. Martin Heidegger, *Being and Time: A Translation of* Sein und Zeit, trans. Joan Stambaugh (Albany: State University of New York Press, 1996), 5; and *Being and Time*, trans. John Macquarrie and Edward Robinson (Oxford: Blackwell, 1962), 26 (*Sein und Zeit*, 17th ed. [Tübingen: Niemeyer, 1993], 7). Hereafter S, MR, and SZ, respectively. For the sake of consistency between the various translations of Heidegger's different texts, I will modify Stambaugh's rendering of *Sein* as "being" in lowercase with the admittedly less accurate "Being." I will also revert Stambaugh's "Da-sein" to "Dasein."

5. "Allerdings nur solange Dasein *ist* . . . 'gibt es' Sein" (SZ 212). In Macquarrie and Robinson: "Of course only as long as Dasein *is* . . . 'is there' Being" (MR 255).

6. Martin Heidegger, *Kant and the Problem of Metaphysics*, 5th ed., enlarged, trans. Richard Taft (Bloomington and Indianapolis: Indiana University Press, 1997), 160 (*Kant und das Problem der Metaphysik*, Vol. 3 of *Gesamtausgabe* [Frankfurt am Main: Vittorio Klostermann, 1991], 228–29), translation modified; original emphasis. Further citations will indicate the page number of the English translation followed by the page number of the German text.

7. In §7 of *Being and Time*, Heidegger writes: "*Being is the transcendens pure and simple.** The transcendence of the being of Da-sein is a distinctive one since in it lies the possibility and necessity of the most radical *individuation*. Every disclosure of being as the *transcendens* is *transcendental* knowledge. *Phenomenological truth* (*disclosedness of being*) is *veritas transcendentalis*."

In the marginalia of his own personal copy of *Sein und Zeit*, Heidegger adds (designated in the English translation by an asterisk): "**of course not transcendens—despite every metaphysical resonance—scholastic and greek-platonic *koinon*, rather transcendence as the ecstatic-temporal [*Zeitlichkeit*]—temporality [*Temporalität*]; but 'horizon'! Being has 'thought beyond' ['*überdacht*'] beings. However, transcendence from the truth of being: the event [*das Ereignis*]" (S 33–4/SZ 38).

See also the following from "What Is Metaphysics?," which we will comment upon momentarily: "Being held out into the nothing—as Dasein is—on the ground of concealed anxiety is its surpassing of beings as a whole. It is transcendence" (93).

8. See Jean-Luc Nancy, "Finite History," in *The Birth to Presence*, trans. Brian Holmes and Others (Stanford, CA: Stanford University Press, 1993): "*Finitude* does not mean that we are noninfinite—like small, insignificant beings within a grand universal, and continuous being—but it means that we are *infinitely* finite, infinitely exposed to our existence as nonessence, infinitely exposed to the otherness of our own 'being' (or that being is in us exposed to its own otherness)" (155).

9. For the controversy surrounding this term (or the controversy concerning the *lack* of controversy surrounding it), see the discussion of Jean-Luc Nancy's *Le partage des voix* (Paris: Éditions Galilée, 1982) (translated as "Sharing Voices," in *Transforming the Hermeneutic Context*, eds. Gayle L. Ormiston and Alan D. Schrift [Albany: State University of New York Press, 1990]) in chapter 2. See also Fynsk, *Heidegger: Thought and Historicity*, expanded ed. (Ithaca, NY: Cornell University Press, 1993).

10. As Nancy suggests, there is also a relation of circularity between finitude and relation as such: "Relation is in finitude because it is incompleteness. (Thus it *is* not.) And the thought of finitude is doubtless necessarily, beyond what in Heidegger seems to subject it to a 'unity' (even a nonsubjective one), a thought of relation" ("The Jurisdiction of the Hegelian Monarch," in *The Birth to Presence*, 141).

11. See SZ 42 and 259. See also Jean-Luc Nancy's statement in the essay "The Decision of Existence" in *The Birth to Presence*: "Existence is, as such, the *decision of existence*" (83).

12. See also Michel Haar, *Heidegger and the Essence of Man*, trans. William McNeill (Albany: State University of New York Press, 1993), xxxii–xxxiii, and Jean-Luc Nancy, "Our History," *Diacritics* 20, no. 3 (Fall 1990): 103.

13. Heidegger writes: "We must . . . endeavour to leap into the 'circle,' primordially and wholly, so that even at the start of the analysis of Dasein we make sure that we have a full view of Dasein's circular Being [*das zirkelhafte Sein des Daseins*]" (MR 363/SZ 315).

14. "Depending upon the being which it is not, the human is at the same time not master of the being which it itself is" (*Kant* 155, translation modified).

15. The reverse must be true as well: the wholeness of the metaphysical subject is only illusory because it masks the question of finitude from Dasein. It is for this reason that Heidegger argues that the human sciences (anthropology, psychology, etc.) have failed thus far in raising the question of the finitude of Dasein because they have already assumed it. See SZ §10, SZ 316, and *Kant* 156: "If the human is only human *on the grounds of the Dasein* in them, then in principle the

question as to what is more original than the human cannot be anthropological. All anthropology, even Philosophical Anthropology, has already assumed that the human is human" (translation modified; original emphasis).

16. In fact, there is perhaps no other phrase in *Being and Time* more condemned to the footnote and to the promise of further inquiry. The question of Dasein's relation to alterity and the priority, despite Heidegger's own remarks to the contrary, of *Mitsein* (Being-with) in the constitution of the being of Dasein remains outside the scope of this chapter, although perhaps the problem of finite transcendence and the finitude of Dasein will remain unresolved until the question of alterity in fundamental ontology is confronted. Until then, there are a few guiding texts, only one of which, Jean-Luc Nancy's *Partage des voix*, I will touch upon in this study. There is, however, the first chapter of Fynsk's *Heidegger: Thought and Historicity*, "The Self and Its Witness," which has contributed significantly in drawing attention to this particular passage in Heidegger. There is also Derrida's text, "Heidegger's Ear: Philopolemology (*Geschlecht IV*)," on the themes of *philia* and *polemos* in Heidegger's thought see John Sallis, ed. *Reading Heidegger: Commemorations* (Bloomington and Indianapolis: Indiana University Press, 1993, 163–220.

17. See *Heidegger and the Essence of Man*, 19.

18. See *Heidegger: Thought and Historicity*.

19. Cf. David Nowell Smith, *Sounding/Silence: Martin Heidegger at the Limits of Poetics* (New York: Fordham University Press, 2013), 84. Although I differ from Nowell Smith in my interpretation of Heidegger's theorization of *phonē* and *logos* in *Being and Time*, as will be seen in chapter 2, I follow him in his explication of the way Heidegger conceives *die Stimme* as a "sounding" of *die Stimmung*.

20. See Jean-François Courtine, "Voice of Conscience and Call of Being," in *Who Comes After the Subject?*, ed. Jean-Luc Nancy and Eduardo Cadava (Minneapolis: University of Minnesota Press, 1991), 79–93.

Chapter 2

1. Jean-Luc Nancy, *The Inoperative Community*, ed. Peter Connor, trans. Peter Connor, Lisa Garbus, Michael Holland, and Simona Sawhney (Minneapolis: University of Minnesota Press, 1991), 6–7.

2. Maurice Blanchot, *The Infinite Conversation*, trans. Susan Hanson (Minneapolis: University of Minnesota Press, 1993), 202.

3. One collection that has appeared recently brings together scholars interested in reconstructing Heidegger's early reflections on language, including where these appear in key sections of *Being and Time*. See *Heidegger and Language*, ed. Jeffrey Powell (Bloomington: Indiana University Press, 2013).

4. It is important to state that the opposition Heidegger names here in *Being and Time* between discourse as an originary relation to the sense of Being and

language as the sphere of ontic communication appears differently in his later writings on language, in a way that is even confusing. In those works, most prominently in *Unterwegs zur Sprache* (1959), where he explicitly makes the relation to language a central theme, "discourse" and "language" cease to be technical terms. Instead, Heidegger simply opposes communicative and representative theories of language to a more originary relation between language and human beings. While the former regard language as an instrument for conveying meaning, the latter names an opening—a scene, an event—where human beings attend to, and are claimed by, the call of Being. In these later writings, Heidegger develops an image of "the Saying" (*die Sage*) of language as "the appropriating event" (*Ereignis*) in which Being lays claim to human being. One important theme that remains consistent between these two periods of Heidegger's reflections on language is his appeal to logos. See "The Nature of Language," in *On the Way to Language*, trans. Peter D. Hertz (New York: Harper and Row, 1971), 57–108 ("Das Wesen der Sprache," in *Unterwegs zur Sprache*, vol. 12 of *Gesamtausgabe* [Frankfurt am Main: Klostermann, 1985], 147–204).

5. Aristotle, *Politics* I.2, 1253a 9–17.

6. As Heidegger notes, he takes this distinction as it is found in a number of Aristotle's works, specifically *De interpretatione*, *Metaphysics*, and the *Nicomachean Ethics* (MR 489n4). A more detailed exegesis can be found in Heidegger's 1925 Marburg lecture course and draft of *Being and Time*, *History of the Concept of Time: Prolegomena*, trans. Theodore Kisiel (Indianapolis and Bloomington: Indiana University Press, 1985), 84–85.

7. Jacques Taminiaux's "Voice and Phenomena in Heidegger's Fundamental Ontology" is highly recommended. As a response to Derrida's *Speech and Phenomena*, Taminiaux's analysis reconstructs the ways Heidegger's reading of Aristotle is inflected through Husserl. See "Voice and Phenomena in Heidegger's Fundamental Ontology," in *Heidegger and the Project of Fundamental Ontology*, trans. and ed. Michael Gendre (Albany: State University of New York Press, 1991), and Derrida, *Speech and Phenomena*, trans. David B. Allison (Evanston: Northwestern University Press, 1973).

8. Derrida's critique in *Of Grammatology* (40th anniversary ed., trans. Gayatri Chakravorty Spivak [Baltimore: Johns Hopkins University Press, 2016]) comes immediately to mind. But a related critique can be found in Giorgio Agamben's *Language and Death: The Place of Negativity*, trans. Karen E. Pinkus and Michael Hardt (Minneapolis: University of Minnesota Press, 1991).

9. "Sharing Voices," in *Transforming the Hermeneutic Context*, ed. Gayle L. Ormiston and Alan D. Schrift (Albany: State University of New York Press, 1990). Originally published as *Le Partage des voix* (Paris: Éditions Galilée, 1982).

10. Nancy cites Derrida's formulation of the closure of metaphysics (to be more exact, the closure of representation) from *Writing and Difference*: "But one can conceive the closure of that which is without end. The closure is the circular limit within which the repetition of difference infinitely repeats itself." *Writing*

and Difference, trans. Alan Bass (Chicago: University of Chicago Press, 1978), 250 (*L'Écriture de la différence* [Paris: Les Éditions du Seuil, 1967], 367); "Sharing Voices" 213; 249n5. Derrida's formulation appears at the conclusion of the chapter on Artaud's theater of cruelty, which could serve as an interesting point of reference as we encounter Blanchot's and Deleuze's respective engagements with Artaud in chapters 5 and 6.

11. Nancy also adds Nietzsche and Freud as figures who have been misinterpreted in terms of their contributions to the problem of interpretation ("Sharing" 248n1).

12. *Geschick* is primarily Heidegger's designation for the history/"sending" of Being, so the passage from *Being and Time* invoking Dasein's destiny could be understood as a gesture to tie Dasein's thrown existence to the history of Being. On meanings of *Geschick* and its role in Heidegger's thought, see George Steiner, *Martin Heidegger* (Chicago: University of Chicago Press, 1989), 112; Reginald Lilly's Translator's Introduction to Heidegger's *The Principle of Reason* (Bloomington and Indianapolis: University of Indiana Press), xiv; and the entry on "Fate and Destiny" in Michael Inwood, *A Heidegger Dictionary* (Oxford: Blackwell, 1999), 67.

13. For background on Heidegger's inheritance of the concept of facticity from Dilthey, see Theodore Kisiel's "Hermeneutics of Facticity," in *Martin Heidegger: Key Concepts*, ed. Bret W. Davis (Durham: Acumen, 2010), 17–32.

14. Particularly in *The Inoperative Community*, trans. Peter Connor et al. (Minneapolis: University of Minnesota Press, 1991) (*La communauté désoeuvrée* [Paris: Bourgois, 1986]; and "The Being-with of Being-there," *Continental Philosophy Review* (2008): 41, 1–15 ("L'être-avec de l'être-là." *Lieu-Dit* 19 "*Communauté*" [Novembre 2003]). I examine these works in detail in chapter 4.

15. "A Dialogue on Language between a Japanese and an Inquirer," in *On the Way to Language*, 1–54 ("Aus einem Gespräch von der Sprache: Zwischen einem Japaner und einem Fragenden," in *Unterwegs zur Sprache*, vol. 12 of *Gesamtausgabe*, 79–146).

Chapter 3

1. I attend to the social-political implications of the link between human finitude and specularity in chapter 4, specifically in that chapter's overview of Lacoue-Labarthe's critique of "onto-typology" in Heidegger's thought.

2. See Fynsk, *Heidegger: Thought and Historicity*, 150. Although Fynsk and I depart somewhat regarding the implications of this evaluation with respect to Lacoue-Labarthe's critique of Heidegger (which I go into detail analyzing in chapter 4), my reading of Heidegger's artwork essay is nonetheless shaped significantly by his interpretation.

3. I am thankful to Christopher Fynsk for prompting me to think of this connection.

4. Martin Heidegger, *Hölderlin's Hymn "The Ister,"* trans. William McNeill and Julia Davis (Bloomington and Indianapolis: Indiana University Press, 1996), 119 (*Hölderlins Hymne »Der Ister«*, vol. 53 of *Gesamtausgabe*, 2nd ed. [Frankfurt: Klostermann, 1993], 149). Hereafter HH and GA53, respectively.

5. Heidegger, "The Origin of the Work of Art," in *Off the Beaten Track*, trans. and ed. Julian Young and Kenneth Haynes (Cambridge: Cambridge University Press, 2002), 37–38 ("*Der Ursprung des Kunstwerkes*," in *Holzwege* [Frankfurt: Klostermann, 1980], 49–50); original emphasis. Hereafter "Origin" and "*Ursprung*," respectively.

6. Although Heidegger explicitly refers to a specific "temple at its site in Paestum" ("Origin" 20), Jeff Malpas notes, citing Babette Babich, that there is evidence Heidegger instead had the temple of Apollo at Bassae in mind. See Malpas, *Heidegger and the Thinking of Place: Explorations in the Topology of Being* (Cambridge, MA: MIT Press, 2012), 336n14, and Babich, "From Van Gogh's Museum to the Temple at Bassae: Heidegger's Truth of Art and Schapiro's Art History," *Culture, Theory & Critique* 44 (2003): 151–69.

7. Heidegger, *An Introduction to Metaphysics*, trans. Ralph Manheim (New Haven, CT: Yale University Press, 1987), 155 (*Einführung in die Metaphysik*, vol. 40 of *Gesamtausgabe* [Frankfurt: Klostermann, 1983], 155). Hereafter IM and EM, respectively. (I wish to acknowledge that there exists a more recent translation of the work by Gregory Fried and Richard Polt. However, even though I modify Manheim's translation in certain instances, I have chosen to work with his edition of the text over the newer edition because his decisions generally align more closely with my own reception of the original. Cf. Heidegger, *Introduction to Metaphysics*, 2nd ed. Rev. and expanded ed., trans. Gregory Fried and Richard Polt [New Haven, CT: Yale University Press, 2014].)

8. Whether this originary sight Heidegger ascribes to tragedy really differs in essence from the speculative vision of modern science and metaphysics forms the crux of Lacoue-Labarthe's critique of the figure in Heidegger, which I discuss in depth in chapter 4.

9. Since I go into great detail reconstructing Heidegger's translation of the ode and how his translation responds to that of Hölderlin's, I have chosen to include an appendix to this chapter that reproduces the original Greek text of the ode, Jebb's translation, Heidegger's and Hölderlin's translations, and finally, English translations of Heidegger's and Hölderlin's German translations.

10. I describe *Auseinandersetzung* here as an "oppositional affinity" in order to underscore Heidegger's emphasis that the terms in these conceptual pairings in *Antigone*'s First Choral Ode are drawn together in their difference rather than stand in exclusionary opposition to each other. Christopher Fynsk translates *Auseinandersetzung* as "reciprocal confrontation." See his *Heidegger: Thought and Historicity*, 120, 124.

11. See Andrzej Warminski, "Monstrous History: Heidegger Reading Hölderlin," in *The Solid Letter: Readings of Friedrich Hölderlin*, ed. Aris Fioretos (Stanford, CA: Stanford University Press, 1999), 201–14.

12. As Cornelius Castoriadis indicates, it is worth noting that Heidegger leaves out the line's concluding phrase here, *to mellon* (the future, what is to come). Castoriadis claims that Heidegger must do this in order to give plausibility to his translation/interpretation. Where Heidegger translates the line as "Everywhere journeying, inexperienced and without issue, he comes to nothingness" (*Überall hinausfahrend unterwegs, erfahrungslos ohne Ausweg kommt er zum Nichts*), Castoriadis translates the line in the following way: "Capable of going everywhere, of going through everything, of finding the answers to everything, he advances toward nothing of what is to come without having some resource." Castoriadis, *Figures of the Thinkable*, trans. Helen Arnold (Stanford, CA: Stanford University Press, 2007), 3.

13. See chapter 2 for another formulation where Heidegger connects Dasein's destiny with the history of Being via Dasein's facticity.

14. See Christopher Fynsk's discussion of the meaning of the term *Verderb* in this section of *Introduction to Metaphysics* and the text's Nietzschean allusions in his *Heidegger: Thought and Historicity*, 122–30. In chapter 6, we will have an opportunity to compare Heidegger's and Deleuze's respective receptions of Nietzsche's saying yes.

15. Nietzsche, *The Birth of Tragedy*, in *The Birth of Tragedy and Other Writings*, ed. Raymond Geuss and Ronald Speirs, trans. Ronald Speirs (Cambridge: Cambridge University Press, 1999), 18.

16. Nietzsche, *The Birth of Tragedy*, 30.

17. See Christopher Fynsk, *Language and Relation: . . . that there is language* (Stanford, CA: Stanford University Press, 1996), on the notion of *der Brauch* (usage, need) in Heidegger.

18. Heidegger will of course elaborate these themes at much greater length in his *Nietzsche* lectures. See especially his 1937 lecture course on the eternal return in Heidegger, *Nietzsche*, vol. 2, *The Eternal Recurrence of the Same*, trans. David Farrell Krell (San Francisco: Harper & Row, 1984), 28–31.

19. G. S. Kirk and J. E. Raven, *The Presocratic Philosophers* (Cambridge: Cambridge University Press, 1957), 270.

20. *An Introduction to Metaphysics* is just one of a number of places where Heidegger undertakes an interpretation of the Presocratics, including Parmenides's sixth fragment. As Richard Capobianco points out, Heidegger elaborates his interpretation of the fragment's "eventful" aspects in *What Is Called Thinking?* (1951–52, published in 1954) by translating *eon* as *das Anwesende* (that which is present) and *emmenai* as *anwesen* (presencing). *What Is Called Thinking?*, trans. J. Glenn Gray (New York: Harper and Row, 1968), 233 (*Was Heißt Denken?*, vol. 8 of *Gesamtausgabe* [Frankfurt am Main: Vittorio Klostermann, 2002], 237). Cited in Richard Capobianco, *Engaging Heidegger* (Toronto: University of Toronto Press, 2010), 26–27.

21. This is actually a common refrain within the history of modern German letters. From Winckelmann to Nietzsche, one finds a call to emulate (i.e., mimetically replicate) a kind of Greek ethos.

22. Ralph Manheim translates the passage as follows: "To accomplish this the exegete must use violence. He must seek the essential where nothing more is to be found by the scientific interpretation that brands as unscientific everything that transcends its limits." I do not believe that it is too much to suggest, however, that such a rendering is detrimental to Heidegger's project because it inserts a subject (a humanistic subject, not a grammatical one) where there is none. It also translates *eigentlich* as essential, practically ignoring the previous research in *Being and Time* as well as the later work on language, thought, and the appropriating event—*Ereignis*.

23. There is another way in which translation is a question in both the 1935 and 1942 readings, which I will not pursue, although I do wish to acknowledge it. Criticisms regarding Heidegger's translation of *Antigone*, and how his translation affects the political issues of his thought, have been raised by various commentators, including: Marc Froment-Meurice, *That is to Say: Heidegger's Politics*, trans. Jan Plug (Stanford, CA: Stanford University Press, 1998), 121–48, and Castoriadis, *Figures of the Thinkable*, 2–3. Also, Daniel Coppieters de Gibson, "Les Grecs et la question de l'homme. À propos d'une lecture de Sophocle par Heidegger," in *Qu'est-ce que l'homme? Hommage à Alphonse de Waelhens* (Brussels: Facultés Universitaires Saint-Louis, 1982), 53–70, cited in Castoriadis.

24. As Richard Sieburth explains in a note to his translation of "*Der Ister*," "The Ister (Istros) is the ancient Greek name for the Danube" (Friedrich Hölderlin, *Hymns and Fragments*, trans. Richard Sieburth [Princeton, NJ: Princeton University Press, 1984] 267).

25. Heidegger's emphasis here on the *zwie* also anticipates what he will call in his later work the "twofold" (*Zwiefalt*) relation between Being and beings. See "Moira (Parmenides VIII, 34–41)" in Martin Heidegger, *Early Greek Thinking*, trans. David Farrell Krell and Frank A. Capuzzi (Harper San Francisco, 1984), 79–101.

26. There exist two versions of Hölderlin's translation of the choral ode, one a draft from 1800–1801 and a fully published edition from 1804. They are reproduced in the Appendix to this chapter. For a discussion of Heidegger's references to the two versions, see Dennis J. Schmidt, *On Germans and Other Greeks: Tragedy and Ethical Life* (Bloomington and Indianapolis: Indiana University Press, 2001), 255–56.

27. I repeat here the translation from *An Introduction to Metaphysics*. The actual English edition of *Hölderlins Hymne »Der Ister«* provides a more literal rendering of Heidegger's translation: "Manifold is the uncanny" (HH 52).

28. I have modified the translation from the English edition, which reads "the whole of what Hölderlin has passed on to us," which, in my opinion, omits the distinction Heidegger is making between translation as *Übersetzung* and translation as *Übertragung*.

29. The English edition of *Hölderlin's Hymn "The Ister"* translates *ungeheuer* as "extraordinary," which I have preserved here. But "monstrous" is more consistent with Hölderlin's thought on tragedy in general—as indicated by his "*Anmerkungen zum*

Oedipus," where, in a difficult passage, he refers to the monstrous as the becoming-one of god and the human: "Die Darstellung des Tragischen beruht vorzüglich darauf, daß das Ungeheuere, wie der Gott und Mensch sich paart, und grenzenlos die Naturmacht und des Menschen Innerstes im Zorn Eins wird, dadurch sich begreift, daß das grenzenlose Eineswerden durch grenzenloses Scheiden sich reiniget. *Tes physeos grammateus en ton kalamon apobrechon eunoun*" (*Sämtliche Werke*, Grosse Stuttgarter Ausgabe, ed. Friedrich Beissner, vol. 5. [Stuttgart: Kohlhammer, 1952], 201). ("The presentation of the tragic rests primarily on that in which the monstrous—how god and man mate and how natural force and man's innermost boundlessness become one in wrath—conceives itself as purifying itself in boundlessly becoming-one through boundless separation. *Tes physeos grammateus en ton kalamon apobrechon eunoun* [Nature's scribe, dipping the well-meaning quill]" [*Friedrich Hölderlin: Essays and Letters on Theory*, trans. and ed. Thomas Pfau (Albany: State University of New York Press, 1998), 107; translation modified].) *Ungeheuer* as "monstrous" is also consistent with its meaning in Kant, as in his discussion of *das Ungeheuer* in the course of his exegesis on the sublime (*das Erhabene*) in §26 of the *Critique of Judgment*.

30. Although it cannot be performed here, it seems that this passage calls out for its own "*Auseinandersetzung,*" as Christopher Fynsk has phrased it, with Benjamin's notion of *Relationsbegriff*, the "concept of relation" signaled, in the case of translation, by language's "translatability," the communication of language itself to itself. See Fynsk's "The Claim of History," in *Language and Relation . . . that there is language* (Stanford, CA: Stanford University Press, 1996), 211–26.

31. Whereas in *An Introduction to Metaphysics*, Heidegger's focus is on Oedipus as the main tragic figure. Froment-Meurice attributes this change to a transformation in Heidegger's conception of the political between 1935 and 1942. See *That is to Say: Heidegger's Politics* 121–48.

32. See Christopher Fynsk's *Infant Figures: The Death of the 'Infans' and Other Scenes of the Origin* (Stanford, CA: Stanford University Press, 2000).

33. As we will see, Lacoue-Labarthe's critique stresses the ways Heidegger's reliance on the figure perpetuates the legacy of speculative metaphysics. Although he will also touch on the role the figure of the feminine plays in this legacy, no one has done more to expose the work the feminine has been made to perform for speculative thought than Luce Irigaray. See in particular her *Speculum of the Other Woman*, trans. Gillian C. Gill (Ithaca, NY: Cornell University Press, 1985), as well as her essay "The Power of Discourse and the Subordination of the Feminine," in *This Sex Which is Not One*, trans. Catherine Porter with Carolyn Burke (Ithaca, NY: Cornell University Press, 1985), 68–85.

34. Sophocles, *The Antigone of Sophocles*, 2nd ed. Edited (with introduction and notes) by Sir Richard Jebb (Cambridge: Cambridge University Press, 1891), 68–76. The romanization that follows is based on this excerpt from the Jebb edition.

35. *Einführung in die Metaphysik*, GA40, 155–57.

36. From *An Introduction to Metaphysics*, trans. Ralph Manheim, 146–48.

37. Friedrich Hölderlin, *Sämtliche Werke*, 5:42.
38. Hölderlin, *Sämtliche Werke*, 5:219–20.
39. Translated in Dennis J. Schmidt, *On Germans and Other Greeks* (Indianapolis and Bloomington: Indiana University Press, 2001), 269–70.

Chapter 4

1. See Jean-Luc Nancy and Aurélien Barrau, *What's These Worlds Coming To?*, trans. Travis Holloway and Flor Méchain (New York: Fordham University Press, 2015).

2. Philippe Lacoue-Labarthe and Jean-Luc Nancy, "Scène." *Nouvelle Revue de Psychanalyse*, no. 46 (Autumn 1992): 73–98. Published as *Scène* suivi de *Dialogue sur le dialogue* (Paris: Éditions Christian Bourgois, 2013). "*Scène*" appears as "Scene: An Exchange of Letters," in *Beyond Representation: Philosophy and the Poetic Imagination*, ed. Richard Eldridge (Cambridge and New York: Cambridge University Press, 1996), 273–302. Hereafter "Scene" and "*Scène*," respectively.

3. Jean-Luc Nancy, *The Inoperative Community*, ed. Peter Connor, trans. Peter Connor, Lisa Garbus, Michael Holland and Simona Sawhney (Minneapolis: University of Minnesota Press, 1991) (*La Communauté désoeuvrée* [Paris: Éditions Christian Bourgois, 1986]); Philippe Lacoue-Labarthe and Jean-Luc Nancy, "The Nazi Myth." *Critical Inquiry* 16, no. 2 (1990): 291–312.

4. In the English translation of "*Il faut*," *dé-figuration* is rendered as "disfiguration." See Lacoue-Labarthe, "*Il faut*," in *Heidegger and the Politics of Poetry*, trans. Jeff Fort (Urbana and Chicago: University of Illinois Press, 2007), 54–55 (*Heidegger. La Politique du poème* [Paris: Galilée, 2002], 106–7).

5. Heidegger, *An Introduction to Metaphysics*, trans. Ralph Manheim (New Haven: Yale University Press, 1959), 199.

6. Lacoue-Labarthe, "The Caesura of the Speculative," in *Typography: Mimesis, Philosophy, Politics*, trans. Christopher Fynsk (Stanford, CA: Stanford University Press, 1998), 234–35.

7. Blanchot, *The Unavowable Community*. trans. Pierre Joris (Barrytown, NY: Station Hill, 1988) (*La Communauté inavouable* [Paris: Éditions de Minuit, 1983]). (Blanchot's response is to the version of *The Inoperative Community* that Nancy first published as an essay under the title "La Communauté desoeuvrée" in February 1983 in the journal *Aléa* [4: 11–49].) See Robert Bernasconi, "On Deconstructing Nostalgia for Community within the West: The Debate between Nancy and Blanchot." *Research in Phenomenology* 23 (1993): 3–21, and Andrew J. Mitchell and Jason Kemp Winfree, "Editors' Introduction: Community and Communication," in Andrew J. Mitchell and Jason Kemp Winfree, eds., *The Obsessions of Georges Bataille: Community and Communication* (Albany: State University of New York Press, 2009), 1–18. I present some more details of Nancy's revitalization of their debate following Blanchot's death in chapter 5.

8. These other scholars working on community include: Giorgio Agamben, *The Coming Community*, trans. Michael Hardt (Minneapolis: University of Minnesota Press, 1991) (*La comunità che viene* [Turin: Einaudi, 1990]) and Roberto Esposito, *Communitas: The Origin and Destiny of Community*, trans. Timothy Campbell (Stanford, CA: Stanford University Press, 2010) (*Communitas. Origine e destino della comunità* [Turin: Giulio einaudi editore, 1998]). See also *Roberto Esposito, Community and the Proper*, special issue of *Angelaki*, ed. Greg Bird and Jonathan Short 18, no. 3 (2013).

9. For one of the notable exceptions, see Ignaas Devisch, *Jean-Luc Nancy and the Questions of Community* (New York: Bloomsbury, 2013).

10. *Being Singular Plural*, trans. Robert D. Richardson and Anne E. O'Byrne (Stanford, CA: Stanford University Press, 2000) (*Être singulier pluriel* [Paris: Éditions Galilée, 1996]).

11. *Continental Philosophy Review* (2008) 41:1–15. ("L'Être-avec de l'être-là." *Lieu-Dit* 19 "*Communauté*" [Spring 2003].)

12. Although that exact phrase does not appear in the *Beiträge*, the translator of Nancy's essay connects Nancy's rendition to section 196 of that work, "*Da-sein und Volk*" ("Da-sein and a people"), where Heidegger writes, "*Das Wesen eines Volkes ist aber seine 'Stimme'*" ("The essence of a people, however, is its 'voice'") (*Beiträge zur Philosophie [Vom Ereignis]*. vol. 65 of *Gesamtausgabe* [Frankfurt am Main: V. Klostermann, 2003]), 319 [*Contributions to Philosophy (Of the Event)*, trans. Richard Rojcewicz and Daniela Vallega-Neu (Bloomington: Indiana University Press, 2012), 252]).

13. *Guilty*, trans. Bruce Boone (Venice, CA: Lapis, 1988), 23. Cited in editor's introduction to *The Obsessions of Georges Bataille: Community and Communication*, ed. Andrew J. Mitchell and Jason Kemp Winfree (Albany: State University of New York Press, 2009), 5.

14. Christopher Fynsk elucidated this relation of "being-(and dying-) with" at the heart of Dasein's thrownness in *Heidegger: Thought and Historicity*, and he has continued to do so most recently in terms of Blanchot's *Le Pas-au-déla* (*The Step/Not Beyond*) in *Last Steps: Maurice Blanchot's Exilic Writing* (New York: Fordham University Press, 2013).

15. As Bataille describes in *Guilty*,

With any tangible reality, for each being, you have to find the place of sacrifice, the wound. A being can only be touched where it yields. For a woman, this is under her dress; and for a god it's on the throat of the animal being sacrificed. Once you've come to hate the egotism of being alone, once you've ecstatically tried to lose yourself, you've had your hands around the empty reaches of heaven's throat: heaven has to howl, has to let its blood flow. (26)

Bataille's choice in this passage to illustrate the exposure of existence with an exposing image of a woman is a telling one. Such a gesture identifying the dissimulation of identity with the feminine is one that will be repeated habitually throughout the texts we are reading in this study (we saw some of this already in Heidegger's figuration of Antigone). While we will note that Lacoue-Labarthe draws our attention to this habitual gesture and its implications for speculative thought, it nonetheless persists as an interrogated premise in the other texts we will treat.

16. See, for example, this passage from "Sacrifices" (1936), in which Bataille invokes Heidegger's theorization of temporality as the horizon of existence:

> Thus the nature of time as object of ecstasy reveals itself in accordance with the ecstatic nature of the *me* that dies. For the one and the other are pure change and both take place on the plane of an illusory existence.
>
> But if the avid and obstinate question "what exists?" still traverses the immense disorder of living thought in the mode of the *me* that dies, what will be the meaning, at this moment, of the answer: "time is only an empty absurdity"?—or of all the other answers that refuse the being of time?
>
> Or what will be the meaning of the opposite answer: "being is time"?

(see *Visions of Excess*, ed. Allan Stoekl, trans. Allan Stoekl with Carl R. Lovitt and Donald M. Leslie Jr. [Minneapolis: University of Minnesota Press, 1985], 135).

17. In "The Unsacrificeable" (1990), Nancy cites this passage from *La limite de l'utile*, in which Bataille describes sacrifice as "a kind of mimeticism": "In a certain sense, sacrifice is a free activity. A kind of mimeticism. Man takes up the rhythm of the Universe"; see *Œuvres complètes* VII, 255, cited in Nancy, *A Finite Thinking*, ed. Simon Sparks (Stanford, CA: Stanford University Press, 2003), 59.

18. See Nancy, "Finite History" 149; *The Inoperative Community* 15.

19. See Georges Bataille, "L'Art, exercise de la cruauté," *Œuvres complètes*, vol. 11 (Paris: Gallimard, 1988), 480–86.

20. "The moment when *anticipation dissolves into* NOTHING"; see Bataille, *The Accursed Share*, 2 vols., trans. Robert Hurley (New York: Zone Books, 1993), 207.

21. "Hegel, Death, and Sacrifice," in *The Bataille Reader*, Fred Botting and Scott Wilson, eds. (Malden, MA: Blackwell, 1997), 287 (*Œuvres complètes*, vol. 12 [Paris: Gallimard, 1988], 337; original emphasis).

22. "The Unsacrificeable" 64–65. See "The Origin of the Work of Art," in *Off the Beaten Track*, 37 (GA 5 *Holzwege* [Frankfurt am Main: Klostermann, 1977], 49).

23. See "The Unsacrificeable" 327n30.

24. *The Muses*, trans. Peggy Kamuf (Stanford, CA: Stanford University Press, 1996), 17.

25. *The Ground of the Image*, trans. Jeff Fort (New York: Fordham University Press, 2005), 2.

26. Blanchot's "Two Versions of the Imaginary" (*The Space of Literature*, trans. Ann Smock [Lincoln: University of Nebraska Press, 1982]) is another example of this elevation I am identifying. And even though Nancy wants to say the image exceeds the visual, encompassing the "musical, poetic, even tactile, olfactory or gustatory, kinaesthetic, and so on" (*Ground* 4), he restricts his treatment largely to Western painting. We thus see a repetition of the high-low art dichotomy that is present in texts ranging from Heidegger to Adorno but that is traceable to the Kantian tradition. Although right now we are simply following Nancy in his theorization of the image (not yet offering a critical assessment of this theorization), if I am to be honest, this is where I find his contention regarding the communication of the fact of sense most tenuous, if not altogether forced. Nowhere in this opening chapter, which was written as a catalogue essay for a traveling exhibition titled *Heaven*, does Nancy worry that what he is saying is projected within the very limited context of Western art history. See *Heaven*, ed. Doreet LeVitte Harten (Ostfildern-Ruit: Hatje Cantz Verlag, 1999).

27. Both inflections involve an idea of participation. In Greek theater, *methexis* refers to a group sharing or ritual. In Plato, *methexis* concerns the participation of the particular in the universal, as in the Form or Idea (*eidos*). Of course, it is perhaps not a coincidence that Nancy's revision of mimesis has a theatrical/scenic connotation as opposed to the more philosophical (and Platonic) meaning of imitation.

28. Collected in *Le Sujet de la philosophie: Typographies I* (Paris: Aubier-Flammarion, 1979) and in English in *The Subject of Philosophy*, ed. Thomas Trezise (Minneapolis: University of Minnesota Press, 1993).

29. *La Fiction du politique* (Paris: Christian Bourgois, 1987) (*Heidegger, Art, and Politics: The Fiction of the Political*, trans. Chris Turner [Oxford and Cambridge, MA: Blackwell, 1990]).

30. "Typography" in *Typography: Mimesis, Philosophy, Politics*, trans. Christopher Fynsk (Stanford, CA: Stanford University Press, 1998), 43–138. First published as "Typographie" in Sylviane Agacinski et al., *Mimesis des articulations* (Paris: Flammarion, 1975).

31. Collected in *Le Sujet de la philosophie* and in English in *Typography*.

32. *Musica Ficta (Figures of Wagner)*, trans. Felicia McCarren (Stanford, CA: Stanford University Press, 1994); "The Scene is Primal" is collected in *Le Sujet de la philosophie* and in English in *The Subject of Philosophy*.

33. Lacoue-Labarthe addresses his analysis primarily to: "Who is Nietzsche's Zarathustra?," in *The New Nietzsche: Contemporary Styles of Interpretation*, ed. David Allison, trans. Bernd Magnus (New York: Dell, 1977), 64–79; *What Is Called Thinking?*, trans. J. Glenn Gray (New York: Harper and Row, 1968); and "On the Question of Being," in *Pathmarks*, ed. William McNeill (Cambridge: Cambridge University Press, 1998), 291–322.

34. Here it is worth noting the different ways Nancy and Lacoue-Labarthe attend to the theme of fictioning. Where Lacoue-Labarthe sees Heidegger's inter-

pretation of Nietzsche through *Er-denken* as an appropriation of mimesis, Nancy, as we recall from our discussion, sees in Schelling's conception of mythic fictioning an enunciative opening of community.

35. Ernst Jünger, *The Worker: Dominion and Form*, trans. Bogdan Costea and Laurence Paul Hemming (Evanston: Northwestern University Press, 2017) (*Der Arbeiter. Herrschaft und die Gestalt* [Stuttgart: Klett-Cotta, 1981]).

36. Quoted in "Typography" 54–55 from *The Question of Being*, trans. William Kluback and Jean T. Wilde (New York: Twayne, 1958), 51 ("On the Question of Being," *Pathmarks* 298; original emphasis).

37. "Typography" 55. In *Heidegger, Art, and Politics*, Lacoue-Labarthe uses more forceful language, stating it is not until the letter to Jünger that Heidegger "*denounced* onto-typology" (86).

38. See "On the Question of Being" (*Pathmarks* 299–303) for the pages Lacoue-Labarthe is reading in this section of "Typography."

39. The *Nietzsche* lectures also take place before the "*Ge-Stell*" Bremen lecture from 1949. But the fact that Lacoue-Labarthe does not engage with "The Origin of the Work of Art" in "Typography" is more than curious, as we shall soon see.

40. Quoted in "Typography," 60; Martin Heidegger, *Nietzsche*, vols. 3–4, trans. David Farrell Krell (New York: Harper and Row, 1991), 96 (GA 6.1, *Nietzsche I*, Brigitte Schillbach, ed. [Frankfurt am Main: Klostermann, 1996], 585).

41. "Typography" 70. Lacoue-Labarthe is reading Heidegger's reading of Fragment 515 of *The Will to Power*. See *Nietzsche*, 3–4:71 and Friedrich Nietzsche, *The Will to Power*, trans. Walter Kaufmann and R. J. Hollingdale (New York: Vintage, 1968), 278.

42. Nietzsche, KSA 13, *Nachgelassene Fragmente: 1887–1889*, ed. Giorgio Colli and Mazzino Montinari (Munich: Deutscher Taschenbuch Verlag, 1999), 334 (*Will to Power* 515, 278).

43. GA 6.1, 585; quoted and translated in "Typography" 69n37. Although I cannot pursue the connection here, we might notice how this notion of fictioning resonates with (but is also distinct from) the meaning of fictioning that Nancy attends to in *The Inoperative Community*, which we reviewed in the first part of this chapter.

44. "Typography" 64. Lacoue-Labarthe rehearses this list, with slight revisions and amendments, in *Heidegger, Art, and Politics* 85–86. Among the amendments, however, is a citation of "The Origin of the Work of Art" in place of the works Lacoue-Labarthe examines to support his reading in "Typography" (*Heidegger, Art, and Politics* 90n18). The change is not insignificant. How does the change in sources affect Lacoue-Labarthe's argument from the time of the writing of "Typography" (1975) to *Heidegger, Art, and Politics* (*La Fiction du politique* [1987])? To resolve this question here would take my analysis too far afield, so I must forgo doing so and simply affirm my plan to reconstruct Lacoue-Labarthe's argument in "Typography" and follow its implications, assuming a degree of soundness to his interpretation and withholding comment otherwise, for better or worse. However, I wish to note this

lacuna in Lacoue-Labarthe's text in order to acknowledge a place where we might put pressure on him regarding his interpretation of Heidegger's conceptualization of the artwork, specifically in terms of his interpretation of *Ge-stell*. For a reading that would challenge Lacoue-Labarthe's, I would refer the reader to the fourth chapter of Fynsk's *Heidegger: Thought and Historicity.*

45. "Typography" 65. Somewhat in the spirit of my previous note, Gregory Schufreider questions Lacoue-Labarthe's method of reading Heidegger's conception of *Gestalt* in "The Origin of the Work of Art" retrospectively through Heidegger's critique of *Gestalt* in Jünger, as well as from the notion of *Ge-stell*, both of which Heidegger formulates after the artwork essay. See Schufreider's "Sticking Heidegger with a Stela: Lacoue-Labarthe, Art and Politics," in *French Interpretations of Heidegger: An Exceptional Reception*, ed. David Pettigrew and François Raffoul (Albany: State University of New York Press, 2008), 190–91.

46. "Typography" 65; see "The Question Concerning Technology" 21, in Martin Heidegger, *The Question Concerning Technology and Other Essays*, trans. William Lovitt (New York and London: Garland, 1977).

47. Lacoue-Labarthe considers this repetitive reversal exclusively in Platonic terms, but it may be worth comparing his reading to Jacques Taminiaux's treatment of the artwork essay, which frames Heidegger's conception of art as an Aristotelian inheritance. See Taminiaux's "The Origin of 'The Origin of the Work of Art,'" in *Reading Heidegger: Commemorations*, ed. John Sallis (Bloomington and Indianapolis: Indiana University Press, 1993), 392–404.

48. Or is it Plato? Or is the choice really rather between "Socrates" and "Plato" (which is the actual figure here)? This is one of the points Lacoue-Labarthe is trying to make regarding speculative thought and figuration and also one of the aspects of Plato's text that Lacoue-Labarthe claims Heidegger curiously overlooks—that is, its literary character.

49. 596c. Plato, *Republic*, Books 6–10, Plato VI, Loeb Classical Library, trans. Paul Shorey (Cambridge, MA: Harvard University Press, 2000).

50. I am being deliberately (but also regrettably) general here regarding "The Echo of the Subject." For the sake of maintaining focus on the primary discussion, I must limit my description to that of an outline. For more sustained analyses of "The Echo of the Subject," see my "The Sonic Turn and Theory's Affective Call." *Parallax* 23, no. 3 (2017): 316–29, and also Christopher Fynsk's *Philippe Lacoue-Labarthe's Phrase: Infancy, Survival* (Albany: State University of New York Press, 2017). For a clear and detailed study of Lacoue-Labarthe's occupation with the subject's dissolution and return in Western thought, see John Martis, *Philippe Lacoue-Labarthe: Representation and the Loss of the Subject* (New York: Fordham University Press, 2005).

51. See "Typography" 93n80, where Lacoue-Labarthe recounts Heidegger's effort in the essay "Science and Reflection" to bring *theoria* into alignment with *aletheia*.

52. "Transcendence Ends in Politics," in *Typography*, 297.

53. Adopted from Adorno's concept of *"Entkunstung"* (de-artification) and Benjamin's notion of the *Verlagerung des Mythologischen* (the "setting down" or "deposing of the mythological"), which Lacoue-Labarthe will remind us of later on in the exchange ("Scene" 281). See Lacoue-Labarthe, "*Il faut*," in *Heidegger and the Politics of Poetry*, trans. Jeff Fort (Urbana and Chicago: University of Illinois Press, 2007), 50–51.

54. Most immediately, the writings collected in the volume *Retreating the Political*, ed. Simon Sparks (London and New York: Routledge, 1997). As we will discuss, in addition to serving as a set of reflections on the problem of figuration in the wake of Heidegger's text, these writings also elaborate Derrida's "concept" of the trace (*trait*).

55. See, however, *Dialogue sur le dialogue*, where Nancy returns to the question of resemblance and the "difference" it makes when he retraces the steps Heidegger takes in *Unterwegs zur Sprache* relating the solitude (*Einsamkeit*) of language's speaking to *sammeln* (gathering) and the Greek *hama*. Nancy connects these further to the Latin *simul* and the French "assembler *ou* rassembler" and ultimately to community as *Gemeinsamkeit* (100; emphasis added).

56. "Oedipus as Figure," trans. David Macey, *Radical Philosophy* 118 (March/April 2003): 7–17.

57. Alison Ross elucidates the contradictory aspect of Heidegger's reliance on figuration, especially as it concerns his conception of finite transcendence and his appeals to the Greek relation to/conception of Being. If finite transcendence eschews imitation, then how are we to follow the Greek example of thinking if not by imitating it? See *The Aesthetic Paths of Philosophy: Presentation in Kant, Heidegger, Lacoue-Labarthe, and Nancy* (Stanford, CA: Stanford University Press, 2007), 120–21; 126–27.

58. Rodolphe Gasché, "Joining the Text: From Heidegger to Derrida," in *The Yale Critics: Deconstruction in America*, ed. Jonathan Arac, Wlad Godzich, and Wallace Martin (Minneapolis: University of Minnesota Press, 1983), 156–75.

59. Gasché shows how the *retrait*'s repetition follows Heidegger right up to his reflections on rhythm and language, although Derrida inflects the *retrait* further through Mallarmé and Benvéniste ("Joining the Text" 162). This raises interesting questions regarding how much the *retrait* could be thought separable from the metaphysics of presence, for as we saw above, Lacoue-Labarthe casts a good deal of suspicion on rhythm and music as defining a realm outside the order of representation. Cf. "The Echo of the Subject."

60. See Jean-Luc Nancy, "Our History." *Diacritics* 20, no. 3 (Fall 1990): 102.

61. See "Transcendence Ends in Politics": "There is not, in other words, an exteriority of the political in relation to the philosophical—doubtless not even a true division between the philosophical and the political: every philosophical determination of the essence of the political obeys a political determination of essence; and the latter inversely presupposes a gesture that one can only characterize as

political. This belonging-together of the philosophical and the political is as old as philosophy (and as old as what is still for us called politics). And this is what Heidegger always submits to, even in his desire to subjugate the political, or at any rate to circumscribe it" (288).

62. Philippe Lacoue-Labarthe and Jean-Luc Nancy, "The Unconscious is Structured Like an Affect (Part 1 of 'The Jewish People Do Not Dream')." *Stanford Literary Review* 6 no. 2 (1989): 196. See Simon Sparks's note to "Opening Address" in *Retreating the Political*, 180n9.

63. Christopher Fynsk explores this path in *Philippe Lacoue-Labarthe's* Phrase, as well as in *Last Steps*.

64. In addition to what we read of this identification in "Typography" (129) and *Musica Ficta* (105–7), see also "The Echo of the Subject," in *Typography*, 203–6. See in addition "The Scene is Primal," in *The Subject of Philosophy*, ed. Thomas Trezise (Minneapolis: University of Minnesota Press, 1993), 111. Alison Ross provides an exemplary explanation of how in "Typography" Lacoue-Labarthe reveals speculative thought's attempt to master its resentment of the feminine's power of reproduction through the repression and assumption of mimesis, which gives the subject the appearance of being able to engender itself without any reliance on a maternal origin. See her *The Aesthetic Paths of Philosophy: Presentation in Kant, Heidegger, Lacoue-Labarthe, and Nancy*, 116–17.

Nonetheless, despite Lacoue-Labarthe's clear awareness of philosophy's appropriation of the feminine, he repeats this appropriation not only in his collaboration with Nancy but also in his work *Phrase* with the invocation of "*la kère*," the feminine figure of death from Greek mythology. See "Phrase VI" in *Phrase* (Paris: Christian Bourgois, 2000), 49–51 (*Phrase*, trans. Leslie Hill [Albany: State University of New York Press, 2018], 33–34). On the figure of Ker, see Jean-Pierre Vernant, *Mortals and Immortals: Collected Essays*, ed. Froma I. Zeitlin (Princeton, NJ: Princeton University Press, 1991), 95–110.

65. See Ross, *The Aesthetic Paths of Philosophy*, 116–17.

66. See Luce Irigaray, *The Forgetting of Air in Martin Heidegger*, trans. Mary Beth Mader (Austin: University of Texas Press, 1999). See Ronell's remarks on the scene of the mother's call in Heidegger's *What Is Called Thinking?* in Avital Ronell, *The Telephone Book: Technology, Schizophrenia, Electric Speech* (Lincoln: University of Nebraska Press, 1989), 20–25. See also Barbara Johnson's analysis of the gendered figuration of the jug in Heidegger's "The Thing" (1950) in her *Persons and Things* (Cambridge, MA: Harvard University Press, 2010), and see Andrew Parker, *The Theorist's Mother* (Durham, NC: Duke University Press, 2012).

Chapter 5

1. "Phrase V," in Philippe Lacoue-Labarthe, *Phrase* (Paris: Christian Bourgois, 2000), 43–48 (*Phrase*, trans. Leslie Hill [Albany: State University of New York Press,

2018], 29–32). Reprinted in Philippe Lacoue-Labarthe, *Agonie terminée, agonie interminable. Sur Maurice Blanchot. Suivi de L'émoi*, ed. Aristide Bianchi et Leonid Kharlamov (Éditions Galilée, 2011) (*Ending and Unending Agony: On Maurice Blanchot*, trans. Hannes Opelz [New York: Fordham University Press, 2015]).

2. I should take a moment to state again a qualification that I make earlier in the introduction to the present study that these pairings I am pursuing in the book's last two chapters—Blanchot with Lacoue-Labarthe and Deleuze with Nancy—are not intended to be completely clean mappings of these thinkers onto one another. While I justify their alignments textually, I do not view these pairings as exclusionary. Blanchot can be read as engaging with aspects of Nancy's position in his debate with Lacoue-Labarthe as well, particularly in terms of the question of community, as I will indicate momentarily.

3. My reference to "steps" here is of course a kind of pun. One of Blanchot's major works, *Le Pas au-delà* (Paris: Gallimard, 1973) (*The Step/Not Beyond*, trans. Lycette Nelson [Albany: State University New York Press, 1992]) plays on the idea of a step (*pas*) that is simultaneously a form of denial or refusal. And although I will not be undertaking any focused reading of Blanchot's literary works (his *récits*), I do want to acknowledge that those writings are not simply realizations of his theoretical reflections (theory put into practice, as it were) but modes of theorizing in themselves, just as his theoretical works travel the boundary between philosophy and literature.

4. *The Infinite Conversation*, trans. Susan Hanson (Minneapolis: University of Minnesota Press, 1993) (*L'Entretien infini*. [Paris: Gallimard, 1969]). Hereafter IC and EI, respectively.

5. Michel Foucault, *The Order of Things: An Archaeology of the Human Sciences* (New York: Vintage, 1994), 387.

6. See chapter 1.

7. See Jacques Derrida, "Heidegger's Ear: Philopolemology (*Geschlecht* IV)," in *Reading Heidegger: Commemorations*, ed. John Sallis, trans. John P. Leavey Jr. (Indianapolis: Indiana University Press, 1993), 163–218; Philippe Lacoue-Labarthe, "The Echo of the Subject," in *Typography: Mimesis, Philosophy, Politics*, ed. Christopher Fynsk (Stanford, CA: Stanford University Press, 1998), 139–207.

8. As we will see in chapter 6, this essay will prove to be immensely influential to Deleuze.

9. Blanchot's presentation of the conversation makes it challenging to quote from it. He uses em dashes to signal changes in the different voices speaking, and he also encloses the entire chapter in quotation marks, which Wittgenstein and others who employed similar dialogue forms in their writings, such as Jean-François Lyotard in *The Differend* (1988/*Le Différend* [1983]), do not do, hence my use here of quotation marks within quotation marks. It is unknown whether Blanchot foresaw the challenges of quoting from his text, but doing so engenders a dizzying proliferation of voices and a difficulty in establishing each voice's origin, which in a curious way matches up with the book's section title ("Plural Speech"). See also

Leslie Hill's remarks on Blanchot's use of quotation marks in his *récit L'Arrêt de morte* [*Death Sentence*] (Leslie Hill, *Blanchot: Extreme Contemporary* [London and New York: Routledge, 1997], 155–56). Following Hill, we might say that these dialogues in *The Infinite Conversation* stand as *récits* within the theoretical work.

10. This is one place where we might begin to compare Nancy's and Blanchot's conceptions of community, especially with respect to what Blanchot, thinking of Derrida's "Of an Apocalyptic Tone Recently Adopted in Philosophy," alludes to as the "apocalyptic voice" of community. See *The Unavowable Community*, trans. Pierre Joris (Barrytown: Station Hill, 1988), 57n5 (*La Communauté inavouable* [Paris: Éditions de Minuit, 1983], 26n1); Derrida, "Of an Apocalyptic Tone Recently Adopted in Philosophy," trans. John P. Leavey Jr., in *Derrida and Negative Theology*, ed. Harold Coward and Toby Foshay (Albany: State University of New York Press, 1992) (*D'un ton apocalyptique adopté naguère en philosophie* [Paris: Galilée, 1983]). As we will soon see, however, such comparison is not so straightforward.

11. G. W. F. Hegel, *The Phenomenology of Spirit*, trans. Terry Pinkard (Cambridge: Cambridge University Press, 2018), para. 19, 13 (*Werke*, ed. Eva Moldenhauer and Karl Markus Michel, 20 vols. [Frankfurt am Main: Suhrkamp, 1970], III, 24). Hereafter PS and WIII, respectively.

12. "Literature and the Right to Death," trans. Lydia Davis, in *The Work of Fire*, trans. Charlotte Mandell (Stanford, CA: Stanford University Press, 1995), 300; translation modified (*La Part du feu* [Paris: Éditions Gallimard, 1949], 293). Hereafter WF and PF, respectively.

13. See, respectively, Martin Heidegger, "Language," in *Poetry, Language, Thought*, trans. Albert Hofstadter (New York: Harper, 1971), 188 (*Unterwegs zur Sprache*, vol. 12 of *Gesamtausgabe* [Frankfurt am Main: Klostermann, 1985], 10; GA12 hereafter), and "The Way to Language," in Martin Heidegger, *Basic Writings*, ed. David Farrell Krell, rev. ed. (New York: HarperCollins, 1993), 398; original emphasis. I refer to the translation in *Basic Writings* because Peter D. Hertz's translation in *On the Way to Language* (New York: Harper & Row, 1971) (hereafter OW) renders the phrase "*die Sprache als Sprache zu Sprache bringen*" as "to speak about speech *qua* speech," which amounts to a distortion of Heidegger's turn to language. See GA12, 230, and OW 112.

14. "Language" was first given as a lecture by Heidegger in 1950, and he also originally presented "The Way to Language" as a lecture in 1959. Both were published in 1959 in *Unterwegs zur Sprache* (*On the Way to Language*). By comparison, an earlier version of "La Littérature et le droit à la mort" was published in the journal *Critique* in 1948 (*Critique* 20 [January 1948]: 30–47) before appearing in *La Part du feu* in 1949. For an exhaustive bibliography of Blanchot's works, see Leslie Hill, *Blanchot: Extreme Contemporary* (London and New York: Routledge, 1997), 274–98.

15. Alexandre Kojève, *Introduction to the Reading of Hegel: Lectures on the Phenomenology of Spirit*, ed. Allan Bloom, trans. James H. Nichols Jr. (Ithaca, NY: Cornell University Press, 1980).

16. Blanchot's rendering, "*La vie qui porte la mort et se maintient en elle*" (PF 324), is actually a paraphrase of Hegel's statement: "*Aber nicht das Leben, das sich vor dem Tode scheut und von der Verwüstung rein bewahrt, sondern das ihn erträgt und in ihm sich erhält*" (WIII 36) ("However, the life of spirit is not a life that fears death and austerely protects itself from ruin; rather, it bears death and sustains itself in it" [PS, para. 32, 20–21; translation modified]).

17. Yet, as Blanchot notes, this death in and to language would not be possible were there not some essential relation between language and human finitude. "My language does not kill anyone," Blanchot concedes. "But if this woman were not really capable of dying, if she were not threatened by death at every moment in her life, bound and joined to death by an essential bond, I would not be able to carry out that ideal negation, that deferred assassination which is what my language is" (WF 323).

18. That Blanchot figures this possibility through the example of the death of an anonymous, abstract "woman" is the matter for another (although much needed) analysis that I will need to pursue on a separate occasion. See chapter 4, notes 15 and 64. As I outline in those notes and in my concluding remarks in chapter 4, Nancy and Lacoue-Labarthe repeat philosophy's historical drive of appropriating the feminine as part of constituting its identity as "Philosophy." This moment in "Literature and the Right to Death" is a brief appearance of that same drive and of a similar repetition in Blanchot's work, which we will see in more pronounced fashion with his appeal to the myth of Orpheus and Eurydice. The feminine occupies a fraught place in many of his *récits* as well, as in the figure of J. in *Death Sentence* (1948), who may be considered a precursor to Blanchot's Eurydice. In *The Unavowable Community* (1983), Blanchot equates "the absolutely feminine" with the "absolutely other." One lone analysis that has attempted to question the appearance of the feminine in Blanchot is Lynne Huffer, "Blanchot's Mother," *Yale French Studies*, no. 93 (1998): 175–95.

19. "What Is Metaphysics?," in *Pathmarks*, ed. William McNeill (Cambridge: Cambridge University Press, 1998), 90. PM hereafter.

20. "Zeit und Sein" (1962), in *Zur Sache des Denkens*, vol. 14 of *Gesamtausgabe* (Frankfurt am Main: Klostermann, 2007) ("Time and Being," in *On Time and Being*, trans. Joan Stambaugh [Harper & Row: New York, 1972]).

21. Emmanuel Lévinas, *Existence and Existents*, trans. Alphonso Lingis (Pittsburgh: Duquesne University Press, 2001), 57 (*De l'existence à l'existant*, Seconde edition augmentée [Paris: Vrin, 2013]). Hereafter EE and DE, respectively. As many commentators have noted, the "origin" of the *il y a* as a concept in Blanchot's and Lévinas's work is difficult to pin down. When Blanchot touches on the *il y a* in the note just quoted from "Literature and the Right to Death," he refers to Lévinas's *Existence and Existents*. Yet, when one turns to *Existence and Existents*, one finds Lévinas theorizing the *il y a* from his reading of Blanchot's *Thomas the Obscure* (*Thomas l'Obscur* [1941]) (*Existence and Existents*, 58). Despite this mutual

referencing between Blanchot and Lévinas, Blanchot can be found thematizing the phrase as early as 1935 in his *récit* "Le Dernier mot." For more on the discursive circuit of the *il y a* between Blanchot and Lévinas, see Leslie Hill, *Blanchot: Extreme Contemporary* (London and New York: Routledge, 1997); Christopher Fynsk, *Language and Relation . . . that there is language* (Stanford, CA: Stanford University Press, 1996); Simon Critchley, *Very Little . . . Almost Nothing: Death, Philosophy, Literature*, 2nd ed. (London and New York: Routledge, 1997); William Large, "IMPERSONAL EXISTENCE: A Conceptual Genealogy of the 'There Is' from Heidegger to Blanchot and Lévinas." *Angelaki* 7, no. 3 (2002):131–42; and Arthur Cools, "Revisiting the *Il y a*: Maurice Blanchot and Emmanuel Lévinas on the Question of Subjectivity," *Paragraph* 28, no. 3 (2005): 54–71.

22. There is evidence that the *es gibt* occupied Heidegger's thinking as early as 1919 (*Zur Bestimmung der Philosophie* [GA 56/57] / *Towards the Definition of Philosophy* [2000]), and although he invokes it in a way that equates it with the French *il y a* in the "Letter on Humanism" (1947), as previously noted, Heidegger does not reflect on the *es gibt* at length until "Zeit und Sein" (1962) (in *Zur Sache des Denkens* [GA 14] / "Time and Being," in *On Time and Being* [1972]).

23. *Being and Time*, §40.

24. Leslie Hill's interpretation of *Thomas the Obscure* features a detailed explanation of the figure of the night in that work and the insomnia that accompanies it. Hill also points out that the night appears again in *The Space of Literature* as "the *other* night" (SL 163–76). See Hill, *Blanchot: Extreme Contemporary*, 58–60, 238n4. (The figure of the "*other* night" also appears in *The Infinite Conversation* [190, 210; original emphasis].)

25. See Fynsk, *Language and Relation*, 231–32. As Fynsk notes, the figure of Lazarus connects with the figure of the cadaver Blanchot writes about in "Two Versions of the Imaginary" in *The Space of Literature*.

26. See Hill, *Blanchot: Extreme Contemporary*, 113.

27. See Hill, *Blanchot: Extreme Contemporary*, 63, 113.

28. Although I do think Blanchot's conception of literature achieves the image of atheistic writing he calls for, I also believe it exposes itself to a criticism that Jean-Luc Nancy makes in *The Inoperative Community* about the way the concept of community can be appropriated for a politics of nostalgia about the loss of community. In this way, community takes on the appearance of the *deus absconditus*, an absent or hidden God (*Inoperative Community* 10), and also shows how an atheism of the *il y a* can flip back into its opposite, into a negative theology or theism that Nancy describes elsewhere as an "absentheism" (*The Creation of the World or Globalization*, trans. François Raffoul and David Pettigrew [Albany: State University of New York Press, 2007], 50–51). This is a criticism that Nancy applies directly to Blanchot and repeats in many ways his and Lacoue-Labarthe's critique of Heidegger's participation in National Socialism by reading Blanchot's theorization of community through his far-right political writings of the 1930s. (See *La Communauté affrontée* [Éditions Galilée, 2001]) ("The Confronted Community,"

in Andrew J. Mitchell and Jason Kemp Winfree, eds., *The Obsessions of Georges Bataille: Community and Communication* [Albany: State University of New York Press, 2009], 19–30); *Maurice Blanchot: Passion politique* (Éditions Galilée, 2011); *La Communauté désavouée* (Éditions Galilée, 2014) (*The Disavowed Community*, trans. Philip Armstrong [New York: Fordham University Press, 2016].) I cannot go into more detail in the present context, but it is nonetheless a terribly fraught debate, one that would require bringing in Derrida's reflections on negative theology, as found in his "Of an Apocalyptic Tone Recently Adopted in Philosophy" (1983) and Blanchot's reference to that work as previously noted. For some guidance on the relevant exchanges that constitute it, see Leslie Hill, *Nancy, Blanchot: A Serious Controversy* (London and New York: Rowman & Littlefield, 2018) and Christopher Fynsk, *Last Steps: Maurice Blanchot's Exilic Writing* (New York: Fordham University Press, 2013), 279–81n20.

29. *The Space of Literature*, trans. Ann Smock (Lincoln: University of Nebraska Press, 1982), 214 (*L'Espace littéraire* [Paris: Gallimard, 1955], 223). Hereafter SL and EL, respectively. Hegel's original reads as follows: "*Bleibt die Kunst nach der Seite ihre höchsten Bestimmung für uns ein Vergangenes*" (*Werke*, Eva Moldenhauer and Karl Markus Michel, eds., 20 vols. [Frankfurt am Main: Suhrkamp, 1970], XIII, 25); "Art, considered in its highest vocation, is and remains for us a thing of the past" (see *Hegel's Aesthetics: Lectures on Fine Art*, vol. 1, trans. T. M. Knox [Oxford: Clarendon, 1975], 11). See "The Origin of the Work of Art," in *Off the Beaten Path*, ed. and trans. Julian Young and Kenneth Haynes (Cambridge: Cambridge University Press, 2002), 51.

30. See Hill, *Blanchot: Extreme Contemporary*, 121–27.

31. See Jeff Fort, *The Imperative to Write: Destitutions of the Sublime in Kafka, Blanchot, and Beckett* (New York: Fordham University Press, 2014); Christopher Fynsk, *Last Steps: Maurice Blanchot's Exilic Writing* (New York: Fordham University Press, 2013); Leslie Hill, *Maurice Blanchot and Fragmentary Writing: A Change in Epoch* (London and New York: Continuum, 2012); Martin Crowley, "Even Now, Now, Very Now," in *Blanchot Romantique*, ed. Hannes Opelz and John McKeane (Bern: Peter Lang, 2011), 247–61; Lars Iyer, *Blanchot's Communism: Art, Philosophy and the Political* (New York: Palgrave Macmillan, 2004). On the theme of *malheur* in modernism, see Shane Weller, *Language and Negativity in European Modernism* (Cambridge: Cambridge University Press, 2018).

32. See note 18 on death and the figure of woman. See also Shane Weller, "Voidance: Linguistic Negativism in Maurice Blanchot's Fiction," *French Studies: A Quarterly Review* 69, no. 1 (January 2015): 30–45. What also deserves attention is the place of Simone Weil in Blanchot's conception of suffering. See Phillip Tolliday, "Maurice Blanchot: Suffering and Affliction as Epiphany," *Culture, Theory and Critique* 52, nos. 2–3 (2011):199–211.

33. In *Last Steps*, Christopher Fynsk analyzes *malheur* in *The Step/Not Beyond* as an experience (at the limit of experience) of the neuter and connects it directly to Heidegger's conception of *die Stimmung* (164–66). I have no cause to doubt the

connection Fynsk makes in this respect. However, I will simply note that where Fynsk reads the relationship between Heidegger and Blanchot with a stress on the continuity between their thought (and in a way that is less concerned than I am by the modernist sensibility I am noting here), I am seeking to draw out Blanchot's inversion of Heidegger's central formulations of human finitude and its appearance in relation to language and the voice. For me, the continuity between Blanchot's *malheur* and Heidegger's *Stimmung* may indicate the limits of how successful Blanchot was in realizing an inversion of Heidegger in this respect.

34. "Artaud" (1959), trans. Ian Maclachlan, in *The Blanchot* Reader, ed. Michael Holland (Oxford: Blackwell, 1995), 129–35. The French text was republished in 1959 in *Le Livre à venir* (Paris: Gallimard) [Maurice Blanchot, *The Book to Come*, trans. Charlotte Mandel (Stanford, CA: Stanford University Press, 2003)]. All references will be to the translation in *The Blanchot Reader*.

35. *What Is Called Thinking?*, trans. J. Glenn Gray (New York: Harper & Row, 1968), 4; original emphasis.

36. As we will see in chapter 6, this constellation of Heidegger, Blanchot, and Artaud will be formative for Deleuze's pursuit of a new image of thought.

37. "*Un impouvoir à cristalliser inconsciemment,*" writes Artaud in *Le Pèse-nerfs* (*The Nerve Meter*) (1925), "*le point rompu de l'automatisme à quelque degré que ce soit.*" ("A powerlessness to crystallize unconsciously the broken point of the mechanism to any degree at all.") *Œuvres complètes*, vol. 1, 2nd suppl. ed. (Paris: Gallimard, 1970), 111 ("A Powerlessness . . ." from *The Nerve Meter* [1925], in *Antonin Artaud: Selected Writings*, ed. Susan Sontag, trans. Helen Weaver [Berkeley and Los Angeles: University of California Press, 1988], 82).

38. "Correspondence with Jacques Rivière"(1923–24), in *Antonin Artaud: Selected Writings*, 31.

39. Here Blanchot is quoting from (though not citing) Artaud's *Fragments of a Diary from Hell* (1925): "For me there is perpetual pain and darkness, the night of the soul, and I have no voice to cry out" (*Antonin Artaud: Selected Writings*, 96).

40. The letter is to Peter Watson, dated January 27, 1946, for which, incidentally, Blanchot neglects to provide a citation. Also noteworthy is that Blanchot confuses passages from this letter with passages from the correspondence with Rivière. See "To Peter Watson," in Antonin Artaud's *Watchfiends & Rack Screams: Works from the Final Period*, ed. and trans. Clayton Eshleman with Bernard Bador (Boston: Exact Change, 1995), 86.

41. It is worth noting that Blanchot's theorization of the narrative voice is couched within a mini-commentary on Marguerite Duras. That fact, combined with his statement that in "speak[ing] the neutral" the narrative voice upsets community (IC 386), shows Blanchot anticipating in this text the reflection on community he will undertake via a reading of Duras in *The Unavowable Community*.

42. *The One Who Was Standing Apart From Me*, trans. Lydia Davis (Barrytown, New York: Station Hill, 1993), 317; translation modified. (*Celui qui ne m'accompagnait*

pas [Paris: Gallimard, 1953], 125–26.) A partial translation of this passage appears in Michel Foucault, *Maurice Blanchot: The Thought from Outside*, trans. Brian Massumi, in *Foucault/Blanchot* (New York: Zone, 1987), 22–23 ["La Pensée du dehors," in Michel Foucault, *Dits et Écrits*, vol. 1, 1954–1988, ed. Daniel Defert and François Ewald [Paris: Gallimard, 1994], 518–39).

43. Maurice Blanchot, *The Writing of the Disaster*, trans. Ann Smock (Lincoln: University of Nebraska Press, 1983), 5, 75. (The disaster is also a name Blanchot uses to retrieve the immemorial memory of the outside [*The Writing of the Disaster*, 3].)

Chapter 6

1. Gilles Deleuze, *Negotiations*, 1972–1990, trans. Martin Joughin (New York: Columbia University Press, 1995), 88.

2. See Michael Hardt, *Gilles Deleuze: An Apprenticeship in Philosophy* (Minneapolis: University of Minnesota Press, 1993), 123n3. Hardt considers it potentially useful to stage a confrontation between Deleuze's and Heidegger's respective ontologies, but he does not entertain the idea that Heidegger could have influenced Deleuze. Daniel Smith comes closer to considering such a possibility when he states that Deleuze's project in *Difference and Repetition* is a response to the problem of ontological difference as Heidegger initially framed it (Daniel W. Smith, "The Doctrine of Univocity: Deleuze's Ontology of Immanence," *Essays on Deleuze* [Edinburgh: Edinburgh University Press, 2012], 27–42). See also Constantin V. Boundas, "Martin Heidegger," in *Deleuze's Philosophical Lineage*, ed. Graham Jones and Jon Roffe (Edinburgh: Edinburgh University Press, 2009), 321–38. One essay that stages a brief comparison of Heidegger and Deleuze (but not yet a sustained analysis of Heidegger's influence on Deleuze) is Sjoerd van Tuinen's "Difference and Speculation: Heidegger, Meillassoux, and Deleuze on Sufficient Reason," in *Gilles Deleuze and Metaphysics*, ed. Alain Beaulieu, Edward Kazarian, and Julia Sushytska (New York: Lexington, 2014). Other recent texts that have undertaken sustained comparisons of Heidegger and Deleuze are: Gavin Rae, *Ontology in Heidegger and Deleuze: A Comparative Analysis* (New York: Palgrave Macmillan, 2014) and Janae Sholtz, *The Invention of a People: Heidegger and Deleuze on Art and the Political* (Edinburgh: Edinburgh University Press, 2015).

3. Gilles Deleuze, *Cinema 2: The Time-Image*, trans. Hugh Tomlinson and Robert Galeta (Minneapolis: University of Minnesota Press, 1989), 167–68 (*Cinéma 2. L'Image-temps* [Paris: Les Éditions de Minuit, 1985], 218). Hereafter TI.

4. Gilles Deleuze, *Difference and Repetition*, trans. Paul Patton (New York: Columbia University Press, 1994), xv. Hereafter DR.

5. Deleuze's relationship to modernity is a matter that is far from settled. In *Difference and Repetition*, he seems to be arguing that modern life exposes the ontological condition of difference that was already there; he is not making a

historical argument, in other words. In the *Cinema* project, though, it is less clear whether the disruptions to perception that he says are reflected in the cinema of the postwar period constitute a historical development or an ontological revelation. In addition, his conception of modernity is highly specific, relying heavily on European literary modernism. See Garin Dowd, "*The Movement-Image, The Time-Image*, and the Paradoxes of Literary and Other Modernisms," in *Understanding Deleuze, Understanding Modernism*, ed. Paul Ardoin, S. E. Gontarski, and Laci Mattison (New York: Bloomsbury, 2014), 90–109.

6. Deleuze, *Nietzsche and Philosophy*, trans. Hugh Tomlinson (New York: Columbia University Press, 1983), 184. Hereafter NP. (For a provocative analysis of Deleuze's aesthetics in relationship to Kantian aesthetics, see Dorothea Olkowski, "Deleuze's Aesthetics of Sensation," in *The Cambridge Companion to Deleuze*, ed. Daniel W. Smith and Henry Somers-Hall (Cambridge: Cambridge University Press, 2012), 265–85.

7. It might be worth acknowledging at this moment that the conceptual lines of inheritance Deleuze will follow (or indeed assume) between Nietzsche and Artaud are tested in the ways Deleuze treats tragedy and theater as interchangeable. At the risk of repeating Deleuze's inattention to their possible differences, I have chosen not to push at this apparent slippage in Deleuze's text here in this study, if only because this slippage underscores the disagreement between Nancy and Lacoue-Labarthe, which I am about to comment on here briefly, concerning whether tragedy requires a scene/spectacle or needs to be performed on a stage (*opsis*) in order to accomplish the tragic transport. I thank an anonymous reader of this manuscript for alerting me to this issue.

8. See Malcolm Wilson, *Aristotle's Theory of the Unity of Science* (Toronto: University of Toronto Press, 2000).

9. See Allan T. Bäck, *Aristotle's Theory of Predication* (Leiden: Brill, 2000).

10. See, for example, Mary Hesse, "Aristotle's Logic of Analogy." *The Philosophical Quarterly* 15, no. 61 (October 1965): 333. On the "focal meaning" of Being, see G. E. L. Owen's coining of the concept in his "Logic and Metaphysics in Some Earlier Works of Aristotle," in *Aristotle and Plato in the Mid-Fourth Century*, ed. I. Düring and G. E. L. Owen (Gothenberg: Elanders, 1960), 163–90. On "pros hen equivocation," see Joseph Owens, *The Doctrine of Being in the Aristotelian Metaphysics*, 2nd rev. ed. (Toronto: Pontifical Institute of Medieval Studies, 1963).

11. See Edward C. Halper, *One and Many in Aristotle's Metaphysics: Books Alpha-Delta* (Las Vegas: Parmenides, 2009), 297–307. Although it should be noted that according to Halper the analogy of Being is not the same as the *pros hen* conception of Being in Aristotle. He asserts that Aristotle only argued for the latter and that the former is a refinement initiated by Aquinas. However, this does not seem to be a distinction Deleuze makes in his overview. See Halper, *One and Many in Aristotle's Metaphysics: Books Alpha-Delta*, 144.

12. Aristotle, *Metaphysics*, Book III, 3, 998b20–27; *Topics*, VI, 6, 144a35–40; cited in *Difference and Repetition* 308n4.

13. See Herbert Granger, "Aristotle and the Genus-Species Relation." *Southern Journal of Philosophy* 18, no. 1 (Spring 1980): 38–50.

14. See James Blachowicz, *Essential Difference: Toward a Metaphysics of Emergence* (Albany: State University of New York Press, 2012), 67.

15. With few exceptions, Deleuze's point still seems to go overlooked in much of the secondary literature. Cf. Nathan Widder, "The Rights of Simulacra: Deleuze and the Univocity of Being," *Continental Philosophy Review* 34 (2001): 437–53. Despite its value in correcting Alain Badiou's clearly misguided attempt in his *Deleuze: The Clamour of Being* (1997) to reduce Deleuze's thought of univocity to a Platonist One or "One-All," Widder's essay nevertheless seems to overlook the distinction Deleuze makes between Plato and Aristotelian Platonism. In terms of exceptions, see Daniel W. Smith, "The Concept of the Simulacrum: Deleuze and the Overturning of Platonism." *Continental Philosophy Review* 38 (1–2): 89–123, and Marco Altamirano, "Deleuze's Reversal of Platonism, Revisited." *Deleuze Studies* 9, no. 4 (2015): 503–28.

16. Gilles Deleuze, *The Logic of Sense*, trans. Mark Lester with Charles Stivale, ed. Constantin V. Boundas (New York: Columbia University Press, 1990), 254–55. LS hereafter.

17. See Steven P. Marrone, "Henry of Ghent and Duns Scotus on Knowledge of Being." *Speculum* 63, no. 1 (January 1988): 22–57. Marrone describes how Scotus crafted univocity in response to Henry of Ghent's notion of voice (*vox*), an earlier conception of univocity that Henry formulated in his account of divine illumination. However, because Henry's account still appealed to analogy to explain the relation between the finite and the infinite, it did not, in Scotus's estimation, offer a rigorous conception of univocity.

18. Gilles Deleuze, *Expressionism in Philosophy: Spinoza*, trans. Martin Joughin (New York: Zone, 1992), 63, emphasis in original. EP hereafter.

It is perhaps worth pointing out that Deleuze's interpretation of Scotus relies primarily on Étienne Gilson's *Jean Duns Scot: Introduction à ses positions fondamentales* (Paris: Vrin, 1952). Although he cites from Scotus's *Ordinatio* (*Opus Oxoniense*), Deleuze only does so directly in *Expressionism in Philosophy*, and not at all directly in *Difference and Repetition*. It thus makes it likely that he finds his references through Gilson's work, which, as scholars of medieval philosophy and theology have pointed out, has been monumental but also deeply flawed. See Stephen D. Dumont, review of *The Cambridge Companion to Duns Scotus*, ed. Thomas Williams, *Notre Dame Philosophical Reviews* (website) October 10, 2003, https://ndpr.nd.edu/news/the-cambridge-companion-to-duns-scotus/.

In this section, I will hew exclusively to Deleuze's depiction of Scotus's conception of univocity without attempting to make any assessment of the correctness of his interpretation.

19. "Lecture on *Anti-Oedipe* et *Milles Plateaux*," *Cours Vincennes* (website), January 14, 1974, https://www.webdeleuze.com/textes/175.

20. See Hardt, *Gilles Deleuze*, 60.

21. Here in *Difference and Repetition*, Deleuze imports his reading of Scotus from *Expressionism in Philosophy* (67), where he directly cites the conclusion of one of Scotus's arguments regarding the univocity of Being. This appears to be the place in Scotus's text where Deleuze finds his "neutral" conception of univocity. Referring to the question of whether human beings can know if God is either finite or infinite, created or uncreated, Scotus contends the concept of Being is neither (*neuter*) infinite nor finite, created nor uncreated, but is included in (i.e., assumed by) both sets of differentia and is therefore univocal: "*Et ita neuter ex se, sed in utroque illorum includitur; ergo univocus*" (*Opus Oxoniense* I.iii.2 (a4n6); cited in *Expressionism* 360n29). For a detailed discussion of Scotus's attempts to account for differentiation between individuals, see Nathan Widder's "The Rights of Simulacra: Deleuze and the Univocity of Being."

22. See *Ethics* I.D3, in Benedict de Spinoza, *The Collected Works of Spinoza*, vol. 1, ed. and trans. Edwin Curley (Princeton, NJ: Princeton University Press, 1985); See Hardt, *Gilles Deleuze*, 62–63.

23. See Articles 51–52 of Part I of Descartes's *The Principles of Philosophy*, in *The Philosophical Writings of Descartes*, vol. 1, trans. John Cottingham, Robert Stoothoff, and Dugland Murdoch (Cambridge: Cambridge University Press, 1985).

24. ST I.ii.22–25; E I.15s, cited in *Expressionism in Philosophy*, 363.

25. Of course, it is possible to draw normative implications from Spinoza's *Ethics*, which some have done. See, for example, Michael LeBuffe, *From Bondage to Freedom: Spinoza on Human Excellence* (Oxford: Oxford University Press, 2010) (especially chapter 10 "Spinoza's Normative Ethics"), and John Carriero, "The Ethics in Spinoza's *Ethics*," in *Essays on Spinoza's Ethical Theory*, ed. Matthew J. Kisner and Andrew Youpa (Oxford: Oxford University Press, 2014).

26. Gilles Deleuze, *Spinoza: Practical Philosophy*, trans. Robert Hurley (San Francisco: City Light Books, 1988), 125. SPP hereafter.

27. It is worth keeping in mind that French readers of Spinoza have disagreed with Deleuze's interpretation of the affects. Simon Duffy highlights the idiosyncrasies of Deleuze's reading by comparing it with Pierre Macherey's treatment of the *Ethics*. See Simon Duffy, "The Joyful Passions in Spinoza's Theory of Relations," in *Spinoza Now*, ed. Dimitris Vardoulakis (Minneapolis: University of Minnesota Press, 2011), 51–64.

28. "Now I shall relate the history of *Zarathustra*. The fundamental conception of this work, the idea of the eternal recurrence, this highest formulation of affirmation that is at all attainable, belongs in August 1881: it was penned on a sheet with the notation underneath, '6000 feet beyond man and time.' That day I was walking through the woods along the lake of Silvaplana; at a powerful pyramidal rock not far from Surlei I stopped. It was then that this idea came to me" (*Ecce Homo*, trans. Walter Kaufmann [New York: Vintage, 1989], 295).

29. *Thus Spoke Zarathustra*, trans. Walter Kaufmann, in *The Portable Nietzsche*, ed. and trans. Walter Kaufmann (New York: Penguin, 1983), 329.

30. Aphorism 341, titled "*The Greatest Weight*," in *The Gay Science*, trans. Walter Kaufmann (New York: Vintage, 1974), 273–74; original emphasis.

31. See Richard Schacht, *Nietzsche* (London and New York: Routledge, 1992), 253–66.

32. In a passage that Heidegger will later comment on, Nietzsche writes, "This, indeed this alone, is what *revenge* is: the will's ill will against time and its 'it was'" ("On Redemption," in *Thus Spoke Zarathustra*, 252). See *What Is Called Thinking?*, 93.

33. See *On the Genealogy of Morals*, trans. Walter Kaufman and R. J. Hollingdale (New York: Vintage, 1989).

34. *The Birth of Tragedy*, trans. Walter Kaufmann (New York: Vintage, 1967). See *Ecce Homo*, 306.

35. *The Birth of Tragedy*, §10, 73. See also *The Will to Power* 1049 (1885–1886):

> *Apollo's* deception: the eternity of beautiful form; the aristocratic legislation, *"thus shall it be for ever!"*
> *Dionysus:* sensuality and cruelty. Transitoriness could be interpreted as enjoyment of productive and destructive force, as *continual* creation.
> (ed. Walter Kaufmann, trans. Walter Kaufmann and R. J. Hollingdale [New York: Vintage, 1968], 539; original emphasis)

See Marcel Detienne, *Dionysos at Large*, trans. Arthur Goldhammer (Cambridge, MA: Harvard University Press, 1989); Radcliffe Edmonds, "Tearing Apart the Zagreus Myth: A Few Disparaging Remarks on Orphism and Original Sin." *Classical Antiquity* 18, no. 1 (April 1999): 35–73.

36. See chapter 2, "Active and Reactive," in *Nietzsche and Philosophy*, 39–72. Deleuze bases his reading of the eternal return largely on *Thus Spoke Zarathustra* and the uncorrected French editions of *The Will to Power* (*La volonté de puissance* [1935; 1937]). On the versions of Nietzsche's manuscripts Deleuze consults, see Paolo D'Iorio, "The Eternal Return: Genesis and Interpretation." *Lexicon Philosophicum*, no. 2 (2014): 41–96.

37. As Deleuze indicates, his reading of Nietzsche is guided in large part by Pierre Klossowski, whose influence we can also see informing Deleuze's appeal to the concept of simulacra (DR 312n19). On Klossowski's reading of Nietzsche, see Daniel W. Smith, "Klossowski's Reading of Nietzsche: Impulses, Phantasms, Simulacra, Stereotypes." *Diacritics* 35, no. 1: 8–21.

38. *Différence et répétition* (Presses Universitaires de France, 1968), 54.

39. DR 66. Deleuze refers to Heidegger's critique of the eternal return in this passage, which Deleuze seems to suggest marks a limit as to how far he can travel with Heidegger, presumably because of how much his attempts to arrive at a concept of difference are in dialogue with Nietzsche. See Heidegger, *Nietzsche*, vols.

3–4, trans. David Farrell Krell (New York: Harper & Row, 1991), 166. See Taylor Carmen, "Heidegger's Nietzsche." *Inquiry* 63, no. 1: 104–16.

40. See "On the Essence of Truth," trans. John Sallis, in *Pathmarks*, ed. William McNeill (Cambridge: Cambridge University Press, 1998), 136–54 (*Vom Wesen der Warheit*, in GA9 *Wegmarken* [Frankfurt am Main: Vittorio Klosterman, 1976], 177–202). See John D. Caputo, "Dark Hearts: Heidegger, Richardson, and Evil," and William J. Richardson, S. J., "Heidegger's Fall," in *From Phenomenology to Thought, Errancy, and Desire: Essays in Honor of William J. Richardson, S.J.*, ed. Babette E. Babich (Dordrecht: Springer, 1995), 267–75; 277–300.

41. "On the Essence of Ground," trans. William McNeill, in *Pathmarks*, ed. William McNeill (Cambridge: Cambridge University Press, 1998), 97. The English-language edition of *Difference and Repetition* cites the English translation of *Vom Wesen des Grundes* from 1969 (*The Essence of Reasons*, 3rd ed., trans. Terrence Malick [Evanston, IL: Northwestern University Press, 1969]) (DR 64).

42. "On the Essence of Ground," 97 (*Vom Wesen des Grundes*, in GA9 *Wegmarken* [Frankfurt am Main: Vittorio Klosterman, 1976], 123).

43. *Was heißt Denken?* GA8 (Frankfurt am Main: Vittorio Klosterman, 2002), 200 (*What Is Called Thinking?* 197; 240–41). See *Introduction to Metaphysics*, 2nd ed., rev. and expanded ed., trans. Gregory Fried and Richard Polt (New Haven: Yale University Press, 2014), 145, and *Identity and Difference*, trans. Joan Stambaugh (New York: Harper & Row, 1967).

44. See *Introduction to Metaphysics*, 2.

45. "What Is Metaphysics?" (1929), trans. David Farrell Krell, in *Pathmarks*, ed. William McNeill (Cambridge: Cambridge University Press, 1998), 90.

46. In a most recent example, D. J. S. Cross examines Deleuze and Guattari's theorization of a minor literature in terms of affect, but he does not depart from prior treatments that regard minor literature as a kind of exceptional transformation of language. My view is that Deleuze's conception of literature (and of art generally) is similar to that of Heidegger's in the sense that, for Heidegger, the "work" the work of art performs is not an exception to our quotidian forms of subject-object relations but instead makes those relations possible. In the same way that, for Heidegger, poetry reveals the essential relation the human Dasein has to language, Deleuze's conception of literature reveals an essential relation to the being of Becoming, which linguistic models of language occlude or suppress. Cf. D. J. S. Cross, *Deleuze and the Problem of Affect* (Edinburgh: Edinburgh University Press, 2021). On the other side of the language-affect divide, works such as Jean-Jacques Lecercle's *Deleuze and Language* (New York: Palgrave Macmillan, 2002) contribute to an understanding of Deleuze's attention to language, but with only passing connections made to his theorization of affect.

47. This is one other site in the works we have been studying where we encounter the figure of the feminine and particularly the use the feminine serves for contemporary Continental thought. As with those other sites, Deleuze's use of the figure of the little girl will have to be analyzed in a separate study. See

Dorothea Olkowski's *Gilles Deleuze and the Ruin of Representation* (Los Angeles: University of California Press, 1999) for an evaluation of feminist critiques, as well as appropriations, of Deleuze (and Deleuze and Guattari).

48. It should be noted that Artaud's engagement with Carroll is not the pure aesthetic confrontation that Deleuze portrays it to be. Although Deleuze seems to ignore the circumstances surrounding Artaud's encounter with Carroll, Artaud did not choose to translate Carroll on his own but was given the task, and specifically the assignment to translate "Jabberwocky," by his doctor at Rodez, Gaston Ferdière, who not coincidentally was one of the inventors of art therapy. See Ann Tomiche, "Artaud, Madness and/in Translation." *Translation Studies* 12, no. 1: 24–35; Robert Mark Causey, "Deleuze and 'la neutralisation de "ce pauvre M. Antonin Artaud,"'" *Dalhousie French Studies* 96 (Fall 2011): 25–36.

49. Letter to Henri Parisot, *Lettres de Rodez* (Paris: G. L. M., 1946); original emphasis, cited in LS 84. See "To Henri Parisot (September 20, 1945)," in *Antonin Artaud: Selected Writings*, ed. Susan Sontag (New York: Farrar, Straus and Giroux, 1976), 446–48.

50. Lewis Carroll, *Through the Looking-Glass*, in *The Complete Works of Lewis Carroll* (New York: Penguin, 1939), 197.

51. *L'Arbalète* (1947), no. 12; cited in LS 342n2.

52. See Causey, "Deleuze and 'la neutralisation de "ce pauvre M. Antonin Artaud,"'" for this comparison.

53. For a survey of criticism that accuses Deleuze of unreflectively taking Artaud as a schizophrenic case and effectively using him to make a philosophical point without any regard for the circumstances of Artaud's actual life, see Causey, "Deleuze and 'la neutralisation de "ce pauvre M. Antonin Artaud."'" Not unrelatedly, Causey likens these critiques to Derrida's critique of Blanchot's use of Artaud in "La parole soufflée," in *Writing and Difference*, trans. Alan Bass (Chicago: University of Chicago Press, 1978), 169–95.

54. See *Francis Bacon: The Logic of Sensation*, trans. Daniel W. Smith (Minneapolis: University of Minnesota Press, 2005).

55. Despite what I take to be a clear line from Deleuze's theorization of univocity to his attraction to literature, there are few scholarly works that explore this connection. One exception is André Pierre Colombat's "Deleuze and Signs," in *Deleuze and Literature*, ed. Ian Buchanan and John Marks (Edinburgh: Edinburgh University Press, 2000), 14–33. Although Colombat's article does not reflect on how literature influences Deleuze's theorization of univocity, it does link Deleuze's reading of Spinoza to his conception of signs. Another significant exception is Sholtz's *The Invention of a People*, which reflects at length on Heidegger, Deleuze, and their shared attention to the question of the work of art and includes discussions of Deleuze's theorization of univocity as part of that reflection.

56. Gilles Deleuze and Félix Guattari, *Kafka: Toward a Minor Literature*, trans. Dana Polan (Minneapolis: University of Minnesota Press, 1986), 45. Hereafter K.

57. *Kafka: Pour une littéraire mineur* (Paris: Éditions de minuit, 1975), 41. This is one site in Deleuze and Guattari's collaborative project where we might trace echoes with Deleuze's discussion of Artaud in *The Logic of Sense* and his attention to the figures of meat, becoming-animal, and the rendering of the scream or cry in *Francis Bacon: The Logic of Sensation*. For a treatment of Deleuze's reading of Bacon and the general theme of finitude in relation to the scream in Bacon, see Christopher Fynsk, *Infant Figures: The Death of the 'Infans' and Other Scenes of Origin* (Stanford, CA: Stanford University Press, 2000), 11–48.

58. *A Thousand Plateaus*, trans. Brian Massumi (Minneapolis: University of Minnesota Press, 1987), 101. Hereafter TP.

59. See Deleuze's 1976 interview with *Cahiers du Cinéma*, "Three Questions on *Six Times Two*": "The key thing," Deleuze says, "is Godard's use of AND [*et*]. This is important, because all our thought's modeled, rather, on the verb, 'to be,' IS [*est*]. . . . AND, 'and . . . and . . . and . . .' is precisely a creative stammering, a foreign use of language, as opposed to a conformist and dominant use based on the verb 'to be'. . . . AND is neither one thing nor the other, it's always in-between, between two things; it's the borderline, there's always a border, a line of flight or flow" (Gilles Deleuze, *Negotiations*, trans. Martin Joughin [New York: Columbia University Press, 1995], 44–45). I conduct a much more detailed reading of Godard and Deleuze in "Numéro un et *Numéro deux:* It was Outside, the Rejection of the Image," in *I Said I Love: That Is the Promise: The TVideo Politics of Jean-Luc Godard*, ed. Gareth James and Florian Zeyfang, Critical Readers in Visual Cultures no. 4 (Berlin: b_books, 2003).

60. See Deleuze's "He Stuttered," in *Essays Critical and Clinical*, trans. Daniel W. Smith and Michael A. Greco (Minneapolis: University of Minnesota Press, 1997), 107–14 ("Bégaya-t-il," in *Critique et clinique* (Paris: Éditions Minuit, 1993], 135–43).

61. Deleuze's application of Charles Sanders Peirce's semiotics in the *Cinema* books is of course commonly studied. I would argue, however, that Deleuze's interest in and contribution to a theory of signs is not the same thing as his interest in language. But I will need to postpone making that argument here and pursue it on another occasion.

Epilogue

1. I have referred to this elsewhere as "institutional schizophasia." See my "Institutional Schizophasia and the Possibility of the Humanities' 'Other Scene': Guattari and the Exigency of Transversality," *Deleuze Studies* 6, no. 2 (2012): 328–52. At the same time, I should be careful to note that there are affect theorists who engage with affect yet nonetheless remain suspicious of the affective turn, such as Clare Hemmings, who I discuss in my introduction.

2. On Western feminist theory's inheritance and perpetuation of the progress narrative form, in which the turn to affect has most recently played a part, see Clare Hemmings, "Telling Feminist Stories," *Feminist Theory* 6, no. 2: 115–39; and Hemmings, *Why Stories Matter: The Political Grammar of Feminist Theory* (Durham, NC: Duke University Press, 2011).

3. As I stated in my introduction, Lacan is certainly another thinker of the voice with whom I could have engaged. In fact, Heidegger's theorization of language is an important source for Lacan's own reflections on the place language occupies in psychoanalysis, as evidenced by his famous "Rome Discourse" of 1953 ("The Function and Field of Speech and Language in Psychoanalysis," in *Écrits: The First Complete Edition in English*, trans. Bruce Fink [New York and London: W.W. Norton, 2006], 237–68). However, as I note further on in this epilogue, there is an abundance of writings on the voice in psychoanalysis, and as a result, I felt my contribution would be more substantial if I focused my attention on how the voice is theorized in one of the main sources of the post-Freudian psychanalytic reflection on language, namely Heidegger's corpus.

4. Mladen Dolar, *A Voice and Nothing More* (Cambridge, MA: MIT Press, 2006), 10–11. See also Michel Chion, *The Voice in Cinema*, trans. Claudia Gorbman (New York: Columbia University Press, 1999).

5. Dolar, 10. Cf. Michael Hardt, "Foreword: What Are Affects Good For?," in Patricia Ticento Clough, ed. *The Affective Turn* (Durham and London: Duke University Press, 2007), ix, and as discussed in this book's introduction.

6. Kaja Silverman, *The Acoustic Mirror: The Female Voice in Psychoanalysis and Cinema* (Bloomington and Indianapolis: Indiana University Press, 1988).

7. In *What Is Called Thinking?*, Heidegger likens the call of thinking with the mother's disciplining voice: " 'You just wait—I'll teach you what obedience means!' ['*Warte, ich werde dich lehren, was gehorchen heißt*'], calls a mother to her boy who won't come home" (GA 8, 51, translation mine). See Avital Ronell, *The Telephone Book: Technology, Schizophrenia, Electric Speech* (Lincoln: University of Nebraska Press, 1989), 20–25.

8. In both affect studies and new materialism, for example, the names of Foucault and Deleuze are ubiquitous and function as basic shibboleths to the fields.

Bibliography

Agamben, Giorgio. *The Coming Community*. Translated by Michael Hardt. Minneapolis: University of Minnesota Press, 1991.
———. *La comunità che viene*. Turin: Einaudi, 1990.
———. *Language and Death: The Place of Negativity*. Translated by Karen E. Pinkus and Michael Hardt. Minneapolis: University of Minnesota Press, 1991.
Altamirano, Marco. "Deleuze's Reversal of Platonism, Revisited." *Deleuze Studies* 9, no. 4 (2015): 503–28.
Aristotle. *The Complete Works of Aristotle*. 2 vols. Revised Oxford Translation. Edited by Jonathan Barnes. Princeton, NJ: Princeton University Press, 1985.
Artaud, Antonin. "'A Powerlessness . . .' from *The Nerve Meter*." In *Antonin Artaud: Selected Writings*, edited by Susan Sontag, 82. Translated by Helen Weaver. Berkeley and Los Angeles: University of California Press, 1988.
———. "Correspondence with Jacques Rivière" (1923–24). In *Antonin Artaud: Selected Writings*, edited by Susan Sontag, 31–49. Translated by Helen Weaver. Berkeley and Los Angeles: University of California Press, 1988.
———. *Fragments of a Diary from Hell*. In *Antonin Artaud: Selected Writings*, edited by Susan Sontag, 91–96. Translated by Helen Weaver. Berkeley and Los Angeles: University of California Press, 1988.
———. *Œuvres complètes*. Vol. 1, 2nd supplemental ed. Paris: Gallimard, 1970.
———. "To Henri Parisot (September 20, 1945)." In *Antonin Artaud: Selected Writings*, edited by Susan Sontag, 446–48. New York: Farrar, Straus and Giroux, 1976.
———. "To Peter Watson." In Antonin Artaud, *Watchfiends & Rack Screams: Works from the Final Period*, edited and translated by Clayton Eshleman with Bernard Bador, 79–89. Boston: Exact Change, 1995.
Babich, Babette. "From Van Gogh's Museum to the Temple at Bassae: Heidegger's Truth of Art and Schapiro's Art History." *Culture, Theory & Critique* 44 (2003): 151–69.
Bäck, Allan T. *Aristotle's Theory of Predication*. Leiden: Brill, 2000.

Bataille, Georges. *The Accursed Share*. 2 vols. Translated by Robert Hurley. New York: Zone, 1993.

———. "L'Art, exercise de la cruauté." In Vol. 11 of *Œuvres complètes*, 480–86. Paris: Gallimard, 1988.

———. *Guilty*. Translated by Bruce Boone. Venice, CA: Lapis, 1988.

———. "Hegel, Death, and Sacrifice." In *The Bataille Reader*, edited by Fred Botting and Scott Wilson, 279–95. Malden, MA: Blackwell, 1997.

———. *Œuvres complètes*. Vol. 7. Paris: Gallimard, 1976.

———. *Œuvres complètes*. Vol. 11. Paris: Gallimard, 1988.

———. *Œuvres complètes*. Vol. 12. Paris: Gallimard, 1988.

———. "Sacrifices." In *Visions of Excess*, edited by Allan Stoekl, 130–36. Translated by Allan Stoekl with Carl R. Lovitt and Donald M. Leslie Jr. Minneapolis: University of Minnesota Press, 1985.

———. *Visions of Excess*. Edited by Allan Stoekl. Translated by Allan Stoekl with Carl R. Lovitt and Donald M. Leslie, Jr. Minneapolis: University of Minnessota Press, 1985.

Bernasconi, Robert. "On Deconstructing Nostalgia for Community within the West: The Debate between Nancy and Blanchot." *Research in Phenomenology* 23 (1993): 3–21.

Bird, Greg, and Jonathan Short, eds. *Roberto Esposito, Community and the Proper*. Special issue of *Angelaki* 18, no. 3 (2013).

Blachowicz, James. *Essential Difference: Toward a Metaphysics of Emergence*. Albany: State University of New York Press, 2012.

Blanchot, Maurice. "Artaud." Translated by Ian Maclachlan. In *The Blanchot Reader*, edited by Michael Holland, 129–35. Oxford: Blackwell, 1995.

———. *The Book to Come*. Translated by Charlotte Mandel. Stanford, CA: Stanford University Press, 2003.

———. *Celui qui ne m'accompagnait pas*. Paris: Gallimard, 1953.

———. *La Communauté inavouable*. Paris: Éditions de Minuit, 1983.

———. *L'Entretien infini*. Paris: Gallimard, 1969.

———. *L'Espace littéraire*. Paris: Gallimard, 1955.

———. *The Infinite Conversation*. Translated by Susan Hanson. Minneapolis: University of Minnesota Press, 1993.

———. "Literature and the Right to Death." Translated by Lydia Davis. In *The Work of Fire* by Maurice Blanchot, 300–44. Translated by Charlotte Mandell. Stanford, CA: Stanford University Press, 1995.

———. "La Littérature et le droit à la mort." In *La Part du feu*, by Maurice Blanchot, 291–331. Paris: Éditions Gallimard, 1949.

———. *Le Livre à venir*. Paris: Gallimard, 1959.

———. *The One Who Was Standing Apart From Me*. Translated by Lydia Davis. Barrytown, NY: Station Hill, 1993.

———. *La Part du feu*. Paris: Éditions Gallimard, 1949.

———. *Le Pas au-delà*. Paris: Gallimard, 1973.

———. *The Space of Literature*. Translated by Ann Smock. Lincoln: University of Nebraska Press, 1982.

———. *The Step/Not Beyond*. Translated by Lycette Nelson. Albany: State University of New York Press, 1992.

———. "Two Versions of the Imaginary." In *The Space of Literature*, by Maurice Blanchot. Translated by Ann Smock. Lincoln: University of Nebraska Press, 1982.

———. *The Unavowable Community*. Translated by Pierre Joris. Barrytown, NY: Station Hill, 1988.

———. *The Work of Fire*. Translated by Charlotte Mandell. Stanford, CA: Stanford University Press, 1995.

———. *The Writing of the Disaster*. Translated by Ann Smock. Lincoln: University of Nebraska Press, 1983.

Blechman, Max, Anita Chari, and Rafeeq Hasan, "Democracy, Dissensus, and the Aesthetics of Class Struggle: An Exchange with Jacques Rancière." *Historical Materialism* 13, no. 4: 285–301.

Boundas, Constantin V. "Martin Heidegger." In *Deleuze's Philosophical Lineage*, edited by Graham Jones and Jon Roffe, 321–38. Edinburgh: Edinburgh University Press, 2009.

Capobianco, Richard. *Engaging Heidegger*. Toronto: University of Toronto Press, 2010.

Caputo, John D. "Dark Hearts: Heidegger, Richardson, and Evil." In *From Phenomenology to Thought, Errancy, and Desire: Essays in Honor of William J. Richardson, S.J.*, edited by Babette E. Babich, 267–75. Dordrecht: Springer, 1995.

Carmen, Taylor. "Heidegger's Nietzsche." *Inquiry* 63, no. 1: 104–16.

Carriero, John. "The Ethics in Spinoza's *Ethics*." In *Essays on Spinoza's Ethical Theory*, edited by Matthew J. Kisner and Andrew Youpa, 20–40. Oxford: Oxford University Press, 2014.

Carroll, Lewis. *Through the Looking-Glass*. In *The Complete Works of Lewis Carroll*. New York: Penguin, 1939.

Castoriadis, Cornelius. *Figures of the Thinkable*. Translated by Helen Arnold. Stanford, CA: Stanford University Press, 2007.

Causey, Robert Mark. "Deleuze and 'la neutralisation de "ce pauvre M. Antonin Artaud."'" *Dalhousie French Studies* 96 (Fall 2011): 25–36.

Chion, Michel. *The Voice in Cinema*. Translated by Claudia Gorbman. New York: Columbia University Press, 1999.

Clough, Patricia Ticento, ed. *The Affective Turn*. Durham: Duke University Press, 2007.

Colombat, André Pierre. "Deleuze and Signs." In *Deleuze and Literature*, edited by Ian Buchanan and John Marks, 14–33. Edinburgh: Edinburgh University Press, 2000.

Coole, Diana, and Samantha Frost, eds. *New Materialisms: Ontology, Agency, and Politics*. Durham: Duke University Press, 2010.

Cools, Arthur. "Revisiting the *Il y a*: Maurice Blanchot and Emmanuel Levinas on the Question of Subjectivity." *Paragraph* 28, no. 3 (2005): 54–71.

Coppieters de Gibson, Daniel. "Les Grecs et la question de l'homme. À propos d'une lecture de Sophocle par Heidegger." In *Qu'est-ce que l'homme? Philosophie/psychanalyse: hommage à Alphonse de Waelhens*, 53–70. Brussels: Facultés Universitaires Saint-Louis, 1982.

Courtine, Jean-François. "Voice of Conscience and Call of Being." In *Who Comes After the Subject?*, edited by Jean-Luc Nancy and Eduardo Cadava, 79–93. Minneapolis: University of Minnesota Press, 1991.

Critchley, Simon. *Very Little . . . Almost Nothing: Death, Philosophy, Literature*, 2nd ed. London and New York: Routledge, 1997.

Cross, D. J. S. *Deleuze and the Problem of Affect*. Edinburgh: Edinburgh University Press, 2021.

Crowley, Martin. "Even Now, Now, Very Now." In *Blanchot Romantique*, edited by Hannes Opelz and John McKeane, 247–61. Bern: Peter Lang, 2011.

de la Cadena, Marisol. *Earth Beings: Ecologies of Practice Across Andean Worlds*. Durham: Duke University Press, 2015.

Deleuze, Gilles. "Bégaya-t-il." In *Critique et clinique*, 135–43. Paris: Éditions Minuit, 1993.

———. *Cinéma 2. L'Image-temps*. Paris: Les Éditions de Minuit, 1985.

———. *Cinema 2: The Time-Image*. Translated by Hugh Tomlinson and Robert Galeta. Minneapolis: University of Minnesota Press, 1989.

———. *Différence et répétition*. Paris: Presses Universitaires de France, 1968.

———. *Difference and Repetition*. Trans. Paul Patton. New York: Columbia University Press, 1994.

———. *Expressionism in Philosophy: Spinoza*. Translated by Martin Joughin. New York: Zone, 1992.

———. *Francis Bacon: The Logic of Sensation*. Translated by Daniel W. Smith. Minneapolis: University of Minnesota Press, 2005.

———. "He Stuttered." In *Essays Critical and Clinical*, 107–14. Translated by Daniel W. Smith and Michael A. Greco. Minneapolis: University of Minnesota Press, 1997.

———. "Lecture on *Anti-Oedipe* et *Milles Plateaux*," Cours Vincennes—St Denis (January 14, 1974), *Webdeleuze*, www.webdeleuze.com/textes/175.

———. *The Logic of Sense*. Edited by Constantin V. Boundas. Translated by Mark Lester with Charles Stivale. New York: Columbia University Press, 1990.

———. *Negotiations, 1972–1990*. Translated by Martin Joughin. New York: Columbia University Press, 1995.

———. *Nietzsche and Philosophy*. Translated by Hugh Tomlinson. New York: Columbia University Press, 1983.

———. *Spinoza: Practical Philosophy*. Translated by Robert Hurley. San Francisco: City Lights, 1988.
Deleuze, Gilles, and Félix Guattari. *Kafka: Pour une littéraire mineur*. Paris: Éditions de minuit, 1975.
———. *Kafka: Toward a Minor Literature*. Translated by Dana Polan. Minneapolis: University of Minnesota Press, 1986.
———. *A Thousand Plateaus*. Translated by Brian Massumi. Minneapolis: University of Minnesota Press, 1987.
Derrida, Jacques. *D'un ton apocalyptique adopté naguère en philosophie*. Paris: Galilée, 1983.
———. *L'Écriture de la différence*. Paris: Les Éditions du Seuil, 1967.
———. "Heidegger's Ear: Philopolemology (*Geschlecht IV*)." In *Reading Heidegger: Commemorations*, edited by John Sallis, 163–218. Bloomington and Indianapolis: Indiana University Press, 1993.
———. "La Parole soufflée." In *Writing and Difference* 169–95. Translated by Alan Bass. Chicago: University of Chicago Press, 1978.
———. *Memoires for Paul de Man*. Rev. ed. Trans. Cecile Lindsay, Jonathan Culler, Eduardo Cadava, and Peggy Kamuf. New York: Columbia University Press, 1989.
———. "Of an Apocalyptic Tone Recently Adopted in Philosophy." Translated by John P. Leavey Jr. In *Derrida and Negative Theology*, edited by Harold Coward and Toby Foshay, 25–71. Albany: State University of New York Press, 1992.
———. *Of Grammatology*, 40th Anniversary Edition. Translated by Gayatri Chakravorty Spivak. Baltimore: Johns Hopkins University Press, 2016.
———. *Speech and Phenomena*. Translated by David B. Allison. Evanston, IL: Northwestern University Press, 1973.
———. *Writing and Difference*. Translated by Alan Bass. Chicago: University of Chicago Press, 1978.
Descartes, René. *The Principles of Philosophy*. In Vol. 1 of *The Philosophical Writings of Descartes* 177–291. Translated by John Cottingham, Robert Stoothoff, and Dugland Murdoch. Cambridge, UK: Cambridge University Press, 1985.
Detienne, Marcel. *Dionysos at Large*. Translated by Arthur Goldhammer. Cambridge, MA: Harvard University Press, 1989.
Devisch, Ignaas. *Jean-Luc Nancy and the Questions of Community*. New York: Bloomsbury, 2013.
D'Iorio, Paolo. "The Eternal Return: Genesis and Interpretation." *Lexicon Philosophicum* 2 (2014): 41–96.
Dolar, Mladen. *A Voice and Nothing More*. Cambridge, MA: MIT Press, 2006.
Dowd, Garin. "*The Movement-Image, The Time-Image*, and the Paradoxes of Literary and Other Modernisms." In *Understanding Deleuze, Understanding Modernism*, edited by Paul Ardoin, S. E. Gontarski, and Laci Mattison, 90–109. New York: Bloomsbury, 2014.

Duffy, Simon. "The Joyful Passions in Spinoza's Theory of Relations." In *Spinoza Now*, edited by Dimitris Vardoulakis, 51–64. Minneapolis: University of Minnesota Press, 2011.

Dumont, Stephen D. Review of *The Cambridge Companion to Duns Scotus*, edited by Thomas Williams, *Notre Dame Philosophical Reviews*, October 7, 2003. https://ndpr.nd.edu/news/the-cambridge-companion-to-duns-scotus/.

Edmonds, Radcliffe. "Tearing Apart the Zagreus Myth: A Few Disparaging Remarks on Orphism and Original Sin." *Classical Antiquity* 18, no. 1 (April 1999): 35–73.

Eng, Michael. "Art and the Heideggerian Repression: Rancière, Nancy, and a Communism of the Image." *Comparative & Continental Philosophy* 5, no. 1 (May 2013): 19–35.

———. "Institutional Schizophasia and the Possibility of the Humanities' 'Other Scene': Guattari and the Exigency of Transversality." *Deleuze Studies* 6, no. 2 (2012): 328–52.

———. "Numéro un et *Numéro deux:* It Was Outside, the Rejection of the Image." In *I Said I Love. That Is the Promise: The TVideo Politics of Jean-Luc Godard*, edited by Gareth James and Florian Zeyfang, 247–321. Critical Readers in Visual Cultures 4. Berlin: b_books, 2003.

———. "The Sonic Turn and Theory's Affective Call." *Parallax* 23, no. 3 (2017): 316–29.

Esposito, Roberto. *Communitas: The Origin and Destiny of Community*. Translated by Timothy Campbell. Stanford, CA: Stanford University Press, 2010.

———. *Communitas. Origine e destino della comunità*. Turin: Giulio einaudi editore, 1998.

Feola, Michael. *The Powers of Sensibility: Aesthetic Politics through Adorno, Foucault, and Rancière*. Evanston, IL: Northwestern University Press, 2018.

Fort, Jeff. *The Imperative to Write: Destitutions of the Sublime in Kafka, Blanchot, and Beckett*. New York: Fordham University Press, 2014.

Foucault, Michel. *The Archaeology of Knowledge*. Translated by A. M. Sheridan Smith. New York: Pantheon, 1972.

———. *Maurice Blanchot: The Thought from Outside*. In *Foucault/Blanchot*, 7–58. Translated by Brian Massumi. New York: Zone, 1987.

———. *The Order of Things: An Archaeology of the Human Sciences*. New York: Vintage, 1994.

———. "La Pensée du dehors." In Vol. 1 of *Dits et Écrits*, 1954–1988, edited by Daniel Defert and François Ewald, 518–39. Paris: Gallimard, 1994.

Froment-Meurice, Marc. *That is to Say: Heidegger's Politics*. Translated by Jan Plug. Stanford, CA: Stanford University Press, 1998.

Fynsk, Christopher. *Heidegger: Thought and Historicity*. Expanded ed. Ithaca, NY: Cornell University Press, 1993.

———. *Infant Figures: The Death of the 'Infans' and Other Scenes of the Origin*. Stanford, CA: Stanford University Press, 2000.

———. *Language and Relation . . . that there is language*. Stanford, CA: Stanford University Press, 1996.

———. *Last Steps: Maurice Blanchot's Exilic Writing*. New York: Fordham University Press, 2013.

———. *Philippe Lacoue-Labarthe's Phrase: Infancy, Survival*. Albany: State University of New York Press, 2017.

Gage, Mark Foster, ed. *Aesthetics Equals Politics: New Discourses across Art, Architecture, and Philosophy*. Cambridge, MA: MIT Press, 2019.

Gasché, Rodolphe. "Joining the Text: From Heidegger to Derrida." In *The Yale Critics: Deconstruction in America*, ed. Jonathan Arac, Wlad Godzich, and Wallace Martin, 156–75. Minneapolis: University of Minnesota, 1983.

Gilson, Étienne. *Jean Duns Scot: Introduction à ses positions fondamentales*. Paris: Vrin, 1952.

Gopinath, Gayatri. *Unruly Visions: The Aesthetic Practices of Queer Diaspora*. Durham: Duke University Press, 2018.

Granger, Herbert. "Aristotle and the Genus-Species Relation." *Southern Journal of Philosophy* 18, no. 1 (Spring 1980): 38–50.

Gregg, Melissa, and Gregory J. Seigworth, eds. *The Affect Theory Reader*. Durham: Duke University Press, 2011.

Haar, Michel. *Heidegger and the Essence of Man*. Translated by William McNeill. Albany: State University of New York Press, 1993.

Hallward, Peter. "Anything is Possible." *Radical Philosophy* 152 (November/December 2008): 51–57.

Halper, Edward C. *One and Many in Aristotle's Metaphysics: Books Alpha-Delta*. Las Vegas: Parmenides, 2009.

Hardt, Michael. "Foreword: What are Affects Good For?" In *The Affective Turn*, edited by Patricia Ticento Clough, xi–xiii. Durham, NC: Duke University Press, 2007.

———. *Gilles Deleuze: An Apprenticeship in Philosophy*. Minneapolis: University of Minnesota Press, 1993.

Harten, Doreet LeVitte, ed. *Heaven*. Ostfildern-Ruit: Hatje Cantz Verlag, 1999.

Hegel, G. W. F. *Hegel's Aesthetics: Lectures on Fine Art*. Vol. 1. Translated by T. M. Knox. Oxford: Clarendon, 1975.

———. *The Phenomenology of Spirit*. Trans. Terry Pinkard. Cambridge: Cambridge University Press, 2018.

———. *Werke*. Vol. 3. Edited by Eva Moldenhauer and Karl Markus Michel. 20 vols. Frankfurt am Main: Suhrkamp, 1970.

———. *Werke*. Vol. 13. Edited by Eva Moldenhauer and Karl Markus Michel. 20 vols. Frankfurt am Main: Suhrkamp, 1970.

Heidegger, Martin. "Aus einem Gespräch von der Sprache: Zwischen einem Japaner und einem Fragenden." In *Unterwegs zur Sprache*. Vol. 12 of *Gesamtausgabe*, 79–146. Frankfurt am Main: Klostermann, 1985.

———. *The Basic Problems of Phenomenology*. Translated by Albert Hofstadter. Bloomington: Indiana University Press, 1982.

———. *Basic Writings*. Translated by David Farrell Krell. Rev. and expanded ed. New York: HarperCollins, 1993.

———. "Bauen, Wohnen, Denken." In *Vorträge und Aufsätze*. Vol. 7 of *Gesamtausgabe*. Frankfurt am Main: Klostermann, 1977.

———. *Being and Time*. Translated by John Macquarrie and Edward Robinson. New York: Harper and Row, 1969.

———. *Being and Time: A Translation of* Sein und Zeit. Translated by Joan Stambaugh. Albany: State University of New York Press, 1996.

———. *Beiträge zur Philosophie (Vom Ereignis)*. Edited by Friedrich-Wilhelm von Hermann. Vol. 65 of *Gesamtausgabe*. Frankfurt am Main: Klostermann, 2003.

———. "Building, Dwelling, Thinking." In *Basic Writings*. Translated by David Farrell Krell. 2nd ed. New York: HarperCollins, 1993.

———. *Contributions to Philosophy (Of the Event)*. Translated by Richard Rojcewicz and Daniela Vallega-Neu. Bloomington: Indiana University Press, 2012.

———. "A Dialogue on Language between a Japanese and an Inquirer." In *On the Way to Language*, 1–54. Translated by Peter D. Hertz. New York: Harper and Row, 1971.

———. *Early Greek Thinking*. Translated by David Farrell Krell and Frank A. Capuzzi. Harper San Franscisco, 1984.

———. *Einführung in die Metaphysik*. Vol. 40 of *Gesamtausgabe*. Frankfurt am Main: Klostermann, 1983.

———. *The End of Philosophy*. Translated by Joan Stambaugh. New York: Harper & Row, 1973.

———. *The Essence of Reasons*. 3rd ed. Translated by Terrence Malick. Evanston, IL: Northwestern University Press, 1969.

———. *The Fundamental Concepts of Metaphysics: World, Finitude, Solitude*. Translated by William McNeill and Nicholas Walker. Bloomington and Indianapolis: Indiana University Press, 1995.

———. *History of the Concept of Time: Prolegomena*. Translated by Theodore Kisiel. Indianapolis and Bloomington: Indiana University Press, 1985.

———. *Hölderlins Hymne »Der Ister«*. Vol. 53 of *Gesamtausgabe*. Frankfurt am Main: Klostermann, 1984.

———. *Hölderlin's Hymn "The Ister."* Translated by William McNeill and Julia Davis. Bloomington and Indianapolis: Indiana University Press, 1996.

———. *Holzwege*. Vol. 5 of *Gesamtausgabe*. Frankfurt am Main: Klostermann, 1977.

———. *Identity and Difference*. Translated by Joan Stambaugh. New York: Harper & Row, 1967.

———. *An Introduction to Metaphysics*. Translated by Ralph Manheim. New Haven: Yale University Press, 1987.

———. *Introduction to Metaphysics*. 2nd ed. Rev. and expanded ed. Translated by Gregory Fried and Richard Polt. New Haven, CT: Yale University Press, 2014.

———. *Kant und das Problem der Metaphysik*. Vol. 3 of *Gesamtausgabe*. Frankfurt am Main: Vittorio Klostermann, 1991.

———. *Kant and the Problem of Metaphysics*. 4th ed. Translated by Richard Taft. Bloomington and Indianapolis: Indiana University Press, 1990.

———. "Language." In *Poetry, Language, Thought*, 185–208. Translated by Albert Hofstadter New York: Harper, 1971.

———. "Letter on Humanism." In *Pathmarks*, ed. William McNeill, 239–76. New York and Cambridge: Cambridge University Press, 1998.

———. "Moira (Parmenides VIII, 34–41)." In *Early Greek Thinking*. Translated by David Farrell Krell and Frank A. Capuzz, 79–101. San Francisco: Harper San Franscisco, 1984.

———. "The Nature of Language." In *On the Way to Language*, 57–108. Tranlated by Peter D. Hertz. New York: Harper and Row, 1971.

———. *The Eternal Recurrence of the Same*. Vol. 2 of *Nietzsche*. Translated by David Farrell Krell. San Francisco: Harper & Row, 1984.

———. *Nietzsche*. 2 vols. Translated by David Farrell Krell. New York: Harper and Row, 1991.

———. *Nietzsche I*. Vol. 6.1 of *Gesamtausgabe*. Edited by Brigitte Schillbach. Frankfurt am Main: Klostermann, 1996.

———. "On the Essence of Ground." In *Pathmarks*, edited by William McNeill, 97–135. Translated by William McNeill. Cambridge: Cambridge University Press, 1998.

———. "On the Essence of Truth." In *Pathmarks*, edited by William McNeill, 136–54. Translated by John Sallis. Cambridge: Cambridge University Press, 1998.

———. "On the Question of Being." In *Pathmarks*, edited by William McNeill, 291–322. Translated by John Sallis. Cambridge, UK, and New York: Cambridge University Press, 1998.

———. *On Time and Being*. Translated by Joan Stambaugh. Harper & Row: New York, 1972.

———. *On the Way to Language*. Translated by Peter D. Hertz. New York: Harper and Row, 1971.

———. "The Origin of the Work of Art." In *Off the Beaten Track*, edited and translated by Julian Young and Kenneth Haynes, 1–56. Cambridge: Cambridge University Press, 2002.

———. *Pathmarks*. Edited by William McNeill. New York and Cambridge: Cambridge University Press, 1998.

———. *Poetry, Language, Thought*. Translated by Albert Hofstadter. New York: Harper & Row, 1971.

———. *Ponderings II–IV: Black Notebooks 1931–1938*. Bloomington and Indianapolis: Indiana University Press, 2016.

———. *Ponderings VII–XI: Black Notebooks 1938–1939*. Bloomington and Indianapolis: Indiana University Press, 2017.

———. *Ponderings: XII–XV: Black Notebooks 1939–1941*. Bloomington and Indianapolis: Indiana University Press, 2017.

———. "Postscript to *What Is Metaphysics?*" In *Pathmarks*, edited by William McNeill, 231–38. New York and Cambridge: Cambridge University Press, 1998.

———. *The Principle of Reason*. Translated by Reginald Lilly. Bloomington and Indianapolis: University of Indiana Press, 1996.

———. "The Question Concerning Technology." In *The Question Concerning Tehcnology and Other Essays*, 2–35. Translated by William Lovitt. New York and London: Garland, 1977.

———. *The Question of Being*. Translated by William Kluback and Jean T. Wilde. New York: Twayne, 1958.

———. *Sein und Zeit*. 17th ed. Tübingen: Niemeyer, 1993.

———. *Schelling's Treatise on the Essence of Human Freedom*. Translated by Joan Stambaugh. Athens: Ohio University Press, 1985.

———. "Time and Being." In *On Time and Being*, 1–24. Translated by Joan Stambaugh. Harper & Row: New York, 1972.

———. *Towards the Definition of Philosophy*. Translated by Ted Sadler. London: Athlone Press, 2000.

———. *Überlegungen II–VI (Schwarze Hefte 1931–1938)*. Vol. 94 of *Gesamtausgabe*. Frankfurt am Main: Vittorio Klostermann, 2014.

———. *Überlegungen VII–XI (Schwarze Hefte 1938–1939)*. Vol. 95 of *Gesamtausgabe*. Frankfurt am Main: Vittorio Klostermann, 2014.

———. *Überlegungen XII–XV (Schwarze Hefte 1939–1941)*. Vol. 96 of *Gesamtausgabe*. Frankfurt am Main: Vittorio Klostermann, 2014.

———. *Unterwegs zur Sprache*. Vol. 12 of *Gesamtausgabe*. Frankfurt am Main: Klostermann, 1985.

———. "Der Ursprung des Kunstwerkes." In *Holzwege*. Vol. 5 of *Gesamtausgabe*, 1–74. Frankfurt am Main: Klostermann, 1977.

———. *Vom Wesen des Grundes*. In *Wegmarken*. Vol. 9 of *Gesamtausgabe*, 123–76. Frankfurt am Main: Klostermann, 1976.

———. *Vom Wesen der Warheit*. In *Wegmarken*. Vol. 9 of *Gesamtausgabe*, 177–202. Frankfurt am Main: Klostermann, 1976.

———. *Vorträge und Aufsätze*. Vol. 7 of *Gesamtausgabe*. Frankfurt am Main: Klostermann, 1977.

———. *Was Heißt Denken?* Vol. 8 of *Gesamtausgabe*. Frankfurt am Main: Klostermann, 2002.

———. "The Way to Language." In *On the Way to Language*, 111–36. Translated by Peter D. Hertz. New York: Harper and Row, 1971.

———. "The Way to Language." In *Basic Writings*, edited by David Farrell Krell, 393–426. Rev. and expanded ed. New York: HarperCollins, 1993.

———. *Wegmarken*. Vol. 9 of *Gesamtausgabe*. Frankfurt am Main: Klostermann, 1976.

———. "Das Wesen der Sprache." In *Unterwegs zur Sprache*, vol. 12 of *Gesamtausgabe*, 147–204. Frankfurt am Main: Klostermann, 1985.

———. *What Is Called Thinking?* Translated by J. Glenn Gray. New York: Harper & Row, 1968.

———. "What Is Metaphysics?" Translated by David Farrell Krell. In *Pathmarks*, edited by William McNeill, 82–96. New York and Cambridge: Cambridge University Press, 1998.

———. "Who Is Nietzsche's Zarathustra?" In *The New Nietzsche: Contemporary Styles of Interpretation*, edited by David Allison, 64–79. Translated by Bernd Magnus. New York: Dell, 1977.

———. "Zeit und Sein." In *Zur Sache des Denkens*. Vol. 14 of *Gesamtausgabe*, 3–30. Frankfurt am Main: Klostermann, 2007.

———. *Zur Bestimmung der Philosophie*. Vols. 56–57 of *Gesamtausgabe*. Frankfurt am Main: Klostermann, 2000.

———. *Zur Sache des Denkens*. Vol. 14 of *Gesamtausgabe*. Frankfurt am Main: Klostermann, 2007.

Hemmings, Clare. "Invoking Affect: Cultural Theory and the Ontological Turn." *Cultural Studies* 19, no. 5 (September 2005): 548–67.

———. "Telling Feminist Stories." *Feminist Theory* 6, no. 2: 115–39.

———. *Why Stories Matter: The Political Grammar of Feminist Theory*. Durham, NC, and London: Duke University Press, 2011.

Hesse, Mary. "Aristotle's Logic of Analogy." *Philosophical Quarterly* 15, no. 61 (October 1965): 328–40.

Hill, Leslie. *Blanchot: Extreme Contemporary*. London: Routledge, 1997.

———. *Maurice Blanchot and Fragmentary Writing: A Change in Epoch*. London and New York: Continuum, 2012.

———. *Nancy, Blanchot: A Serious Controversy*. London: Rowman & Littlefield International, 2018.

Hinderliter, Beth, William Kaizen, Vered Maimon, Jaleh Mansoor, and Seth McCormick, eds. *Communities of Sense: Rethinking Aesthetics and Politics*. Durham, NC: Duke University Press, 2009.

Hölderlin, Friedrich. "*Anmerkungen zum Oedipus*." In Vol. 5 of *Sämtliche Werke* (Grosse Stuttgarter Ausgabe), edited by Friedrich Beissner, 195–202. Stuttgart: Kohlhammer, 1952.

———. *Friedrich Hölderlin: Essays and Letters on Theory*. Translated and edited by Thomas Pfau. Albany: State University of New York Press, 1998.

———. *Hymns and Fragments*. Translated by Richard Sieburth. Princeton, NJ: Princeton University Press, 1984.

Huffer, Lynne. "Blanchot's Mother." *Yale French Studies* 93 (1998): 175–95.

Inwood, Michael. *A Heidegger Dictionary*. Oxford: Blackwell, 1999.

Irigaray, Luce. *The Forgetting of Air in Martin Heidegger*. Translated by Mary Beth Mader. Austin: University of Texas Press, 1999.

———. "The Power of Discourse and the Subordination of the Feminine." In *This Sex Which Is Not One*, 68–85. Translated by Catherine Porter with Carolyn Burke. Ithaca, NY: Cornell University Press, 1985.

———. *Speculum of the Other Woman*. Translated by Gillian C. Gill. Ithaca, NY: Cornell University Press, 1985.

Iyer, Lars. *Blanchot's Communism: Art, Philosophy and the Political*. Basingstoke, UK, and New York: Palgrave Macmillan, 2004.

Johnson, Barbara. *Persons and Things*. Cambridge, MA: Harvard University Press, 2010.

Jünger, Ernst. *Der Arbeiter. Herrschaft und die Gestalt*. Stuttgart: Klett-Cotta, [1932] 1981.

———. *The Worker: Dominion and Form*. Translated by Bogdan Costea and Laurence Paul Hemming. Evanston, IL: Northwestern University Press, 2017.

Kant, Immanuel. *Critique of Judgment*. Edited by Nicholas Walker. Translated by James Creed Meredith. Oxford: Oxford University Press, 2007.

Kirk, G. S., and J. E. Raven. *The Presocratic Philosophers*. Cambridge: Cambridge University Press, 1957.

Kisiel, Theodore. "Hermeneutics of Facticity." In *Martin Heidegger: Key Concepts*, edited by Bret W. Davis, 17–32. Durham, NC: Acumen, 2010.

Kojève, Alexandre. *Introduction to the Reading of Hegel: Lectures on the* Phenomenology of Spirit. Edited by Allan Bloom. Translated by James H. Nichols Jr. Ithaca, NY: Cornell University Press, 1980.

Kompridis, Nikolas, ed. *The Aesthetic Turn in Political Thought*. New York: Bloomsbury, 2014.

Lacan, Jacques. "The Function and Field of Speech and Language in Psychoanalysis." In Jacques Lacan, *Écrits: The First Complete Edition in English*. Translated by Bruce Fink, 237–68. New York and London: W.W. Norton, 2006.

Lacoue-Labarthe, Philippe. *Agonie terminée, agonie interminable. Sur Maurice Blanchot. Suivi de L'émoi*. Edited by Aristide Bianchi and Leonid Kharlamov. Paris: Éditions Galilée, 2011.

———. "The Caesura of the Speculative." In *Typography: Mimesis, Philosophy, Politics*, edited and translated by Christopher Fynsk, 208–35. Stanford, CA: Stanford University Press, 1998.

———. *Ending and Unending Agony: On Maurice Blanchot*. Translated by Hannes Opelz. New York: Fordham University Press, 2015.

———. *Heidegger, Art, and Politics: The Fiction of the Political*. Translated by Chris Turner. Oxford and Cambridge, MA: Blackwell, 1990.

———. "The Echo of the Subject." In *Typography: Mimesis, Philosophy, Politics*, edited and translated by Christopher Fynsk, 139–207. Stanford, CA: Stanford University Press, 1998.

———. "*Il faut.*" In *Heidegger and the Politics of Poetry*, 38–59. Translated by Jeff Fort. Urbana and Chicago: University of Illinois Press, 2007.
———. "*Il faut.*" In *Heidegger. La politique du poème*, 79–115. Paris: Galilée, 2002.
———. *La Fiction du politique*. Paris: Christian Bourgois, 1987.
———. *Mimesis des articulations*. Paris: Flammarion, 1975.
———. *Musica Ficta (Figures of Wagner)*. Translated by Felicia McCarren. Stanford, CA: Stanford University Press, 1994.
———. "Oedipus as Figure." Translated by David Macey. *Radical Philosophy* 118 (March/April 2003): 7–17.
———. *Phrase*. Paris: Christian Bourgois, 2000.
———. *Phrase*. Translated by Leslie Hill. Albany: State University of New York Press, 2018.
———. "The Scene is Primal." In *The Subject of* Philosophy, edited by Thomas Trezise, 99–115. Translated by Karen McPherson. Minneapolis: University of Minnesota Press, 1993.
———. *The Subject of* Philosophy. Edited by Thomas Trezise. Translated by Thomas Trezise, Hugh J. Silverman, Gary M. Cole, Timothy D. Bent, Karen McPherson, and Claudette Sartiliot. Minneapolis: University of Minnesota Press, 1993.
———. *Le Sujet de la philosophie: Typographies I*. Paris: Aubier-Flammarion, 1979.
———. "Typography." In *Typography: Mimesis, Philosophy, Politics*, edited and translated by Christopher Fynsk, 43–138. Stanford, CA: Stanford University Press, 1998.
———. *Typography: Mimesis, Philosophy, Politics*. Edited and translated by Christopher Fynsk. Stanford, CA: Stanford University Press, 1998.
Lacoue-Labarthe, Philippe, and Jean-Luc Nancy. "The Nazi Myth." *Critical Inquiry* 16, no. 2: (1990): 291–312.
———. *Retreating the Political*. Edited by Simon Sparks. London and New York: Routledge, 1997.
———. *Scène suivi de Dialogue sur le dialogue*. Paris: Éditions Christian Bourgois, 2013.
———. "Scene: An Exchange of Letters." In *Beyond Representation: Philosophy and the Poetic Imagination*, edited by Richard Eldridge, 273–302. Cambridge: Cambridge University Press, 1996.
———. "The Unconscious is Structured Like an Affect (Part 1 of 'The Jewish People Do Not Dream')." Translated by Brian Holmes. *Stanford Literary Review* 6, no. 2 (1989): 191–209.
Large, William. "IMPERSONAL EXISTENCE: A Conceptual Genealogy of the 'There Is' from Heidegger to Blanchot and Levinas." *Angelaki* 7, no. 3 (2002): 131–42.
LeBuffe, Michael. *From Bondage to Freedom: Spinoza on Human Excellence*. Oxford: Oxford University Press, 2010.

Lecercle, Jean-Jacques. *Deleuze and Language*. New York: Palgrave Macmillan, 2002.

Lévinas, Emmanuel. *De l'existence à l'existant*. 2nd rev. ed. Paris: Vrin, 2013.

———. *Existence and Existents*. Translated by Alphonso Lingis. Pittsburgh: Duquesne University Press, 2001.

———. *Otherwise Than Being or Beyond Essence*. Translated by Alphonso Lingis. Pittsburgh: Dusquesne University Press, 2006.

Leys, Ruth. "The Turn to Affect: A Critique." *Cultural Inquiry* 37 (Spring 2011): 434–72.

Lyotard, Jean-François. *The Differend: Phrases in Dispute*. Translated by Georges Van Den Abbeele. Minneapolis: University of Minnesota Press, 1988.

MacKendrick, Karmen. *The Matter of Voice: Sensual Soundings*. New York: Fordham University Press, 2016.

Malpas, Jeff. *Heidegger and the Thinking of Place: Explorations in the Topology of Being*. Cambridge, MA: MIT Press, 2012.

Massumi, Brian. "The Autonomy of Affect." In *Deleuze: A Critical Reader*, edited by Paul Patton. Oxford: Blackwell, 1996, 217–39.

———. *Parables for the Virtual: Movement, Affect, Sensation*. Durham, NC: Duke University Press, 2002.

Marrone, Steven P. "Henry of Ghent and Duns Scotus on Knowledge of Being." *Speculum*, Vol. 63. No. 1 (Jan. 1988): 22–57.

Martis, John. *Philippe Lacoue-Labarthe: Representation and the Loss of the Subject*. New York: Fordham University Press, 2005.

Massumi, Brian. *Parables for the Virtual: Movement, Affect, Sensation*. Durham, NC: Duke University Press, 2002.

Meillassoux, Quentin. *After Finitude: An Essay on the Necessity of Contingency*. Translated by Ray Brassier. London: Continuum, 2008.

Mitchell, Andrew J., and Jason Kemp Winfree, "Editors' Introduction: Community and Communication." In *The Obsessions of Georges Bataille: Community and Communication*, ed. Andrew J. Mitchell and Jason Kemp Winfree, 1–17. Albany: State University of New York Press, 2009.

Moran, Dermot. "What Does Heidegger Mean by the Transcendence of Dasein?" *International Journal of Philosophical Studies* 22, no. 4 (2014): 491–514.

Muñoz, José Estaban. "Feeling Brown, Feeling Down: Latina Affect, the Performativity of Race, and the Depressive Position." *Signs* 31, no. 3. New Feminist Theories of Visual Culture (Spring 2006): 675–88.

Nancy, Jean-Luc. "A Finite Thinking." In *A Finite Thinking*, ed. Simon Sparks, 3–30. Stanford, CA: Stanford University Press, 2003.

———. "The Being-with of Being-there." *Continental Philosophy Review* 41 (2008): 1–15.

———. *Being Singular Plural*. Translated by Robert D. Richardson and Anne E. O'Byrne. Stanford, CA: Stanford University Press, 2000.

———. *The Birth to Presence*. Translated by Brian Holmes, Xavier Callahan, David Carroll, Mary Ann Caws, Peter Caws, Thomas Harrison, Nathalia King, Christine Laennec, Katherine Lydon, Juliet Flower MacCannell, et al. Stanford, CA: Stanford University Press, 1993.
———. *La Communauté affrontée*. Paris: Éditions Galilée, 2001.
———. *La Communauté désavouée*. Paris: Éditions Galilée, 2014.
———. *La Communauté désoeuvrée*. Paris: Éditions Christian Bourgois, 1986.
———. "The Confronted Community." In *The Obsessions of Georges Bataille: Community and Communication*, ed. Andrew J. Mitchell and Jason Kemp Winfree, 19–30. Albany: State University of New York Press, 2009.
———. *The Creation of the World or Globalization*. Translated by François Raffoul and David Pettigrew. Albany: State University of New York Press, 2007.
———. "The Decision of Existence." In *The Birth to Presence*, 82–109. Translated by Brian Holmes, Xavier Callahan, David Carroll, Mary Ann Caws, Peter Caws, Thomas Harrison, Nathalia King, Christine Laennec, Katherine Lydon, and Juliet Flower MacCannell. Stanford, CA: Stanford University Press, 1993.
———. *The Disavowed Community*. Translation by Philip Armstrong. New York: Fordham University Press, 2016.
———. "L'Être-avec de l'être-là." *Cahiers philosophiques* no. 111 (October 2007): 66–78.
———. *Être singulier pluriel*. Paris: Éditions Galilée, 1996.
———. "Finite History." In *The Birth to Presence*, 143–66. Translated by Brian Holmes, Xavier Callahan, David Carroll, Mary Ann Caws, Peter Caws, Thomas Harrison, Nathalia King, Christine Laennec, Katherine Lydon, and Juliet Flower MacCannell. Stanford, CA: Stanford University Press, 1993.
———. *The Ground of the Image*. Translated by Jeff Fort. New York: Fordham University Press, 2005.
———. *The Inoperative Community*. Edited by Peter Conno. Translated by Peter Connor, Lisa Garbus, Michael Holland, and Simona Sawhney. Minneapolis: University of Minnesota Press, 1991.
———. "The Jursidiction of the Hegelian Monarch." In *The Birth to Presence*, 110–42. Translated by Brian Holmes, Xavier Callahan, David Carroll, Mary Ann Caws, Peter Caws, Thomas Harrison, Nathalia King, Christine Laennec, Katherine Lydon, and Juliet Flower MacCannell. Stanford, CA: Stanford University Press, 1993.
———. *Maurice Blanchot: Passion politique*. Paris: Éditions Galilée, 2011.
———. *The Muses*. Translated by Peggy Kamuf. Stanford, CA: Stanford University Press, 1996.
———. "Our History." Translated by Cynthia Chase, Richard Klein, and A. Mitchell Brown. *Diacritics* 20, no. 3 (Fall 1990): 97–115.
———. *Le Partage des voix*. Paris: Éditions Galilée, 1982.

———. "Sharing Voices." In *Transforming the Hermeneutic Context*, edited by Gayle L. Ormiston and Alan D. Schrift, 211–59. Albany: State University of New York Press, 1990.

———. "The Unsacrificeable." In *A Finite Thinking*, edited by Simon Sparks, 51–77. Stanford, CA: Stanford University Press, 2003.

Nancy, Jean-Luc, and Aurélien Barrau. *What's These Worlds Coming To?* Translated by Travis Holloway and Flor Méchain. New York: Fordham University Press, 2015.

Nietzsche, *The Birth of Tragedy*. Translated by Walter Kaufmann. New York: Vintage, 1967.

———. *The Birth of Tragedy and Other Writings*. Edited by Raymond Geuss and Ronald Speirs. Translated by Ronald Speirs. Cambridge: Cambridge University Press, 1999.

———. *Ecce Homo*. Translated by Walter Kaufmann. New York: Vintage, 1989.

———. *The Gay Science*. Translated by Walter Kaufmann. New York: Vintage, 1974.

———. *Nachgelassene Fragmente: 1887–1889*. Edited by Giorgio Colli and Mazzino Montinari. KSA 13. Munich: Deutscher Taschenbuch Verlag, 1999.

———. *On the Genealogy of Morals*. Translated by Walter Kaufman and R. J. Hollingdale. New York: Vintage, 1989.

———. *Thus Spoke Zarathustra*. In *The Portable Nietzsche*, edited and translated by Walter Kaufmann, 103–439. New York: Penguin, 1983.

———. *The Will to Power*. Translated by Walter Kaufmann and R. J. Hollingdale. New York: Vintage, 1968.

Olkowski, Dorothea. "Deleuze's Aesthetics of Sensation." In *The Cambridge Companion to Deleuze*, edited by Daniel W. Smith and Henry Somers-Hall, 265–85. Cambridge: Cambridge University Press, 2012.

———. *Gilles Deleuze and the Ruin of Representation*. Los Angeles: University of California Press, 1999.

Owen, G. E. L. "Logic and Metaphysics in Some Earlier Works of Aristotle." In *Aristotle and Plato in the Mid-Fourth Century*, edited by I. Düring and G. E. L. Owen, 163–90. Gothenburg: Elanders, 1960.

Owens, Joseph. *The Doctrine of Being in the Aristotelian Metaphysics*, 2nd rev. ed. Toronto: Pontifical Institute of Medieval Studies, 1963.

Parker, Andrew. *The Theorist's Mother*. Durham, NC: Duke University Press, 2012.

Pearson, Keith Ansell. *Germinal Life: The Difference and Repetition of Gilles Deleuze*. London and New York: Routledge, 1999.

Plato, *Republic*, Books 6–10, Plato VI, Loeb Classical Library. Translated by Paul Shorey. Cambridge, MA: Harvard University Press, 2000.

Povinelli, Elizabeth. *Economies of Abandonment: Social Belonging and Endurance in Late Liberalism*. Durham, NC: Duke University Press, 2011.

Powell, Jeffrey, ed. *Heidegger and Language*. Bloomington: Indiana University Press, 2013.

Rae, Gavin. *Ontology in Heidegger and Deleuze: A Comparative Analysis*. New York: Palgrave Macmillan, 2014.

Rancière, Jacques. *Disagreement: Politics and Philosophy*. Translated by Julie Rose. Minneapolis: University of Minnesota Press, 1999.

———. *La Mésentente. Politique et philosophie*. Paris: Éditions Galilée, 1995.

———. *Le Partage du sensible. Esthétique et politique*. Paris: La Fabrique-éditions, 2000.

———. *The Politics of Aesthetics: The Distribution of the Sensible*. Translated by Gabriel Rockhill. New York: Continuum, 2004.

Richardson, William J., S. J. "Heidegger's Fall." In *From Phenomenology to Thought, Errancy, and Desire: Essays in Honor of William J. Richardson, S.J.*, edited by Babette E. Babich, 277–300. Dordrecht: Springer, 1995.

———. *Heidegger: Through Phenomenology to Thought*. The Hague: Martinus Nijhoff, 1963.

Ronell, Avital. *The Telephone Book: Technology, Schizophrenia, Electric Speech*. Lincoln: University of Nebraska Press, 1989.

Ross, Alison. *The Aesthetic Paths of Philosophy: Presentation in Kant, Heidegger, Lacoue-Labarthe, and Nancy*. Stanford, CA: Stanford University Press, 2007.

Schacht, Richard. *Nietzsche*. London and New York: Routledge, 1992.

Schmidt, Dennis J. *On Germans and Other Greeks: Tragedy and Ethical Life*. Bloomington and Indianapolis: Indiana University Press, 2001.

Schufreider, Gregory. "Sticking Heidegger with a Stela: Lacoue-Labarthe, Art and Politics." In *French Interpretations of Heidegger: An Exceptional Reception*, ed. David Pettigrew and François Raffoul, 187–214. Albany: State University of New York Press, 2008.

Sedgwick, Eve Kosofsky and Adam Frank. "Shame in the Cybernetic Fold: Reading Silvan Tomkins." In *Shame and Its Sisters: A Silvan Tomkins Reader*, edited by Eve Kosofsky Sedgwick and Adam Frank, 1–28. Durham, NC: Duke University Press, 1995.

———. *Touching Feeling: Affect, Pedagogy, and Perfomativity*. Durham, NC: Duke University Press, 2003.

Sholtz, Janae. *The Invention of a People: Heidegger and Deleuze on Art and the Political*. Edinburgh: Edinburgh University Press, 2015.

Silverman, Kaja. *The Acoustic Mirror: The Female Voice in Psychoanalysis and Cinema*. Bloomington and Indianapolis: Indiana University Press, 1988.

Smith, Daniel W. "The Doctrine of Univocity: Deleuze's Ontology of Immanence." In *Essays on Deleuze*, 27–42. Edinburgh: Edinburgh University Press, 2012.

———. "Klossowski's Reading of Nietzsche: Impulses, Phantasms, Simulacra, Stereotypes." *Diacritics* 35, no. 1 (2005): 8–21.

———. "The Concept of the Simulacrum: Deleuze and the Overturning of Platonism." *Continental Philosophy Review* 38, nos. 1–2 (2005): 89–123.

Spinoza, Benedict de. *The Collected Works of Spinoza*. Vol. 1. Edited and translated by Edwin Curley. Princeton, NJ: Princeton University Press, 1985.

Sophocles, *The Antigone of Sophocles*. 2nd ed. Edited (with introduction and notes) by Sir Richard Jebb. Cambridge: Cambridge University Press, 1891.

Steiner, George. *Martin Heidegger*. Chicago: University of Chicago Press, 1989.

Taminiaux, Jacques. "The Origin of 'The Origin of the Work of Art.'" In *Reading Heidegger: Commemorations*, edited by John Sallis, 392–404. Bloomington and Indianapolis: Indiana University Press, 1993.

———. "Voice and Phenomena in Heidegger's Fundamental Ontology." In *Heidegger and the Project of Fundamental Ontology*, edited and translated by Michael Gendre, 55–68. Albany: State University of New York Press, 1991.

Thrift, Nigel. "Understanding the Material Practices of Glamour." In *The Affect Theory Reader*, edited by Melissa Gregg and Gregory J. Seigworth, 289–308. Durham, NC: Duke University Press, 2011.

Tolliday, Phillip. "Maurice Blanchot: Suffering and Affliction as Epiphany," *Culture, Theory and Critique* 52, nos. 2–3 (2011): 199–211.

Tomiche, Ann. "Artaud, Madness and/in Translation." *Translation Studies* 12, no. 1 (2019): 24–35.

van Tuinen, Sjoerd. "Difference and Speculation: Heidegger, Meillassoux, and Deleuze on Sufficient Reason." In *Gilles Deleuze and Metaphysics*, edited by Alain Beaulieu, Edward Kazarian, and Julia Sushytska, 63–90. New York: Lexington, 2014.

Vernant, Jean-Pierre. "Feminine Figures of Death in Greece." In *Mortals and Immortals: Collected Essays*, edited by Froma I. Zeitlin, 95–111. Princeton, NJ: Princeton University Press, 1991.

Warminski, Andrzej. "Monstrous History: Heidegger Reading Hölderlin." In *The Solid Letter: Readings of Friedrich Hölderlin*, edited by Aris Fioretos, 201–14. Stanford, CA: Stanford University Press, 1999.

Weller, Shane. *Language and Negativity in European Modernism*. Cambridge: Cambridge University Press, 2018.

———. "Voidance: Linguistic Negativism in Maurice Blanchot's Fiction," *French Studies: A Quarterly Review* 69, no. 1 (January 2015): 30–45.

Widder, Nathan. "The Rights of Simulacra: Deleuze and the Univocity of Being." *Continental Philosophy Review* 34 (2001): 437–53.

Wilson, Malcolm. *Aristotle's Theory of the Unity of Science*. Toronto: University of Toronto Press, 2000.

Index

Adorno, Theodor W., 259n53
aesthetic turn, 1–2, 7–14, 29–30, 49, 229–39; *See also* affect; affective turn
aesthetics, 18, 70, 120, 122, 141, 176, 237; and politics, 10–11; of subjectivization, 236. *See also* Benjamin, Walter; Rancière, Jacques
affect, 1, 7–14, 15, 165; and becoming, 8–10, Deleuzean, 8–10, 21, 45, 191, 210, 214; Heideggerian, 17, 45, 178, 214, 215, 216, 218; modernist, 178; Spinozist, 206–7, 270n27. *See also* affective turn; attunement; *Stimmung*
affective turn, 1–2, 7–14, 29–30, 45, 49, 178, 207, 219, 229–39; critiques of 11–12. *See also* aesthetic turn, affect
aisthesis, 45
aletheia, 69, 71, 120, 133–41, 142, 174–75, 176, 177; *Unverstelltheit* as, 138
Antigone (character), 18; as *deinon*, 90; as figure, 70; as "the purest poem itself," 90
Antigone (play), 18, 73–87
Aristotle, 192, 247n6–7; and the analogy of Being, 196, 198–203; on the *opsis*, 143–44

Artaud, Antonin, 157, 175–85, 189–90, 192, 195, 214, 215, 219–24, 226, 273n48, 273n53; *cris-souffles* (howls-breaths) in, 223, 224; the cry in, 274n57; and nothingness, 182; and theater of cruelty, 192, 195, 218, 223; translation of "Jabberwocky," 221–23; 273n48
artwork, 18–19, 69, 70–73, 118–24, 156, 165, 176, 194, 195, 220, 227, 272n46; and facticity, 120. *See also* work
attunement, 45. See also *Stimmung*
Auseinandersetzung, 23, 76, 83, 90, 126, 191, 249n10. See also *explication*
Auslegung (interpretation), 41, 50, 59, 61, 63, 81. *See also* facticity; interpretation; *Selbstauslegung*

Bacon, Francis, 274n57
Badiou, Alain, 269n15
Bataille, Georges, 109; and art, 118–20; and communication, 115; and sacrifice, 116, 254n15
Benjamin, Walter, 107, 252n30; and the aestheticization of the political, 155; and demythologization (*Entmythologisierung*), 107; and

Benjamin, Walter *(continued)*
deposition of the mythological
(*Verlagerung des Mythologischen*), 145,
259n53
Bestimmen, 89
Blanchot, Maurice, 20–21, 24, 48,
189–90, 195, 196, 214, 215, 218,
226, 256n26; on Artaud, 157,
175–85, 273n53; and community,
109, 266n41; the cry in, 184;
and discontinuity, 229–39; and
Marguerite Duras, 266n41;
and essential solitude, 182; and
fascination, 178; and the day,
169; and the language of research,
229–39; the murmur in, 184; and
the narrative voice, 156, 162, 174,
183, 226, 266n41; and the neuter,
156, 161, 174, 183, 184; and the
night, 20, 156, 177, 184, 264n24;
and the nothing in speech, 170; and
speech, 183; Work (*l'Oeuvre*), 156,
164, 173, 182, 183
body, 8, 14; and affect, 8–10; Deleuzian,
8–10. See also affect; Spinoza

call: of Being, 247n4; of conscience,
44, 52, 56; of the eternal return,
212; of thinking, 23, 208, 214–18,
235, 238; of the voice, 23, 51, 63
care (*Sorge*), 33, 39
Carroll, Lewis, 219–24, 273n48
Castoriadis, Cornelius, 250n12
causality, 7, 10, 11–12, 238. See also
freedom
Causey, Robert Mark, 273n53
Clough, Patricia Ticineto, 7–9, 12
communication, 29, 48, 52, 53, 113,
223. See also Bataille, Georges;
Deleuze and Guattari
community, 5, 16, 19, 23, 106,
109–24; as interruption, 109–24;
and negative theology, 264–65n28.

See also myth; spectacularization;
voice; *Volk*
Cross, D. J. S., 272n46

Darstellen. See *Darstellung*
Darstellung (presentation), 65, 122,
125, 133–34, 135–41, 144, 194.
See also *Herstellen*
Dasein: ancient Greek vs. modern, 69,
74, 80, 81
deconstruction, 147, 155; and
Heidegger's project of *Destruktion*,
147, 155
deinon, 76, 83, 85, 88; See also
uncanny
Deleuze, Gilles, 21–22; the affective
turn and, 8–10; on the artwork,
272n46; on Becoming, 191, 195,
201, 207, 272n46; and cruelty, 218;
and free indirect discourse, 226;
the Idea in, 219; image of thought
in, 190, 191, 214, 220, 226, 227;
and insomnia, 213; and language,
219; on literature, 272n46; and
modernity, 193, 194, 267–68n5;
and powers of the false, 194
Deleuze and Guattari, 223–25;
and communication, 223; and
deterritorialization, 224; and minor
literature, 223–25, 272n46; and
style, 226
dēmiourgos, 136–38
Derrida, Jacques, 1, 23, 24, 126,
246n16, 247n7, 247–48n10,
273n53, 275n8; and *archi-écriture*,
146; and community, 262n10; and
retrait, 147, 259n59; and text,
147
désoeuvrement, 20, 113, 114, 156;
voice of, 158, 164
dialogue, 61, 62, 63, 64, 86, 87; as
dia-logos, 63, 68; as *Zwiesprache*,
83–84, 87

difference, 16, 19, 20, 24, 62, 106, 115, 125, 157, 178, 191, 192, 197, 207, 211, 212, 214, 215, 216, 217, 225, 237; Being as, 204; concept of, 194, 197; conceptual, 193, 197–202; in-itself, 201–2; ontological, 62, 193, 215, 216, 217, 267n2; and simulacra, 201

Dilthey, Wilhelm, 248n13

discourse (*Rede*). *See* language

distribution of the sensible 12. *See also* Rancière, Jacques

Duns Scotus, John, 196, 202–4, 270n21

dwelling, 7, 13, 14, 230, 243n21

earth, 18, 71, 120

ecstasis, 33, 116; and ek-sistence, 115

effacement, 20–21, 145, 148, 153–85, 196

errancy: in Deleuze, 213, 215; in Deleuze and Guattari, 225; in Heidegger, 215

explication, 23, 126, 191. *See also Auseinanderseztung*

existentiale, 36–38. *See also* ontological

existentiell, 36–38. *See also* ontic

facticity, 4, 15, 59, 60, 61, 72, 86, 114, 132, 248n13; and figuration, 120–21; and the work of art, 120. *See also Auslegung*; figuration; interpretation; *Selbstauslegung*

fantasy, 235–36, 238–39

fascination, 178, 239. *See also* spectacularization

feminine, 18, 90, 141, 148, 178, 195, 238, 252n33, 254–55n15, 260n64, 263n18, 265n32, 272–73n47

fictioning, 113, 116, 128–29, 132, 133, 136, 140, 196, 256–57n34, 257n43; as auto-fictioning, 114

figuration, 14–15, 18, 68, 124–49, 230; as auto-figuration, 114; and facticity, 120–21; and finitude, 18; interruption of, 106. *See also* facticity

figure: Carroll's Alice as, 220; of Apollo, 209, 271n35; of Dionysus, 195, 209, 210, 271n35; eternal return as, 195, 208; Eurydice as, 177, 263n18; of the friend, 45; Heidegger's conception of, 71; hermeneutic circle as, 50, 61; Lazarus as, 173, 177; of the Mother in Klein, 220; Oedipus as, 75, 252n31; Orpheus as, 173, 177, 263n18; philosophical, 127; of the *schizo*, 220, 222; Socrates as, 127; and typography, 127; the voice as, 3–4, 14, 15–24, 30; Zarathustra as, 127–28, 208

finite transcendence, 29–30, 31–34, 60, 215; circle as figure of, 34; scene of, 74

finitude, 2, 3, 4, 15, 18, 29–30, 31–34, 215; and figuration, 18; forgetting of, 34–36, 38;and language, 15, 20, 30; interpretation as scene of, 61

Foucault, Michel, 126, 158–59, 160, 243n24, 275n8

freedom, 2, 4, 6, 9, 10, 11–12, 14, 78. *See also* causality

Freud, Sigmund, 248n11

Froment-Meurice, Marc, 252n31

Fynsk, Christopher, 32, 45, 244n2–3, 246n16, 248n2, 249n10, 252n30, 254n14, 264n25, 265–66n33, 274n57

Gasché, Rodolphe, 146–47, 259n59

Guattari, Félix, 274n1. *See also* Deleuze and Guattari

Geschick, 60, 77

298 / Index

Gestalt, 69, 71, 127–32, 141, 231, 258n45
Gestaltung, 130, 175, 231
Ge-stell, 69, 71, 72, 129–34, 141, 258n45
Gewalt, 76
Geworfenheit. See thrownness
Gilson, Étienne, 269n18
Godard, Jean-Luc, 225–26
Gregg, Melissa, 9–10, 13

Haar, Michel, 45
Halper, Edward C., 268n11
Hardt, Michael, 7, 267n2
hearing (*Hören*), 54, 162, 163; modern, 74, 80, 81, 82. See also keeping silent (*Schweigen*)
Hegel, Georg Wilhelm Friedrich, 115–16, 124, 165, 166, 198, 233, 236; and art, 176; and negation, 169–71
Heidegger, Martin, 177, 178, 181, 189–90, 191, 193–97, 214–18, 226, 233–34, 267n2, 271n32, 275n7; and fundamental ontology, 58; on the voice of conscience (*die Stimme des Gewissens*), 16–17; on Nietzsche, 127–43; and nothingness, 171; on Plato, 135–41; on the work of art, 18, 70–73, 176. See also Antigone (character); *Antigone* (play)
Hemmings, Clare, 11–12, 13, 242n15, 275n2
hermēneia, 61, 64–65, 87.
hermeneutic circle, 37, 58; as figure, 50, 61
Herstellen, 133–34, 136–41. See also *Darstellung*
Herstellung. See *Herstellen*
Hill, Leslie, 264n24
Hölderlin, Friedrich, 20, 75, 82–87, 107, 251–52n29

il y a, 167, 171–75, 183, 184, 264n28; vs. *es gibt*, 167, 171, 177; and insomnia, 172, 174, 264n24; night of vs. Heideggerian anxiety, 172
impouvoir, 156, 174, 175–85, 190, 214, 218
interpretation, 50–51, 60, 81, 82, 223–24; and figuration, 51; *hermēneia* as, 61; modern interpretation of, 58. See also *Auslegung*; facticity; *Selbstauslegung*
Irigaray, Luce, 148, 252n33

Johnson, Barbara, 260n66
Jünger, Ernst, 129–30

Kafka, Franz, 223–25
Kant, Immanuel, 122, 233, 252n29
keeping silent (*Schweigen*), 41–42, 51–56, 162
Kierkegaard, Søren, 233–34
Klossowski, Pierre, 271n37

Lacan, Jacques, 238, 243n24, 275n3
Lacoue-Labarthe, Philippe, 16, 19–20, 191, 195, 196, 197, 200; and architheater, 144, 146; and caesura of the speculative, 20, 107, 125, 126, 148; and de-figuration (*dé-figuration*), 107, 143–49, 196; *l'émoi*, 154; on the feminine, 252n33; and mimetology, 139, 141, 143; on music, 141–42; *phrase*, 154
language, 6; and affect, 49, 192, 219, 225, 229–39, 272n46; antagonism of, 17, 45, 51–57, 166, 223; and death, 169, 172, 263n17; and difference, 160; and discourse (*Rede*), 41, 45, 49, 53, 54, 55, 56, 246–47n4; experience of/with, 3, 15, 17, 20, 46, 156; the fact of, 3; and

finitude, 15, 20, 29; and form, 231; of metaphysics, 45; metaphysics of, 45, 48; and nothingness, 169, 171; and onto-theology, 160; philosophy of, 236; and progress, 232; question of, 49, 229–39; and questioning, 235; Saying of, 247n4; and sense, 219–27; speaking of, 168, 224; and the voice, 3, 15, 29; writing as the effacement of, 164, 184. *See also* logos; *phonē*

Lévinas, Emmanuel, 167, 171–75, 235, 243n24

Leys, Ruth, 12

limit-experience, 48, 165, 173, 183

linguistic turn, 1–2, 7, 10, 154, 230

literature, 20, 156, 165, 190, 192, 215, 219, 220; and affect, 165, 174, 272n46; and impossibility, 168; and negation, 160–75. *See also* work

logos, 17, 24, 49–51, 53, 61, 246n19. *See also* voice. *See also under* language: antagonism of

Lyotard, Jean-François, 243n24

malheur, 156, 174, 178, 182, 265n31, 265–66n33

Marrone, Steven P., 269n17

Massumi, Brian, 11, 242n15

metaphysics, 130; closure of, 46, 57, 128, 147, 155, 247–48n10; of presence, 24, 49, 57, 61, 105, 155, 162, 173, 174, 178, 193, 217, 259n59

methexis, 122, 123, 256n27

mimesis, 5, 16, 19–22, 107–8, 118–43, 177, 178, 193–94, 195, 196, 197, 200, 201, 210, 212, 213, 217, 225, 230, 238; metaphysical judgment of, 135; and music, 141–42; narrative voice as, 175; as voice, 141

mise-en-abyme, 65, 69, 139, 195

Mitdasein, 110–13

Mitsein, 63, 110–13, 114, 115, 117, 246n16

modernism, 168, 178, 265n31

myth, 16, 19, 200–1; interruption of, 106

Nancy, Jean-Luc, 16, 17, 19–20, 48, 190, 191, 192, 195, 196, 200, 202, 246n16, 262n10,; and archi-dialogue; critique of Blanchot, 264–65n28; and compearance, 114; and literary communism, 117, on modern hermeneutics, 58, 59; and ontological mimesis, 19, 144; and plural worlds, 105, 121

narrative voice, 16, 20

need (*Not*), 79, 80; vs. *Brauch*, 250n17; as *chrē*, 80

new, 10, 12, 178, 237

new materialism, 1, 2

Nietzsche, Friedrich, 79, 126, 127, 131–32, 134, 159, 194, 195, 201, 202, 207–14, 233–34; and the eternal return, 201, 207–9, 210, 211, 212, 220, 270n28, 271n36; and modern hermeneutics, 248n11; and *ressentiment*, 209, 211–12

nothing, 42–44, 170, 215, 216–17. *See also* nothingness; notness; nullity

nothingness: language and, 169

notness (*Nichtheit*), 42–44, 216–17. *See also* nothing; nothingness; nullity

nullity, 42–44. *See also* nothing; nothingness; notness

object-oriented ontology, 1

Olkowski, Dorothea, 268n6, 273n47

ontic, 35, 36–38, 52–54. *See also* existentiell

ontological, 36–38, 52–54. *See also* existentiale
onto-theology, 145, 158–66; and language, 160
onto-typology, 19, 106, 124–49, 197
outside (*le dehors*), 20, 156, 164, 173, 174, 175–85, 226

Parmenides, 74, 80, 128, 197, 250n20
partage, 12–13, 14, 17, 51, 63, 83, 107, 108–24, 146
passivity, 158
Philosophy, 5, 20, 127, 178, 194, 213, 239; and the feminine, 263n18; and madness, 126–28; narcissism of, 127; and teaching, 233–34; and writing, 233. *See also* Theory
phonē, 17, 49, 53, 246n19. *See also* voice. *See also under* language: antagonism of
physis, 73–74, 76, 81, 195
Plato, 123, 126, 127, 131, 134, 135, 200–2; 256n27
Platonism, 131, 136, 192, 197–202, 219
poiesis, 131, 133, 135–41; vs. the poetic, 132
political: image of, 108; *retrait* of, 143, 147–48. *See also retrait*

Rancière, Jacques, 10–11, 12–13, 242n12. *See also* distribution of the sensible
retrait, 122, 143–49, 164
return to the aesthetic. *See* aesthetic turn
Riß (rift-design), 71
rhythm, 29, 30, 38, 72, 120, 141–42, 176–77, 255n17, 259n59
Rivière, Jacques, 179–81, 218
Ronell, Avital, 148; and oedipedagogy in Heidegger, 238
Ross, Alison, 259n57, 260n64

Rousseau, Jean-Jacques, 233

sacrifice, 110, 113, 118–24; *Aufgeben* as, 112; *Selbstaufgabe* as, 115, 116. *See also* Bataille, Georges
Sade, D. A. F., 233
Same, 157, 160, 161, 193, 210, 211, 214, 215–16, 217; vs. the identical, 215–16
Schelling, Friedrich Wilhelm Joseph von, 114
Schufreider, Gregory, 258n45
scenic, 4, 14–24, 65, 77, 106, 140, 143–49; vs. the figure, 157; and tragedy, 79
Sedgwick, Eve Kosofsky 11, 242n12, 242n15
Seigworth, Gregory J., 9–10, 13
Selbstauslegung, 41, 63. *See also Auslegung*; facticity; interpretation
sense, 2, 3, 13–14, 15, 36, 48, 61, 207; community of, 63; cruelty of, 219–27
sensibility, 36, 48, 49
Sholz, Janae, 273n55
Silverman, Kaja, 238
simulacra, 21–22, 189–227
Smith, Daniel W., 267n2
Sorge. *See* care
spectacularization: and the aural, 162; and fascination, 105; and the figure of community, 5; of mimesis, 140; and specular capture, 19, 125; and speculation, 4, 14, 19, 105–6, 141, 142; and the speculative, 4, 14, 19, 134, 139, 161. *See also* fascination; Lacoue-Labarthe, Philippe; Nancy, Jean-Luc
specular, 68, 125, 143–49, 162. *See also* spectacularization
specularization. *See* spectacularization
speculation, 59, 105, 124, 128, 161, 166, 227, 252n33; and tragedy, 75, 249n8. *See also* spectacularization

speculative realism, 1, 2
speech: and discontinuity, 236; institutional, 229–39; plural, 225, 231, 235; and teaching, |234
Spinoza, Benedict de, 9, 10, 204–7, 242n11; and affect, 206–7; and power (*potential*), 206; and substance, 205
Stimme, 17, 30, 36, 45, 89; *des Gewissens*, 38. See also voice
Stimmung, 17, 30, 36, 38, 45, 55, 89, 178, 265–66n33. See also affect: Heideggerian; attunement
strife (*Streit*), 69
sublime, 252n29

Taminiaux, Jacques, 247n7, 258n47
technē, 64, 76, 78
theater, 195, 209; vs. tragedy, 268n7. See also Artaud, Antonin
Theory, 5, 139, 140, 141–43, 178; and atheism, 146; and theater, 146. See also Philosophy
thinking, 23–24, 165, 175–85, 189–90, 202, 212, 220, 226; and affect, 214, 229–39; and language, 229–39; the matter (*die Sache*) of, 215; and questioning, 217–18
thrownness (*Geworfenheit*), 33, 35; and ecstasis, 33, 34, 42, 45
translation, 69; as *Übersetzung*, 82–87; as *Übertragung*, 82–87
tragedy, 18, 69, 70, 72, 79, 107; as speculation, 75, 249n8; vs. theater, 268n7

uncanny 42, 45, 83, 88, 89, 90. See also *deinon*; *Unheimlichkeit*
Ungeheuere, 85, 251–52n29
Unheimlichkeit, 77, 83, 84, 85, 88
University, 24, 229–39

univocity, 16, 21, 191, 192, 193–207, 208, 220, 222

voice: as aesthetic relation, 29–30; and affect, 3, 29–30, 166; *Anspruch* (claim) of, 70; and *Auslegung* 41; of Being, 31, 196; call of, 3, 16–17, 23, 36, 51; of community, 113, 117, 262n10; of conscience, 16–17, 31, 41, 61; and difference, 196; as dissimulation, 105; as figure, 3–4; of the friend, 45; as interruption, 106; of language, 184; as logos, 17; of madness, 183; and music, 225; as *phonē* 17; of "Science," 160; and *Selbstauslegung* 41; silent, 51; of simulacra, 192; as testimony/witness, 36, 40; of the Work (*l'Oeuvre*), 182. See also univocity
Volk, 5, 110, 111, 114, 115, 116

Warminski, Andrzej, 76, 85, 86
Weil, Simone, 265n32
Widder, Nathan, 269n15
work, 69; of the dialectic, 166, of death, 115; of history, 176; of literature, 166; *oeuvre* vs. *travaille*, 166; as *part* (share); and *partage*, 115; of the work of art, 69, 72, 118, 120, 176, 178. See also Blanchot, Maurice
world, 3, 7, 13, 14, 18, 33, 34, 69, 71, 120, 230, 243n21; Being-in-the-, 34; plural, 105
writing, 6, 16, 20, 147–48, 191, 192, 197, 215, 218, 220, 235; and affect, 236; atheistic, 146, 156, 158–66, 174, 264–65n28; of community, 19–20, 117; and discontinuity, 236; and effacement, 164, 184; and interruption, 182–83; and madness, 181; and myth, 19; as other voice, 162

www.ingramcontent.com/pod-product-compliance
Lightning Source LLC
Chambersburg PA
CBHW021651230426
43668CB00008B/588